1985

W9-DFF-387

speech communication

FUNDAMENTALS AND PRACTICE

RAYMOND S. ROSS Ph.D.

Professor of Speech Communication, Theatre and Journalism
Wayne State University

fifth edition

PRENTICE-HALL, INC., Englewood Cliffs, New Jersey 07632

SPEECH
COMMUNICATION
fundamentals
and practice

Library of Congress Cataloging in Publication Data

Ross, Raymond Samuel
    Speech communication.

    Includes bibliographical references and index.
    1. Oral communication. 2. Public speaking.
I. Title.
PN4121.R689 1980   808.5   79-22769
ISBN 0-13-827493-2

THE PRENTICE-HALL SERIES IN SPEECH COMMUNICATION
Larry L. Barker / Robert J. Kibler, *consulting editors*

speech communication
FUNDAMENTALS AND PRACTICE

fifth edition
Raymond S. Ross

Printed in the United States of America
10 9 8 7 6 5 4 3 2 1

Editorial/production supervision: Jeanne Hoeting
Interior Design: Judith Winthrop
Cover Design: Bill Agee
Manufacturing Buyer: Harry P. Baisley

PRENTICE-HALL INTERNATIONAL, INC., *London*
PRENTICE-HALL OF AUSTRALIA PTY. *Limited, Sydney*
PRENTICE-HALL OF CANADA, LTD., *Toronto*
PRENTICE-HALL OF INDIA PRIVATE LIMITED, *New Delhi*
PRENTICE-HALL OF JAPAN, INC., *Tokyo*
PRENTICE-HALL OF SOUTHEAST ASIA PTE. LTD., *Singapore*
WHITEHALL BOOKS LIMITED, *Wellington, New Zealand*

12.95

CONTENTS

THE NATURE OF HUMAN COMMUNICATION
part one

117,520

THE PSYCHOLOGY OF PERSUASION
part three

INTERPERSONAL AND GROUP COMMUNICATION
part four

PREFACE

The goal of this book is to enable its readers to better appreciate the crucial importance of the arts and skills of speech communication as agents of social control.

Responsible speech communication, whether as rhetoric, symbolic interaction, art, or science, seeks to generate agreement among people and cultures. To communicate is usually the beginning of understanding.

In more specific terms the goals are: to increase one's ability to communicate clearly and persuasively; to develop self-confidence; and to make it easier for people to get along with one another.

This book, now in its fifth edition, reflects the realities of the unusual times in which we are living. In the years since the first edition (yea, even the last edition), there have been some substantial changes in the communication field. Less attention is being paid to some of the traditional areas such as group dynamics, leadership, public communication, and even attitude change. We stress interpersonal attraction, social perception theory, and, like other social psychologists, attribution theory.

Most of these cycles are normal, but the last ten years have been unusual. However, none of these developments mean necessarily that some traditional topics are now unimportant, nor that some of the new interests are all-important. Because some areas are not receiving a lot of attention right now is not a sufficient reason for deleting them. The classic works on speech fundamentals are still enormously valuable. They are part of the body of knowledge that all communication students should know. The soundness of the traditional speech communication curriculum has *not* been deemphasized. Purpose, delivery, preparation, outlining, arrangement, logic, and anxiety are all discussed fully.

The book reflects the changes and issues of current interest. Listening is now a full chapter; nonverbal communication is handled differently; interpersonal communication is half of Part Four. The persuasion chapter has a new view of attitudes, but still retains the notion.

The text is not meant to be an encyclopedia of current research. It includes many references to recent work as well as the classic references. It is meant to be an eclectic perspective which reflects the new with redefinitions and reevaluations of the old. This edition attempts to be readable, interesting, and above all, relevant to the student's life.

I should like to thank my colleagues who took the time to complete a detailed marketing survey intended to make this fifth edition the best yet. I found your responses, especially those pertaining to book organization, very helpful. You will find SC5 organized more like my recommendations to your students.

Those of you familiar with the earlier editions will note that the fifth edition is divided into four, not five, parts:

Part One—The Nature of Human Communication
Part Two—Public Speaking: Preparation and Delivery
Part Three—The Psychology of Persuasion
Part Four—Interpersonal and Group Communication

There is a short introduction to interpersonal communication in Part Four which should be helpful in follow-up courses in group discussion and interpersonal communication.

Reflecting current learning theory, each of the four parts attempts to help the student by indicating the general objectives sought. In addition to a thorough summary, each chapter now concludes with a list of (1) speech communication principles, (2) specific learning outcomes, (3) communication competencies (written as behavioral objectives),[1] and (4) projects and tasks. The projects and tasks are practical materials and assignments culled from years of experience and suggestions of many veteran teachers.

There are two appendices. The first is a collection of communication models for those students and teachers who prefer such an emphasis or for class discussion. The second includes additional model speech outlines as requested by numerous users.

I have also responded to requests for an expanded *Instructor's Manual.* It now includes seven different syllabi incorporating four approaches to teaching a course based on this book; additional projects

---

[1] For those who prefer even more precision in these matters see Robert J. Kibler, Donald J. Cegala, Larry L. Barker, and David T. Miles, *Behavioral Objectives and Instruction* (Boston: Allyn & Bacon, 1974); Donald J. Cegala, Robert J. Kibler, Larry L. Barker, and David T. Miles, "Writing Behavioral Objectives: A Programmed Article," *The Speech Teacher,* XXI, no. 3 (September, 1972), 151–68.

and tasks; suggestions for evaluation and criticism; an extensive pretested item file and model examinations. I should like to thank its author, Mark G. Ross of Kent State University, for its improvement.

Finally, much love and appreciation to my toughest critic and the world's best business agent—Ricky Ross.

RSR

speech communication

FUNDAMENTALS AND PRACTICE

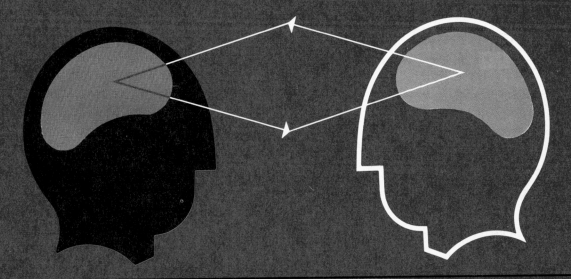

part one

THE NATURE
OF HUMAN
COMMUNICATION

Suppose you communicate a rumor to two of your friends; then suppose that they each relay the rumor to two of their friends. Allowing fifteen minutes for each communication and assuming a hypothetical chain of contacts that is neither duplicated nor broken, this rumor would reach every person in the world in only eight hours and thirty minutes. Talk about a grapevine! If you have ever played the game of passing along a message orally to see how much distortion takes place by the time it reaches the last person at your party, you can guess what would probably happen in our hypothetical, worldwide grapevine. One wonders how we achieve any understanding at all.

If you would like to speed up the rumor mill, consider that newspaper pages and photographs are now transmitted from coast to coast, using regular telephone lines, in about four minutes.

That is slow compared with a new laser-writing method. It takes just four seconds. The device also can transmit documents, X-ray photographs, color photographs, and a three-dimensional "stereo" picture.

Attempting to understand the nature of human communication is an eternal quest. If we are to survive in the world as we find it, we must have some acquaintance with the process of communication, audience psychology, language habits, nonverbal communication, and listening. These are the five chapters of part 1: The Nature of Human Communication.

We first need to know something about the communication process, which more than anything else gives humans their special place among all living things. Our overwhelming need to communicate and express ourselves is as characteristic a part of our nature as our physiology is. We are unique among all other forms of animals because of our rationality and our sophisticated system of communication. These assets have permitted us to record the discoveries of yesteryear so that others yet unborn may profit from the past. This ability, in conjunction with human creativeness, has led to an information explosion.

The amount of material to be stored and communicated in this period of our history is enormous. One scholar has estimated that we have accumulated more knowledge within the last fifty years than during all the centuries before, and that knowledge has more than doubled within the last century! Furthermore, it is estimated that 95 percent of all the world's scientists are alive today! Our libraries at Wayne State University house some 1,300 technical journals. The costs of American scientific research exceed twenty-five billion dollars a year. Our present specialization of knowledge adds to our problems. Communication must somehow bridge these isolated islands of specialization.

The sheer amount of communication is fantastic. Surveys indicate that we spend seventy-five percent of our waking time in some communication activity, in listening, speaking, reading, and writing. When one considers the telephone system and the mass media, the volume of messages becomes astronomical. It is estimated that the American public makes some 288 billion telephone calls a year, or nearly 6,000 per second. Washington, D.C. has over 130 phones per 100 persons.[1]

Communication is vitally important to business and industry. Research tells us that business managers may spend 75 to 90 percent of their time doing nothing but communicating, and that about three-quarters of that time is spent in oral, face-to-face situations. This importance is reflected in the establishment of communications departments in many companies and in requests for special training courses and increased numbers of professional consultants. Those who think dialogue will replace rhetorical persuasion haven't reckoned with the advertising agencies! Look at these statistics:

10 LEADING NATIONAL ADVERTISERS[2]
(Ad dollars in millions)

1	Proctor & Gamble	$460
2	General Motors Corp.	312
3	General Foods Corp.	300
4	Sears, Roebuck & Co.	290
5	K mart	210
6	Bristol-Myers Co.	203
7	Warner-Lambert Co.	201
8	Ford Motor Co.	184
9	Philip Morris, Inc.	184
10	American Home Products Corp.	171

Source: Advertising Age

Consider the $250,000 cost of a thirty-second spot commercial during the Superbowl. If one assumes there are 90 million viewers, that is $2.78 per 1,000 viewers per minute (CPM). This kind of communication is indeed big business, and somebody thinks it is effective.

The importance of speech communication training to you, the student, is indicated by its requirement in many schools. Research shows that you can improve your speech skills significantly by taking such a course.[3] Moreover, testimonials by successful individuals have affirmed the value of speech training, and research has indicated its usefulness to you in better understanding your other university courses. Charles Hurst studied 157 college sophomores, 70 with speech training and 87 without such training. He described the educational implications of the relationships between formal instruction in a basic speech course and increased readiness to undertake work at the next academic level. He discovered that there definitely is a significant and positive relationship between these two

[1] *Detroit News,* January 8, 1975, p. 12C.

[2] *Ibid.,* September 6, 1978, p. 4E.

[3] Anthony Mulac, "Effects of Three Feedback Conditions Employing Videotape and Audiotape on Acquired Speech Skill," *Speech Monographs,* 41, no. 3 (August 1974), 205–14.

factors. Further, the speech group was found to be superior on a measure of study skills and practices. A finding of interest to all grade-conscious students was that the achievement of the speech group in classroom work, as measured by comparison of mean honor-point averages, was found to be superior to that of the nonspeech group. In fact, the speech group showed a net gain, compared with a net loss for the nonspeech group. Hurst concluded that "the basic speech course provides students with a basis for orderly thinking and for improved control of the various elements that make up the total personality."[4]

Another scholar defines speech as "a tool of social adjustment, which reflects the efficient personality."[5] Others suggest that "physical, social, and mental existence depend upon communication. Each affects the other until it would be foolish to try to distinguish where one begins and the other leaves off. Communication shapes personality and personality determines the pattern of communication."[6] Perhaps for our purposes we can say that speech training can have as much impact on personality as personality can have on speech.

In addition to gaining insight into human communication as a process, we need to know something of how humanity perceives itself, how it perceives the rest of the world, and how it reacts to stimuli. This is the purpose of chapter 1.

Crowds, mobs, and strongly stimulated audiences call for a modern classification system. Such a system, using contagion, regression, anonymity, suggestibility, and other active influences, is provided in chapter 2.

How many times have you been offended by a poorly chosen word, a gross generalization, or other language inappropriate to the situation? If you think a "stable" in ghetto talk is for horses, you're in for a surprise! Chapter 3 addresses itself to language habits and semantics.

Do you realize that only 35 percent of communication is verbal? When you speak face-to-face with a person, that person receives 65 percent of your message by means other than the words you use—by your tone of voice, your gestures, even by the way you stand and are dressed.

When we find that a gesture that means "come here" in America means "go away" in Italy, we begin to sense the problem. This is the subject of chapter 4, "Nonverbal Communication."

[4] Charles Hurst, "Speech and Functional Intelligence: An Experimental Study of Educational Implications of a Basic Speech Course" (unpublished doctoral dissertation, Wayne State University, 1961).

[5] Elwood Murray, *The Speech Personality* (Philadelphia: J. B. Lippincott Company, 1944), p. 10.

[6] Gordon Wiseman and Larry Barker, *Speech—Interpersonal Communication* (San Francisco: Chandler, 1967, 1974), p. 5; see also Lee Thayer, *Communication and Communication Systems* (Homewood, Ill.: Richard D. Irwin, 1968), p. 17.

Americans are not good listeners. Some talk more than they listen. Yet, listening is still the most common of the communication skills. Surveys indicate that people may spend as much as 60 to 75 percent of their time listening.[7] Chapter 5, "Listening," is intended to help you improve your listening habits.

General learning outcomes are stated clearly at the opening of each chapter. More specific objectives, along with principles, competencies, and study projects, are found at the end of each chapter.

[7] Ralph G. Nichols and Leonard A. Stevens, *Are You Listening?* (New York: McGraw-Hill Book Company, 1957), pp. 6–8.

GENERAL LEARNING OUTCOMES

1   We should better understand the enormous complexity of the process of human communication.

2   We should gain a working understanding of human communication as a process.

3   We should learn that our field of experience greatly affects the way we perceive the world about us.

4   We should learn the importance of speech communication training to our successful growth and development.

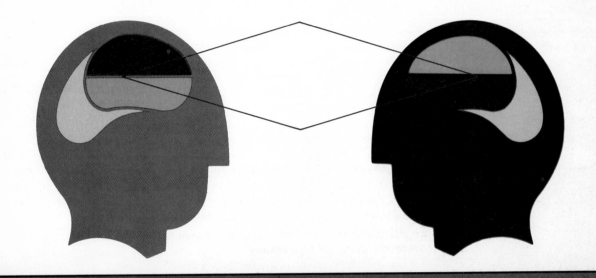

the
communication
process

Before we can consider the skills in speech communication training and practice, we must understand how the communication process works.

When asked to define communication, many people reply that it is the transfer of meaning from one mind to another. Most speech teachers today believe that this definition is not really true, and that it may actually hinder the learning of more specific skills which must be acquired.

DEFINITIONS

Definitions of speech and communication range from "speech is the great medium through which human cooperation is brought about"[1] to the more specific definition of the American College Dictionary, "the imparting or interchange of thoughts, opinions, or information by speech, writing, or signs." Let's examine some other useful definitions.

> Communication is the eliciting of response and successful human speech communication is the eliciting of the desired response through verbal symbolization.[2]

> Human communication is a subtle set of processes through which people interact, control one another, and gain understanding.[3]

> Communication is social interaction through symbols and message systems.[4]

> Communication has as its central interest those behavioral situations in which a source transmits a message to a receiver(s) with conscious intent to affect the latter's behaviors.[5]

> Speech is ongoing multisymbolic behavior in social situations carried on to achieve communication. We define communication as a social achievement in symbolic behavior.[6]

[1] Grace A. de Laguna, *Speech: Its Function and Development* (New Haven: Yale University Press, 1927), p. 19.

[2] From *Business and Professional Speech Communication* by Harold P. Zelko and Frank E. X. Dance. Copyright © 1965, 1978 by Holt, Rinehart & Winston. Reprinted by permission of Holt, Rinehart & Winston, p. 5

[3] Alfred G. Smith, ed., *Communication and Culture: Readings in the Codes of Human Interaction* (New York: Holt, Rinehart & Winston, 1966), p. v.

[4] George Gerbner, "On Defining Communication: Still Another View," *Journal of Communication*, 16, no. 2 (June 1966), 99.

[5] Gerald R. Miller, "On Defining Communication: Another Stab," *Journal of Communication*, 16, no. 2 (June 1966), 92.

[6] A. Craig Baird and Franklin H. Knower, *Essentials of General Speech* (New York: McGraw-Hill Book Company, 1968).

Communication is a process of transmission of structure among the parts of a system which are identifiable in time and space.[7]

Communication is a social function . . . , a *sharing* of elements of behavior, or modes of life, by the existence of sets of rules. . . . Communication is not the response itself but is essentially the *relationship* set up by the transmission of stimuli [signs] and the evocation of responses.[8]

Communication occurs whenever persons attribute significance to message-related behavior.[9]

The problem of too specific or too general a definition seems obvious. Over one-hundred serious attempts at clarification have appeared in print.

All of these definitions are worth considering and even discussing in class. Current definitions seem to agree that ideas must in some way be shared before communication can exist, and, most important, that communication should be thought of as a process and not simply as a transfer of meaning from one mind to another. Let us examine this social process and attempt to develop a working behavioral definition.

There is something necessarily *mutual* about human communication; each party influences the other. Communication is a truly dynamic process. Carl Rogers has stated the same point briefly and clearly: "I have found it of enormous value when I can *permit* myself to understand another person."[10] For a person who is even partially involved in *real* communication, just trying to understand a different point of view may become threatening. We are afraid to *permit* ourselves to understand: "If I let myself really understand another person, I might be changed by that understanding."

Communication involves common experience and mutual influence. Real communication is very difficult if there is not at least some small opportunity for two-way influence. Whether we know it or not, we communicate hoping to influence others to respond as we want them to. This process has no beginning and no end; it is ever changing, dynamic, and mutual.

Although it is impossible to separate the parts of so integrated a process, for our purposes it may be helpful to divide it arbitrarily into a sequence of events. Let's assume we have a message (which might be

---

[7] K. Krippendorf, "Values, Modes and Domains of Inquiry into Communication," *Journal of Communication,* 19 (1969), 107.

[8] Colin Cherry, *On Human Communication* (Cambridge, Mass. and London: The M.I.T. Press, 1966), pp. 6–7.

[9] C. David Mortensen, *Communication* (New York: McGraw-Hill Book Company, 1972), p. 14.

[10] Carl Rogers, *On Becoming a Person* (Boston: Houghton Mifflin Company, 1961), p. 18 (emphasis added).

referred to as an *idea* or *concept* or *meaning*) that we wish to convey to another person. Our brain now sorts through our storehouse of knowledge, experience, feelings, and previous training to select and refine the precise meaning we are seeking to communicate. Before we transmit this meaning, we encode it; we put it into signs and symbols that we commonly think of as language. (Gesture, facial expression, and tone of voice may also be considered as signs, symbols, or codes.) We might transmit our meaning by means of a sign language, a foreign language, or even international Morse code. The way in which the message is coded, the medium or channel chosen for its transmission, and the skill with which it is transmitted influence the meaning it will have for the receiver. Assuming that the medium for this illustration is simply the air between you and the listener, we now have the encoded message, its transmission, and its reception by the other person. The receiver then decodes the signal, or at least attempts to decode it. The listener sorts out, selects, and elicits meanings from *his* or *her* storehouse of knowledge, experience, and training until there has been created in his or her own mind a replica of the images and ideas contained in the mind of the sender. However, if the signal is in a code with which the listener is not familiar, such as a foreign language, not much communication will take place.

To the extent that this replica is similar to the sender's images and ideas, we have achieved communication. The idea, concept, or meaning in the mind of the listener is therefore very dependent upon, if not restricted to, the knowledge and experience he or she can apply to the code. The value of knowing your listener and the value of audience analysis now become evident.

Thus, our working definition of intentional communication is *a process of sorting, selecting, and sending symbols in such a way as to help a listener elicit from his or her own mind a meaning or response similar to that intended by the communicator.* We now see why seemingly obvious meanings (in *our* minds) are often distorted or misunderstood by others. Perhaps this is what is meant by the saying, "One cannot teach a man what he does not already know"; and perhaps this better explains the old teaching rule, "Go from the known to the unknown."

MODELS

The word *model* generally refers to a representation of a thing or a process. We have relatively little trouble producing a model of a physical object. We can learn much about the physical behavior of trains, boats, and airplanes by building models of them. In addition, models such as the flight trainer shown in figure 1.1 can be used for training purposes. However, when we attempt to make models of more abstract things—things that are difficult to measure physically—we often oversimplify to the point of poor or danger-

Figure 1.1 A flight trainer that reportedly permits the trainee to experience aircraft operation under actual flight conditions. Special attachments and pivots make it possible for the student pilot to control movement of the aircraft— permitting the student to experience take-off, "flight," left and right banks, and yaw. *From* Training *(New York: Gellert Publishing Corp., September, 1974), p. 6.*

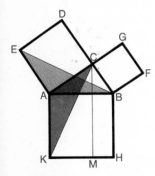

Figure 1.2
The square of the hypotenuse of a right triangle is equal to the sum of the squares of the legs, or AKHB = ACDE + BFGC.

ous representation, or we may simply be unable to agree on exactly what it is we are modeling.

The advantages of using a model are quickly evident. The model gives you another, different, closer look. It provides a frame of reference, suggests informational gaps, underlines the problem of abstraction, and expresses a problem in symbolic language if there is some advantage in using figures or symbols. Of course there are some drawbacks, such as oversimplification and other dangers inherent in gross abstraction, to using models.

We may use words, numbers, symbols, and pictures to illustrate our models of things, theories, or processes. In geometry we accept the theorem that the square of the hypotenuse of a right triangle is equal to the sum of the squares of the legs. This statement is a form of verbal model. If we draw a picture of this theorem as well (figure 1.2), we have a verbal-pictorial model. Communication experts have used mostly verbal-pictorial models in trying to give us a closer and more scientific look at the communication process. The working definition of communication suggested earlier for this text is really a verbal model, one that will shortly be illustrated. First, let's

```
WHO
SAYS WHAT
IN WHAT CHANNEL
TO WHOM
WITH WHAT EFFECT
```

Figure 1.3 Lasswell model. *From H. D. Lasswell, "The Structure and Function of Communication in Society," in* The Communication of Ideas, *ed. Lyman Bryson (New York: Harper & Row, Publishers, Inc., 1948), p. 37.*

look at several models that appear to agree about human communication. Each of these models give you a slightly different perspective. For instance, figure 1.3 is a simple verbal model posed as five questions. Figure 1.6 is my own model and is explained on page 14. Additional models that you may wish to study and discuss are shown in Appendix A.

The encoder and decoder can perform their functions only in terms of

Figure 1.4 Berlo model.[11]

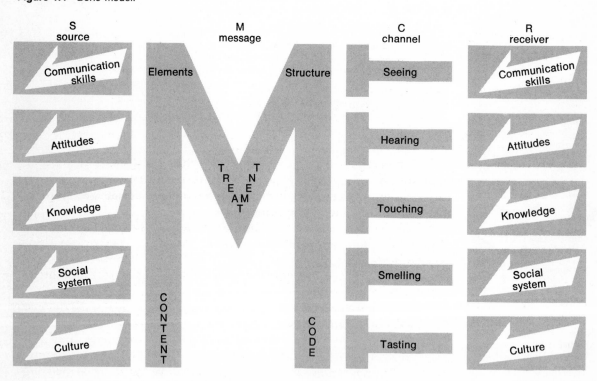

[11] From *The Process of Communication: An Introduction to Theory and Practice,* by David K. Berlo. Copyright © 1960 by Holt, Rinehart & Winston. Reprinted by permission of Holt, Rinehart & Winston.

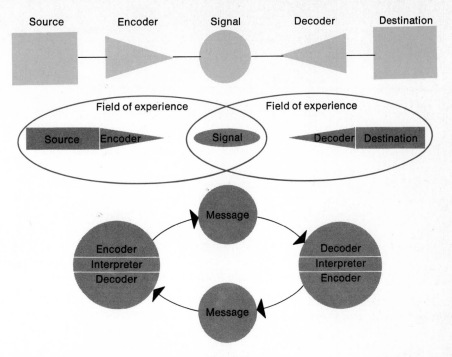

Key: 1. Encoding: putting the information or feeling into a form that can be transmitted.
2. Sending: transmitting the encoded message.
3. Decoding: relating the received message to "one's picture in the mind."

Figure 1.5 Three Schramm models. *From Wilbur Schramm, "How Communication Works," in* The Process and Effects of Mass Communication, *ed. Wilbur Schramm (Urbana, Ill.: University of Illinois Press, 1955), pp. 4–8.*

their own fields of experience. In this sense, then, the decoder and encoder both are limited by their experience. Nevertheless, there must be some experience common to both in order for the communication to be useful for the intended message to be conveyed.

The decoding of a message by the receiver starts that person's process of encoding. Whether or not this encoding results in an overt communication depends upon the barriers to communication. The communication process is continuous. A single communication is merely part of a greater network of communication.

The roles of encoder and decoder are interchangeable. Thus, each person in the communication process is encoder and decoder as well as interpreter.

Since no model of anything, much less a complicated process, can ever be completely accurate, you are not expected to agree totally with the previous models or with the one I am about to describe. However, with the previous material as a frame of reference, perhaps more insights are now available to you as you decode the Ross model (see figure 1.6, page 14).

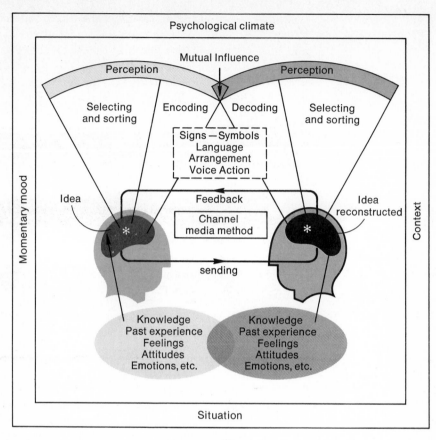

Figure 1.6 Ross communication model. (1980)

The Ross model focuses on the *human* organism and particularly human sign-symbol behavior.[12] In interpreting this model, remember that we are capable of being both sender and receiver at the same time; we are, as Zelko and Dance[13] would say, *transceivers*.

The frame of the model tries to show everything, including the world in which this communication takes place. The picture frame suggests the importance of situation, mood (or set), context, and psychological climate.

The *situation* could range from a date to a simple exchange of home-work information. It could then make a real difference. *Mood* refers to

---

[12] Some writers are interested primarily in mathematical theories and models applied to electrical engineering: see C. E. Shannon and W. Weaver, *The Mathematical Theory of Communication* (Urbana, Ill.: University of Illinois Press, 1949), p. 98. Others are interested in animal communication: see Jon J. Eisenson, J. Jeffery Auer, and John V. Irwin, *The Psychology of Communication* (New York: Appleton-Century-Crofts, 1963), chap. 10.

[13] From *Business and Professional Speech Communication* by Harold P. Zelko and Frank E. X. Dance. Copyright © 1965, 1978 by Holt, Rinehart & Winston, pp. 6–7.

feelings of the moment. At different times our mood might be happy, angry, tense, and so on. Our mood can greatly affect what we say or hear and how we say or hear something. *Context* is the framework of other words or ideas into which yours fit. If you are talking about paper, note how the word changes in these contexts: The paper was late today (newspaper). The paper is crooked (wallpaper). It is an *A* paper (homework). *Psychological climate* is a lot like weather or physical climate. Just as our weather might be bitterly cold, so too might the psychological mood (climate) of a classroom, a meeting, or a date be cold. An unhappy, impersonal (cold) psychological climate would hinder rather than help communication. Sometimes climate is the most important part of a message.

Let's assume that the person on the left side of the model in figure 1.6 is a woman who wishes to communicate a message (a concept or an idea) to the other person. The idea is represented by the star inside her brain. Let's suppose the concept is an abstract one, such as *love*. The fan projecting from each brain represents our 12 billion brain cells. In this woman's brain are stored her knowledge and past experience, her feelings, attitudes, emotions, and many more things that make her the person she is.

> The brain, composed of 12 billion working parts, has enough storage capacity to accept 10 new facts every second. It is conservatively estimated that the human brain can store an amount of information equivalent to 100 trillion different words (which would mean acquiring one word per second continuously for 1,000,000 years). In a lifetime of 70 years, a human being may store information roughly equivalent to a mere trillion words.[14]

Our sender now sorts through and selects from her storehouse of knowledge and past experience, choosing items that help her define and refine what she is trying to say. She has to have a basis upon which to perform this operation, a program if you will. We can think of the brain in some ways as a computer. The forebrain, for example, becomes a kind of input regulator into which we feed the program. This woman's program had better include at least three questions, or she is already in trouble! These are: (1) What do I have stored under *love*? (2) What do I know about the other person? and (3) What do I have filed for this particular situation and context? You can almost visualize the program in action: assessing, accepting, rejecting, cross-referencing, and synthesizing the information in the storehouse—in short, selecting and sorting the appropriate knowledge, past experience, and so on.

Although there is some confusion among scholars as to exactly how, and in particular *when*, the encoding takes place, it is useful, if only for instructional purposes, to think of it as a sequence. Our sender must now choose her codes and should apply at least the same program or questions discussed previously. More will be said of this critical process of encoding in

[14] Al Cohn, *Detroit News*, March 16, 1975, p. 1D.

chapter 3. The sender now transmits the message, which, let's assume, is mainly oral. (She might, of course, have chosen to write a memo or use a blackboard.) Let us also assume that there is no unusual distraction or noise and that the sensory abilities of each person are adequate. Since our message concerns *love,* the situation itself may be fairly critical, to say nothing of the characteristics of the other person.

Finally (and this whole operation may last but seconds), the message is received by the other person. The resulting *sensations* experienced by the receiver are the first part of human perception; the second part is the *interpretation* of those sensations in this particular situation. More will be said of this process of perception in our discussion of feedback, which follows shortly.

The model suggests that our receiver now *decodes* the signs, symbols, and language of the sender, sorting through his or her storehouse of knowledge and experience and selecting those meanings that will allow him or her to create a message concerning love. To the extent that this re-creation is similar to the sender's intended message, we have communication. This reconstructed idea, then, is dependent upon a person's prior knowledge and experience.

The term *feedback* in the model requires a moment of important consideration. In engineering, feedback refers to some of the transmitted energy being returned to the source. The automatic pilot used in airplanes is an example of self-correcting machinery that uses feedback. The analogy between this kind of feedback and the feedback used in human communication breaks down a bit when we consider the kind of electronic feedback all of us have observed in public-address systems or tape recorders (in which a reentry of some of the sound from the speaker to the microphone causes a howl or loud noise). For speech purposes we may think of feedback as useful in a self-correcting, or perhaps we should say adaptive, sense. As our transmitted signal is "bounced off" our receiver, it feeds back information that allows us to correct and refine our signal. A quizzical look, a frown, a yawn, the sound of our own voice—any of these may cause us to reevaluate and recode our signals. On the other hand, speech fright to the point of emotional disintegration (such as forgetting) can be compared to intense feedback of the public-address system type, which momentarily—but completely—shorts out the sending device. The complicated phenomenon of speech fright will be covered in chapter 10. For now, let us think of feedback as something that we should make work for us.

The problem of near-zero feedback is caught in the clever sketches in figure 1.7. Comic-strip character Funky Winkerbean illustrates another form of feedback in figure 1.8.

As stated earlier, the model shows that communication assigns meaning, and that it *works well* when the person receiving a message interprets it in the *same* way that the sender intends it.[15] It is clear that human commu-

[15] For a detailed discussion of the elements of a model, see Leonard C. Hawes, "Elements of a Model for Communication Processes," *Quarterly Journal of Speech,* 59, no. 1 (February 1973), 11–21.

Figure 1.7 Making a point. *Drawings by David John McKee, by permission of* The Times Educational Supplement *(London), March 27, 1964. Published in the United States by* Saturday Review *(New York), Sept. 19, 1964, p. 68.*

Figure 1.8 Funky Winkerbean. *"Funky Winkerbean"* by Tom Batiuk, courtesy of Publishers Hall Syndicate.

nication is not really a transfer of meaning at all. It is *a process of sorting, selecting, and sending symbols in such a way as to help a receiver find in his or her own mind a meaning similar to that intended by the sender.* That we seldom have perfectly clear communication and probably should not expect it now seems obvious.

PERCEPTION AND COMMUNICATION

An understanding of how people receive, decode, and assign meaning to messages is critical to our understanding of communication. Listening is much more than keen hearing. All of our senses may be called upon to help us interpret even an oral signal. For our purposes, the perception process is identical to the communication process except that the emphasis is on receiving instead of on sending. The receiver, or perceiver, apparently makes hypotheses regarding the meaning of the message, hypotheses that he or she then accepts or rejects on the basis of personal constructs based on prior learning and experience.

Sensation and Interpretation

Have you ever been on a train that was stopped next to other trains in a railroad terminal? Have you then felt, seen, and heard all the signs indicating movement, only to find that it was the other trains that were moving? Perhaps you discovered this by noticing that the other trains were gone, or by fixing your gaze on something you *knew* was not moving, such as the ceiling of the station, a roof support, or the ground.

The point of this is that perception is essentially two things: (1) the *sensation* caused by the stimulation of a sense organ and (2) the *interpretation* of that sensation. In our study of speech we are concerned mainly with the interpretation. As we stated earlier, it is through our knowledge and experience that we interpret or attach meaning to a symbol.

The complexity of human communication is indicated also by the various levels of perception now thought to exist. *Subliminal* or *subthreshold* perception, for example, is the reception of impressions below the level of conscious awareness. This is not to be confused with so-called extrasensory perception. Many experiments have been conducted in this field, most of them with images projected so fast that, although we are subconsciously aware of them, we cannot consciously recognize them. Such experiments are complicated by the fact that people vary in their perceptual abilities and that a person perceives better at some levels of perception than at others. The best-known of all subthreshold experiments[16] was the projection of nonsense syllables and the simultaneous application of an electric shock to the subject. When these stimuli were later presented at speeds so rapid that the subjects could not consciously identify them, the subjects' emotional reactions were more intense than their reactions to nonsense syllables not previously associated with a shock. The subjects were thus able to identify the stimuli unconsciously before they could do so consciously. During a six-week experiment in a New Jersey theater in 1957, sales of popcorn and soft drink allegedly were increased by the use of subthreshold messages superimposed over the regular film. No adequate account of the procedures used is available for us to examine, however.[17] A more recent study of subthreshold flashing of the word *Doctor* on one person in a video-tape discussion indicated significant influence.[18]

A person's *mood (or set),* or one's readiness to perceive a stimulus in a certain way affects one's ability to perceive and how to accept a stimulus. The consciousness defends itself by apparently refusing to accept certain messages. On the other hand, we may wish so much to hear something that, regardless of the actual message, we hear, interpret, and attach meaning to it according to what we wish to hear. One of the great barriers to good communication is our tendency to hear what we wish to hear, see what we wish to see, and believe what we wish to believe.

A closely related perceptual and communication problem arises from our normal tendency toward *completeness.* In communications that appear to be only partially complete, we often fill in the unsaid part or complete the pattern. If we do not have a sense of completeness about something, we often feel upset, ill at ease, confused, and unhappy about it. This tendency can be an important way to motivate people. Perhaps you have had a teacher

[16] R. S. Lazarus and R. A. McCleary, "Automatic Discrimination without Awareness: A Study in Subception," *Psychological Review,* 58 (1951), 113–22.
[17] H. Brean, "'Hidden Sell' Technique Is Almost Here," *Life,* March 31, 1958, pp. 102–4.
[18] J. Douglas Gibb, "An Experimental Study of the Effects of a Subthreshold Prestige Symbol in Informative and Persuasive Communication" (unpublished doctoral dissertation, Wayne State University, 1966).

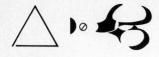

Figure 1.9
Pattern-closing tendencies.

who communicates just enough knowledge in a stimulating way to motivate you to do further reading and research so that you can complete or close the pattern. A problem arises when we close incomplete communication patterns in ways not intended by the speaker, or when we become frustrated by a lack of details. It is easier to see figure 1.9 as a *complete* triangle and its companion as six strange marks—or can you fill in the missing information and find the scissors?

Sometimes our habits and previous experiences cause us to leave things out. Read the three messages in figure 1.10 quickly.

Figure 1.10

Many people see nothing unusual about these messages even after two or three readings. The good, rapid readers seem to have the most trouble. Why should this be so? A group of second and third graders had no trouble finding the double words in each message. We perceive to a certain extent what our habits, our emotions, and our prior knowledge and experience let us perceive. A good reader has learned to skim and to ignore nonessential words. The beginning reader sees one word at a time.

Test your perceptual ability in figure 1.11. Do you see anything familiar or identifiable? Do you see a message?

Figure 1.11

You should see a word in white on a partial black field. Your experience is usually just the opposite of this pattern, in which the area *between* the letters is black instead of the letters themselves.[19] Even after you see the message, it may escape you momentarily as your long-standing habits and previous patterns of experience assert themselves.

[19] This is referred to as a *figure-ground transformation*. The word is *LEFT*.

Experience should help you the next time. Let's see. Can you decode figure 1.12? You've had practice! The color field is reversed from that of figure 1.11.

Figure 1.12

Figure 1.13
From David Krech and Richard S. Crutchfield, Elements of Psychology *(New York: Knopf, Inc., 1958), p. 93.*

Figure 1.13 should be easy for you if you stretch your experience a little.

As we noted above, your *mental set*—that is, your readiness to interpret a message in a certain way has a lot to do with what you "see." Look for faces in the lamps in figure 1.14. You should find some quickly because faces are, after all, what you are looking for.

Figure 1.14

Keep studying the lamps. You should find six faces, two of them animal. Did you get the message?

A group of professional photographers found it almost impossible to "see" the photograph in figure 1.15 (page 22). What do you see?

Don't proceed until you see a cow looking right at you! If you haven't seen it by now, you may actually become annoyed, particularly if you've asked for help and your friends see the cow immediately. Communication is like that. We don't do our best when we begin to feel awkward, stupid, or left

Figure 1.15

out. How are you doing with *LEFT* and *THE*? Have you lost them? When experiences are new to us, we may understand or "see" one moment and "not see" the next. This would be a good time to review the communication models again.

Their set or mood causes them to select for attention those things that agree with such a set. The three photographs in figure 1.16 all are reproduced from the same negative; they are shown as they might appear to three different individuals.

Perhaps what you notice depends upon where you live, as shown in figure 1.17. Some things are barely noticed in New York City!

In figure 1.18 our friend Charlie Brown illustrates humorously how others' perceptions and subsequent communications affect our own.

Figure 1.16 Selective perception. *Reprinted with permission of Macmillan Publishing Co., Inc. from* Communications: The Transfer of Meaning *by Don Fabun. Copyright © 1968, Kaiser Aluminum & Chemical Corporation.*

A young man "on the town"   A person needing to cash a check   Someone who is late for an appointment

Figure 1.17 *Photo by World Wide Photos*

Figure 1.18 Peanuts. © *1960 United Feature Syndicate, Inc.*

For Carl Rogers, every individual exists in a continually changing world of experience of which he is the center. Whether this world is called the phenomenal field or the experiential field, humans exist in a sea of experiences, both conscious and unconscious. For Rogers, this is a private world that can really be known only by the individual. The way each person perceives his or her private world is reality for that person. We do not react to absolute reality but rather to our perception of reality. "We live by a perceptual 'map' which is never reality itself." [20]

[20] Carl R. Rogers, *Client-Centered Therapy* (Boston: Houghton Mifflin Company, 1951), p.485.

1 SUMMING UP

Theoretically, human communication is capable of fantastic speeds. The amount of communication we use is tremendous. Practices in government, industry, and colleges and universities reflect the growing importance of speech and communication training. The literature cited in this chapter underlines the growing systemization and the interdisciplinary character of the study of communication. The importance of speech training to college students in their (1) work in other courses, (2) learning, (3) study habits, (4) grades, and (5) personality has been demonstrated experimentally. The point of view of this book is that communication is not simply a transfer or transmission of meaning from one mind to another. It is a process intimately related to human perception and it involves the sorting, selecting, and sending of symbols in such a way as to help a listener elicit from his or her own mind a meaning similar to that contained in the mind of the communicator.

A knowledge of the processes of communication and perception is essential to those who want to learn communication skills. The model we have used to analyze the communication process (figure 1.6) includes (1) an idea or concept, (2) selecting and sorting, (3) encoding, (4) transmitting, (5) receiving and decoding, (6) selecting and sorting, and (7) a reconstructed idea or concept. Feedback is information being returned from our receivers which is vital to the correction and refining of the signals we send.

Perception may be divided into (1) sensation and (2) interpretation. Past experience, knowledge, set, all have a great impact upon perception. Wishful thinking is the cause of much distortion in perception and therefore interferes with communication. Perception is a result of internal as well as external signals or forces.

Speech Communication Principles

1 Human communication is a process of sorting, selecting, and sharing symbols in such a way as to help another person select from his or her own experiences a meaning similar to that intended by the source.

2 We all are the center of our own field of experience; the way we perceive that field is our own reality.

3 Our mood, our set or readiness to perceive a stimulus in a certain way influences our ability to perceive and to accept a stimulus.

4 Our field of experience significantly affects the way we perceive all kinds of stimuli, ranging from optical illusions to complex nonverbal behavior.

Specific Learning Outcomes

1 In a five-minute report we should be able to explain and illustrate the process of human communication.

2 In a three-page report we should be able to reproduce and explain the main features of any two of the models illustrated in chapter 1.

3 We should be able to explain orally or in a short essay the relationship between the process of perception and the process of communication.

Communication Competencies

1 We should develop an ability to adapt to feedback in classroom communication, to the satisfaction of peers familiar with the material in this chapter.

2 We should be able to "see" the hidden messages in the perceptual tests in chapter 1 and better assess the effect of past experience on communication.

3 We should be able to apply a communication model to a specific incident or interaction in order to understand the process of communication, and we should be able to demonstrate this application orally and pictorially to the satisfaction of our instructor.

Study Projects and Tasks

1 Develop your own verbal-pictorial model of the human communication process. Figure 1.19 is presented as an example. See Appendix A for more ideas.

2 Apply one of the communication models to a specific incident, event, or interaction. Report (verbally and/or pictorially) the insights or lessons of this exercise. Pay special attention to feedback. See figures 1.19, 1.20, and 1.21.

3 Using the optical illusions in chapter 1 or other perceptual abnormalities you may find, test a few people outside class and record what they see. Assess the reasons for any differences and be prepared to share your experiences in class. Is self-image involved?

4 Reread the various definitions of communication offered in chapter 1 and be prepared for a classroom discussion of the drawbacks and merits of each.

5 With a classmate, prepare an eight- to ten-minute dialogue in the form of an interview or role play (for instance, a job interview, a dialogue with an arresting officer,

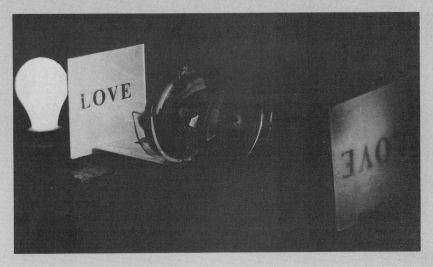

Figure 1.19 Speaker analogy model. *From a radio-TV-film student, William Kennedy, Wayne State University.*

a doctor's appointment, a conversation with a friendly bartender), so as to introduce each of you to the rest of the class.

6 Create a seven- or eight-word message and whisper it to one class member, who in turn whispers it to the next person. Have the last class member repeat the message aloud and compare it to the original. Discuss the results.

Figure 1.20 Police communication model. *From a model by student John H. Kim, Wayne State University.*

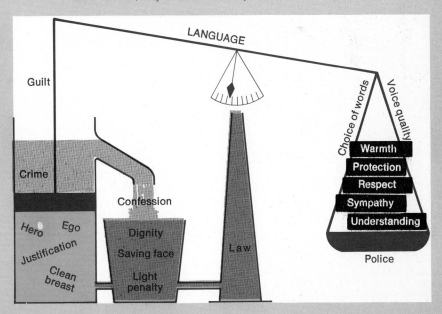

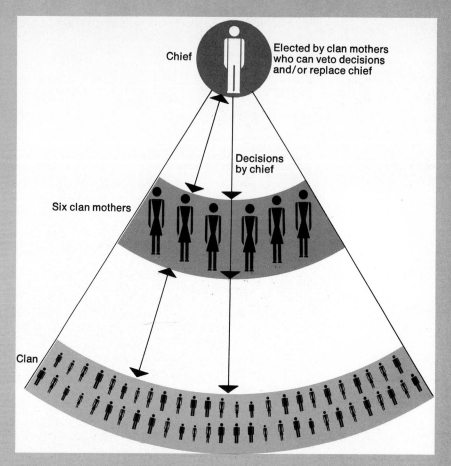

Figure 1.21 Iroquois Indian (Wolf Clan) communication model. *From a model by student Glenn Mosley, Wayne State University.*

7 Read the following message once and count the *f*s in it. Compare your count with those of other class members and discuss any differences. Would an illiterate person have as much trouble making the correct count?

> The necessity of training farm hands on first-class farms in the fatherly handling of farm livestock is foremost in the minds of farm owners. Since the forefathers of the farm owners trained the farm hands on first-class farms in the fatherly handling of farm livestock, the farm owners feel they should carry on with the family tradition of training farm hands on first-class farms in the fatherly handling of farm livestock, because they believe it is the basis of good fundamental farm management.

8 Note how past experience interferes with this simple instruction: connect all nine dots with four connecting straight lines. Discuss the implications of such interference for communication theory.

9 Prepare an oral report or essay in which you attempt to prove or disprove any of the speech communication principles listed in this chapter.

10 Communication models often serve very specific purposes—instruction, prediction, research, classification, and so on. Study the models in Appendix A, and try to determine the specific purpose of each. Evaluate their success. Prepare for a class discussion on communication models.

11 Keep a communication log. Guidelines are listed below.

Communication Log

The communication log is a record and analysis of your personal communication experiences. Minimum standards (for a grade of B on the log) are as follows:

1 *Number of entries:* Entries should be made on *at least* four days of each week. Date your entries.

2 *Nature of entries:* Each week, at least one entry should describe something that occurred in class and at least one entry should be of something that occurred outside class. Some of the entries may be brief (for example, one sentence). Other entries should be much longer in order to demonstrate that you are growing in the ability to understand and analyze the communication problems of both yourself and others. In either case, try to explain why a speech or discussion went well or poorly. Your efforts to explain what occurred in a discussion are the principal criterion for distinguishing between "A" and "B" logs.

In the first two weeks of the course, you *must* make one entry that describes your strengths and weaknesses in communicating with others and that states what you expect to accomplish in this course. Be specific.

During the last week, one entry *must* describe again what you think your strengths and weaknesses are and what you think you have accomplished during the term.

3 *References to the textbook:* The log must show that you have read the text. This requirement can be met by making a *minimum* of ten references to the text in your log entries.

GENERAL LEARNING OUTCOMES

1 We should be able to distinguish among mobs and audiences and to gain insight into the influence of such groups on speech communication.

2 We should become familiar with the importance of audience analysis to audience configurations, seating arrangements, and audience characteristics affecting speech communication.

3 We should be able to explain the differences between dyadic and audience models of the communication process.

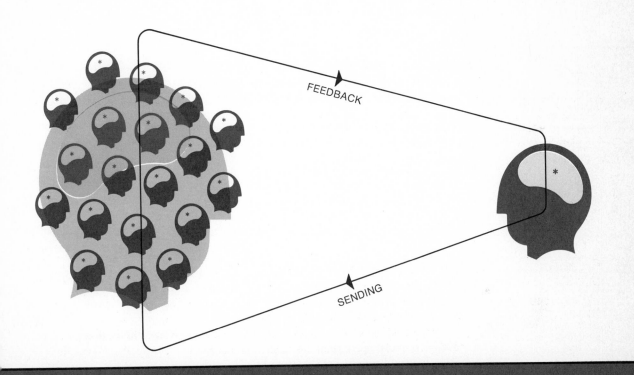

FEEDBACK

SENDING

audience psychology

Our emphasis in speech communication training generally is on passive audiences. However, the modern speaker is also meeting active, expressive, and aggressive collections of people. In recent times we have known demonstrations, panics, riots, and other types of collective behavior that challenge long-standing rhetorical advice. Most of our research and theorizing assumes relatively passive audiences and groups. We can understand more standard audiences by looking at what happens in more stimulated groups.

MOB BEHAVIOR

When an audience becomes a mob, as in a panic, we see people at their worst. The Chicago Iroquois Theatre fire of 1903, as related by the comedian Eddie Foy, who was on stage when it occurred, is a staggering real-life example.

> "Fire!" . . . The crowd was beginning to surge toward the doors and already showing signs of a stampede. . . . They were falling into panic. . . . Especially in the gallery, they had gone mad.
>
> The horror in the auditorium was beyond all description. . . . The fire escape ladders could not accommodate the crowd, and many fell or jumped to death on the pavement below. Some were not killed only because they landed on the cushion of bodies of those who had gone before. . . . Most of the dead were trampled or smothered. . . . In places on the stairways, . . . bodies were piled seven or eight feet deep. . . . The heel prints on the dead faces mutely testified to the cruel fact that human animals stricken by terror are as mad and ruthless as stampeding cattle. Many bodies . . . had the flesh trodden from their bones. . . .
>
> From the start of the fire until all in the audience either escaped, died, or lay maimed in the halls and alleys, took just eight minutes. In that 8 minutes more than 500 perished. . . . Subsequent deaths among the injured brought the list up to 602.[1]

Le Bon suggests that when a crowd is focused into a mob, a *psychological law of mental unity* comes into play.[2] The participants become a sort of "collective mind," and conscious personality is lost; each person thinks and behaves quite differently from the way he or she would if acting alone. This is the same phenomenon that E. D. Martin describes as "crowd mentality."[3]

[1] From the book *Clowning Through Life* by Eddie Foy and Alvin F. Harlow. Copyright, 1928, by E. P. Dutton & Co., Inc. Renewal, © 1956 by Alvin F. Harlow. Published by E. P. Dutton & Co., Inc. and used with their permission.

[2] Gustave Le Bon, *The Crowd* (New York: The Viking Press, 1960), p. 26.

[3] E. D. Martin, *The Behavior of Crowds* (New York and London: Harper & Brothers, 1920), pp 4–5

Martin classified this collective mind into dreams, delusions, and automatic behavior. It is as if our animal nature or id were unleashed. According to Martin the mob becomes "a device for indulging ourselves in a kind of temporary insanity by all going crazy together."[4] For Martin and Le Bon alike, the mob lurks under the skin of us all. In this view mobs may be weapons of revenge. They are always uncompromising in their demands, and in no way do they respect individual dignity. Even their achievements are less a testament to their leadership than a consequence of their unbridled fury.

For Le Bon, Martin, Ross, and others, the mob is a group in which people's normal reactions become secondary to unconscious desires and motivations. The major mechanisms leading to a state of *collective mind* or *mob mentality* appear to be *anonymity, contagion,* and *suggestibility.* One who is lost in the press of the mob loses much of his or her sense of responsibility. This anonymity produces an inflated feeling of power. Contagion was best

[4] *Ibid.,* p. 37.

Figure 2.1
Photo credit: Bill Anderson from Monkmeyer Press Photo Service.

illustrated by the panic attending the Iroquois Theatre fire, described earlier. It is a kind of high-speed, infectious mayhem. A heightened state of suggestibility leads to hasty, thoughtless, and rash action. Many of one's restraining emotions are lost—fear is often gone in battle, pity in a riot or a lynching.

A complete concept of *collective mind* includes, of course, the ethical and legal issues of sanity and guilt or innocence. One can argue that stupidity, suggestibility, and irrationality exist in individuals as much as in mobs and that individuals vary in their degree of participation in mob action.[5] One can also argue, as has Floyd Allport, that mobs simply supply a form of *social facilitation:*[6] individuals' desires are stimulated merely by the sight and sound of others making similar movements.

A modern social psychologist, Roger Brown, argues that "something new is created. To describe this new thing, this 'emergent,' as a 'group mind' does not seem to be seriously misleading. It may be a degree more illuminating to say that what emerges in the crowd is a payoff matrix that does not exist for the members when they do not compose a crowd."[7]

There is still much to uncover about the behavior of crowds and mobs. In a sense, they add a new dimension to modern speech communication.

AUDIENCE ANALYSIS

There is far less emotionality and irrationality in a typical audience than in a mob; the "group mind" is nowhere near as evident, and regressive acts are comparatively rare. Nevertheless, motivational forces are present even in very casually organized audiences. More formal audiences, such as classes of students, church groups, and lecture gatherings, which are intentionally and purposefully organized, are motivated by more identifiable forces.

Audiences, like mobs, can vary considerably in size. We believe that the small group of six or less is special enough to be considered separately in chapter 14. We therefore are most concerned with relatively formal, intentional audiences of roughly twenty or more persons. We are concerned mainly with audiences that are present physically. When we are dealing with vast, unseen audiences as in the mass media, we are for the most part beyond interpersonal influence and must utilize a more sociological and political analysis of primary contacts (such as family and friends), secondary contacts (religious and political affiliations, occupational ties, and so on), and definable *publics*. Nevertheless, much of what is said below will also apply to the mass media audience. Let's try now to adapt the Ross communication model (figure 1.6), a dyadic model, to audiences (figure 2.2).

[5] R. H. Turner and L. M. Killian, *Collective Behavior* (Englewood Cliffs, N.J.: Prentice-Hall, Inc., 1957, 1972).

[6] Floyd N. Allport, *Social Psychology* (Cambridge, Mass.: Riverside Press, 1924).

[7] Roger Brown, *Social Psychology* (New York: Free Press, 1965), p. 760.

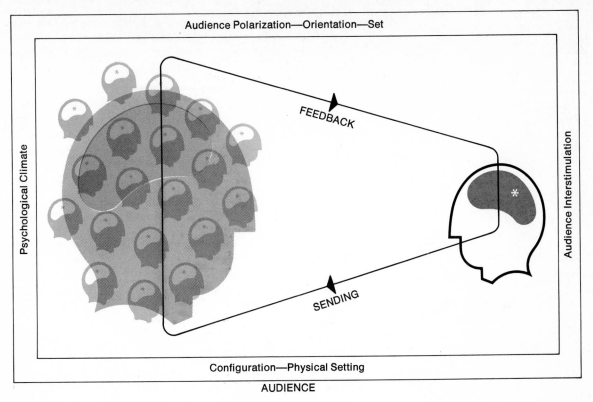

Figure 2.2 Ross communication model, as adapted to audiences.

Most of what was said about the Ross dyadic model in chapter 1 applies directly here. The audience model obviously has a larger potential for interstimulation and its consequences, and the problems of physical setting and feedback are more important. The analysis of audiences by types becomes in part an averaging process, and we must realize that such generalizing inevitably fits some members of the audience poorly and others perhaps not at all. Accordingly, the model in figure 2.2 places some of the members outside of the general audience concept.

The audience frequently has been considered as a statistical concept, as a means of assembling a large amount of information about individuals into manageable form (average age, income, nationality, education, and so forth).[8]

Audiences have also been classified into many general types, such as organized-unorganized, unified, heterogeneous, apathetic, hostile, polarized, and bipolar. More will be said about types of audiences shortly. In general, the audience we are talking about is a fairly formal collection of

[8] Theodore Clevenger, *Audience Analysis* (Indianapolis and New York: The Bobbs-Merrill Co., Inc., 1966), pp. 13–22.

individuals who assemble for a specific purpose. Patterns of interaction are reasonably predictable in such groups, given enough information.

Three of these patterns are *polarization, interstimulation,* and *feedback-response. Polarization* describes unusually homogeneous audience attitudes. When two relatively homogeneous but opposing factions are present in an audience, the audience is referred to as *bipolar.* Debates often attract bipolar audiences. *Interstimulation* refers to some of the volatile behavior characteristic of mobs and more specifically to Allport's concept of social facilitation. It includes ritual, suggestion, and the reinforcement one receives from similar behavior occurring at the same time. When all of those around us are angry, we are apt to be angry; when all are happy, we are apt to be happy. *Feedback-response* is a positive response to the efforts of the speaker; a negative response is quite another matter. If the speaker is strongly reinforced by positive feedback, he or she may become closely identified with some ideal. With strong interstimulation this identification may lead to exceptional, if only temporary, polarization among the speaker's listeners, an enviable situation as long as the persuader can control it and live with the results over a period of time. An aroused audience, let us remember, is only a few steps removed from a mob.

The classic categorization of audiences was made by H. L. Hollingworth, who suggested five types: (1) pedestrian, (2) discussion passive, (3) selected, (4) concerted, and (5) organized audiences. Hollingworth's categories make sense not only for dyadic and small-group siuations but also for more formal settings. Hollingworth used the term *orientation,* by which he meant "the establishment of a pattern of attention, when the group is considered, or a set and direction of interest, when we consider the individuals comprising the group."[9]

The *pedestrian audience* is a temporary audience, such as a group of pedestrians on a busy street corner. No common ties or lines of communication bind the members of the audience to the speaker. The first step, that of catching everyone's attention, is crucial. How far the process goes beyond that varies with the purpose of the speaker.

The *discussion group* or *passive audience* is one whose attention is already secured or guaranteed by rules of order. The persuader's initial problem is more likely to be the second step, that of *holding* attention or interest. Again, how long the persuader can do so depends upon the occasion or the success of the persuader.

The *selected audience* is one whose members are assembled for some common purpose, but not all are sympathetic to one another or to the speaker's point of view. Impression, persuasion, and direction characterize the speaker's undertaking here.

The *concerted audience* is one whose members assemble with a common, active purpose in mind, with sympathetic interest in a mutual enterprise, but

---

[9] H. L. Hollingworth, *The Psychology of the Audience* (New York: American Book Co., 1935, 1977), p. 21.

with no clear division of labor or rigid organization of authority. A sense of conviction and delegation of authority are the speaker's chief responsibilities.

The *organized audience* is a group with a rigid division of labor and authority supported by specific common purposes and interests. The tasks of the members are well learned, having already been assigned by the leader. The persuader has only to issue instructions, since the audience is already persuaded.

Before appearing in front of the audience, according to Hollingworth, the speaker ought to secure as full a knowledge as possible of the mode and degree of the audience's orientation. The speaker must be prepared to shift tactics if the first reactions of the audience show that his or her initial judgment was wrong.

According to Hollingworth, the five fundamental tasks of a persuader are *attention, interest, impression, conviction,* and *direction.* From these we can gain a better picture of what distinctions Hollingworth saw among the five types of audiences. We shall have more to say about the five tasks in part 4. In figure 2.3 we have listed the five tasks under the types of audiences to which they are most relevant. For instance, the principal tasks of a person

Figure 2.3 Hollingworth's categorization of audiences and tasks.
From H. L. Hollingworth, The Psychology of the Audience
(New York: American Book Co., 1977), p. 21.

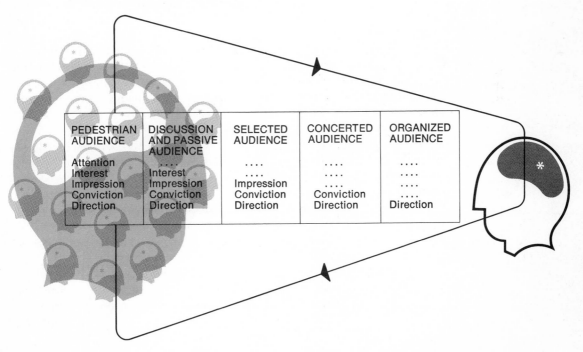

speaking before a concerted audience are to instill conviction and to delegate authority.

According to Hollingworth , the craving for an audience is one of humanity's fundamental needs. One of the most significant characteristics of an individual is the type of audience that most readily motivates his or her thought and conduct.

Closely related to both interpersonal communication and speaker-audience interaction is Hollingworth's observation that there is often a striking conflict between our craving for an audience and our fear of it. We probably seek a certain amount of confrontation or encounter and at the same time resist it.

Audience configuration (seating arrangement, closeness, and the like) is thought to be an important aspect of collective behavior and audience analysis. In somewhat polarized or formal audiences, the occasion and associated *ritual* may become an overwhelming part of the configuration. This is an important point. The Japanese auto worker who as a ritual does five minutes of company-coordinated calisthenics every morning, sings songs, and cheers his or her second-shift replacement is a different breed from most of the auto workers in Detroit.

We take the rituals of our social clubs, veterans' organizations, and churches well in stride. However, speakers had better be cautious and pragmatic about the rituals of their audiences. The old public-speaking adage against using foul language is probably a useful one, especially when ritual is part of the audience configuration. The most foul-mouthed among us often becomes the purest of tongue in such situations. The audience's resentment of the blasphemer who misassesses its temper is devastating. If a mob can become animalistic, some if not most audiences can, in a flash become holier than thou! More will be said of verbal obscenity in chapter 3.

The *physical setting* is part of the occasion and ritual. The pulpit in a church adds something to the minister's message. In like manner the raised dais in the House of Representatives imparts extra authority to the Speaker's words. The old Globe Theatre was no ordinary house! What we do with lighting, music, and pomp is also part of the physical setting and ritual. The same message uttered in a church, a restaurant, and a fraternity house might be sacrilege in the first, rudeness in the second, and understatement in the third! People have different expectations in different settings as well as in different situations. The proximity of the speaker to the audience is also thought to be important to audience psychology. If you are on an elevated platform far removed from the first row of the audience, your style of delivery should be different from the style you would use if you were close to the group.

The *arrangement* of the audience also affects how it reacts to persuasion and influence, although there is mixed evidence as to how it does. Fixed seating, recorded messages, or institutionalized environments, in which much of the "groupness" is at a minimum to begin with, all are important. Apparently, compactness itself does not mean that an audience will be more receptive to all types of messages. Logical, factual persuasion is probably most effective when listeners are separated, and emotional appeals are probably most successful when listeners are close together.

Several useful questions relating to *audience-message analysis* have been suggested by Jon Eisenson and his associates:[10]

1 *What is the significance of the subject for the audience?* Is its interest in the subject only casual, or is it motivated by real needs and wants? How far has its thinking about the problem progressed?

2 *What does the audience know about the subject?* Does it have essential factual information, or only opinions and sentiments? Are its sources of information sound ones, unbiased and complete?

3 *What beliefs or prejudices does the audience have about the subject?* In either case, what are the probable sources or influences in the formation of these existing notions?

4 *What is the attitude of the audience toward the subject?* Is it possible to estimate the percentage who are favorable, neutral, or unfavorable toward the problem?

Some *general descriptive measures* worth considering in audience analysis are:

1 *Age.* It is obvious that an audience of ten-year-olds will call for considerably different preparation by the speaker than will a group of forty-year olds, even if the subject is Little League baseball. Merely a few children in an otherwise all-adult audience sometimes presents a problem. Even if you choose (or are advised) to ignore them, you can be certain that the *audience* will not; rather, they will establish norms of appropriateness and understanding based on the presence of the youngsters. A risqué story is less well received when even a single child is present.

2 *Sex.* An audience of twenty men often differs considerably in outlook from an audience of twenty women. Likewise, an audience of ten men and ten women is different from either of the homogeneous audiences. An audience of nineteen men and one woman may cause a male speaker to alter many of his jokes and examples, not necessarily *because* of the one woman but because of nineteen men's expectations that the speaker will be conscious of the one woman. If you ignore the women in your audience, the men will be unhappy.

3 *Education.* A person's education is the sum of that person's learning. Do not confuse schooling with education, for schooling is no guarantee of an education. There are many uneducated college graduates! Nevertheless, formal schooling is in many cases a faster and more systematic way of acquiring knowledge than other ways are. A person's level of schooling may therefore be useful information to consider in planning your speech. Your language and vocabulary should be adapted to your audience's educational level and previous schooling. Moreover, an audience with a highly technical education will require a different approach than one with a religious or a liberal arts background. Here again, the problem of variable educational

---

[10] Jon Eisenson, J. Jeffery Auer, and John V. Irwin, *The Psychology of Communication* (New York: Appleton-Century-Crofts, 1963), p. 279.

levels presents itself. Time invested in this kind of audience analysis is usually well spent.

4 *Occupation.* Typing a person by his or her occupation is as dangerous as classifying a person according to schooling. Nevertheless, knowing one's occupation is often useful. For instance, the average income level of your audience can often be predicted by knowing the occupation of most of its members. Furthermore, you can predict that teachers will have college degrees, top management executives may have similar opinions of pieces of labor legislation, and so on.

5 *Primary group memberships.* Most of us belong to so many groups that to predict the groups represented in even a uniform audience is often shaky at best. For example, an audience at a political convention may be one-hundred percent Republican or one-hundred percent Democratic and yet may represent many religious, ethnic, and occupational groups, not to mention attitudes toward key issues. However, the more you can learn about the groups to which an audience does or does not belong, the more intelligently you can prepare your speech.

6 *Special interests.* Whatever its differences in primary group membership, audiences are often highly polarized if they all have some special interest in common. A small community with a winning high-school basketball team may unceremoniously ignore a guest speaker if he or she is unaware of this special interest. Sometimes these interests are temporary, but a speaker will do well to seek out and become familiar with any special interests about which the audience *expects* him or her to know something.

7 *Audience-subject relationships.* This part of your analysis concerns an audience's *knowledge* of your speech topic, its *experience* and *interest* in the subject, and its *attitude* toward your specific purpose. It is often valuable to know the extent of audience uniformity in these matters.

Audiences are sometimes very firm in their beliefs, whatever their level of knowledge or experience. Specific strategies for such a situation are covered at length in part 3. In general, an audience is interested in or apathetic toward your speech *subject,* but the audience's attitudes are directed toward your *purpose.* A useful scale for determining the general audience attitude toward the purpose of your speech is shown in figure 2.4.

Your preparation of your speech and your arrangement of its material will depend heavily upon this kind of analysis.

Figure 2.4

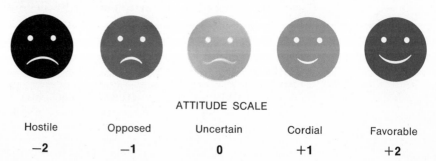

ATTITUDE SCALE

Hostile	Opposed	Uncertain	Cordial	Favorable
−2	−1	0	+1	+2

2 SUMMING UP

Audience behavior includes that observed in *mobs, audiences,* and *small groups.* When a crowd turns into a mob, suggests Le Bon, a psychological law of mental unity or "collective mind" makes a mob think and behave quite differently from the way in which the members would act individually. The major mechanisms that alter the mob members' behavior appear to be anonymity, contagion, and suggestibility. Mobs stimulate and aid in the expression of individuals' repressed desires.

In an audience, the "group mind" is nowhere near as evident, regressive acts are less gross, and emotionality and irrationality are generally less widespread. More formal audiences, such as classes of students, church groups, and lecture gatherings, which are intentionally and purposefully organized, are groups whose motivating forces are more identifiable than those of casual groups. Three reasonably predictable patterns of interaction are *polarization, interstimulation,* and *feedback-response.*

H. L. Hollingworth enumerates five types of audiences: (1) pedestrian, (2) discussion-passive, (3) selected, (4) concerted, and (5) organized. In his view, persuaders undertake five fundamental tasks (attention, interest, impression, conviction, and direction), all of which are necessary when speaking to nonpolarized, pedestrian audiences and only one of which (direction) is necessary in speaking to highly polarized, organized audiences.

Audience configuration considerations include ritual, physical setting, and seating arrangement.

Some general descriptive measures usually considered in analyzing an audience are age, sex, education, occupation, primary group membership, special interests, and audience-subject relationships.

Speech Communication Principles

1   The major mechanisms influencing the psychology of mobs are anonymity, contagion, and suggestibility.

2   Polarization, interstimulation, and response to feedback are reasonably predictable patterns of interaction in groups.

3   Formal audiences that are intentionally and purposefully organized are groups whose motivating forces are more identifiable than those of casual groups.

4   Distinctions between types of audiences are critical to a reality-based theory of speech communication.

5   There appears to be a conflict between our need for an audience and our fear of it. We seek and yet resist a certain amount of confrontation.

6   In highly polarized or formal audiences, the occasion and its associated ritual often become an all-important part of the audience configuration.

7   Assuming some homogeneity in the audience, logical, factual messages are more effective when listeners are separated; physical closeness is more apt to enhance emotional messages.

Specific Learning Outcomes

1   We should learn about various types of audiences and about various patterns of audience interaction (for instance, polarization, interstimulation, and response to feedback).

2   We should understand the categories of audiences delineated by H. L. Hollingworth (pedestrian, discussion-passive, selected, concerted, and organized).

3   We should understand the general descriptive measures utilized in audience analysis and be able to explain their usefulness in preparing a message.

Communication Competencies

1   We should be able to evaluate a real or hypothetical group of people and determine whether it is a mob or an audience, and of what specific kind.

2   We should be able to develop an awareness of our own interstimulation in group situations, relate this awareness to the models described, and write an objective analysis of our own feelings and behavior.

3   We should be able to assess the general impact of setting, seating arrangements, and ritual in most audiences with which we are familiar.

4   We should be able to apply the general descriptive measures for audience analysis to the audience to whom we will speak, and to check our assessment against the facts which are ultimately determined through class discussion and/or records.

Study Projects and Tasks

1   Observe live or televised groups of people until you find two clear-cut examples of (1) a mob and (2) an audience. Describe each in a page or less.

2   Describe in one page an audience situation about which you know that approached the "crowd [mob] mentality" description of E. D. Martin.

3 Remain near the center of an active group (for instance, a demonstration, revival meeting, athletic event, fight, or political rally) until you feel a sense of interstimulation (anonymity, contagion, suggestibility) or collective mind. Leave, and write the most detailed account possible of how you felt, what impulses came over you, what seemed to cause these impulses, and how one might have avoided them.

4 Attend the meeting of a relatively ritualized group (for example, a church service, an award ceremony, a graduation, or a funeral service), and write a short report on the influence of ritual and audience arrangement on communication.

5 Prepare a two-minute speech to counter-persuade a hypothetical crowd of twenty-five. Assume your listeners are in a suggestible, active, aggressive, turbulent mood. (For example, assume they are faced with a fire, flood, or other threatening situation which does not *really* warrant panic; or assume they form an angry, menacing mob whose actions are about to get out of hand.) Some heckling might make this project more realistic.

GENERAL LEARNING OUTCOMES

1   We should learn the fundamental importance of language habits and semantics as they relate to meaning and one's total communication effectiveness.

2   We should learn about the sensitive nature of words and language segments and their impact upon human behavior and understanding.

3   We should learn that language habits affect and reflect our personality.

4   We should learn that unless we become aware of abstraction, generalization, and semantics, we are not meeting the ethical responsibilities of an educated communicator.

3

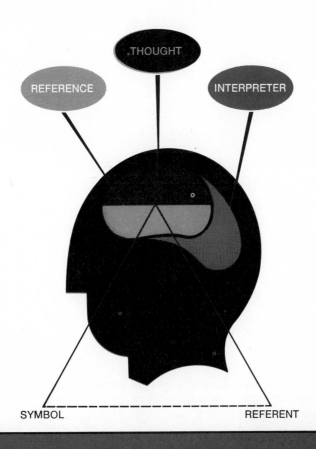

REFERENCE

THOUGHT

INTERPRETER

SYMBOL   REFERENT

language habits

CODE AND SYMBOL

It is in the use of oral language that we need our most rigorous training, for there is an infinitely larger number of oral means available to the listener than to the reader. This is because of the *concomitant* signals—those that accompany and operate at the same time as the words. Your voice, for example, is a wonderfully sensitive instrument with a powerful influence upon the meaning the listener attaches both to your words and to you, the speaker. Your correct use of your voice and your articulation is thus very important. Funky Winkerbean is a good example.

The appearance of the speaker—dress, movements, facial expressions, and gestures—is another signal that affects the decoding by the listener. Neither the customer's language nor his appearance seemed to sit well with Id's bartender!

Another, less obvious point to be made is that these codes and signals affect one another. Sometimes they work together and strengthen the meaning intended by the speaker. At other times, however, they conflict with one another and distort the intended meaning to the point at which the listener is confused, suspicious, or frustrated. Consider the sloppy student presenting a speech on the value of personal neatness, or the professor with a frozen grin discussing the possibility of a student's failing her course. We often act in a way contrary to what we really intend. The cause may be tension, emotional involvement, or simply poor speech training.

Figure 3.1 *"Funky Winkerbean"*
by Tom Batiuk, courtesy of Field Enterprises, Inc.

Figure 3.2 By permission of Johnny Hart and Field Enterprises, Inc.

Let's turn now to the all-important symbols we call *words*, remembering that the codes and symbols previously discussed will affect their intended meaning in ways other than those described here. Words are symbols which are conventionally used to represent certain things. They are convenient labels which help us to classify things. It is obvious that there are more things and concepts in the world than there are words. So you think a rat is a rat. Try the definitions in figure 3.3.

As another example, if each chair in the world had its own label, we would have to have dictionaries of chairs. Even with the general classifying word *chair,* we have developed a large vocabulary of chair-words (for example, Windsor, Hitchcock, stuffed, swivel, rocking). In short, if we did not use a limited number of words to represent an infinite number of things, we could communicate hardly at all. Despite our useful and necessary dictionaries, no word has real meaning except in the particular context in

Figure 3.3

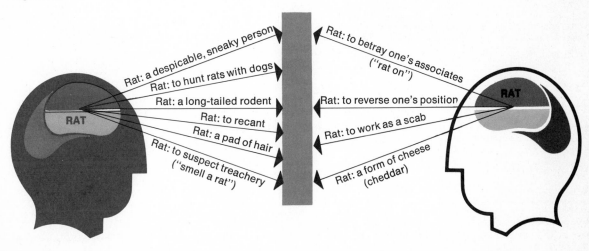

which it is used. The meaning of a word is never quite the same from one occasion to another, although the variation in meaning may not always be great. Word meanings change when we take words for granted and think of them as actual things rather than as what they really are—representations of things. A good speaker must always ask, "What does *this* word mean to *this* audience in *this* situation, in *this* context, as used by *this* speaker at *that* time?"

A word may be considered, then, as a representation or generalization with its meaning matching its context. When we arrange words into the context of a sentence—that is, when we create *syntax*—we are really fitting generalizations together. The meaning of an English sentence is determined not by its words alone but by the whole arrangement and sequence of the words. Even this meaning may be vague if the relationship of the sentence to the paragraph or chapter is not known.

In one sense, the communication pattern of a sentence is the systematic exclusion of meanings the listener might attach which are *not* intended by the speaker. In short, the sentence may define meanings *not* intended.

Ever-changing black slang is a good example of how words can be confusing if you are not familiar with them. Try yourself on some of these.

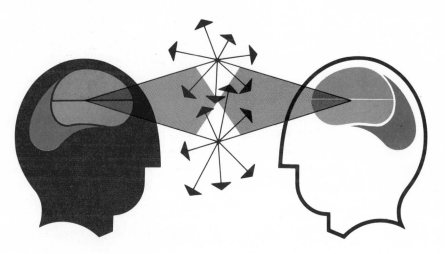

bad:	bad or good (used to mean good)
bleach:	bribe money
down home:	jail or prison (used to mean the South)
early:	late
Rufus:	the first all-black state (future)
LeRoy:	capital of Rufus
q:	rescue, barbecue, etc. (q sound)
stay:	go
xylophone:	cello

In light of the above, it is not difficult to understand why there are sensitivities to certain words and why people may sometimes react negatively to words not intended to be derogatory. If Americans were more aware of the words and phrases likely to provoke anger, there might be better communication between us.

Were Confucius alive today, he might well be pained by our fascination with slang. He once said, "The first step in finding out the truth is to call things by their right names."

Verbal obscenity is also a part of the modern scene. Words can hurt us. According to James Michener, the National Guardsmen involved in the Kent State tragedy were particularly enraged by the obscenities shouted by female demonstrators.

Michener quoted a guardsman, Sergeant Gordon R. Bedall, a supervisor for a trucking company, who rode a jeep in the midst of the disturbances:

> I sort of suspected there might be some rock-throwing, but what happened was much worse. The coeds in the crowd began yelling at us, and I wouldn't dare repeat what they said. It was incredible. I'd never heard such filth from our truck drivers. . . . I looked at Dennis Lutey, who was riding right-hand shotgun, and he sat with his mouth open. We couldn't believe that such language was coming from young ladies. . . . A very pretty girl stuck her hand right under my nose, gave me the finger, and uttered four words I've never used myself. I've been on riot duty before, but I've never encountered such language, not even among the raunchiest whores on Wooster Avenue.[1]

"To hear obscenities in common usage from girls who could have been their sisters produced a psychic shock which ran deep," Michener relates. "To many of the guardsmen these girls had removed themselves from any special category of 'women and children.'"[2]

What is clear from researched accounts is that language contributes hugely to tensions such as those at Kent State. No one claims that people shoot because they are being called names. Events are usually much more complex than that. But shockingly obscene words have a way of stunning the rationality of both those who use them and those to whom they are addressed.

In more recent research the male-female assumptions were not supported, indicating some shifting beliefs regarding appropriate language for males and females. However, this same research[3] did find that speakers using obscene phrases were rated lower in "socio-intellectual status" and "aesthetic quality."

[1]James A. Michener, "Kent State: What Happened and Why," *Reader's Digest,* April 1971, p. 232.
[2]*Ibid.;* see also S. I. Hayakawa, "The Uses of Obscenity," *Saturday Evening Post,* Spring 1972, p. 123.
[3]Anthony Mulac, "Effects of Obscene Language upon Three Dimensions of Listener Attitude," *Communication Monographs,* 43, no. 4 (November 1976), 300–7. However, no differences were found for speaker "dynamism."

The riots at the 1968 Democratic National Convention in Chicago entailed much obscenity and counter-obscenity. John Bowers and Donovan Ochs say flatly that "the tactic that probably prompted the 'police riot,' the violent suppression witnessed by millions on television, was the use of obscenity."[4]

How we should regard verbal obscenity in our study of rhetoric is a difficult question. The ancient rhetoricians stated without qualification that it should be rejected as a legitimate rhetorical strategy. J. Dan Rothwell, however, suggests that:

> neither denunciation nor suppression of its use is an adequate response to the fact of verbal obscenity; the students of rhetoric must seek to understand the purposes and effects of this rhetorical strategy. Despite centuries of negative criticism, verbal obscenity has become a more frequent rhetorical device. It is successful in creating attention, in discrediting an enemy, in provoking violence, in fostering identification, and in providing catharsis. Its effects are governed by a variety of circumstances which need to be understood more fully. It has precipitated a police riot, brutal beatings, and even death. Hoping it will go away will not make it so. It is time to accept verbal obscenity as a significant rhetorical device and help discover appropriate responses to its use."[5]

Modern research tells us that using profanity in a communication generally has a detrimental effect on the credibility of the speaker.[6] Suitable language is a necessary part of human social behavior.[7]

Because emotions are attached to language, careful audience analysis and word selection by the speaker are necessary. Words are not things or emotions, but we often act as if they are. Rather, language is abstract: it only represents real things.

ABSTRACTION

The heart of the difficulty with language is the confusion of the word with the thing for which it stands. The further we are from this thing—the *referent*—the more problems of meaning that arise. Meaning is thought to have three elements: a person having thoughts, a symbol (or sign), and a referent. The triangle of Ogden and Richards (figure 3.4) is a classic explanation.

[4]John Bowers and Donovan Ochs, *The Rhetoric of Agitation and Control* (Reading, Mass.: Addison-Wesley Publishing Co., Inc., 1971) p. 70.
[5]"Verbal Obscenity: Time for Second Thoughts," *Western Speech*, 35, no. 4 (1971), 242.
[6]Robert N. Bostrom, John R. Basehart, and Charles M. Rossiter, Jr., "The Effects of Three Types of Profane Language in Persuasive Messages," *Journal of Communication*, 23 (December 1973), 461–75.
[7]Edward A. Mabry, "A Multivariate Investigation of Profane Language," *Central States Speech Journal*, 26, no. 1 (1975), 39–44.

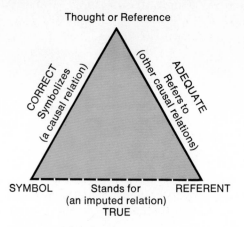

Figure 3.4 Ogden and Richards model.
From C. K. Ogden and I. A. Richards, The Meaning of Meaning *(New York: Harcourt, Brace, 1936; London: Routledge & Kegan Paul, 1936), p. 11.*

When we receive a symbol or sign, it travels to our *thought or reference* center. As in our communication model, figure 1.6, we consult our store-house of experience to find the thing or *referent* to which the symbol refers. The triangle in figure 3.4 is represented as having no base to make the crucial point that the symbol and its referent are not *directly* related. The word is not the thing! You cannot sit on the word *chair* or write with the word *pencil!*

Line A in figure 3.5 indicates what a person ideally perceives as a *correct* symbol, in this case the word *chair*. Line B represents the cognitive selecting and sorting of knowledge and experience which ideally represents an *adequate* referent. The broken line C indicates that the *word* chair and a *real* chair are not the same. Clear communication calls for a referent, a reference, and a symbol, which leads us to the subject of misuse of abstractions.

Abstracting is a process of thinking in which we selectively leave out details about concrete or real things. Perception has at least two elements, (1) sensation and (2) interpretation of this sensation. This interpretation is controlled by our individual knowledge, experience, and emotional set. For this reason, as well as because of the limitations of our language system discussed previously, all language contains an element of abstraction.

The process of abstraction occurs at different levels. For example, we have cars, sports cars, and Corvettes. The Corvette is a first-order abstraction; that is, it is a specific type of sports car, which in turn is a type of car. As we move from lower- to higher-order abstractions, we tend to consider fewer and fewer details of the specific, original object. Another way of looking at abstraction is to consider firsthand observations as facts, but as facts that may never be described completely. If we move away from

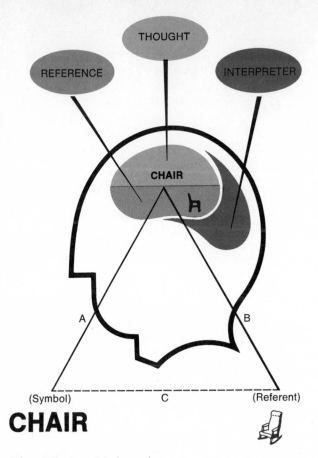

Figure 3.5 A model of meaning.

firsthand descriptions, we will be in a different order of abstraction—*inference*. Most simply, an inference goes beyond what is observed. If an ambulance is in your driveway when you return home, you may say, "One of my family has been seriously hurt." This is an inference. You must go into the house to see if it is valid. Upon entering the house, you may find a close friend excitedly telling your healthy family about his new business venture of converting station wagons into ambulances. Suppose you have been told by a resort owner that the fishing is great on the edge of some weeds. If you are a veteran fisherman, you will ask, "What does 'great' mean?" You will want more than inferences—namely, descriptions of this great fishing (such as, "Just this morning a fellow took five bass in two hours"). Of course, in dealing with fishermen one might be just a little suspicious of the reliability of the description (another inference)! When we are in the realm of inference, then, we are dealing with probability rather than with certainty.

SPECIFICITY

When we support our inferential statements with specific descriptive statements and examples, we use not only more accurate but probably more interesting language. The question of how specific to be is not always an easy one. For example, in explaining atomic fission to us a physicist might choose only terms that are closely related to his other referents—highly specific, technical, and scientific terms. The physicist in one sense is using accurate language, but the message may be very long (because of the detail) and for nonphysicists very difficult to understand. Should the physicist decide to eliminate detail in an effort to use less time and to avoid technical language in an effort to sustain interest, he or she will then lose precision of meaning; listeners may attach a wider range of meanings from their own experiences than was intended, and this might lead to serious distortion, confusion, or contradiction. Even seasoned commuters experienced confusion with the overload of specific suggestions that appear in figure 3.6.

Figure 3.6 Westbound motorists leaving the Ford Freeway at the Addison Road-Ford Road exit are confronted by this apparent contradiction in traffic control signs.
The conflicting signs may confuse drivers who see them for the first time, but commuters who pass that way regularly know that the top two signs prohibit right turns onto Cabot, the street before the signs (not shown). The bottom sign is for motorists, like those above, who continue past Cabot to Addison Road. *Photo by* The Detroit News.

For the speaker, the answer to this dilemma is usually found in the interest, previous knowledge, and experience of the audience. Just how important is it to be precise in speaking on this subject to this audience? Is there potential danger, such as in a speech on drug prescriptions or hypodermic injections to an audience of student nurses? Time is another factor: classroom speeches tend to be short, and this alone may foster overgeneralization, lack of specificity, and inaccuracy of meaning. It is probably easier to give a long speech than a short one.

LANGUAGE AND PERSONALITY

Language and the particular character you give it through your language usage is obviously important to your messages. Language habits alone often suggest our personality (or assumed personality) to the listener. For example, extreme cases of talkativeness or silence are often indications of emotional maladjustment. Any of us may exhibit these behaviors in moments of distress, peril, or unhappiness, but a consistent pattern of them may call for professional help. As we indicated in chapter 1, the problem of interpreting communication only in terms of one's desires is a serious problem; when practiced consistently, it is thought to indicate what the psychiatrist calls paranoia. One of the most characteristic language patterns of schizophrenics is an apparent confusion between words and things. The words are taken not as representations of reality, but as reality itself. Because objective, systematic abstraction is difficult for the schizophrenic, he or she tends to be extremely one-sided and opinionated. The sobering thought in discussing the extreme language habits of maladjusted individuals is that we all exhibit these habits to some degree. It behooves us to be aware of our language patterns lest we too represent a one-value world of words without referents. All "normal" speakers should ponder Wendell Johnson's compelling description of the linguistically irresponsible behavior of schizophrenics in the figure that follows.

(1) An "emotional flatness," an unresponsive, poker-faced air of detachment; (2) a grotesque confusion of sense and nonsense, essentially the same tone of voice, facial expression, and general manner being employed in making sensible remarks as in uttering the purest gibberish; (3) an apparent lack of self-criticism, a striking failure to show any glimmer of curiosity about whether the listener understands or agrees; and (4) a general confusion or identification of level of abstraction, as though all levels were one and the same, there being no apparent differentiation between higher and lower orders of inference and between inference and description.[8]

If this paragraph frightened you a little, this is a healthy sign, for your powers of evaluation had to go beyond just the words. Remember that your language habits reflect your personality. Let's now examine some practical suggestions for improving our language and avoiding linguistic behavior patterns that convey unintended and undesirable meanings.

IMPROVING OUR LANGUAGE HABITS

Almost any good course in speech, whatever its context (radio, television, public speaking, persuasion, oral interpretation, rhetoric, correction, theater, communication, discussion, or debate), puts a high premium on language habits. The instructor will criticize you diligently, knowing that proper language habits will make it easier for you to adjust to the linguistic demands of college life.

Reading and listening, when done systematically, will help improve your language behavior. In both reading and listening, you are essentially in the receiving and decoding aspect of communication. Critical, objective listening and reading habits have been an important base in the training of almost all famous speakers.[9]

When you read or listen to a speech, try to determine what the words mean to the speaker and how the timing of the communication, when it is said, morning, evening, happy time, and so forth, might alter the meaning. All the communication signals and cues have to be considered in critical listening; as was discussed earlier, the nonword signals (gestures, visual aids, vocal emphasis, and others) are an essential part of the message. The way in which an idea is stated cannot be divorced from the idea itself. Perhaps the most important aspect of listening, as well as reading, is the listener's awareness of his or her own beliefs, prejudices, or lack of knowledge; *what* we believe profoundly influences our ability to perceive objectively. This is not to suggest that one should not believe anything. Were this the case, we might never make a necessary decision. The point is simply to know more

---

[8]Wendell Johnson, *People in Quandaries* (New York: Harper & Row, Publishers, Inc., 1946), p. 275.
[9]See W. N. Brigance, ed., *History and Criticism of American Public Address* (New York: McGraw-Hill Book Company, 1943), p. vii.

precisely *what* we believe and be aware of its effect on our listening and reading habits.

It should be evident by this time that it is impossible for a person to "say exactly what he means." Much of our language behavior is what S. I. Hayakawa calls *presymbolic*[10]—that is, it may function even without recognizable speech, or perhaps with symbols approaching an *idiom* (an accepted expression with a meaning different from the literal). A grunt from my office partner at 8:00 A.M. means, "Good morning, it's good to see you." When you pass a friend on the street and she says "Hi," how does this really differ from "How are you?" Does "Nice day" mean just that and no more?

A favorite illustration of many teachers regarding this point concerns a man staring sadly at a very flat tire. A smiling farmer comes up and asks, "Got a flat tire?" If we take his words literally, his communication appears stupid indeed and we might answer, "Can't you see, birdbrain?" However, a famous psychiatrist interprets "Got a flat tire?" as follows:

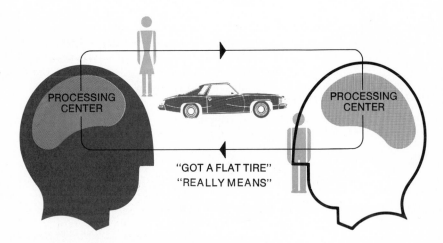

"GOT A FLAT TIRE"
"REALLY MEANS"

Hello—I see you are in trouble. I'm a stranger to you but I might be your friend now that I have a chance to be if I had any assurance that my friendship would be welcomed. Are you approachable? Are you a decent fellow? Would you appreciate it if I helped you? I would like to do so but I don't want to be rebuffed. This is what my voice sounds like. What does your voice sound like?[11]

When language is used in a presymbolic sense, we have to look considerably beyond the words to obtain the real meaning intended. In our efforts to become alert, critical listeners we must take care not to become so literal that we mistake tact and social grace for foolishness, hypocrisy, or

[10]S. I. Hayakawa, *Language in Thought and Action* (New York: Harcourt, Brace & World, 1949), p. 77.
[11]Karl Menninger, *Love against Hate* (New York: Harcourt, Brace & World, 1942), pp. 268–69.

stupidity. Much of what we refer to as small talk is in part presymbolic language. In order to become an objective and honest receiver or listener, we must strive to distinguish presymbolic from symbolic language.

SEMANTICS AND GENERAL SEMANTICS

In this section we are concerned with meaning. Some confusion is really unbelievable. Here are the exact words of a witness in an arbitration case. See if you can figure them out.

> Now, there is two obligations on them here in the plan, and I think one is more controlling over the other, and that is to do what they said they were going to do, and if they can't do what they said they were going to do in the manner in which they said they were going to do it, I don't feel that they are relieved from the obligation of doing what they said they were going to do, even if it had to be done in a manner other than what they said they were going to do, inasmuch as doing what they said they were going to do is consistent with their obligation under the agreement to do what they said they were going to do, and anything else would be inconsistent.

S. I. Hayakawa defines *semantics* as

> (1) in modern logic, the study of the laws and conditions under which signs and symbols, including words, may be said to be meaningful; semiotic [pertaining to signs]; and (2) the study of the relation between words and things, later extended into the study of the relations between language, thought and behavior, that is, how human action is influenced by words, whether spoken by others or to oneself in thought; significs. The word was originally used to mean (3) in philology, the historical study of changes in the meaning of words; semasiology [study of semantic change].[12]

The term *general semantics* is credited to Alfred Korzybski and is amplified in his book *Science and Sanity*.[13] If semantics concerns mainly meaning and changes in meaning, general semantics will extend these concepts to include relationships between symbols and behavior. Korzybski was interested in a human's total response to his or her environment—in particular, how a person evaluates and uses language and how language affects his or her attitudes, feelings, and behavior. Korzybski believes that much of the misunderstanding in the world has been caused by too dogmatic an acceptance of the assumptions of basic Aristotelian logic, particu-

[12]S. I. Hayakawa, *Language, Meaning and Maturity* (New York: Harper & Row, Publishers, Inc., 1954), p. 19.
[13]Alfred Korzybski, *Science and Sanity* (Lancaster, Pa.: Science Press, 1933).

larly in the human social realm. Since understanding and objective communication depend upon the relationship between language and reality, Korzybski believed that any system that was oversimplified "in the sense that words were confused with things" presented a threat to one's psychological and emotional flexibility, maturity, and sanity.[14]

The propositional nature of language can be a problem in some language systems. Even absurd statements can be grammatically correct. Try this!

Red is Green

Figure 3.7 B.C.
by permission of Johnny Hart and Field Enterprises, Inc.

The rules of formal logic have an obvious usefulness, as we shall see in chapter 12. The problem is that because of the propositional nature of language, we may become too literal and too rigid in our evaluation of words. These characteristics lead ultimately to poor logic, poor language habits, emotional imbalance, and misunderstanding. The principles of general semantics combat such dangers by allowing a communicator to judge his or her own evaluative process through the following kinds of checks or rules.

The $\boxed{\text{is}}$ *problem* is related to the principle of nonidentity. Simply stated, words are *not* things, even though we must use them as substitutes for things. The map is not the territory, as anyone who has ever been misled by an old map can readily tell you. You cannot write with the word *pencil.* Hayakawa comments that the injunction to "call a spade a spade" is profoundly misleading because it implies that we call it a spade because that's what it is. Language and thought are not identical. Words are not the things signified (the referents). Dictionaries do *not* give the referents, but only the meanings that people have given to words.

[14]For an excellent discussion of semantics, see Hayakawa, *Language, Meaning and Maturity;* see also his *Language in Thought and Action;* and Stuart Chase, *The Tyranny of Words* (New York: Harcourt, Brace, 1938).

The ⬚etc.⬚ or *et cetera rule* is related to the principle of nonallness. In a sense, this rule also refers to the awareness of abstracting—an awareness that we are leaving something out. One cannot say everything or the last word on a given matter; there is always more to be said. Thus, the good speaker leaves listeners with the impression that he or she has not attempted to say the last word on a subject. The speaker should avoid appearing to be a naive know-it-all, blinded by zeal or prejudice.

The ⬚index⬚ *rule* relates to overstatement and overgeneralization. All Democrats are not alike, nor are all Republicans alike. This rule would have us *think* in terms of, if not actually index or catalogue Democrat 1, Democrat 2, Democrat 3, and so on. It is a warning against taking stereotypes seriously and failing to appreciate individual differences.

One of the most widespread communication faults of student speakers is *false generalization*. This is the problem of selectively leaving out details and concluding after only a superficial examination that a thing is true beyond any shadow of doubt. If upon driving into Detroit for the first time you (1) witnessed a serious accident, (2) observed a truck exceeding the speed limit, and (3) had your fender dented at a busy intersection, you might be tempted to draw some strong conclusions, and speak in strong language about Detroit drivers. At the least, however, you would have to examine comparative safety records, driver education programs, and driver insurance rates before participating in any intelligent discussion about Detroit drivers. Even then, you might want to hedge your generalizations by noting that Detroit has more cars per person than any other city in the world.

A violently antiunion student speaker opened one of his class speeches with the words, "Unions are ruining this country. I am going to prove to you that they are entirely corrupt and more dangerous than hijackers." This language was enough for his opponents to throw up an emotional communication barrier, and as a result he was not very persuasive. The most interesting part of this story is that the promanagement listeners were most critical of the speech. Even when a sophisticated audience largely agrees with your point of view, it can be offended by extreme overstatement and overgeneralization, for these are indications of immaturity, emotional insecurity, or stupidity.

The irony and tyranny of overgeneralization is that it is usually not intended—it seems so obvious that all Detroit drivers are crazy! When a person speaks from firsthand experience in a sincere and friendly voice without being aware of faulty abstracting or generalizing, that person is faced with a serious problem. The communication problems of generalization are complicated, frustrating, and often dangerous. Once you understand this clearly, you have already solved much of the practical problem, for it is in being *aware* of abstracting and generalizing that you begin to restrain your own overstatement and reckless generalization. A practical way of using this awareness is to qualify and index your statements with great care.

The speaker carries an ethical responsibility proportionate to his or her reputation. Perhaps this is why sophisticated persons with high ethical standards are often accused of qualifying things to the point of vagueness—which raises the ethical question of how much you can qualify before you completely dodge your obligations and responsibilities.

Dating your language is another form of indexing worthy of a special rule. Often, the date of an event significantly affects the meaning a listener will attach to it. "At last the Japanese people have taken the actions that will restore their rightful dignity." Certainly, we would attach different meanings to this hypothetical statement by the Emperor of Japan according to whether it was uttered on:

January 7, 1925 (no special significance)
December 7, 1941 (Pearl Harbor)
September 2, 1945 (surrender of Japan)
July 1, 1968 (return of Okinawa)

A favorite exam question of one psychology professor was, "What are Thorndike's laws of learning?" This question is challenging because Thorndike changed his mind about some of his laws of learning and made this clear in his writings only after 1930. The student who had read only his pre-1930 writings would inevitably give the wrong answer.

When we respond to words or language apart from meaning and in an almost automatic, emotional way, we are guilty of *signal response*. If we can delay signal responses even a split second, we may get closer to the referents by understanding the total context. Did she *really* intend what I'm thinking? Was it just poor word choice? Am I a little oversensitive?

The either-or *response* is a type of overgeneralization that indicates that one's language habits are concealing differences of degree. The absolute ruler and the demagogue use this device regularly. All of us in moments of frustration or desperation seem to revert to "They're all no good," "You're either for me or against me," or "You'll never understand." When we routinely use words such as *all, nobody, everybody,* and *never,* we are guilty of a false-to-fact use of language. The speaker guilty of these exaggerations runs great risks of creating resentment, particularly among sophisticated audiences.

An extremely irritating form of this either-or response is what we might call *arrogant dismissal*. Irving Lee illustrates this most clearly in the following pattern of disagreement:

> The mood of dismissal [is that] in which a man makes it clear that he wishes to go no farther, to talk no more about something which is to him impossible, unthinkable, wrong, unnecessary, or just plain out of the question. He has spoken and there is little use in trying to make him see otherwise. If he has his way there will be no more discussion on the matter. "It won't work and that's all there is to it. . . . I refuse to listen to any more of this nonsense. . . .

Anybody who comes to such a conclusion has something wrong with him. . . . We've never worked that way before and we aren't going to start."[15]

Individuals who engage in this kind of behavior consistently are considered by Wendell Johnson to have serious "quandaries." Simplistic language such as that cited by Lee, usually reflects simplistic thinking or a high degree of emotional involvement.

Finally (and that itself is a dangerous word), try to think like the listener; try to understand your subject and position from *his* or *her* point of view. Audience analysis is a critical part of public speaking. Knowing what you think is equally important. If you do not care what the audience thinks, are not very sure of your own purpose, and are unaware of your preferences, your beliefs, and your word meanings, you are in for a difficult and frustrating series of speeches. The meaning of any speech is really in the mind of the listener. You must so manipulate your language to help the listeners sort and select from their word representations something approximating your purpose.

> Humpty-Dumpty said: "There's glory for you." "I don't know what you mean by 'glory,'" Alice said. Humpty-Dumpty smiled contemptuously. "Of course you don't—till I tell you." . . . "But 'glory' doesn't mean 'a nice knock-down argument,'" Alice objected. "When I use a word," Humpty-Dumpty said in a rather scornful tone, "It means just what I choose it to mean, neither more nor less."[16]

---

[15]Irving J. Lee, *How to Talk with People* (New York: Harper & Row, Publishers, Inc., 1952), p. 46.
[16]Lewis Carroll, *Through the Looking-Glass* (Cleveland: World Publishing, 1946), p. 245.

3 SUMMING UP

We have discussed language in the context of code and symbol. Oral language calls for more rigorous training than other forms of language do because of its larger number of concomitant signals. Voice, for example, has a powerful influence upon meaning. A speaker's appearance and gestures are other concomitant signals that affect the listeners.

A word is a kind of symbol. A word is a generally accepted representation of a thing. There are obviously more things and concepts in the world than there are words, so a word may be thought of as a representation or generalization with a meaning in accordance with its context. A speaker should ask, "What does *this* word mean to *this* audience in *this* situation, in *this* context, as used by *this* speaker at *this* time?" A good sentence systematically excludes meanings the listener might attach that are not intended by the speaker—in short, it qualifies by defining meanings *not* intended.

How we should approach verbal obscenity in rhetoric is a difficult problem. The ancient rhetoricians believed that verbal obscenity should be rejected as a rhetorical strategy, but recent commentators are beginning to question this view.

Abstraction is that process of thinking in which we selectively omit details about concrete or real things. The heart of the difficulty with language is the confusion of the word with the thing for which it stands. The further we are from the referent, the more problems of meaning that arise. Short speeches may foster overgeneralization, and this is why short speeches often call for more preparation than long ones do.

Language habits reflect your personality. Seriously maladjusted individuals can often be identified by their language habits. Speech courses, together with attentive reading and listening, will help you learn proper language behavior.

The *way* in which you say something is often as important as *what* you say. Listeners as well as speakers should be aware of their own beliefs, prejudices, or lack of knowledge. It is almost impossible to say *exactly* what you mean. We must be careful not to become so literal that we mistake tact and social grace for hypocrisy or stupidity. We must strive to distinguish presymbolic from symbolic language.

Semantics may be defined as the study of the laws and conditions under which signs and symbols may be said to be meaningful. It is the study of the relationship between words and things and, further, of how human action is influenced by words. Semantics concerns principally meaning and changes in meaning.

The propositional nature of language can be a problem in some language systems. If one becomes too literal and rigid, logic and language habits may be impaired and misunderstanding and emotional imbalance may result. Such dangers may be combated through sufficient appreciation of the *is* problem, the need for indexing and dating one's statements, and the need to avoid signal responses and either-or responses.

Sophisticated audiences are offended by overstatement and overgeneralization, even when they agree with the speaker's point of view. The speaker has a tremendous ethical responsibility. It is in being conscious of abstraction, generalization, and semantics that you begin to meet this responsibility. Qualify your statements appropriately. Try to think like the listener. Select your language so as to help the listener sort and select from his or her word representations something approximating your meaning.

Speech Communication Principles

1 Despite the existence of dictionaries, which are both useful and necessary, no word has real meaning except in the particular context in which it is used.

2 There is an emotional dimension to words. Words can hurt us.

3 The heart of the difficulty with language is the confusion of the word with the thing for which it stands: words are not their referents; one cannot say everything about anything; we use words to talk about words.

4 Language habits often convey our personality (or assumed personality) to the listener.

5 It is impossible for a person to "say exactly what he means."

6 Much of our language behavior is presymbolic; we must look beyond the words for the meaning.

7 Often, the date of an event or statement significantly affects the meaning a listener will attach to it.

8 If one becomes too literal and rigid, one will likely display poor logic, bad language habits, misunderstanding, and even emotional imbalance.

Specific Learning Outcomes

1 We should learn and be able to illustrate the emotional and cultural dimension of words through personal experience.

2 We should learn and be able to illustrate how context determines meaning.

3 We should learn and be able to reproduce the triangle of Ogden and Richards (see figure 3.4).

4 We should learn the difference between presymbolic and symbolic language and be able to produce several examples showing why the difference is important.

5 We should learn the three checks of general semantics and be able to define and illustrate each in a short oral or written report.

Communication Competencies

1 We should be able to illustrate, in a ten-minute dialogue, how context determines language meaning, to the satisfaction of an audience of fifteen to twenty-five persons who are familiar with the context of this chapter.

2 We should develop a sensitivity toward words and language as they affect meaning and interpersonal communication, to the satisfaction of the rest of the class and/or the instructor.

3 Our language behavior should be characterized by awareness of the *is* problem and the *et cetera* and *indexing* rules.

4 Our listening and critical behavior should be characterized by a more objective and flexible language sensitivity than is usually required.

5 We should learn to look for meanings in people, not just in symbols.

Study Projects and Tasks

1 Collect two examples of context confusion that caused language to mean different things to different individuals.

2 In one page, list five words or short language segments that annoy you (almost regardless of context), and try to explain why.

3 Interview a person of a different race or culture (or subculture) regarding the language he or she finds most offensive. Report results in one page or less.

4 Find an advertisement or commercial that you feel is racially, sexually, or culturally debasing (linguistically), and explain your choice.

5 Language can be quite tricky when it deliberately takes advantage of its propositional function, context, and the receiver's experience. See if you can untangle and answer the following. Discuss.

a How many members of each species did Moses take aboard the Ark?

b If you take two apples from three apples, how many do you have?

c How many outs are there in an inning in baseball?

d Can a man living in North Carolina be buried west of the Mississippi?

e Can a man in South Carolina marry his widow's sister?

f If a farmer lost all but nine of his seventeen sheep, how many would he have?

g If a doctor told you to take three pills, one every half-hour, how many hours would they last?

h Does England have a Fourth of July?

i How many birthdays does a man have in his average lifetime?

j How many months have twenty-eight days?

6 Discuss these examples of language breakdown, and try to recall instances of breakdown that you experienced.

> There is a story that the Japanese verb mokusatsu was responsible for the loosing of American atom bombs on Hiroshima and Nagasaki. The verb can mean either "no comment" or "to kill with silence" and was used in the Japanese newspaper accounts of the Japanese government's reaction to the American demand for unconditional and immediate surrender. By the time reports reached the Allied authorities, the second meaning was accepted, so it seemed that Premier Suzuki had rejected the ultimatum as "unworthy of notice." What he actually said, so the story goes, was that his government had decided to postpone action and withhold comment pending clarification of the demand for surrender.[17]

> DERBY, England—(UPI)—The men who referee women's soccer games have had enough. The ladies' language is too much for them.
>
> "The trouble is that some of the ladies do not behave like ladies," said Frank Hardwood, secretary of the 354-member Derby District Referees Society. "The language can be quite startling."
>
> He said the society is going to train women to referee women's matches from now on.[18]

[17]Mario Pei, *The Story of Language*, 2nd ed. (Philadelphia: J. B. Lippincott Company, 1965), p. 405.
[18]*The Detroit Sunday News*, November 5, 1972, p. 4D.

GENERAL LEARNING OUTCOMES

1 We should learn that nonverbal signals greatly affect how an audience interprets what we say.

2 We should learn the major areas of nonverbal communication.

3 We should learn the five major characteristics of nonverbal communication.

4 We should learn the standards of appropriate body action and facial expression in communication.

5 We should learn the impact on communication of the nonverbal signals of voice and articulation.

6 We should learn to make practical evaluations of the vocal and articulatory processes and pronunciation.

7 We should learn that we express attitudes through body action, voice, what we wear and own, and our use of time and space.

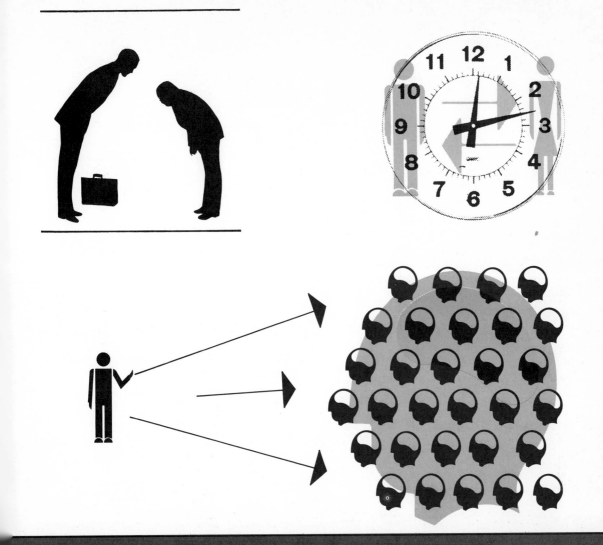

nonverbal communication

IMPORTANCE OF NONVERBAL COMMUNICATION

Do you realize that only 35 percent of communication may be verbal? When you speak face-to-face with a person, that person may be receiving 65 percent of your message by means other than the words you use—by your tone of voice, your gestures, even by the way you stand and are dressed.[1]

In one view, the relative ability or impact of the facial nonverbals may reach 55 percent and the vocal nonverbals 38 percent.[2] It may be that the blending of channels has more to do with meaning than the simple summing of all the channels.[3] In other words, the verbal is still critical to how we interpret the nonverbal.

When we find that a gesture that means "come here" in America means "go away" in Italy, we begin to sense the problem. There is evidence that in our own culture, black and white job applicants behave quite differently nonverbally, even though their intent is the same.[4] One writer suggests that white people "run white" and blacks "run black."[5] Perhaps a culture or subculture creates its own system of nonverbal communication. There is also evidence that the sexes differ in their nonverbal behaviors, and that they are in line with societal role expectations.[6]

When combined with the verbal message, nonverbal signals are quite effective in conveying ideas, particularly emotional concepts such as love and hate. People display quite different nonverbal responses to various emotional situations. One study found that some people are more sensitive than others to nonverbal signals, and that such individuals tend to function better socially and intellectually. The same study also found that young people were less sensitive to nonverbal signals than older people were.[7] No wonder that in some speech communications our voices and our actions speak so loudly that our words are often unheard or are not very persuasive.

Apparently, in the long run we cannot avoid acting nonverbally, and therefore we cannot avoid communicating at least nonverbally. That our

[1]Randall Harrison, "Nonverbal Communication: Exploration into Time, Space, Action, and Object," in *Dimensions in Communication,* ed. J. H. Campbell and H. W. Hepler (Belmont, Calif.: Wadsworth Publishing Co., Inc., 1965), p. 101.
[2]Albert Mehrabian, *Nonverbal Communication* (Chicago: Aldine-Atherton, 1972), p. 182.
[3]Timothy G. Hegstrom, "Message Impact: What Percentage is Nonverbal?" *The Western Journal of Speech Communication,* 43, no. 2 (Spring 1979), 134–142.
[4]William Kloman, "E. T. Hall and the Human Space Bubble," *Horizon,* 9 (Autumn 1967), 43.
[5]Frances S. Dubner, "Nonverbal Aspects of Black English," *Southern Communication Journal,* 37, no. 4 (Summer 1972), 366.
[6]Marianne LaFrance and Clara Mayo, "A Review of Nonverbal Behaviors of Women and Men," *The Western Journal of Speech Communication,* 43, no. 2 (Spring 1979), 96–107.
[7]Robert Rosenthal and others, "Body Talk and Tone of Voice—the Language without Words," *Psychology Today,* September 1974, pp. 64–68.

nonverbal behavior may be unintentionally contrary to our verbal message should be considered by speakers. We express our attitudes through our body action, our voice and articulation patterns, the objects we wear or own, our use of time and space, and our language and thoughtfully prepared messages. The speech communication act, then, includes an almost countless number of channels. Making the nonverbal communication process work for us by improving our messages is the major objective of chapter 4.

Areas or aspects of nonverbal communication most relevant to speech communication are: *body communication* (kinesics), *voice and articulation* (paralanguage), *objects* (clothes and things), *space,* and *time.* Of these, kinesics and paralanguage are the most important to speakers.

CHARACTERISTICS OF NONVERBAL COMMUNICATION

Our nonverbals of whatever kind, conscious or unconscious, may be characterized as follows:

1 They always communicate something.
2 They are bound to the situation.
3 They are believed.
4 They are seldom isolated.
5 They affect our relationships.

1. THEY ALWAYS COMMUNICATE SOMETHING   Assuming some kind of human interaction, one cannot *not* behave, and since behavior is nonverbal communication—*one cannot not communicate.* A blank stare communicates something to the decoder, even if it is just confusion. This is not always appreciated by less sensitive personalities. These behaviors may be consciously or unconsciously conveyed, but one way or another they communicate.

2. THEY ARE BOUND TO THE SITUATION   The context or situation makes a lot of difference. The baby's smile might indicate pleasure in one situation or gas in another. A thumb in the air might mean A-OK on the launch pad or a request for a ride on the highway. When the context or situation is not appreciated or considered, nonverbals can be confusing indeed! When it is obvious, our nonverbals are most clear. Is there any doubt about what our hero is expressing in the following photograph?

Figure 4.1 Reprinted with the permission of UPI.

3. THEY ARE BELIEVED   Perhaps they should not be, but this tendency exists. Con men have taken advantage of this fact from the beginning. Perhaps nonverbals are harder to fake for most of us, but certainly not for good actors. When what you *say* disagrees with how you *look* or *sound,* people tend to believe the nonverbals. "She said no-no, but there was yes-yes in her eyes!"

Figure 4.2 Copyright, 1975, Universal Press Syndicate.

"Times must be getting tough. I thought I saw that clerk smile."

4. They are Seldom Isolated It is very difficult for most of us to be boiling mad and yet control our actions and voice so that we appear calm. A glisten of perspiration, a faster eye-blink, a slight tremble, a dryness in the voice—these and more give us away. Even when you are laughing on the outside (and crying on the inside), the character of your laughter probably gives you away. These other nonverbals tend to be related, consistent, and supportive of one another. When they are not, suspicions about intent are raised. Except in pictures or audio-tapes, nonverbals are difficult to isolate.

5. They Affect our Relationships We decide three important things about people largely on the basis of nonverbal communication. These are (1) personal liking or attraction, (2) evaluation of power relationships, and (3) our feelings about the response we get from others.

Let's review each of these as nonverbal codes:

(1) Sometimes by nonverbal cues alone, we might feel attracted toward another. That person seems a "likeable sort," "a good guy," and is easy to be with. That the opposite also happens is all too clear. More will be said about attraction in chapter 13.

(2) Power assessment is your evaluation of the other person's status, influence, or clout. Nonverbal cues become important, particularly in the absence of verbal information. Several of these will be discussed shortly.

(3) Another nonverbal area of this interpersonal decision making is your perception of a responsive listener, a person who can and will appreciate your position or your problem.

These three nonverbal decisions about people lead us in and out of a lot of communication trouble.

BODY ACTION LANGUAGE (KINESICS)

In chapter 1 we learned that our audience interprets the total message that we present to them. What they see may seriously affect how they interpret what we say. An actor's clever pantomime is sometimes much clearer and more emphatic than what the actor says. Body action language may therefore be important to the total impression made by the speaker.

Unconscious Nonverbal Communication

We use body action constantly in our everyday conversation. It is a definite part of our communication system. The way a person walks or *sits* at a given moment may demonstrate that person's mood more adequately than her words do. When we try to avoid looking awkward, it usually communicates even more awkwardness and looks unnatural and ridiculous. In addition, such holding back may lead to poor control of one's emotions. A lack of action often makes the message less clear. There is no point in trying

Figure 4.3 *Detroit News* photo by Drayton Holcomb.

to avoid body action; there are many good reasons to try to understand it, control it, and use it.

Communication by Stereotypes

The communication of stereotyped—stylized—gestures and facial expressions has been studied experimentally. Landis performed an experiment designed to discover whether subjects' reported emotions are accompanied by definite and easily recognized facial expressions. His subjects were photographed while they were being exposed to various emotional situations; they were not simply portraying emotions, as an actor would. After comparing the reactions of many subjects to these situations, Landis reported: "With no verbal report of a given emotion did a muscle, group of muscles, or expression occur with sufficient frequency to be considered characteristic of that emotion. There is no expression typically associated with any verbal report."[8]

A study similar to the one described above was conducted by Feleky, but with one difference: emotions were artificially portrayed by the subjects who were photographed. The experimenter found in this case that those

---

[8]C. Landis, "Experimental Studies of the Emotions: The Work of Cannon and Others," in *Great Experiments in Psychology*, ed. Henry E. Garrett (New York: Appleton-Century-Crofts, 1941), p. 331. For an interesting discussion of the role of the face and eyes in communicating emotion, see Mark L. Knapp, *Nonverbal Communication in Human Interaction* (New York: Holt, Rinehart & Winston, 1978), pp. 263–312.

who viewed the posed photographs identified the emotions correctly, indicating that we may interpret an individual's emotional state with reasonable accuracy from a posed photograph,[9] that is, a stereotype.

A more recent study by Williams and Tolch[10] indicated that there are two elements in the perception of acted facial expressions, *general evaluation* and *dynamism*. By general evaluation they meant a viewer's evaluation of those characteristics of an expression that reveal such ethical qualities as goodness, gratefulness, kindness, and the like. Dynamism is an evaluation of qualities such as active or passive, fast or slow, interesting or boring, and so on. Acted facial expressions based on only these two elements were differentiated successfully by viewers. However, an acted "no message—neutral" expression introduced into the study was usually seen as having both *evaluative* and *dynamic* qualities.

Schlosbery suggests that facial expression can be evaluated in terms of what he calls pleasantness or unpleasantness, sleep or tension, and rejection or attention.[11]

Moe and Savage cut up pictures of stereotyped emotions (such as terror, love, and hate) and asked students to look at the hand gestures and facial expressions separately. Recognition of the emotion portrayed was better than chance in both cases, indicating that there are stylized expressions of the hands as well as of the face.[12]

On the basis of these experiments, we can say that acted or stylized emotions can be identified with some reliability, whereas real emotions cannot be recognized with any certainty.

Good actors and capable speakers appear to communicate emotions regularly. The actor has the play, the set, the other actors, and the stylized conceptions of the audience as aids. If the cause of whatever emotion the actor is portraying also is seen (for example, a gun and fear), the communication is easier to interpret. One study suggests that acted emotions are even more recognizable when used with oral signals.[13]

Although certain expressions of emotion have become stylized, these expressions may vary so much from person to person and from sender to receiver that it remains difficult, except perhaps in skilled acting, to communicate the precise emotion intended.

[9]Garrett, ed., *Great Experiments in Psychology*, p. 330; see also J. Frois Wittman, "The Judgment of Facial Expression," *Journal of Experimental Psychology*, 13 (1930), 113–51; and D. Dusenbury and F. H. Knower, "Experimental Studies of the Symbolism of Action and Voice—I: A Study of the Specificity of Meaning in Facial Expression," *Quarterly Journal of Speech*, 24, no. 3 (1938), 435.

[10]F. Williams and J. Tolch, "Communication by Facial Expression," *Journal of Communication*, 15, no. 1 (March 1965), 17; see also J. Tolch, "The Problem of Language and Accuracy in Identification of Facial Expression," *Central States Speech Journal*, 14 (February 1963), 12–16.

[11]Harold Schlosbery, "Three Dimensions of Emotion," *Psychological Review*, 61 (1954), 81–88.

[12] J. Moe and N. Savage, "Recognizability of Emotions as Expressed by Facial Expressions and Hand Gestures" (unpublished pilot study, Speech 0726, Wayne State University, 1967).

[13]Kenton L. Burns and Ernest G. Beier, "Significance of Vocal and Visual Channels in the Decoding of Emotional Meaning," *Journal of Communication*, 23 (March 1973), 118–30.

There is also new evidence that we tend to communicate (nonverbally) more stereotypically when we know we are not alone.[14]

In review, research into the portrayal and recognition of emotions such as anger, love, and fear has shown that we rely on previous experience in interpreting these highly abstract messages. The expression on the face of a person photographed while being stuck with a needle may be incorrectly identified as portraying love. If the viewer also sees the needle, however, his chances of identifying the emotion are much better. If a person is asked to act as though he is in great pain, viewers usually get the message.

As suggested earlier, certain cultures and subcultures stereotype patterns of body action in ways different from our own. In some cultures a smile does not always indicate amusement, but rather politeness.[15] The American Indians had an elaborate sign language that the pioneers had to interpret correctly before they could communicate with the Indians effectively.

These observations lead to the question of how much stereotyping a speaker should use. One needs enough stereotyping to be understood, but not so much as to appear artificial. American speech education in the nineteenth century suffered from a highly mechanical approach. This was a period of flamboyant language and highly stylized gestures. Delsarte, a French scholar, contributed a system of gesturing during this time which contained some eighty-one gestures for practically all parts of the body, including specific ones for the nose, eyebrows, and feet. In answer to this movement, the famous School of Expression of S. S. Curry was born. This view taught that "every action of face or hand . . . is simply an outward effect of an inward condition. Any motion or tone that is otherwise is not expression."[16] In other words, a speaker should be so involved in her subject that her expression is always dynamic and spontaneous. At present, we recognize that in our communicative body action, we do rely on certain learned, general stereotypes which we use in natural and relatively spontaneous ways.

The conclusion of all this research is that "meaning" is in the eyes, ears, and other senses of the receiver, but even more it is in the receiver's store of experience, knowledge, attitudes, and emotions.

Empathy

If your instructor runs his fingernails sharply across the blackboard, you probably cringe and grit your teeth. If you've ever huddled in the stands, alternately shivering and cheering as the Detroit Lions made a goal-line stand against the Green Bay Packers or the Dallas Cowboys, you can understand empathy. If you've ever seen a youngster take a violent and

---

[14]William Kennedy, "The Communication of Affect via Facial Expression" (unpublished doctoral dissertation, Wayne State University, 1978).

[15]Weston LaBarre, "The Cultural Basis of Emotions and Gestures," *Journal of Personality,* 16, no. 1 (1947), 49–69.

[16]S. S. Curry, *Foundations of Expression* (Boston: The Expression Co., 1920), p. 10.

Figure 4.4 *Detroit News* photo by George Waldman.

bruising fall, you probably "felt" the pain as you projected yourself into the youngster's situation. Can you empathize with our tennis heroine?

This projection is the basis of empathy. Empathy includes a muscular reaction: to an extent, an audience imitates the actions of the speaker. When a speaker appears mortally afraid and tense, the audience dies a little. When the speaker acts tired, the audience feels tired or bored. When a person paces the floor like a caged lion, the audience usually tires before the speaker does. The speaker should take the audience into account when considering body action. Attempt to use the kind and amount of action that will help achieve the purpose of your speech.

Emotion

One can drain pent-up tension by body action. This is why some speakers pace the floor or fidget constantly. Instead of acting in distracting ways, try to use meaningful body action that will help you control your speech fright at the same time that it helps communicate your message.

General Impression

The general impression you create is a combination not only of all the signals that you communicate to your audience, but also of the things over which you may not always have control—for example, the lighting, the building, the platform, and the person who introduces you. However, there are some relatively simple things over which you *do* have some control, things that may contribute much to the general impression you make. Dress is one of these. In considering what to wear, the watchword is *appropriate*. You don't want to appear conspicuous, yet you do wish to live up to your audience's expectations regarding the dress of its speakers. Your physical and psychological comfort affect your body action. However, there's a lesson to be learned if the audience remembers your leotard instead of your speech.

Another problem is whether to address the audience from a sitting or a standing position. You might feel awkward standing on a platform with only three or four listeners at your feet, and some small informal audiences may prefer that you sit while speaking to them. However, other small groups are insulted if the speaker sits. The impression they receive, apparently, is that they are not considered important enough for a stand-up speech. Your decision depends a lot upon how well you know the group and how well they know you. As a general rule there is less risk in standing, even before a very small group. If the audience appears uncomfortable, it is much easier to sit down after a speech has started than to stand up. In an "Effective Supervision" course in which eight to twelve students rated the teachers, the evaluations of the instructors favored those who stood while speaking. Whether you're sitting, standing, or walking, the way you do it is revealing. It can draw people to you or drive them away.

All of the elements of body action contribute to the general impression you create. Let's take a look at some of the more important elements or types.

The Types of Bodily Action

In this section we shall discuss the patterns of physical behavior that make up total body action. Although these patterns most often occur at the same time, we are separating them here for the purpose of explanation.

POSTURE Posture is an important part of the general impression you make: it affects the empathy of the audience and what they conclude from your signals. The prize-winning photo on page 77 is a good example. The way you carry yourself tends to show whether or not you have confidence in yourself. Whether you slouch and cower or whether you stand with military bearing affects your outlook and sense of power and your control over yourself. A slouching posture can tire the audience as quickly as it can the speaker.

In general, good posture involves the distribution of your body weight in a comfortable and poised way consistent with the impression you wish to make as a speaker. You should be erect without looking stiff, comfortable without appearing limp. Your bearing should be alert, self-possessed, and communicative. Good posture and poise reflect a kind of cool unconcern. The great danger, as with all stylized body action, is appearing artificial, overly noticeable, or out of place.

Figure 4.5 Photo by Andrew Hosie, *Glasgow Daily Record,* Scotland.

A satisfactory standing position should be a balanced one: it should allow you to recover quickly if you were suddenly pushed. Your feet should be fairly close together, one foot slightly ahead of the other. Keep your hips straight, shoulders back, and chin in. Try to find a poised, natural speaking stance. There is no one way that is right for every speech! The stance you finally select will have to be modified to meet changing speech circumstances, such as the size and nature of the audience, the formality of the occasion, and so on.

WALKING   Actors have long known the importance of walk to express various moods and degrees of emphasis. The *femme fatale* has a walk that clearly communicates her role; the sneaky villain also has a stylized walk. The child about to be spanked walks quite differently from the way he would on his way to the movies. Zsa-Zsa, a sexy woman with an undulating walk and a come-hither look in her eyes, complains that all men are after the "same thing" and none respects her mind. Which part of the message are we to believe, the verbal or the nonverbal?

Walking may serve as a form of physical punctuation. Transitions and pauses may be strengthened by a few steps to the side, emphasis by a step

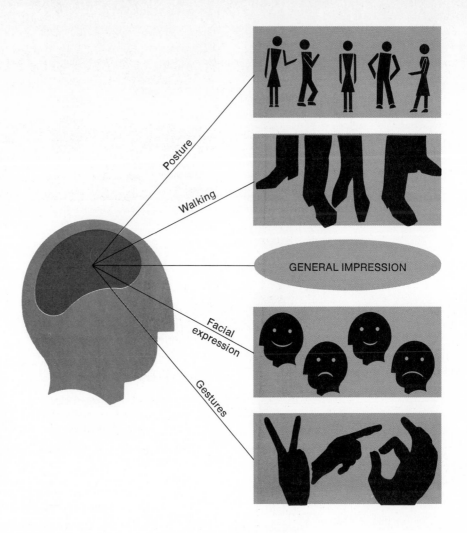

forward. Like the actor, the speaker wishes to appear natural, not awkward. If your walking is ungraceful or mechanical, it will distract from its intended purpose; if it is random, it will distract from the general purpose of your speech. In short, the way you walk tells a lot about you. It can show energy, enthusiasm, sloppiness, indifference, fatigue—or any number of other things about you.

Walking also has empathic value: it can offer physical relief to a suffering audience. On the other hand, too much walking can wear an audience out. The right amount of planned, purposeful walking is an outlet for muscular tension for both the speaker and the audience.

The question of the desirable amount and kind of walking requires the same considerations that apply to all body action: the subject, the speaker, the size of the audience, the formality of the occasion, and so on. In general, the more formal the speech, the less pronounced your walking should be. The larger the audience, the more definite your steps may be.

Remember also that walking, like all body action, begins before you actually start to speak. When you leave your chair to approach the speaker's stand, your communication has already begun: you are not finished until you have walked off the platform.

FACIAL EXPRESSION   In the studies of the portrayal and recognition of emotion, most of the photographs were of facial expressions. This was because the researchers thought that the face was the most expressive and quickly altered part of our body. This may very well be so. We all have heard of "the face that launched a thousand ships," and that "the eyes are the mirror of the soul."

The problem is that the speaker may unintentionally use stylized facial expressions or ones unsuitable to the subject. A student in a speech class once had a temporary facial disorder that caused her eye to wink uncontrollably about every sixty seconds when she was speaking. Even after the class discovered the real cause of the winking, the signal confusion remained alarming. Once the student learned to blink both her eyes, most of the problem was solved. Closing one eye in a wink has a stereotyped meaning. Closing both eyes at the same time in a blink has no stereotyped meaning (unless done in rapid succession), and was not confusing or particularly distracting when done by this student.

An emotionally tense person may tighten the jaw and unconsciously take on a crocodile grin. This usually passes as one relaxes, but the first moments of a serious speech by a grinning speaker can be most confusing.

The speaker's eyes, at least for relatively small audiences, are very communicative, as was indicated in our discussion of winking. Audiences are wary of shifty eyes: "She avoids my eyes" is a frequent classroom criticism. The audience expects to be looked at, not stared at constantly, but looked at occasionally. Directness of delivery is defined by many, and not unrealistically, as based on eye contact.

Simply stated, the lessons to be learned are to (1) avoid unintentional or inappropriate facial stereotypes, (2) make eye contact with the audience, and (3) free your natural and spontaneous facial expressions so that they may strengthen your message. The nonverbal experts call these "affect displays."[17]

GESTURES   Your gestures reveal more than meets the eye. Observe the gestures of people you know well and see if their actions reveal to you their real personality.

Nervous gestures are often annoying to others. The wringing hands is often a sign of nervousness or indecision. Drumming on the table or kicking the chair are messages that may indicate boredom or impatience.

In discussing gestures, we'll be concerned mostly with the hands and arms, but always keep in mind that you gesture with your entire body and

[17]P. Ekman and W. V. Friesen, "The Repertoire of Nonverbal Behavior: Categories, Origins, Usage, and Coding," *Semiotica* 1 (1969), 49–98.

personality. In a very general sense, we all use gestures for two rhetorical purposes—to reinforce an idea or to help describe something.

REINFORCING GESTURES   It seems natural to clench our fist or perhaps even pound the lectern when trying to communicate a strong feeling. Such actions emphasize our words. In disagreeing verbally, we might routinely turn our palms down or out. In appealing we might naturally turn our palms up or in. These types of gestures reinforce through emphasis. Other gestures reinforce through a kind of suggestion. In communicating a scolding attitude toward the other political party, we might wag a finger in much the same stereotyped way that the teacher does. Speakers may emphasize a separation of points by using first one hand ("On the one hand it can be said . . .") and then the other. Or we might use only one hand, suggesting several categories by slicing the air with a vertical palm and moving our hand on a level plane from left to right. No two persons use these reinforcing gestures exactly alike, but the stereotype is usually recognized. These also are called "Emblems."[18] They usually are translated rather directly as with the hitchhike or A-OK sign.

DESCRIPTIVE GESTURES   When we are asked to describe the size or shape of something, it is natural to use our hands to indicate the dimensions. If we could not use our hands, it would be difficult to describe a circular staircase to a person who had never seen one. All descriptive gestures are also partly reinforcing. The person describing a blind date with gestures communicates more than just size and shape; we might, for example, quickly pick up a message of approval or disapproval. Ekman and Friesen refer to these as "Illustrators."

Sometimes our gestures are part emblem and part illustrator as with those shown below.

[18]*Ibid.*

Figure 4.6   *Detroit News* photos by Edwin C. Lombardo.

Standards of Good Body Action

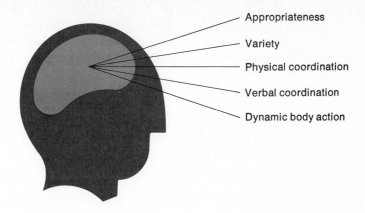

- Appropriateness
- Variety
- Physical coordination
- Verbal coordination
- Dynamic body action

APPROPRIATENESS   Your subject, your physical makeup and personality, and, most important, the size and nature of your audience determine what kind of body action is appropriate. A very formal subject, particularly when combined with a formal occasion and a small, older audience, generally calls for poised but relatively restricted body action. Grand sweeps of the arms and other showy movements would be out of place. Other things being equal, the larger the audience, the more unrestricted your body action may be.

Most speakers use too little body action, whatever the speech occasion. When you are finally free of your inhibitions on body action, however, remember to match your body actions with the expectations of your audience.

VARIETY   Any body action, but particularly gestures, should be varied occasionally. Otherwise, the routineness of the action may call attention to itself and not only cease to carry meaning but also become a distraction. A speaker who pounds the table *every* time she makes a point, regardless of its importance, soon loses the reinforcing effect of that gesture. A random gesture used in moderation does not harm your communication, but monotony of action, whether the action is illustrative or not, is usually distracting. All of us tend to repeat our favorite gestures, and these mannerisms often reflect our personalities. We must periodically ask ourselves if we are overworking some of our gestures and if our body action really reflects the personality we would like to project. We are typically unaware of over-using a favorite gesture, particularly if it is principally to release tension. If necessary your instructor will feed back this information to you so that you can correct this distracting monotony.

PHYSICAL COORDINATION   Physical coordination means the combination of all parts of your body in expressing yourself. You can appear ridiculous by locking your elbows to your sides and moving only your forearms and hands. A "detachment" such as this makes you appear mechanical. The whole body is always involved in any body action.

VERBAL COORDINATION   By verbal coordination we mean the timing of words and action so as to achieve the greatest reinforcement of our message. This includes rehearsed or "canned" body action. A lack of verbal coordination can be quite humorous. Try saying "Uncle Sam needs *you*," but instead of pointing on the word *you*, wait three seconds and then point!

DYNAMIC BODY ACTION   By dynamic body action we mean the projection of a lively sense of communication. Body action should be essentially spontaneous; it should be determined by impulses and spontaneous thoughts. To become dynamic and spontaneous in your body action, you sometimes have to prime the pump by including in your speech some details requiring body action, such as visual aids and demonstrations using descriptions of shape or size and imitations of people or animals.

VOICE AND ARTICULATION (PARALANGUAGE)

Voice and Personality

An expert in voice and diction training once said, "Bluntly stated, one may have a dull, uninteresting, or unpleasant voice because his voice is defective or improperly used; but he may also have such a voice because he is a dull, uninteresting, or unpleasant person." Vocal training, like all speech training, cannot take place in a vacuum; rather it is intimately related to one's whole personality. Just as personality affects voice, voice improvement may affect personality.

The voice contributes much to the total communication signal. It may be the single most important code we use. Studies of voice and social status indicate the importance and the communication potential of this nonverbal code. There is evidence that one's social status can be determined in large part by the signals we receive from the voice alone, apart from language.[19] There is also evidence that Americans tend to downgrade a person who speaks with a foreign accent.[20]

As in pantomime, there are certain long-standing stereotypes that we take for granted in the use of the voice. We recognize certain radio roles as voice stereotypes—the mean character, the hero, the sissy, the dunce. The very great danger in using voice stereotypes is that one might take on an

[19]James D. Moe, "Listener Judgments of Status Cues in Speech: A Replication and Extension," *Speech Monographs,* 39, no. 2 (1972), 144–47.

[20]Anthony Mulac, Theodore D. Hanley, and Diane Y. Prigge, "Effects of Phonological Speech Foreignness upon Three Dimensions of Attitude of Selected American Listeners," *Quarterly Journal of Speech,* 60, no. 4 (December 1974), 411–20.

artificial voice permanently. Of course, we all occasionally fail to match the voice we "put on" with the situation in which we find ourselves. Listen to yourself on occasion. If you sound "arty" when talking about fertilizer, your voice habits may be altering your personality in ways that will seriously affect your communication.

Our discussion so far leads to the question of what is abnormal or faulty speech. Charles Van Riper, a highly respected speech clinician, offers a clear answer: "Speech is defective when it deviates so far from the speech of other people that it calls attention to itself, interferes with communication, or causes its possessor to be maladjusted."[21] Speech is faulty when it is overly noticeable, unclear, or *unpleasant*. Van Riper explains that not all deviations from normal speech are defects.

> A child of three who says "wabbit" for "rabbit" has no speech defect, but the adult of fifty who uses that pronunciation would have one because it would be a real deviation from the pronunciation of other adults. If you said *deze, doze,* and *dem* for *these, those,* and *them* in a hobo jungle, none of the other vagrants would notice. If you used the same sounds in a talk to a P.T.A. meeting a good many ears would prickle.[22]

We are not totally consistent in our voice and articulation patterns; we vary and adapt them to moods, subjects, and people, as indeed we should. It is when our deviations become noticeable in ways that damage our intended communication that we have problems.

Many deviations that are not speech defects, strictly speaking, nevertheless call for a remedy. Some common problems that are usually adjusted quickly through normal speech training are fast rate, wrong pitch, loudness, and certain articulation bad habits such as the substitution of a *d* sound for *th* sound (for example, *d*ese for *th*ese). However, certain *organic* and *functional* disorders and some bad habits may call for the services of a qualified speech pathologist. Your instructor is in a position to determine your needs. *Organic disorders* are uncorrected physical conditions such as cleft palate, malocclusion of the teeth, or enlarged tonsils, which *may* cause noticeable deviations. *Functional disorders* are caused by habitual misuse of all or part of the voice and articulation mechanisms; they include poor breathing, tight jaw, and lazy lips. Most articulation problems are functional—they are simply bad habits.

The Vocal Process

The vocal process uses organs of the body whose primary function is physiological. The muscles and bones we use in speaking are responsible, first and foremost, for breathing, chewing, and swallowing. Physical states

---

[21]Charles Van Riper, *Speech Correction,* 6th ed. (Englewood Cliffs, N.J.: Prentice-Hall, Inc., 1978), p. 29.
[22]*Ibid.*

such as exhaustion or inebriation cause noticeable variations in our physical performance. These and other states also affect the sound of the noise and musical notes produced by the human voice. This combination of noise and notes is *voice*, and voice is a large part of communication. For these reasons, a brief description of the speech organs is necessary.

In order to produce modifiable sound, a mechanism with certain functions and characteristics is necessary. In almost any musical instrument an *energy source* is the first requirement, whether it be a violin bow or a saxophone player's lungs. The second requirement is a *vibrator*, such as the violin string or the saxophone reed. The third requirement is to strengthen the resulting sound; this is called *resonation*. The resonators of the violin are its hollow body and its wooden texture. The saxophone, however, has a mainly metal texture which produces a sound easily distinguishable from that of a violin. When we modify the size, shape, and texture of the resonators in some recognizable, consistent, or pleasing way, we make music. Let's now analyze the human vocal process in these same terms.

THE ENERGY SOURCE   Our breathing machinery is the energy source for voice production *(phonation)*. The primary purposes of this machinery are to bring oxygen into the lungs as a source of fuel for the body and to expel waste gases. The physical demands of the body noticeably affect this machinery. When running we need more energy (oxygen), and therefore our breathing becomes harder and faster. It is difficult to speak after running the hundred-yard dash.

We normally speak when exhaling (breathing out) rather than inhaling (breathing in). Thus, we are quite apt to need and notice a heavier-than-usual inhalation cycle in our speaking, particularly if it is public speech and we are under some emotional stress. According to the James-Lange theory of emotion (see pages 243–44), the awareness of an unexplained physical reaction such as this one may lead to speech fright and may *be* the actual emotion. As we indicated, it is normal for the process of inhalation to be different in public speaking. We should, of course, make every effort to operate our breathing machinery or energy source as efficiently as possible. This requires good posture, comfortable clothes, ventilation, bodily rest, and an understanding of the unexpected changes in inhalation which are the source of much speech fright.

THE VIBRATOR   The vocal cords within the *larynx* (Adam's apple) are the vibrators in the voice. The larynx, located on top of the *trachea* (windpipe), has a flap called the *epiglottis*, which closes when you swallow. Air is forced up the trachea through the vocal cords in the larynx, causing them to vibrate and thereby produce sound. Figure 4.7 illustrates the trachea and the *esophagus* (gullet). Probably all of us have had the experience of food going down the "wrong throat," which is usually the result of swallowing food at the instant of starting phonation. You are really asking the epiglottis to be both open and closed at the same time. A physical problem such as this

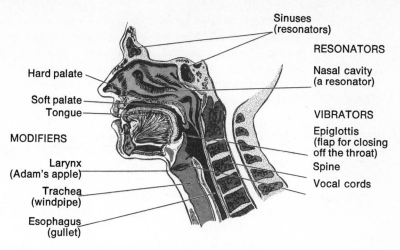

Figure 4.7 Where speech sounds are formed.

is normally taken care of naturally by your body. You automatically cough and drive out the food or liquid from your windpipe. However, this can be quite frightening if it happens during a speech. The dangers of chewing gum or throat lozenges while speaking are evident. The embarrassment is not worth whatever relaxation the chewing may give you.

THE RESONATORS The sound produced by the energy source and the vibrator now fills the entire head, which thereby becomes a *resonator*. Sound changes as the resonators vary in size, shape, and texture. The cavities in your head can be altered quite readily. For example, you can change the size and shape of your mouth and shift your tongue. If you hold your nose, you often notice a change in vocal quality. This is because a certain amount of sound normally escapes through your nose when you speak.[23] The nasal cavity is controlled and changed by the action of the tongue and soft palate. The sinuses in your head are also resonators; when their texture and size are changed, as during a head cold, you quickly become aware of voice changes. We recognize people by their voices in large part because of the inborn qualities of their resonators, but it is also evident that we have considerable control over resonation if we work at it. This is demonstrated by the people who make a living imitating the voices of others.

THE MODIFIERS Resonated sound is made more precise by being modified, interrupted, and separated into standard segments, which we may call speech. The *modifiers* are the lips, teeth, tongue, jaw, and soft palate. Their function is most recognizable in the consonants. Try to say the word *pill* without bringing your lips together. The *p* demands a specific kind of modification of the lips; so do other letters such as *b* or *m*. The consonants

[23]Especially *m, n, ing;* not so for words like *raw, hope, tooth.*

are really voiceless or without speech except for certain mechanical noises that may go with them, such as the hissing of an *s*. The vowels are the voiced sound. The consonants are known through the alteration and specific interruptions of those vowels by the modifiers. The importance of the modifiers to articulation is evident. If physical disorders, such as defective teeth or a cleft palate, are present, acceptable enunciation may be difficult until one has had surgery or has been taught by a qualified pathologist how to make up for the problem. Faulty enunciation is more commonly caused by lack of knowledge, lazy speech habits, or, occasionally, overly precise habits.

Variable Characteristics of Voice

You have considerable control over certain characteristics of voice. You can change your *rate* of speaking; you can adjust your *loudness* almost as you would that of a radio; you can speak at different *pitch* levels; and you can alter the overtones or partial tones of your voice, which represent a kind of *quality* control often called *timbre* or *vocal color*. Along with *intonation*, sounding the vowels, these characteristics are the nonverbal signals that help a listener determine the structure and meaning of what you say.[24] They are also known as vocal qualifiers.

RATE Test passages have been devised for measuring verbal speed in wpm (words per minute). In general, a rate of more than 185 wpm is considered too rapid for a normal public speaking situation, and a rate of less than 140 wpm is considered too slow.[25] The problem of measurement is complex, for certain communications take place at a very rapid verbal rate and others at a slow or mixed rate. A further problem associated with verbal rate is that words are not really separately formed units but tend to flow from one sound to another; this affects both articulation and pronunciation. Take the phrase, "Did you eat?" If really speeded up, it becomes "Jeet?" This process is called *assimilation*. The length of sounds or tones is also a factor in verbal rate, as are pauses, phrasing, and general rhythm patterns.

The *duration* of sounds and words normally varies with our moods. We generally use tones of relatively short duration when expressing anger and more prolonged tones for expressing love. The average duration of the words of good speakers tends to be greater than that of poor speakers. A poor speaker is more apt to use short, abrupt speech consistently.

A person's use of *pauses*[26] and phrases is a factor in his or her rate of

[24]Arthur Wingfield, "Acoustic Redundancy and the Perception of Time-compressed Speech," *Journal of Speech and Hearing Research*, 18, no. 1 (1975), 96–104.

[25]Grant Fairbanks, *Voice and Articulation Drillbook* (New York: Harper & Row Publishers, Inc., 1960), p. 115. Some authorities argue that since listening rates may range from 400 to 800 wpm, a public speaking rate of 200 wpm is not unrealistic.

[26]Norman J. Lass and Marcia Paffenberger, "A Comparative Study of Rate Evaluations of Experienced and Inexperienced Listeners," *Quarterly Journal of Speech*, 57, no. 1 (1971), 89–93.

speaking. The "pregnant pause" is no idle jest; it has much to do with our communication. A phrase is a group of words that forms a thought unit. Pauses occur between words and between phrases, and the number and duration of pauses seriously alter the meaning of what you say. The complexity and nature of your speech material should also affect your decisions regarding the use of phrases and pauses. If you were to use a long pause after a phrase for emphasis, fine, but if the phrase were relatively silly you might appear ridiculous. If you were to use long pauses in a random manner not related to meaning (not an uncommon error), you would then *confuse* your audience. Short pauses generally indicate that there is more to come. If you routinely use a rather intermediate-length pause without consistently relating it to what you are saying, you run the added danger of *monotony,* a tiresome lack of variation. Be sure that your speech pattern of pauses and phrases does not take on a fixed rhythm that interferes with your communication.

Rhythm patterns include all the variable characteristics of voice. Over-used pitch and volume patterns contribute to the rhythmic sing-song, pause-phrase problem so common among improperly trained speakers.

In oral speech you have much more flexibility than grammar permits in written communication. You should be guided by the fine shades of meaning you wish to express, rather than by mechanical rules.

LOUDNESS   A very common fault among beginning speakers is an improper projection of the voice to the audience. Such speakers either project more volume than the situation calls for, or, more typically, they do not project enough. It is essential that your audience be able to hear you. Loudness is a measure of the total signal. You may think of loudness generally as volume, but speech science indicates that volume is related so intimately to pitch that the term loudness may be misleading. Your volume is easier to raise as your pitch goes up. Furthermore, it is possible to speak with more force or intensity without altering your volume proportionately. If the duration of your tones is too short, you may not be speaking loudly enough simply because your voice mechanism has not been given a chance to enhance the tones for you. This may be caused by a restricted energy source or breathing apparatus, but most likely it is related to your pitch selection. More will be said of this in the following discussion on pitch.

Among the psychological reasons for this common lack of voice projection is a form of avoidance of the speech situation. People tend to *withdraw* from threatening situations. Poor projection is a logical and normal device when you find you cannot run away from the speech situation. It may also be a form of *repression:* you hold yourself in check emotionally in order to get through the ordeal. Again, loudness suffers. It is almost as if speaking with a soft, barely heard voice is the next best thing to not being in the speech situation at all.

Your audience will help you adjust your loudness. Look at them for feedback signs. Are they straining to hear? Are they withdrawing?

Much of what we call *vocal variety* is related to loudness. The force with which you utter certain phrases or words is a form of oral punctuation and can add much to your audience's understanding of what you say. The manner in which you apply force to what you say is also a factor in vocal variety. You may use a lot of oral exclamation marks, or you may, through the use of intensity, underline many words. Variety, or the contrast between what is emphasized and what is not, is important. An audible whisper can be a powerful nonverbal as well as verbal emphasis in some speech situations. These are some of the loudness dimensions of vocal variety.

PITCH   The frequency of vibration of the vocal cords determines *pitch*. More simply, pitch refers to a tonal position on a musical scale. When we speak, we use a variety of pitches, which are normally distributed in terms of amount of usage. If we were to plot the number of occurrences of the different pitches we use, we would find a central pitch around which the others vary in relatively predictable amounts. The typical musical range may include two octaves. The problem of *optimum pitch* level for a given person—that person's best general pitch level—is a complex one. To find one's optimum pitch level often necessitates a compromise between mechanical vocal efficiency and what is generally accepted as being pleasing or appropriate. For example, if a man's optimum pitch is exceptionally high for a man in his culture, he may wish to lower his *habitual pitch* level, the level he uses most frequently, even though he may lose some vocal efficiency by doing so. If you lower your pitch unreasonably, however, the resulting loss of vocal efficiency shows up as inflexible pitch or lack of variety and may also reduce your loudness.

For most people, optimum pitch should be the habitual or central pitch. Often, our optimum pitch is found a little below the habitual or normally used pitch because of tensions that restrict the vocal apparatus. However, young men may strive so deliberately for very low voices that the reverse is occasionally true.

Trying to determine your optimum pitch from the viewpoint of vocal efficiency alone is fun (if not always entirely reliable). With the aid of a piano, determine in relation to middle C the lowest and highest note you can sing without a complete loss of quality. This interval is your singing *range*. The average voice will be found to perform best when the speaking level is at approximately the midpoint of the lowest octave of the singing range. The next step is to try to find your habitual pitch by using a sample of your normal speech. Hit the piano keys in the vicinity of the optimum pitch already found. At the same time, speak or read until you achieve a kind of blend between your speech and the notes on the piano. You will then have a rough idea as to whether or not your present general pitch level is adequate.

You can speak at your best all-round pitch and still be a "Johnny-one-note" if you lack pitch variety in the form of *shifts* or *inflections*. A shift is a pitch change that occurs between independent sounds or phonation. An inflection is a pitch change without interruption of a given phonation.

QUALITY Voice quality results from the modification frequency modulation of the vocal-cord tone by the resonators. It is that attribute of tone and sound waves that enables us to distinguish between two sounds that are alike in pitch, duration, and loudness.[27]

Other things being equal, we can easily distinguish the overly nasal, breathy, or harsh voice. In addition, we are able to make nonverbal distinctions of a much more subtle nature: for example, we recognize the voice of a person who is sincerely touched by a tribute or the voice of a person who is suppressing anger. Emotional moods affect voice quality and may have a profound effect upon emphasis and meaning. In this context, voice quality is often referred to as *timbre*.

Voice quality is considered faulty when one's voice contains consistent deviations that detract from the message or its meaning. Certain organic disorders, such as a cleft palate or nasal obstructions, can cause defects in voice quality. Emotional moods may also result in deviations from voice quality which, even if temporary, appear as defects. In addition, voice quality may be affected by the strictly temporary physical problems caused by head colds, sore throats, and the like. However, we are interested here primarily in nonorganic, or *functional,* defects—in other words, with faulty habits.

Some of the more common voice-quality problems are nasality, breathiness, and harshness.

NASALITY This problem is caused by too much nasal resonance, particularly in nonnasal voiced sounds. The vowels are affected most noticeably. Aside from organic defects, the problem is typically caused by not opening the mouth wide enough or by improper use of the soft palate or tongue. Assimilation also is important here. A person may run the nasal sounds right into following vowels, or when the vowel precedes the nasal consonant, he or she may have started the nasal resonance too early—that is, during the phonation of the vowel. This is called *assimilated nasality* and is one of the more frequent bad habits to avoid. Opening the mouth wider and using firmer tongue action help control one's beginning and ending of nasal resonance.

BREATHINESS If your vocal cords do not draw close enough together during phonation, too much unvocalized air escapes, giving your voice a breathy quality. Functional reasons for breathiness may include faulty breathing habits, insufficient loudness, or too low a pitch level. Improper or too frequent inhalation, which is often caused by too rapid a rate may be at fault. Insufficient loudness automatically causes more unvocalized air to escape. A whisper is obviously breathy; on the other hand, it is practically impossible to voice a really loud tone that is breathy. If you are straining for

[27]Fairbanks, *Voice and Articulation Drillbook,* chaps. 1 and 15.

an unusually low pitch, you may affect both loudness and larynx control, either of which can cause breathiness.

Frequent temporary causes of breathiness are overexertion, emotional strain, illness, and certain artificial mannerisms thought to be desirable.

HARSHNESS   By harshness we mean huskiness, hoarseness, and throatiness. These terms and others are specifically defined by voice scientists, but for our purpose we may think of them as describing a rasping, unmusical quality. We all exhibit this quality frequently when grunting, growling, or suffering from a sore throat after cheering at a football game.

A chronic hoarseness is often organic and calls for diagnosis by both a qualified speech pathologist and a physician. The most frequent functional cause is a routine misuse of voice, which if serious enough can lead to physical disorders. This misuse is often accompanied by tension in the laryngeal muscles, which may be caused by general tension and emotional stress (see chapter 10) or by a speaker's too frequent attempts to show strain, emotion, or earnestness in his or her communication. The result is that we constrict our throat while attempting to project loudness (particularly at low pitches) at the same time. This results in a shrill, harsh quality often referred to as "clergyman's throat." General tenseness is probably the most common functional cause of a consistently harsh vocal quality.

The Articulation Process

The word *articulation* refers in general to a flexible fitting of things together. For example, the bones and cartilages in your elbow are said to articulate. The word is well suited to the action of the speech organs as they interact with one another and help join the various sound units into accepted patterns that we call speech.

THE ORGANS OF ARTICULATION   This articulating of bones, muscles, teeth, and so on is responsive to training. Just as the musician, typist, and surgeon must learn certain motor skills and habits in the articulating of the knuckles, bones, and cartilages in their hands, so too must speakers develop good skills and habits with their articulating mechanisms. Musicians who are lazy with their fingers decrease the beauty or acceptability of their effort. Typists who are careless about the use or consistent placement of their fingers may lose their job. Your habits and training in the articulation of such organs as teeth, tongue, lips, palate, and jaw are of great importance to you in speaking.

To some extent, you should adapt your articulation in groups and situations in which a different dialect is spoken, particularly if you are part of such a group. Many students have developed two dialects in order to communicate more easily. Whatever the benefits of such adaptation, take care that you do not develop poor, unplanned articulations which are primarily mechanical. These might call negative attention to yourself, regardless of the situation. You may wish on occasion to make an inventory of your articulation habits to be sure you are not becoming careless.

COMMON ARTICULATORY FAULTS Some of the more common mechanical causes of careless articulation are (1) locked jaw, (2) slack lips, and (3) muffled mouth.

LOCKED JAW This problem is caused by a failure to open the mouth wide enough. The jaw is tight and seems locked in position. The speaker talks through her teeth and nose because the sound has to escape somehow. Projection is reduced; resonance is increased; vowel quality in particular is injured. This may be caused in part by tension and speech fright; but in any case the remedy is the same—unlock your jaw and open your mouth!

SLACK LIPS In this case the lips are so loose that they do not adequately shape the mouth opening for proper vowel production or for proper articulation of the lip consonants (*p, b, m, w, f,* and *v*). The rule is simple: allow your lips to perform their necessary functions. In addition, an inability to see the speaker's lips move is frustrating to many listeners. Unless you are a ventriloquist, free your lips. Articulation, of course, also can suffer from very tight or tense lips.

MUFFLED MOUTH This problem is caused principally by weak or slow tongue activity. Because the tongue is your most important organ of articulation, you may ruin a large part of your speech if you are guilty of this fault. The production of the fine shades of tone that distinguish the vowels from one another is endangered by a muffled mouth, since the tongue position in large part decides the shape and size of the oral cavity. Many consonants also depend upon vigorous and precise tongue action. A *th* sound (*th*ese) easily becomes a *d* sound (*d*ese) if the tongue is lazy and does not move forward far enough to articulate with the teeth. Other consonants, such as *d, l, r,* and *s,* also call for vigorous and specific tongue action. Vigorous and firm articulation of your tongue with your teeth is your best safeguard against muffled quality.

Pronunciation

Pronunciation is the act of expressing the sounds and accents of words so that they conform to accepted standards. In addition to aiding understanding, appropriate pronunciation influences how an audience judges a speaker. Adapting to varying standards and groups to which you may belong again points out the value of using two dialects. In old Milwaukee the word *theater* was typically pronounced "the-*ay*-ter," a compromised carryover from the German pronunciation of "das Theater" (tay-*ah*-ter). In Detroit we hear "th-*uh*-ter." Some localities may say "drammer" for "drama." The extremely valuable dictionary is a little awkward on some pronunciations because there are three generally accepted dialects in the United States (eastern, southern, and standard American). The most wide-spread dialect is standard American, and our dictionaries and national mass media are geared to this dialect. Sometimes, the use of a second dialect has social and practical advantages.[28]

The problem of showing on paper the desired or different pronunciations of a word is awkward at best. One way is to agree upon and memorize a common code of symbols based strictly upon sound, which is how the International Phonetic Alphabet was born. It has one symbol for every different sound in the language. The news services use a system of *respelling* similar to what was used in the previous paragraphs. Dictionaries use *diacritical marks* and relatively stable words as bases of pronunciation. Accent or stress is indicated as primary (ˈ) or secondary (ˌ). A guide to pronunciation and to the diacritical system used in dictionaries is carefully explained in the introduction to any good dictionary[29] and is well worth reading.

EXAMPLES OF PRONOUNCING SYSTEMS

Word	Diacritical System	International Phonetic System	Respelling System
chaotic	/kā-ˈät-ik/	[keˈatik]	kay-otic
theater	/ˈthē-ət-ər/	[ˈθiətə]	the-uh-ter
nativity	/nə-ˈtiv-ət-ē/	[neˈtrvətr]	nay-tiv-ity

Some of the more common pronunciation errors in the English language are improper stress, errors in spelling-phonetics (pronouncing words as they are spelled), sound substitutions, sound additions, sound reversals, and sound subtractions. Illustrations of these errors appear in the following table. These pronunciation errors (p. 93) are used by permission from Webster's New Collegiate Dictionary, © 1977 by G. & C. Merriam Co., Publishers of the Merriam-Webster Dictionaries.

OBJECT LANGUAGE
(CLOTHES AND THINGS)

Research suggests that individuals who appear attractive to the receivers of communication are more successful interpersonally. In one clever study a young woman was dressed and made up attractively for one group of receivers and then was dressed and made up to look unattractive to a similar

[28]Mildred C. Matlock, "Teaching Standard English to Black Dialect Speakers," *Michigan Speech and Hearing Association Journal,* 10, no. 2 (1974), 91–99.
[29]See especially *Webster's New Collegiate Dictionary* (Springfield, Mass.: G. & C. Merriam Co., 1977).

PRONUNCIATION ERRORS

Improper Stress

prag‖matist instead of ‖pragmatist
super‖fluous instead of su‖perfluous
com‖parable instead of ‖comparable
tele‖graphy instead of te‖legraphy

Errors of Spelling-Phonetics

salmon/‖sal-mən/	instead of	/‖sam-ən/
rancid/‖ran-kid/	instead of	/‖ran (t)-səd/
hearth/hürth/	instead of	/‖härth/
zoologist/‖zü-alə-jəst/	instead of	/zo-‖äl-ə-jəst, zə-‖wäl-/

Sound Substitutions

just/jist/	instead of	/‖jəst/
tremendous/tri-‖men-jəs	instead of	/tri-‖men-dəs/
sieve/sēv/	instead of	/‖siv/
ask/äsk/	instead of	/‖ask/
catch/kēch/	instead of	/‖kach, ‖kech/
heinous/‖he-nəs/	instead of	/‖hā-nəs/

Sound Additions

elm/‖el-əm/	instead of	/‖elm/
film/‖fil-əm/	instead of	/‖film/
umbrella/əm-bər-‖rel-ä/	instead of	/ˌəm-‖brel-ə/
wash/‖worsh/	instead of	/‖wosh/
athlete/‖ath-ə-lēt/	instead of	/‖ath-ˌlēt/
indict/in-‖dīkt/	instead of	/in-‖dīt/

Sound Reversals

larynx/‖lar-ningks/	instead of	/‖lar-iŋ (k)s/
cavalry/‖kal-vərē/	instead of	/‖kav-əl-rē/
perspiration/‖pres-pi-rā-shən/	instead of	/ˌpər-spə-‖rā-shən, pər-ˌsprā/
tragedy (trăd‖ĕjĭ)/‖trad-əjē/	instead of	/‖traj-əd-ē/

Sound Subtractions

popular (pŏp‖lēr)/‖päp-lər/	instead of	/‖päp-yə-lər/
eighth/‖at/	instead of	/‖ātth/
geography/‖jäg-rə'fē/	instead of	/jē-‖äg-rə-fē/
history (his‖trī)/‖his-trē/	instead of	/‖his-t (ə-)rē/
picture/‖pich-ər/	instead of	/‖pik-chər/

audience. The young woman was judged to be more believable and was generally found to be more persuasive and more desirable when presented attractively.[30]

Note in figure 4.8 how meanings change when dress code objects are in or out of line with their historical period.

We cannot change everything about our physical appearance through clothing, grooming, and "things" that we put on, hang on, glue on, tie on, or splash on (rings, wigs, eyeglasses, girdles, flowers, lipstick, aftershaves). However, we can do a lot, but it is sometimes a short way from appropriate to inappropriate.

Right or wrong, many stereotypes are associated with "clothes and things." Research helps us define even these. Persons who wear bizarre clothes are considered more radical, activist, and more likely to experiment with drugs. People who wear more conventional dress are associated with

[30]J. Mills and E. Aronson, "Opinion Change as a Function of the Communicator's Attractiveness and Desire to Influence," *Journal of Personality and Social Psychology,* 1 (1965), 73–77; see also R. N. Widgery and B. Webster, "The Effects of Physical Attractiveness upon Perceived Initial Credibility," *Michigan Speech Journal,* 4 (1969), 4–15.

Figure 4.8 Photography by Guy Morrison, Bloomfield Hills, Michigan.

everyday jobs and "traditional fun."[31] The problem is in knowing what kind of "clothes and things" are conventional, in style, or expected of us. That happens to be the problem of all interpersonal communication, whether nonverbal or verbal. The point is that the nonverbals of clothes and things make a big difference in the way we are seen *totally*, that is, socially, vocationally, sexually, and so on. The key word is *appropriate*. We usually do not wish to stand out in a crowd. Yet we want to be fashionable and appropriate to what is expected of us at any given time or in any particular situation. If in a public speech the audience remembers the sunflower in your hair instead of your message . . . , you can draw your own conclusion.

Figure 4.9 © 1966 United Feature Syndicate, Inc.

SPACE AND DISTANCE (PROXEMICS)

Each of us carries a kind of space bubble around us to mark off our personal territory. It varies in size from person to person and according to the culture from which we come. More hostile people are thought to have larger bubbles. They are more easily angered and upset because it is easier to bruise their larger bubbles. People also have different bubbles for different situations. We "occupy" a certain room of the house: my room, Dad's den, and Mom's living room are pretty special at times. Invasions into another's room often make us quite unpopular.

Cultural influence is considerable. Latin Americans and Arabs tend to stand close together when they talk. Most North Americans like to talk at arm's length. What is normal distance for Latin Americans and Arabs is considered intimate by most of us. The possibility of poor or at least confused interpersonal communication is obvious! Within our own culture these appropriate distances change according to the message and how well we know the listeners. We tend to stand farther away from strangers than from friends. Of course, we are apt to stand closer when saying "I love you" than "Hello there!" We also use our voices differently according to distance, message, and mood. Edward Hall has proposed a scale that helps identify these relationships (figure 4.10). Figure 4.11 depicts the various speech situations which a person might encounter.

[31]For more on these matters, see Mark L. Knapp, *Nonverbal Communication in Human Interaction* (New York: Holt, Rinehart & Winston, 1978).

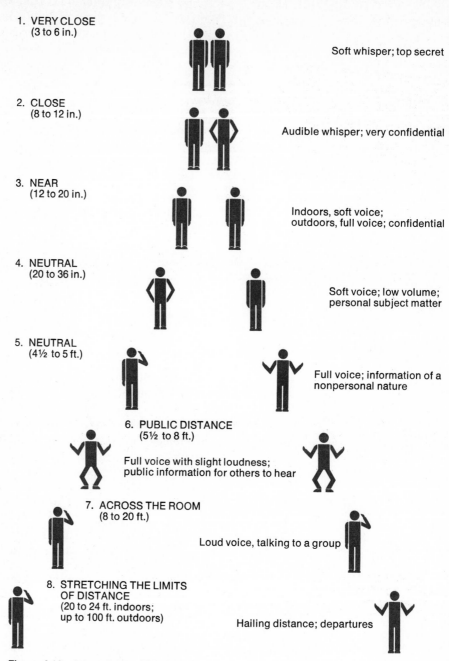

1. VERY CLOSE
   (3 to 6 in.)

Soft whisper; top secret

2. CLOSE
   (8 to 12 in.)

Audible whisper; very confidential

3. NEAR
   (12 to 20 in.)

Indoors, soft voice;
outdoors, full voice; confidential

4. NEUTRAL
   (20 to 36 in.)

Soft voice; low volume;
personal subject matter

5. NEUTRAL
   (4½ to 5 ft.)

Full voice; information of a
nonpersonal nature

6. PUBLIC DISTANCE
   (5½ to 8 ft.)

Full voice with slight loudness;
public information for others to hear

7. ACROSS THE ROOM
   (8 to 20 ft.)

Loud voice, talking to a group

8. STRETCHING THE LIMITS
   OF DISTANCE
   (20 to 24 ft. indoors;
   up to 100 ft. outdoors)

Hailing distance; departures

Figure 4.10 Adapted from Hall, *The Silent Language,* pp. 208-9.

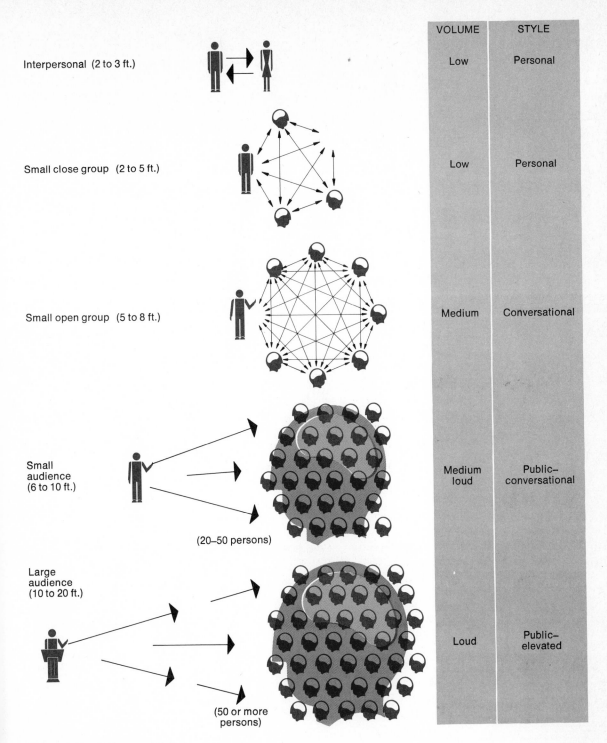

Interpersonal (2 to 3 ft.)

Small close group (2 to 5 ft.)

Small open group (5 to 8 ft.)

Small audience (6 to 10 ft.)

(20–50 persons)

Large audience (10 to 20 ft.)

(50 or more persons)

VOLUME	STYLE
Low	Personal
Low	Personal
Medium	Conversational
Medium loud	Public– conversational
Loud	Public– elevated

Figure 4.11 © Raymond S. Ross.

TIME (CHRONEMICS)

Time is another element over which you have some control. Seldom are you in trouble for being early, but occasionally you may get in trouble for being late! One famous American general who had risen from the ranks claimed that one of the secrets of his success was always being fifteen minutes early for appointments. Almost every interview form includes an evaluation of the subject's dependability, which often translates into his or her attitude toward being on time. Our general culture tends to stress promptness. Television viewers complain by the thousands when a scheduled program is delayed by a news special or a game that runs into overtime.

Lateness suggests low regard for the sender, the situation, or the message. We can often save strained interpersonal relations by giving good reasons when we are late.

" WELL, I SEE MY TIME IS UP. "

Figure 4.12 Reprinted from the *Saturday Evening Post,* © 1959, the Curtis Publishing Company. Used by permission of Joe Zeis.

There are many other nonverbal codes, too many to discuss here. However, the simple but important one of silence also should be mentioned.

The ultimate nonverbal insult is often simply to be ignored! ("Look at me when I speak to you!!") Silence can be a powerful message. The "man who never called" has sent quite a message to the lady involved. Sometimes people remain silent simply because they are confused, tired, embarrassed, or honestly did not hear. Remember this when you are ignored (or think you are) and try one more time.

4 SUMMING UP

Our audience interprets the total message—both verbal and nonverbal—that we present to them. Nonverbals may convey much of the message.

Five important areas of nonverbal communication are: *kinesics* (body communication), *paralanguage* (voice and articulation), *object* language (clothes and things), *proxemics* (space and distance), and *chronemics* (time).

Our nonverbals may be conscious or unconscious and have five important characteristics: (1) they always communicate something; (2) they are bound to the situation; (3) they are believed; (4) they are seldom isolated; and (5) they affect our relationships.

We decide three important things about people largely on the basis of nonverbal communication: (1) personal liking or attraction, (2) evaluation of power relationships, and (3) our feelings of response we get from others.

What your audience sees greatly affects how it interprets what you say. Much unconscious body action accompanies most speeches. A lack of action often makes your message less clear. There is therefore no point in trying to restrain body action, and there are many good reasons for trying to understand it, control it, and use it.

Research into the portrayal and recognition of emotions such as anger, love, and fear has shown that we rely on previous experience to interpret these highly abstract messages. Certain cultures and subcultures have stereotyped patterns of body action different from our own. We use enough stereotyping to be understood, but not so much as to appear artificial.

In general, speakers should be so involved in their subject and audience that their body action language will be both dynamic and spontaneous. It is evident that we communicate through many learned stereotypes of body action and that a speaker must use these stereotypes.

Empathy, the projection of oneself into the situation of another, includes a muscular reaction: the audience imitates, in part, the actions of the speaker. Speakers should adapt their body action to the empathy of the audience. Constant pacing, for example, should be avoided, because it will probably wear out the audience before it does the speaker.

Prolonged restraint on the use of normal body action can result in emotional disintegration. We should use constructive body action to help control our speech fright as well as to communicate our message. The types of bodily action are: posture, walking, facial expression, and gestures.

Posture is an important part of the general impression you make: it affects the empathy of the audience and what they conclude from your speech, and it also reflects your self-concept. Good posture and poise present a picture of cool unconcern. The great danger is in appearing artificial, overly noticeable, or out of place.

Walking is an important way to express various moods and degrees of emphasis. It serves as a form of physical punctuation for the speaker. Walking also has empathic value: it can offer physical relief to a cramped or suffering audience.

Good facial expression includes (1) the avoidance of unintentional or inappropriate facial stereotypes, (2) eye contact with the audience, and (3) natural and spontaneous expressions that will reinforce your message.

Some gestures are used to emphasize parts of the message. These are *reinforcing* gestures. Others are used to describe the shape or size of objects and are called *descriptive* gestures.

The standards of good body action are (1) *appropriateness* to your subject, your physical makeup and personality, and the size and nature of the audience; (2) *variety* of body action, so that monotony does not cause a loss of the reinforcing effect of the action; (3) *physical coordination,* the combination of all parts of your body in expressing yourself; (4) *verbal coordination,* the correct timing of words and action; and (5) *a dynamic and spontaneous* sense of communication.

Paralanguage contributes much to your nonverbal signal and thus to your total communication signal; it may be the most important code you use. Voice and articulation are thought to be faulty when they deviate so far from the norm that they call too much attention to themselves.

Some common problems of voice are fast rate, wrong pitch, improper level of loudness, and faulty articulation.

The vocal process includes an *energy source* (our breathing machinery); a *vibrator* (our vocal cords); *resonators* (such as the cavities in our heads); and *modifiers* (such as our lips, teeth, tongue, jaw, and palate). The alteration of the size, shape, and texture of these agents is the principal factor in the production of speech.

There are certain attributes of voice over which you have considerable control. These are *rate, loudness, pitch,* and *quality.* Rate is influenced by assimilation, duration, pauses, phrases, and rhythm. Loudness is a product of intensity, volume, and vocal variety. There are central, habitual, and optimum levels of pitch. Your pitch range includes all the pitches you can sing without a complete loss of quality. The most critical problems affecting quality are *nasality, breathiness,* and *harshness.*

Articulation is the interacting of the speech organs as they help join the various sound units into accepted patterns that we call speech. Your training of such organs as teeth, tongue, lips, palate, and jaw are of great importance to proper articulation. Some of the more common mechanical faults in articulation are *locked jaw, muffled mouth,* and *slack lips.*

Pronunciation is the act of expressing the sounds and accents of words so that they are best adapted to your total communication. There are three general dialects in the United States: eastern, southern, and standard American. Our mass media and dictionaries are geared to the standard American dialect.

The problem of showing different pronunciations in print is solved in part through pronouncing systems such as the International Phonetic Association alphabet, the respelling system and the diacritical-mark system. The last of these is preferred by our dictionaries.

Some of the more common pronunciation errors in the English language are *improper stress, errors of spelling-phonetics, sound substitutions, sound additions, sound reversals,* and *sound subtractions.*

Object language uses the influence and display of material things. It includes the clothes you wear, the things you wear, the jewelry, cosmetics, and so forth that *say* something. The key word is *appropriate.*

Space and distance (proxemics) are the personal space or territory we deem acceptable. Our preferences are culture-bound. Space and distance are also closely related to the message, situation, and mood. We adapt our voices in rather set ways to these aspects. E. T. Hall suggests an eight-point scale from three inches to one hundred feet. Another scale suggesting proper volume and style according to type of communication situation (interpersonal, small group, audience) is shown.

Time as a nonverbal varies with cultures and situations. In our culture we stress promptness. Lateness suggests a low regard for the sender, the situation, or the message.

1 Our listeners interpret the total message that we present to them. A large amount of the message is conveyed by nonverbal signals.
2 Cultures and subcultures create their own forms of nonverbal communication.
3 When combined with the verbal message, nonverbal signals accurately communicate most emotional concepts.
4 Our actions may speak so loudly that our words are meaningless.
5 We express our attitudes through body action, voice, the clothes we wear and the objects we own and our use of time and space.
6 Much of our nonverbal communication is expressed unconsciously.
7 Acted or stylized emotions can be perceived or identified with some reliability.
8 Real emotions, when presented apart from the total message, are difficult to identify.

9 Empathy includes a muscular reaction: the audience imitates, in part, the actions of the speaker.
10 Good posture and poise take the form of a cool unconcern.
11 Our social status is communicated by signals in our voice.
12 We express our attitudes through our voice and articulation.
13 Just as personality affects voice, voice improvement may affect personality.
14 Speech is faulty when it is too noticeable, unclean, or unpleasant.
15 Most articulation problems are functional matters of habit.
16 The vocal process uses organs of the body whose primary function is physiological.
17 The average duration of the words of good speakers tends to be greater than that of poor speakers.
18 For most people, optimum pitch should be the habitual (central) pitch.
19 A chronic hoarseness is most often organic.
20 To some extent, you should adapt your articulation in groups and situations in which a different dialect is spoken, especially when you are a part of such a group.

21 The most widespread dialect in the United States is standard American.
22 Your voice contributes much to your nonverbal and total communication signal. It may be the most important code you use.
23 Many stereotypes are associated with clothes and things (object language).
24 Culture is a large part of space preferences.
25 The way we project our voice is related not only to our mood and message but also to the distance or space between us and the audience.
26 Promptness is admired in our culture; seldom do we offend anyone by being early.

Specific Learning Outcomes

1 We should become sensitive to unconscious messages as revealed by nonverbal signals, and be able to describe the messages.
2 We should learn the five important characteristics of nonverbal communication.
3 We should learn the technical as well as the common words for the major areas of nonverbal communication.

4   We should become aware that cultures and subcultures vary in their use of nonverbal signals.

5   We should be able to relate the meanings conveyed by nonverbal communication to the process nature of human communication, as described in chapter 1.

6   We should learn that acted or stylized nonverbal emotional signals can be recognized with considerable reliability, though real emotions may easily be misread.

7   We should learn the difference between reinforcing and descriptive gestures and be able to illustrate several of each.

8   We should learn the standards of good body action: appropriateness, variety, verbal coordination, and a dynamic and spontaneous sense of communication.

9   We should learn to describe and explain the vocal process in terms of *energy source, vibrator, resonator,* and *modifiers.*

10   We should learn to describe and explain the variable attributes of voice: *rate, loudness, pitch,* and *quality.*

11   We should learn and be able to apply some of the various pronouncing systems: the respelling system and the diacritical-mark system.

12   We should learn to identify the more common pronunciation errors in the English language: improper stress, errors of spelling-phonetics, sound substitutions, sound additions, sound reversals, and sound subtractions.

13   We should learn to identify common articulatory faults.

Communication Competencies

1   We should learn to adapt our body action to an audience of fifteen to twenty-five students familiar with the content of this chapter.

2   We should be able to use body action to help control speech fright as well as to communicate a message.

3   We should learn to use body movement on the platform as a form of physical punctuation as well as to offer empathic relief to the audience.

4   We should learn to apply the standards of good facial expression: avoid inappropriate facial stereotypes, make eye contact, and be natural.

5   In a short oral exercise, we should be able to adjust our vocal rate, volume, pitch, and quality to the satisfaction of an audience of fifteen to twenty-five students familiar with the content of this chapter.

6   We should be able to employ one of the pronouncing systems in such a way that our pronunciations generally agree with those of our instructor.

7   We should be able to identify our own pronunciation errors in terms of the six common errors, and we should be able to correct these errors as a result of ten-minute drill and practice sessions.

8   We should be able to discover our own optimum pitch and learn to adjust (if necessary) our habitual or central pitch.

9   We should be able to adjust our articulation in a short oral exercise to the satisfaction of an audience of fifteen to twenty-five students familiar with the content of this chapter.

10   We should learn to dress appropriately for our subject and audience.

11   We should learn to adjust our speaking distance, style, and voice to the communication situation, message, and mood.

12   We should learn to take time requirements seriously and start and close formal speech communication exercises on time.

1 Using no props, develop a two-minute pantomime in which you try to communicate an emotion (for instance, fear, love, or rage). Let the class feedback be the measure of your effectiveness.

2 Watch a television show, the first half with only the picture and the second half with only the sound. Describe on one page, for the purpose of class discussion, the effects of having no verbal and no visual signals.

3 Prepare a one-minute pantomime in which you use body action to provoke an empathic response (for example, walking and fatigue, lifting and strain, falling and pain, taste and ecstasy, and so forth).

4 Take turns trying to communicate the following messages through body action language:

    a Don't blame me.
    b I'm the piano tuner.
    c She (he) is really quite something.
    d Will you walk with me?
    e Oh, George (Gladys), let's park here.
    f Oh, George (Gladys), let's not park here.

5 Prepare a two-to-four-minute descriptive speech that requires considerable body action (for instance, a speech on shooting the rapids, water skiing, ski jumping, the big-game play, the close race, the big storm, a frightening episode, a close call, an embarrassing moment).

6 Observe the nonverbal behavior of a speaker (for example, an instructor, preacher, lecturer, or student) and comment upon his or her effectiveness in terms of appropriateness, variety, verbal coordination, and dynamism.

7

FILL IN WHAT THESE ACTIONS INDICATE TO YOU

Slouching _____

_____

Hands clenched _____

_____

Unconscious frown _____

_____

Avoiding your eyes _____

_____

Key twirling _____

_____

8 Record your voice for five minutes, two and a half while reading and two and a half while speaking impromptu. Complete a written report and inventory of your voice and articulation on the basis of the advice given in this chapter.

9 Record your voice, as above, and then write a report on the personality you think others might associate with it. Record it again, attempting to portray a different personality through voice and articulation alone. Write a brief second report explaining your success or lack of it.

10 Find a piano and, following the advice of this chapter, find your *optimum* pitch and compare it to your habitual pitch. Report any wide variations to your instructor.

11 Select a 100-to-300-word poem, scene from a play, passage from a novel, or other material for an oral presentation to the class. Prepare a short extemporaneous introduction for the material, and practice to sharpen your voice, articulation, and pronunciation. Be ready for class feedback. If you want, you may use either of the readings at the end of this chapter.

12 Based upon the impressions you have gained from your classmates' voice and articulation habits, characterize each of your classmates in two or three well chosen sentences. Your instructor may wish to read some of these aloud, not revealing the authors.

13 In the practice readings below, find two words that are relatively new to you. Show how to pronounce them using the diacritical marking system and the respelling system. (If you prefer a more typical message, you may select a paragraph or two of your own.)

Pompeii

Roll back the tide of many hundreds of years. At the foot of vine-clad Vesuvius stands a royal city. Like all cities, both ancient and modern, there exists a number of contrasts, particularly between the splendid palaces of the royalty and the simple dwellings of the plebeians.

Despite the contrasts, life is happy, unhurried. The stately Roman walks the lordly streets, or banquets in the palaces of splendor, or dines simply in a modest home. There is the bustle of busy thousands; you may hear it along the thronged quays; it rises from the amphitheatre and the forum. And there is the sense of quieter moments along the less frequented streets. As a whole, it is the home of luxury, of gaiety, and of joy. The togaed royalty drowns itself in dissipation, the lion roars over the martyred Christian, and the bleeding body of the gladiator dies at the beck of applauding spectators. Little by little the senses are deadened in riotous living. It is a careless, a dreaming, a devoted city.

Lo! There is blackness on the horizon, and the earthquake is rioting in the bowels of the mountain! Listen! A roar! A crash! And the very foundations of the eternal hills are belched forth in a sea of fire! Woe for that fated city! The torrent comes surging like the mad ocean! It boils above wall and tower, palace and fountain, engulfing a screaming, scuttling mass of people! There is hardly time for escape! Many are caught unaware in their beds and are suffocated by the fire and ash that settles over the city. Pompeii, once a city of luxury, of gaiety, and of joy, becomes a massive tomb.

—An adaptation from an anonymous writer

IF—

If you can keep your head when all about you
  Are losing theirs and blaming it on you;
If you can trust yourself when all men doubt you,
  But make allowance for their doubting too;
If you can wait and not be tired by waiting,
  Or, being lied about, don't deal in lies,
Or, being hated, don't give way to hating,
  And yet don't look too good, nor talk too wise;

If you can dream—and not make dreams your master;
  If you can think—and not make thoughts your aim;
If you can meet with triumph and disaster
  And treat those two imposters just the same;
If you can bear to hear the truth you've spoken
  Twisted by knaves to make a trap for fools,
Or watch the things you gave your life to broken,
  And stoop and build'em up with wornout tools;

If you can make one heap of all your winnings
  And risk it on one turn of pitch-and-toss,
And lose, and start again at your beginnings
  And never breathe a word about your loss;
If you can force your heart and nerve and sinew
  To serve your turn long after they are gone,
And so hold on when there is nothing in you
  Except the Will which says to them "Hold on";

If you can talk with crowds and keep your virtue,
  Or walk with kings—nor lose the common touch;
If neither foes nor loving friends can hurt you;
  If all men count with you, but none too much;
If you can fill the unforgiving minute
  With sixty seconds' worth of distance run—
Yours is the Earth and everything that's in it,
  And—which is more—you'll be a Man, my son!

by Rudyard Kipling

Source: "If," Copyright 1910 by Rudyard Kipling, from the book *Rudyard Kipling's Verse: definitive edition.* Reprinted by permission of Doubleday & Company, Inc., and Mrs. George Bambridge.

14 Try an experiment in *object language.* Wear something unusual (for you) and interact with some family or friends. Write a one-page report of what happened to the communication. Discuss it in class.

15 Try a *space and distance experiment.* Sit in someone's favorite chair or place, or stand closer to people than you usually do. Write a one-page report of what happened in the ensuing communication. Discuss it in class.

GENERAL LEARNING OUTCOMES

1 We should learn the importance of listening to human communication and understanding.

2 We should understand the process of listening so that we may improve our own listening behavior.

3 We should learn the factors and attributes of and the barriers to effective listening so that we may improve our own listening and speaking behavior.

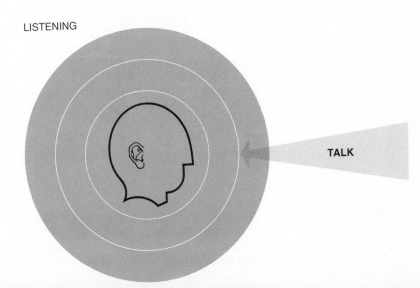

LISTENING

TALK

listening

THE IMPORTANCE OF LISTENING

> **"Listen, My Children . . ."**
>
> "First listen, my friend, and then you may shriek and bluster." (Aristophanes)
> "Hearing is one of the body's five senses. But listening is an art." (Frank Tyger)
> "Hear twice before you speak once." (Scottish saying)
> "The funny thing about human beings is that we tend to respect the intelligence of, and eventually to like, those who listen attentively to our ideas, even if they continue to disagree with us." (S. I. Hayakawa)
> "While the right to talk may be the beginning of freedom, the necessity of listening is what makes the right important." (Walter Lippman)
> "Speech is difficult, but silence is impossible." (Chinese proverb)
> "Shut up, he explained!" (Anonymous)
> "The listener is always right." (Carroll C. Arnold)[1]

Hal Boyle suggests that no one is willing to listen anymore and that there is a tremendous market for good listeners. He humorously offers to rent his ears as follows:

> Whenever anyone grabs me by the lapels and starts wagging his jawbone, I'll silently hand him a printed folder which says:
> "You are speaking to a man who earns his living by listening. So, please button your mouth unless you are willing to pay my rates, which are as follows:
> "Listening to comments on the weather, baseball and politics: 50 cents an hour.
> "Listening to husbands complain about their wives: 75 cents an hour.
> "Listening to wives complain about their husbands: Ditto.
> "Listening to campaign speeches and periodically breaking into loud cheers: $1 an hour.
> "Listening at cocktail parties: $2 an hour before midnight, $4 after midnight, plus two free drinks for the road.
> "Listening to views on Vietnam and other international problems: $5 for 15 minutes.
> "Listening to gossip: No charge—if it's about anyone I know. Otherwise $1 an hour.

[1] William Work, "Eric Report," *Communication Education,* 27, no. 2 (March 1978), 146.

"Listening over the telephone: Double usual rates, payable in advance.

"Listening to your troubles: $15 a morning, money to be refunded if you spend all afternoon listening to my troubles.

"Standby rate for waiting while you make up your mind what you want to talk about: 10 cents a minute.

"Pay up or shut up!"

What do you think of the idea? What, you didn't hear a word I said? See what I mean?

Nobody listens.[2]

From our discussion of the process of perception and its intimate involvement in the process of communication, it seems obvious that although speech training must emphasize skills of delivery (encoding and transmitting), it must also concentrate on listening.

When we describe speech as a process of communication and perception we are also describing listening. Listening is the most used of the communicative skills, and *good* listening is an integral part of the communication process. Listening is therefore an essential factor in *good* speaking. Surveys of communication habits indicate that people may spend as much as 60 to 75 percent of their time listening.[3]

On the average verbal communication breaks down as follows:

Listening	42%
Talking	32%
Reading	15%
Writing	11%

Students have been found to spend 46 percent of an average school day listening; 66 percent of this time was spent listening to their teachers.

Stuart Chase has openly scolded Americans for their listening habits:

> Listening is the other half of talking. If people stop listening, it is useless to talk—a point not always appreciated by talkers.
>
> Americans are not good listeners. In general they talk more than they listen. Competition in our culture puts a premium on self-expression, even if the individual has nothing to express. What he lacks in knowledge he tries to make up for by talking fast or pounding the table. And many of us, while ostensibly listening, are inwardly preparing a statement to stun the company when we get the floor.[4]

[2] Reprinted from "Nobody Listens Any More" by Hal Boyle in *Boston Traveler*, August 17, 1966. © 1966 The Associated Press. Used by permission of The Associated Press.
[3] Ralph G. Nichols and Leonard A. Stevens, *Are You Listening?* (New York: McGraw-Hill Book Company, 1957), pp. 6–8.
[4] Stuart Chase, "Are You Listening?" *Reader's Digest*, December 1962, p. 80.

There is hope! We have evidence that listening can be improved through understanding the process and acquiring better attitudes about social interaction and listening itself. Listening training improved the listening ability among elementary students.[5] College students improved their listening comprehension through a program first designed for industry.[6] Oral reading seems to help.[7] There is even evidence that improving our listening skills may improve our reading skills.[8]

Good listening habits are important. William Work, who synthesized much of the research cited above, reminds us that to a large extent, *we are what we listen to.*

> Nutritionists tell us that we—quite literally—*are* what we eat (and drink and breathe). In terms of our physical being, this is true. In terms of our psychic selves, we—quite literally—*are* what we hear and read and view. As our social structures and systems become more complex, each individual becomes more dependent on the ability to process information effectively. Competence in listening and speaking is central to the achievement of that end. Being a good listener will not guarantee "success" or happiness or the securing of one's life goals, but, for most, poor listening will stand in the way of their attainment.[9]

A LISTENING MODEL

If we can become better listeners by understanding the listening process, the following model may help. Listening is perception, and you will recall that perception was defined as having two broad components: sensation and interpretation. One has to bring one's past experience, attitudes, and emotions to bear on the sensations of which one is aware to make any sense or *interpretation* of them. Your interpretation can, of course, be wrong, or at least unlike the one intended by the sender. Therefore the third step, *comprehension,* is shown in this model. Let us now examine the steps in the model.

In step 1, *Sensation,* we are really talking about hearing. Of course our perceptions are related, and hearing is frequently affected by our other

[5] Susan Fleming Blackburn, "The Construction, the Implementation, and the Evaluation of a Title I Primary Grade Listening Program," "Eric Report," *Communication Education,* 27, no. 2 (March 1978), 150.

[6] Deane Ford Schubach, "An Experimental Evaluation of a Program for Improvement of Listening Comprehension of College Students," "Eric Report," *Communication Education,* p. 151.

[7] Margaret Weidner, "Reading Achievement of Grade Four Students," "Eric Report," *Communication Education,* p. 150.

[8] Robert Lee Lemons, Jr., "The Effects of Passive Listening and Direct Training in Listening upon the Reading and Listening Skills of a Group of Black Fourth Graders," "Eric Report," *Communication Education,* p. 149; Thomas G. Sticht and others, "Auding and Reading: A Developmental Model," "Eric Report," *Communication Education,* p. 149.

[9] Work, "Eric Report," *Communication Education,* p. 152.

Figure 5.1 Steps to Good Listening.

senses. We see as well as hear another person. The *hearing barriers* include items like the following:

Hearing Barriers **Step 1. Sensation**

1 Noise
2 Hearing impairment
3 Fatigue
4 Sensory distraction
5 Sender deficiency

These are reasonably obvious. If someone is operating a jack hammer or beating a drum you may lose the verbal signal in sheer noise. We still give an audiometric screening (hearing test) to our beginning students, and we find young people with hearing losses of which they are not aware. We all have learned that we hear poorly when we are tired. Sensory distraction could be competing noises or other verbal messages. It could also be distraction by the other senses. A really foul smell, temperature extremes, a pretty face—any of these can be barriers to hearing. Sender deficiency refers to a really poor speaker, one who lacks volume, projection, or is so dull as to make hearing actually difficult. More will be said of sender responsibilities later.

We may think of step 1 as mainly auditory sensation, keeping in mind that all of our other senses also contribute to what we finally decode. Listening then is dependent upon our sense of hearing and our ability to hear despite the barriers. Assuming we have overcome the barriers and are willing to stay attentive, we are finally *auding* (or hearing) but not yet seriously listening.

In step 2, *Interpretation*, we are talking about the beginning of *listening* which is assigning of meaning to what we hear. We may never fully comprehend or understand the message, but we are receiving part of it. Our decoding may be quite different from what the sender intended. This leads us to the interesting problem of *listening barriers*. All of the *hearing* barriers of step 1 also affect step 2. The barriers can best be expressed as bad listening habits.

1 Insisting that the topic is stupid or uninteresting.
2 Criticizing the person instead of the message.
3 Permitting negative stereotypes to intrude.
4 Prejudging.
5 Premature outlining.
6 Seeking distractions.
7 Faking attention.

These bad habits are worth more discussion. Are you guilty of any of them?[10]

(1) *Insisting that the topic is stupid or uninteresting.* This is a great way to duck listening. Work hard at relating the topic to something you do like or do find interesting. Some topics are difficult and complex—this is a good way to avoid those also.

(2) *Criticizing the person instead of the message.* Try to disregard a person's appearance or speech mannerisms when they offer you an excuse for not listening to the message. This often takes real effort!

(3) *Permitting negative stereotypes to intrude.* If we hear something that challenges our most deeply rooted prejudices, our brains may become overstimulated in a direction that leads to bad listening. We mentally plan a rebuttal to what we hear, develop a question designed to embarrass the talker, or perhaps simply turn to thoughts that support our own feelings on the subject at hand. This is a kind of closed-mindedness that may cause us to daydream, yawn, or get so upset that we confuse the message. Letting emotionally loaded words distract us belongs here.

(4) *Prejudging*—jumping to the conclusion that the other person's meaning is understood before it is fully expressed. Worse yet, it often means preparing and rehearsing answers to questions or points before fully understanding them. This all too common bad habit can make us appear really stupid or rude.

(5) *Premature outlining.* What you are listening to may not always permit outlining. Listen for awhile and find out. Jot down the key concepts and let them grow into an outline. Outlining too quickly may interfere with listening.

(6) *Seeking distractions.* A dandy way to avoid listening is actively to seek out distractions: looking out the window for something, anything that might be more interesting; concentrating on another person who excites you; daydreaming or actually causing distraction.

(7) *Faking attention*—also called sleeping with your eyes open! You only pretend to listen, and your act gets pretty good. You smile, nod, blink, and

---

[10] These bad habits are adapted from R. G. Nichols and L. A. Stevens, *Are You Listening?* (New York: McGraw-Hill Book Company, 1957), pp. 104–12 and L. Barker, *Listening Behavior* (Englewood Cliffs, N. J.: Prentice-Hall, Inc., 1971), pp. 61–66.

so forth; you may even fool the speaker. That is why this bad habit is so cruel—you may be fooling (and cheating) both yourself and the speaker.

These questions should help you find your bad listening habits.

1 Do you often avoid getting into situations in which you must listen to a speaker you feel is poor?
2 Do you avoid listening to new and different topics which may challenge you?
3 Do you yield easily to physical distractions?
4 Do you become irritated by speaker's mannerisms?
5 Do you find your mind wandering frequently in listening settings?
6 Do you become emotional about what a speaker is saying and not listen to him?
7 Do you try to impose your own thoughts on others when listening to them?
8 Do you frequently fake attention?[11]

If you answered any of the above questions with "yes," you probably need to work on your listening habits.

In step 3, *Comprehension*, we are talking about *understanding* what you are listening to. It also includes critical evaluation. You not only understand the message intended (or most of it) but also are aware of your own reactions. All of the barriers and bad listening habits pertain here, but there are additional ones over which you may not always have as much control as those previously discussed.

Ralph Nichols has listed the factors he believes are most important to listening comprehension.[12] All of them are also critical to helping you better analyze *your* listeners in order to adapt your delivery to them as well as possible.

[11] Barker, *Listening Behavior,* pp. 66–67, (adapted).
[12] Ralph G. Nichols, "Factors in Listening Comprehension," *Speech Monographs,* 15, no. 2 (1948), 161–62.

Figure 5.2 B.C. *by permission of Johnny Hart and Field Enterprises, Inc.*

Intelligence
Reading comprehension
Recognition of correct English usage
Size of the listener's vocabulary
Ability to make inferences
Ability to structuralize a speech (that is, to see the organizational plan and the connection of the main points)
Listening for main ideas, not merely for specific facts
Use of special techniques while listening to improve concentration
Real interest in the subject discussed
Emotional adjustment to the speaker's thesis
Curiosity about the subject discussed
Physical fatigue of the listener
Audibility of the speaker
Speaker effectiveness
Admiration for the speaker
Respect for listening as a method of learning
Susceptibility to distraction
Room ventilation and temperature
Use of only the English language at home
High-school scholastic achievement
High-school speech training
Experience in listening to difficult expository material

IMPROVING LISTENING HABITS

Although perhaps we cannot always change factors like intelligence or even aptitude, we can improve our reading, our vocabulary, our language, and the like. This whole book is, in fact, devoted to just such personal growth and development. Weaver suggests specific ways to enhance even comprehension through improving listening capacity and your sense of evaluation.[13]

enlarging your listening capacity

1 You can reflect the message to the talker.

2 You must guess the talker's intent or purpose.

3 You should strive to bring the quality of your habitual listening up to the level of your optimal capacity.

4 You should try to determine whether your referents for the words of the talker are about the same as his.

5 You should try to determine your purpose in every listening situation.

6 You should become aware of your own biases and attitudes.

7 You should learn to use your spare time well as you listen.

8 You should analyze your listening errors.

9 You should pay attention to the process of cognitive structuring as it occurs and to the time it takes.

[13] Carl H. Weaver, *Human Listening, Processes and Behavior* (Indianapolis and New York: The Bobbs-Merrill Company, Inc., 1972), pp. 99 and 105.

10 You should learn as much as you can about the process of listening.

evaluating
what you hear

1 You should get the whole story before evaluating it.
2 You should be alert to mistaken causal relations.
3 You should ask yourself whether the speaker has done his homework well.
4 You should ask yourself whether the opinions you hear are sound.
5 You should judge how much the speaker's biases are affecting his message.

One expert supplies the following factors and attributes thought useful to improving our listening.

factors

1 An adequate hearing acuity. (Check your hearing.)
2 A recognition on the part of the listener of the problems and obstacles to overcome in order to listen effectively, including such things as improper attitude, boredom, fatigue, and the like.
3 A knowledge of the specific kind of listening situation and the listener's adaptation to it, including such kinds as casual listening and intent listening.
4 The relationship between listening and vocabulary. (Improve your vocabulary.)
5 The judging of what is heard—being able to think and analyze while listening.

attributes

1 A readiness to listen.
2 An ability to discriminate among sounds and ideas.
3 The capacity to give meanings to selected sounds.
4 The ability to relate meanings given to certain sounds to other experiences.
5 The ability to evaluate properly the medium and manner of the sound presentations.
6 The willingness to disregard prejudice.[14]

You listen with more than your ears, and you listen for more than sound—you listen with all appropriate senses in order to perceive the total situation or receive the total communication.

Listening is a difficult process even under the most favorable conditions. One reason for this is that we think much faster than we talk. The average *rate* of conversational speech of most Americans is around 125 words per minute, whereas it has been found that people can listen to speech at more than 300 words per minute without a significant loss in comprehension.[15]

[14] Robert S. Goyer, "Oral Communication: Studies in Listening," *Audio-Visual Communication Review,* 2, no. 4 (Fall 1954), 263–76; see also Sam Duker, *Listening: Bibliography* (New York: Scarecrow Press, 1964). (Parentheses mine.)
[15] Nichols and Stevens, *Are you Listening?* pp. 78–79.

This is not to say that speakers should sound like a machine gun, but too slow a rate does give listeners more free time to distract themselves. All of us occasionally find ourselves checking in and out of a conversation by taking little mental excursions. This is not always critical if we remember to check back in! There is mixed evidence for the value of very rapid speech when it comes to listening.[16] An *appropriate* rate depends in part on the difficulty of the message and your audience analysis.

Although we are counseled to be interested listeners, we have to take care that our own opinions and biases do not get in the way. As stated earlier, when our most deeply rooted prejudices, notions, convictions, mores, or complexes are challenged, our brains may become overstimulated, and not in a direction that leads to good listening. We really do plan a rebuttal to what we hear, often formulating questions designed to embarrass the talker instead of listening.[17]

We can probably do a better job of listening if we remember *why* we are listening. We are not always involved in deep, evaluative listening, or even in informational listening. We often listen for fun and recreation—for enjoyment. We can be a poor listener and a poor conversationalist as well, if we push all social discourse into content analysis. Sometimes people talk just for the sheer joy of it, and *that,* not the words, is the real message. Good listeners must be sensitive to this kind of communication behavior. Does "How are ya?" from a person you pass on the street call for a ten-minute response—or is it simply a form of recognition? How about "nice day." "Like heck it is! What do you mean by that?" Try Lucy's reaction to "Happy New Year" in figure 5.3.

We also listen to actors, oral interpreters, music, and so on. These are

[16] Mary Ann Ihnat, "The Effect of Listening Drills Utilizing Compressed Speech and Standard Speech upon the Listening Comprehension of Second-Grade Children"; Richard W. Woodcock and Charlotte R. Clark, "Comprehension of a Narrative Passage as a Function of Listening Rate, Recall Period, and IQ," "Eric Report," *Communication Education,* p. 148.

[17] Ralph G. Nichols and Leonard A. Stevens, "Listening to People," *Harvard Business Review,* 35, no. 5 (September 1957), 88.

Figure 5.3 © *United Feature Syndicate, Inc.*

PEANUTS®　　　　　　　　　　　　　　　　　　　　　**By Charles M. Schulz**

fun, enriching, often aesthetic experiences, and our listening rules and admonitions have to be applied more gently.

If you are listening to a lecture mostly for information, or to a political candidate for an evaluation of his stand, that, of course, is a different matter. The point is to consider the purpose and then summon the appropriate listening skills. Listening is not easy. It is often very hard work, but it can be fun if one has learned to be good at it.

All speakers are entitled to *some* listening effort by their audience. In the case of a required course that is notoriously dull and taught by an even duller teacher, you may dramatically discover your own listening responsibilities as you fail the mid-semester examination!

As speakers, or senders, we are also responsible to a large extent for both attentive *hearing* and objective *listening* by our audience. An audience that is inattentive and half-asleep may not be *hearing* very efficiently because our voice or delivery pattern is dull and monotonous, or because our subject is dull and monotonous, or both. The audience may not be *listening* for the same reason. However, *listening* is related more closely to subject, organization of material, interest, and linguistic ability. In trying to enhance critical listening, the speaker has the serious ethical responsibility to avoid *name-calling,* the stacking of his or her message's organization and evidence, and the use of abstract language of the *glittering-generality* variety. These devices might improve the audience's hearing or attentiveness, but they make objective listening very difficult.

It behooves the speaker to consider all of the process of listening when organizing and adapting the material, mood, and mode of his or her delivery to a particular group of potential listeners. Remember also that communication is a two-way process. Watch closely for the feedback signs suggested in this chapter. Good listeners usually let you know, one way or another, if you are not being understood.

Nearly one hundred years ago in George Eliot's *Felix Holt,* the Reverend Rufus Lyon counseled the hot-tempered hero as follows: "Therefore I pray for a listening spirit, which is a great mark of grace. . . . The scornful nostril and the high head gather not the odors that lie on the track of truth."[18]

Pflaumer reviews an ideal listener for us as one who:

. . . keeps an open curious mind
. . . listens for new ideas
. . . relates what is heard to what is known
. . . is self-perceptive and listens to others from that self
. . . pays attention to what is said
. . . does not blindly follow the crowd
. . . maintains perspective

[18] George Eliot, *Felix Holt, the Radical: The Personal Edition of George Eliot's Works* (New York: Doubleday, 1901), p. 70.

. . . looks for idea organization and arguments
. . . listens for the essence of things
. . . stays mentally alert, outlining, objecting, approving
. . . is introspective but critically analytical
. . . attempts to understand values, attitudes and relationships
. . . focuses on the speaker's ideas
. . . listens with feeling and intuition.[19]

[19] Elizabeth M. Pflaumer, "Listening: A Definition and Application" (Paper delivered at the International Communication Association Convention, Atlanta, Georgia, April, 1972), p. 7. (Rewritten for rhetorical purposes.)

5 SUMMING UP

The importance of listening is reflected by surveys that indicate that people may spend as much as 60 to 75 percent of their time listening. Americans are not thought to be good listeners. There is evidence that we can improve our listening habits through understanding the listening process and through developing better attitudes toward the task of listening.

A three-step listening model is provided: (1) Sensation, (2) Interpretation, (3) Comprehension. The *hearing* barriers to step 1 are: noise, hearing impairment, fatigue, sensory distraction, and sender deficiency. The *listening* barriers to step 2 are: insisting the topic is stupid or uninteresting, criticizing the person instead of the message, permitting negative stereotypes to intrude, prejudging, premature outlining, seeking distractions, and faking attention. Some of the barriers to step 3, *comprehension,* are: intelligence, reading ability, vocabulary, thinking ability, and experience.

Ways of improving our listening habits include: ten suggestions for enlarging your listening capacity, five suggestions for evaluating what you hear, and five factors and six attributes related to good listeners. We can improve our listening habits by considering the purpose of our listening. We listen for *information,* for *evaluation,* and for *enjoyment.* We can help others improve their listening effectiveness by being good speakers who organize messages clearly, who use elements of interest, and who avoid the distractions of name-calling, evidence-stacking, and glittering-generality language. We can help from either end of the message by asking for or giving feedback.

Listening is an integral part of the processes of communication and perception and is the most used of the communication skills. It may be defined as a conscious cognitive effort using mainly the sense of hearing (reinforced by other senses) which in turn leads to interpretation and understanding.

1 Knowledge of and practice in listening behavior can improve our listening habits.
2 Listening has three basic steps: sensation, interpretation, and comprehension.
3 Some barriers to good listening are inherent; others are simply bad habits.
4 Speakers have a responsibility to help their listeners listen effectively.
5 Evaluating our purpose for listening can increase effectiveness.

Specific Learning Outcomes

1 In a five-minute report we should be able to explain and illustrate a model of the listening process.
2 We should learn the factors and attributes of and the barriers to good listening and be able to apply them to our own behavior.

Figure 5.4 SIER—4 Stage Communication Construct *Lyman K. (Manny) Steil, University of Minnesota, and President, Communication Consultants Associated.*

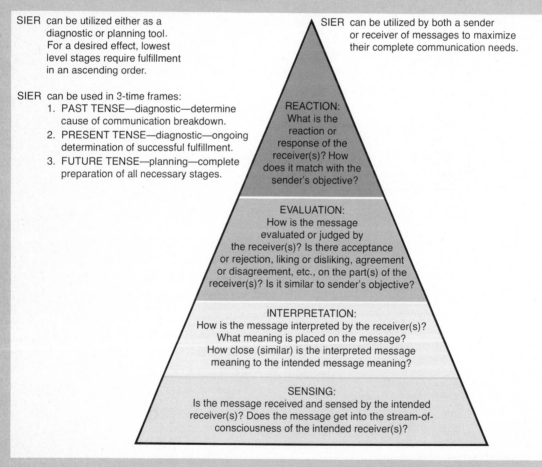

SIER can be utilized either as a diagnostic or planning tool. For a desired effect, lowest level stages require fulfillment in an ascending order.

SIER can be used in 3-time frames:
1. PAST TENSE—diagnostic—determine cause of communication breakdown.
2. PRESENT TENSE—diagnostic—ongoing determination of successful fulfillment.
3. FUTURE TENSE—planning—complete preparation of all necessary stages.

SIER can be utilized by both a sender or receiver of messages to maximize their complete communication needs.

REACTION: What is the reaction or response of the receiver(s)? How does it match with the sender's objective?

EVALUATION: How is the message evaluated or judged by the receiver(s)? Is there acceptance or rejection, liking or disliking, agreement or disagreement, etc., on the part(s) of the receiver(s)? Is it similar to sender's objective?

INTERPRETATION: How is the message interpreted by the receiver(s)? What meaning is placed on the message? How close (similar) is the interpreted message meaning to the intended message meaning?

SENSING: Is the message received and sensed by the intended receiver(s)? Does the message get into the stream-of-consciousness of the intended receiver(s)?

Communication Competencies

1 We should develop better listening habits and a better monitoring system for our own verbal output.

2 We should be able to apply a listening model to a specific incident or interaction in order to obtain greater insight into the process of listening, and we should be able to demonstrate this application orally and pictorially to the satisfaction of our instructor.

Study Projects and Tasks

1 Develop your own verbal-pictorial model of the listening process. (See model in the chapter and figure 5.4 on page 122.)

2 Apply the three-step Ross model to a specific incident you have observed or were part of, and evaluate the listening behavior. Report verbally and/or pictorially what lessons this exercise yielded. Pay special attention to the *bad* listening habits.

3 Make daily entries in your communication log (chapter 1 task) for the next five days, which illustrate one or more of the bad listening habits discussed in this chapter.

BAD LISTENING HABITS	*Frequency* almost always	usually	some-times	seldom	almost never
1. Routinely calling the subject uninteresting	☐	☐	☐	☐	☐
2. Criticizing the speaker personally	☐	☐	☐	☐	☐
3. Being overstimulated by some point within the speech	☐	☐	☐	☐	☐
4. Listening primarily for facts instead of ideas	☐	☐	☐	☐	☐
5. Trying to outline everything	☐	☐	☐	☐	☐
6. Faking attentiveness to the speaker	☐	☐	☐	☐	☐
7. Tolerating or creating distractions	☐	☐	☐	☐	☐
8. Paying little attention to difficult expository material	☐	☐	☐	☐	☐
9. Letting emotion-laden words arouse personal antagonism	☐	☐	☐	☐	☐
10. Daydreaming	☐	☐	☐	☐	☐

4 Try *really* listening to your parents the very next time you have an opportunity. Report in 100 words or less what you have learned about your listening habits (or theirs).

5 Rogerian feedback exercise. Divide into groups of three. Two converse and the third serves as a reporter-observer. After each short communication, the listener attempts to paraphrase the message to the satisfaction of the sender. For example:

Sender: "One of every four persons has been sexually abused."
Listener: I heard, "One of every four women has suffered wife abuse."
Sender: "No, not quite. Let me try again . . ." (and so on until the sender is satisfied with the paraphrase).

The reporter explains what he or she observed.

6 Check yourself on the preceding bad listening habits.[20] Then compare your list with those of other classmates. Discuss. Think of a specific person whom you feel is a bad listener. Check the inventory in a way that best describes that person's behavior. Discuss. (See page 123.)

---

[20] Adapted from the works of Nichols and Stevens cited earlier in this chapter.

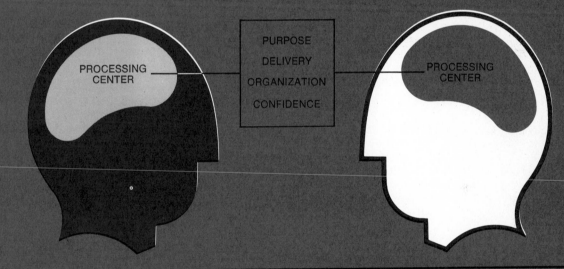

PROCESSING
CENTER

PURPOSE

DELIVERY

ORGANIZATION

CONFIDENCE

PROCESSING
CENTER

part two

PUBLIC SPEAKING:
PREPARATION
AND DELIVERY

It has been estimated that 11,000 speeches are given each week in New York City alone! Obviously this is a skill you may need. Do people take speech making seriously? In a Detroit political poll, 500 voters were asked why they voted for or against a particular candidate. The respondents put party affiliation first, *speaking ability* second, appearance or good looks third, age fourth, race or ethnic background fifth, and the candidate's sex last.[1] Even honesty, intelligence, a grasp of the issues, and previous record were farther down the list.

Are we afraid of speaking in public? You bet! In a national survey of 2,543 male and female adults, respondents were asked to pick out any items (from a list) for which they had some degree of fear. "Speaking before a group" ranked first for 40.6 percent of the respondents.[2]

In part 2 you will learn how to prepare, organize, and deliver speeches. One whole chapter (10) is to help you develop confidence and overcome fear. Speech messages, like machines, musical scores, and fine art, have a classifiable structure and internal consistency. Learning to prepare speech messages systematically is similar to the labor of the engineer, the artist, or the composer. This is not to say that there is no elusive and critical artistry in these persons' works, but all true masters are quick to point out the overwhelming importance of training, practice, purpose, and structure.

In part 1 we learned that speech communication can be verbal; nonverbal; related to signs; related to time, space, actions, and objects; intentional or accidental; and, of course, rhetorical. In part 2 we will be concerned with a carefully planned message purpose and a carefully arranged and organized outline to carry out your general and specific purposes. The message is still the crux of all speech communication. Part 2 is designed not only to assist you in preparing messages intelligently but also to make you more able critics of the messages with which we are bombarded every day.

Purpose and delivery are crucial to all areas of speech communication, but especially to public speaking—hence, the emphasis of chapter 6 on this subject. It's a little like having a specific and realizable goal. If you don't know *where* you're going, how will you know *when* you're there? If you don't know what your purpose is, how will you know if you've achieved it? More to the point, perhaps—how will you go about preparing, organizing, and presenting your message?

Fundamental to the structuring of messages around a purpose is a knowledge of the location of materials, note-taking techniques, the arrangement of materials, the mechanics of outlining, means of achieving

[1] Pete Waldmeir, "Never Mind Talent—Politics Is a Game of Image," *Detroit News,* August 7, 1978, p. 1B.

[2] "What Are Americans Afraid Of? *The Bruskin Report,* no. 53, July 1973, p. 1 (New Brunswick, N.J.: R. H. Bruskin Associates).

clearness and interest, types of supporting materials, and audio-visual aids. These topics, among others, are the subjects of chapters 7 and 8. More will be said about the special psychological arrangement of primarily persuasive messages in part 3.

A well-organized message and outline should help give you the confidence that results from the knowledge that you have done your homework and that you have a system. The systematic structure should make it easier for you to remember your material and easier for the audience to understand and retain it.

When the group is greater than six or seven members, our participation as a speaker becomes of special concern. If questions and interruptions are commonplace or even solicited within the group, the suggestions in chapter 9 will enable us to participate more actively both as participant and as leader. There are six principles of preparation and five rules for handling questions, as well as suggestions for stimulating participation by other members.

Some communication occasions are so special that they have developed almost a ritual. In such situations, intelligent prescription or rules to a point makes some sense. The eulogy is not a place for jokes; the tribute speech is not typically given in a "ha-ha" manner; a speech of introduction should say something informative about the speaker. These special-occasion speeches occur so often and usually have such similar principles that they too are provided. Chapter 9 will describe and discuss speeches of introduction, speeches of presentation and acceptance, speeches of tribute and commemoration, after-dinner speeches, and the adaptation of speech material for presentation on radio and television.

Humans are emotional animals. As such, their communication is often hindered or stimulated by the presence of an audience. When one considers the modern social climate, complete with its unyielding complexity, dogmatic language, emerging cultures, and all-too-frequent substitution of violence for persuasion, perhaps there is good reason for this. The analysis of emotion in chapter 10 is meant to be a practical answer to at least some of the problems of speech fright, which may interfere with effective human communication.

GENERAL LEARNING OUTCOMES

1 We should learn the general purposes and goals of speaking, in order to structure our own messages better and to become a more able critic of the messages of others.

2 We should learn the four principal types of delivery and when each is appropriate.

3 We should learn the characteristics of good delivery and bad delivery.

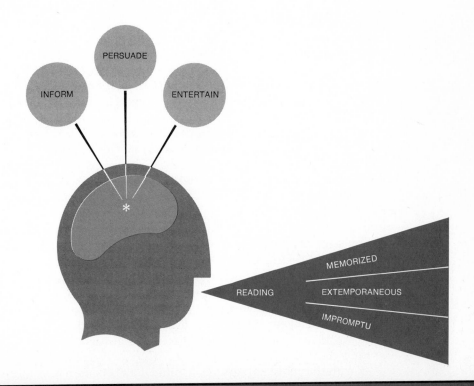

PERSUADE

INFORM

ENTERTAIN

*

MEMORIZED

READING

EXTEMPORANEOUS

IMPROMPTU

purpose and delivery

THE GENERAL PURPOSES OF SPEAKING

In previous chapters we discussed some general theory and knowledge essential to intelligent, objective speech and communication; namely, the process of communication, audience psychology, language, nonverbal communication and listening. In this chapter we shall study the general purposes of speaking and the various ways of delivering a speech. The specific ways of preparing and outlining a speech will be explained and illustrated in chapters 7 and 8.

The insurance agent who comes to your door with policy in hand is interested mainly in selling you the policy. Even though insurance agents may present an armload of objective and practical information that explains the risks of not having insurance and that describes how the policy works, their general purpose is to persuade. A speech billed as an "Informative Talk on the Arts" may turn out to be a highly belittling piece of persuasion on abstract painting, even if most of the material is informative and perhaps very entertaining. These examples illustrate the difficulty of intelligently dividing the purposes of speaking into even the apparent ones of informing, persuading, and entertaining. There is probably no such thing as a purely informative, purely persuasive, or even purely entertaining speech. Even the most overgeneralized, flowery oratory probably presents at least a bit of information. Entertainment ranging from court jesters to comedy players has for ages been the means of subtle and effective persuasion. Some very effective persuasive speeches have sounded like informative talks; some, in fact, have been composed almost wholly of information.

By itself the sheer number of informative, entertaining, or persuasive elements in a speech does not determine the kind of speech or speaker purpose. The arrangement of the material, the knowledge possessed by the audience, the speaker's style and voice, and many more factors also must be considered.

With the above paragraphs in mind, let's become a little more specific. It is practical to discuss one at a time the various purposes of speaking. If your instructor asks you to prepare an informative speech for the next class and you state your purpose as being "to inform the class why it should join the Republican party," you had better be prepared for criticism. The instructor will probably suggest that you save the subject for the persuasive speech assignment and that you then state your purpose more accurately as being "to persuade the class to join the Republican party." You might use as your purpose "to inform the class about the history of the Republican party." The speech then becomes either informative or persuasive, depending upon the treatment and emphasis you use. Certainly this *could* be an excellent, *essentially* informative speech subject.

Your real purpose can be determined by the primary reaction you want from your audience. The general purposes of speaking may be stated as follows:

Purpose	Goals
To inform	Clarity Interest Understanding
To persuade	Belief Action Stimulation
To entertain	Interest Enjoyment Humor

To Inform

One of the most frequent purposes of speaking is to inform people of something about which you either have more knowledge or know in a different or more specific way. This is the purpose of a typing teacher who is showing students how to use the keyboard. The instructor lectures primarily to inform. The speaker who would inform has the obligation of making the information or instruction clear and interesting as well as easy for the audience to learn, remember, and apply. To achieve these goals, a speaker should know something of how humans learn (this will be discussed in detail in chapter 8). Briefly, we learn through our previous knowledge and experience, and we do so more easily when we arrange material in some logical sequence. We remember better because of reinforcement (strengthening the message through repetition), verbal emphasis, organization, effective use of voice, and other techniques. The first goal in informative speaking is *audience understanding;* the key means to this goal are *clarity, interest,* and *organization of material.*

To Persuade

The general goals of a persuasive speech are to convince people to believe something, convince them to do something, and stimulate them to a higher level of enthusiasm and devotion.

These divisions (belief, action, and stimulation), like the general purposes of speaking, often overlap and are not easily recognized at first. When no immediate action is warranted, the speaker may be attempting to convince or to induce *belief.* This purpose might be illustrated by persuasive speeches such as "Foreign Policy," "The Threat of Fascism," or "Uphold the United Nations." No specific and immediate action or performance is asked of the audience. Rather, the listeners are asked to agree with the speaker and to believe and be convinced. This assumes that the audience does not have the power to act except in some distantly related way. If the audience were the United States Congress, these belief purposes could become action purposes.

When the audience is asked to do something specific, immediately following the speech, the purpose is *action*. A speech asking for donations to the Red Cross that is ended by passing a container for contributions among the audience is an obvious example. Election speeches asking people to vote or to sign petitions are further examples. Most sales talks are action speeches—even though the TV announcer does not really expect you to run out and buy a Chevrolet at 11:30 P.M. The desired action is typically specific and typically available in the very near future.

When a speaker is seeking a higher degree of audience involvement, enthusiasm, or devotion on issues and beliefs than the audience already holds, the purpose is one of *inspiration* or *stimulation*. An example might be a speech for party unity at a political convention after the nominee has been selected. In short, the purpose of stimulation is found in those situations in which the speaker is (1) not trying to change any basic attitudes, but rather to strengthen them; (2) not trying to prove anything, but rather to remind the listeners; or (3) not calling for any unusual action, but rather to inspire the listeners to a more enthusiastic fulfillment of the actions to which they are already committed.

To Entertain

When your purpose in speaking is to help people escape from reality, and when you sincerely want them to enjoy themselves, your general purpose is to entertain. The "fun," after-dinner, or radio-television speeches are the most typical examples. These speeches contain jokes, stories, and a variety of humor, all of which depend upon the experience, skill, and personality of both the speaker and the audience. In a speech designed solely to entertain, the audience should understand that purpose and be encouraged to relax and enjoy themselves.

A word of warning is in order for both beginning and experienced speakers. Other things being equal, the speech to entertain is the most difficult kind of speech to give! The feedback is more rapid and far less subtle. There is little doubt when a funny story or joke does not succeed. The effect of such failure on the speaker is often demoralizing, and the presentation and adaptation of the rest of the speech may suffer. Practice is critical.

TYPES OF DELIVERY

The four principal ways of delivering a speech are (1) by reading from a manuscript, (2) by memorization, (3) by impromptu delivery, and (4) by speaking extemporaneously. The subject and the occasion are important factors in determining which one or which combination should be used at a given time.

Reading from a Manuscript

In this type of delivery the speaker presents the subject to the audience by reading word for word a written manuscript. Fortunately, the subjects and occasions that demand this method of delivery and preparation are few, for this is probably the most difficult of all the types of delivery. However, such occasions are increasing in number. An important policy speech by the United States secretary of state may be dissected word by word by foreign governments; therefore, it will call for maximum accuracy in wording and a minimum of opportunity for misstatement. Our mass media make further demands on a speaker's flexibility. Very often, a copy of the manuscript is obtained before the speech is given, and, thus, the newspapers can print or quote the speech almost before it has been delivered. If the speaker then deviates from the manuscript, he or she invites trouble and confusion. Certain highly complicated and technical subjects demanding absolute accuracy may call for manuscript reading. Very rigid time limits may also require reading from a manuscript; this occurs often in radio and television broadcasts.

The problems of manuscript reading, even for a classroom speech, are apparent. The preparation must be painfully accurate; worse, there is little chance for spontaneity or for instant adaptation of the material to the ever changing demands of the audience. The actual delivery, except for very exceptional readers, is hamstrung by a lack of eye contact and directness: the speaker's eyes are typically glued to her manuscript, except for furtive glances into outer space, which only cause her to lose her place. This embarrassment may cause her to lose emphasis and vocal variety. A lively sense of communication is almost impossible to maintain in this situation—for some the word is *dull.*

One of the ironies in speech training is that the beginner, apparently in an effort to avoid the inevitable confrontation with the audience, may use the manuscript as something behind which to hide. This only delays self-development, because it usually results in an unsuccessful audience experience, which is extremely frustrating to the beginner.

When preparing a manuscript that is to be read aloud to an audience, we have to make some fundamental stylistic changes in the writing. The language of writers, for example, is typically less direct. They use *a person, people, the reader;* a speaker uses *I, you, they,* and the like. The other differences are not as obvious. Although we extemporize in short, simple sentences, our tendency is to write in longer, more complex ones. When we are engaged in literary writing (material that will be read silently by the receiver), we have less of a problem with this "longer" style, for the receiver can reread and review. But in a speech, the necessity for shorter, less complex sentences is critical, as is the use of more repetition, restatement, and reinforcement. Remember, the listener, unlike the reader, cannot stop and go back over the material or use a dictionary. The spoken words must be instantly clear to the listener. This requires more illustrations, examples, analogies, contrasts, and vividness than the style for a written essay does. The secret is to write "out loud."

The delivery of the speech from a manuscript is also somewhat different. Normal eye contact and vocal patterns are often disrupted. The manuscript may be hard to see if the lighting is bad or your vision is otherwise reduced. A fan has been known to distract a speaker. The position of the manuscript also creates problems. You either may hold your manuscript in your hand at about waist level or put it on a lectern. In the first case you inhibit your hand gestures; in the other you hide most of your body. Either way, the problem is to let your eyes drop to the paper while keeping your head erect.

Most good manuscript reading requires a generous amount of memorization, but partial memorization only—that is, of blocks of language that are held together for you by meaning. This permits you more time to look at the audience. When your memory fails, you refer back to the manuscript for the next memorized language group. The problem is trying to find your place! Marginal notes, underlining, and various markings can help. The real insurance is a thorough understanding of your message and practice, practice, practice. To achieve successful oral communication, you must learn to spend considerably more time looking at your audience than at your manuscript.

The problems of voice may also be important to manuscript reading. Most people do not read well without practice and training, and this is why we have courses in interpretative reading. Beginners may singsong (speak in a monotonous rhythm of rising and falling tones), use stress and inflection separate from meaning, or project a withdrawal tendency in a sleepy monotone. The varying of rate, loudness, pitch, and quality, along with the careful use of pauses, is essential to manuscript reading. It is most important to join these vocal variations to the pertinent meanings. The secret is to try to develop a *wide-ranging eye-voice correspondence*. (For a more extensive discussion of voice, see chapter 4.)

Memorization

Occasionally, an effective speech is delivered from memory (every single word of a carefully written speech is committed to memory). Except among actors, who work hard at sounding spontaneous despite exact memorization, there is little justification for a completely memorized speech. The effort required for a word-for-word memorization is enormous. The delivery, except by professional actors is typically stilted, overly rhythmical, and impersonal. Moreover, memorization does not offer any easy way to adapt the material to the audience. However, just as they will choose to read from a manuscript, many frightened beginners will undertake the enormous task of memorization. This method can result in panic if one's memory fails. There is neither a place to go nor a specific thing to do. Grade schoolers repeating a memorized poem are in far better shape than most speakers, because they have a prompter. Moreover, it is only a poem, not a personal message, that is in danger.

This is not to say that you should not memorize *parts* of your speech. A dramatic introduction, a conclusion that includes poetry, a piece of testimony, and a complicated group of statistics (when visual aids are unavailable or awkward) are all likely passages for memorization.

Impromptu Delivery

An impromptu speech is one that is delivered on the spur of the moment, without advance notice or time for detailed preparation. Usually, you will not be asked to make even an impromptu speech unless you have some general subject-matter preparation, even if this pertains merely to your special knowledge, experience, or training. If you have some special experience or expertise that makes you vulnerable to unexpected requests for a "few words," you had better carry at least a mental outline with you at all times. In this way you reduce the risks of being caught completely off guard. A student from Kenya once observed that even in the most informal gatherings he was routinely asked to explain something about Kenya and his reaction to America. On these occasions, he eventually found himself in a true speaking situation as more and more people gathered around and as he did more and more of the talking. To improve these presentations, he prepared several highly adaptable speech outlines, committed the outlines to memory, and then tried to anticipate each situation and group in which he was apt to find himself. He explained that he has become so expert at this that he is now disappointed if he *is not* asked to say a few words. People are amazed at his fluent and well organized "impromptu" remarks!

Your instructor may give you some experience in impromptu speaking by simply stating two or three speech topics and then telling you to choose one topic, take a minute to collect your wits, and then start talking. Here are some general rules that may help you if you find yourself in this or any other potentially impromptu situation:

1 Anticipate the situation. Try to avoid having to present a true impromptu speech: figure the odds on your being called, and try to determine on what topic you would be asked to speak.
2 Relate the topic under consideration to your experience. You will tend to speak more easily and confidently about something with which you have had specific experience.
3 When in doubt, summarize. There may be moments when you lose the thread of what you were saying or where you were going. At this moment, a quick review or summary often restores perspective and allows your mind to get back on the right track.

4 Be brief! The less time you speak impromptu, the less chance for you to lose track of what you are saying.

5 Quit when you are ahead! All too often we make a good impromptu speech and then, either because we feel we have not said enough or because our momentary success has given us false confidence, we continue to ramble on until we eventually ruin whatever communication we had achieved.

6 If you really have nothing to say, then don't speak! Better to be thought a fool than to open your mouth and remove all doubt.

Extemporaneous Delivery

The extemporaneous method of speaking involves the preparation of a thorough but flexible outline, the cataloguing of much potentially usable material, and the use of a general outline, which is either memorized or carried by the speaker. The language and wording of the speech are adaptable, as is the use of speech materials and details.

In this method the emphasis is on knowing your subject and knowing your audience. This typically requires collecting a lot more material than you will need. Thus, if one illustration or piece of evidence does not satisfy your audience, you will immediately be able to select another. If one strategy of organization is unclear, you will need a previously determined alternative to adapt to the audience confusion of the moment.

The chief advantage of extemporaneous preparation and delivery is that it gives you the flexibility and adaptability essential to an audience- and communication-sensitive speaker. You are able to respond successfully to the communication problems as they develop. You are thinking on your feet in the best sense of that term.

In general, an extemporaneous speech is most effective when given from a brief but meaningful outline, which is carried either in your head or your hand and which is supported by thorough preparation. This is the type of preparation and delivery expected of you except in those special exercises your instructor may announce.

CHARACTERISTICS OF GOOD DELIVERY

In the preceding section we noted that extemporaneous delivery gives you a potentially more thorough understanding of your subject and the words you use. Furthermore, it gives you flexibility of thought, adaptability of material, and sensitivity (or *empathy*) to your listeners. These are the essential qualities of good conversation and interpersonal communication. These same qualities should be present in all good speeches as well. The speaker who seeks to inspire need not sound artificial or pompous. A speaker can be eloquent without sounding like divine certainty. On the other hand, adapting conversational qualities to public speaking does not mean employing a matter-of-fact voice, poor preparation, or careless language.

A very great speech teacher, James A. Winans, once noted, "It is not true that a public speech to be conversational need sound like conversation. Conventional differences may make it sound very different."[1] We are seeking the best qualities and moods of conversation, not a stylized version of conversation.

Characteristics associated most often with effective speaking include:

1 Clear organization.
2 Clear concepts and precise language and wording.
3 A clear, pleasant voice and articulation.
4 A sense of communication indicated by some direct eye contact.
5 An alertness of body and mind that indicates enthusiasm.
6 Controlled yet flexible bodily activity that reinforces meaning.

CHARACTERISTICS OF BAD DELIVERY

Speech studies undertaken to determine just what specific aspects of delivery are unpleasant, ineffective, or annoying to audiences are most useful in helping us recognize effective delivery. Those aspects considered annoying include:

1 Evident lack of preparation and knowledge.
2 Dangling conclusion: the speaker seems unable or unwilling to close and simply repeats the message.
3 Mumbling of words.
4 General vagueness.
5 Monotonous, stiff reading or delivery from a manuscript.
6 Unnecessary verbalizations such as "ah," "er," and "uh."
7 Too many mispronunciations and grammatical mistakes.
8 Loss of temper over routine disturbances or interruptions.

Other aspects of delivery that lead to ineffective speaking include:

1 Stiff body action.
2 Refusal to look at the audience.
3 Weak, unclear, or monotonous voice.
4 Excessive nervousness or fidgeting.
5 Evident lack of enthusiasm.

[1] James A. Winans, *Speech Making* (New York: Appleton-Century-Crofts, 1938), p. 17.

6 SUMMING UP

The general purposes of speaking are to inform, to persuade, and to entertain. Many speeches combine these purposes and are difficult to classify. By itself, the degree of information, entertainment, or persuasion in a speech does not indicate the speaker's purpose; we must also consider the arrangement of the material, the knowledge possessed by the audience, and the speaker's style and voice. Your real purpose can be determined from the principal reaction you desire from your audience. The first goal in informative speaking is audience understanding. The keys to this goal are clarity, interest, and organization of material. In a speech to persuade, the speaker tries to make people *believe* something, urges them to *do* something, or attempts to *stimulate* them to a higher level of enthusiasm. The goals of a speech to entertain are to help people escape from reality and to enjoy themselves without the threat of some hidden meaning.

The four principal ways of delivering a speech are reading from a manuscript, memorization, impromptu speaking, and extemporaneous speaking. In manuscript delivery the speaker presents the subject to the audience by reading word for word a completely written speech. In memorization the speaker commits every word of the manuscript to memory. An impromptu speech is one that is delivered on the spur of the moment, without advance notice or time for detailed preparation. In the extemporaneous method a thorough but flexible outline is prepared, a wealth of potentially usable material is catalogued, and a general outline is either memorized or carried by the speaker. The language and wording of such a speech may be specific, but they are always adaptable to circumstances, as is the use of speech materials and details.

The characteristics of good delivery include a conversational quality; precise concepts, wording, and pronunciation; a clear, pleasant voice and articulation; direct eye contact; enthusiasm; and controlled yet flexible body action.

The characteristics of bad delivery include evident lack of preparation, dangling conclusions, mumbling, vagueness of meaning, monotonous reading, unnecessary verbalizations, mispronunciation, loss of temper, rigid body action, lack of eye contact, weak voice, fidgeting, and an evident lack of enthusiasm.

Speech Communication Principles

1 The real purpose of your message is determined by the principal reaction you want from your audience.

2 The main goal of an informative message is audience understanding; the keys to this goal are clarity, interest, and organization.

3 The main goals of a persuasive message are to make people *believe* something, make them *do* something, and *stimulate* them to a higher level of enthusiasm.

4 Many speeches combine the three general purposes and are difficult to classify, either by the speaker or by the receiver.

5 Assuming a message of some basic worth, the method of delivery and the credibility of the sender significantly affect how we view the source of the message.

Specific Learning Outcomes

1 We should learn to distinguish between speech purposes on the basis of whether they are mostly informative, persuasive, or entertaining.

2 We should learn to describe *extemporaneous* delivery and compare it with the other three types (reading from a manuscript, memorization, and impromptu speaking).

3 We should become familiar with the characteristics of good delivery: a conversational quality; precise concepts, wording, and pronunciation; a clear, pleasant voice and articulation; direct eye contact; enthusiasm; and controlled yet flexible body action.

4 We should become familiar with the characteristics of bad delivery: an evident lack of preparation, dangling conclusions, mumbling, vagueness of meaning, monotonous reading, unnecessary verbalizations, mispronunciation, loss of temper, rigid body action, lack of eye contact, a weak voice, fidgeting, and an evident lack of enthusiasm.

5 We should learn the general rules for performing well in impromptu speaking situations.

Communication Competencies

1 We should learn and be able to explain (a) the conditions under which a message should be delivered by manuscript reading and (b) the problems and limitations of this method.

2 We should learn the general rules for impromptu speaking and be able to apply them successfully in one or two short classroom exercises.

3 We should learn to identify while observing speech behavior, the characteristics of bad and good delivery.

4 We should be able to distinguish the general purposes of speaking and the specific goals associated with each.

Study Projects and Tasks

1 Write out, word for word, a two-to-three-minute message in your best oral style. Then rehearse it and prepare to read it from a manuscript.

2 Observe a speaker (live, on radio, or on TV) for at least fifteen to thirty minutes. On two separate sheets of paper note the characteristics of good and bad delivery that you observed.

3 From newspapers and magazines select and clip items that are clearly (a) informative, (b) persuasive, (c) entertaining, or (d) a combination of these, and identify the specific purposes of each item.

4 Your instructor will assign you two numbers at random from 1 to 48. These refer to the numbered impromptu topics below. Review the suggestions on pages 000–000 for making good impromptu speeches, choose one of the two topics, take thirty seconds to prepare, and speak impromptu for one minute before the class.

1. Animals I Have Known
2. The Most Valuable Modern Invention
3. A Mystery I Never Solved
4. Things I Want to Learn
5. Learning to Dance
6. Learning to Swim
7. My First "Public Appearance"
8. "It Pays to Advertise"
9. Learning to Play Golf
10. My Hobby
11. What to Do on a Rainy Day
12. The Radio or Television Program I Like Best (or Least)
13. My Favorite Character in Fiction
14. Improvements I Would Suggest for This School
15. How I Taught Someone to Drive
16. How I Got Out of a Difficult Situation
17. The Most Important Story in This Week's News
18. Charisma
19. Improvements I Would Suggest for This City
20. A Joke That Didn't Come Off
21. My Favorite Relative
22. My Pet Superstition
23. Styles Have Changed
24. Books Worth Buying
25. Something I Do Well
26. "Pride Goeth before a Fall"
27. The Best Purchase I Ever Made
28. The Music I Like Best
29. My Last Vacation

GENERAL LEARNING OUTCOMES

1 We should learn how and where to find materials to use in preparing our message.

2 We should learn to differentiate the standard ways of organizing ideas.

3 We should learn the systems for arranging the parts of a message.

4 We should learn the rhetorical principles of unity, coherence, and emphasis.

5 We should learn the basic principles of outlining a message.

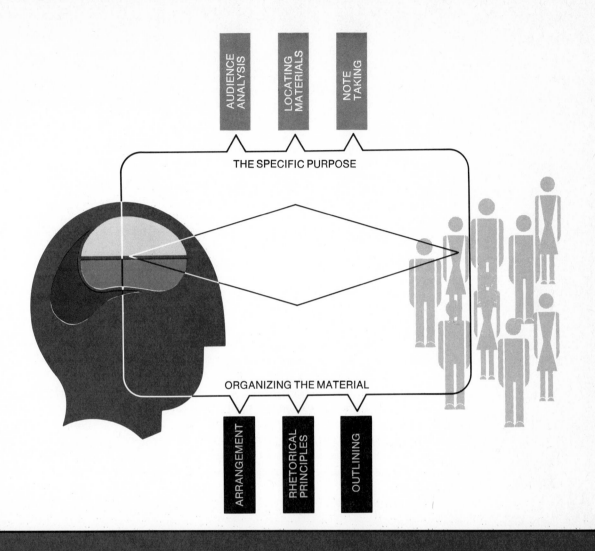

AUDIENCE ANALYSIS

LOCATING MATERIALS

NOTE TAKING

THE SPECIFIC PURPOSE

ORGANIZING THE MATERIAL

ARRANGEMENT

RHETORICAL PRINCIPLES

OUTLINING

preparing and organizing the message

PREPARING THE SPEECH

In Chapter 6 we discussed the *general* purposes of speaking—to inform, to persuade, and to entertain. In this chapter we are concerned with the *specific* purpose of speaking, the specific audience, and methods of finding, organizing, and outlining materials.

The Specific Purpose

The specific purpose is the *outcome, objective,* or *response* that your speech is supposed to achieve. A teacher, for example, talks of lesson plans (outlines); the specific purpose is called a learning outcome (a desired objective or response). A geometry teacher has the general purpose of *informing* (about geometry); the specific purpose or learning outcome for a given class might be to inform the class about the applications of geometry to map and chart reading.

If you are interested in flying, you might start preparing your speech with the general idea (purpose) of informing the class about flying. Obviously, the general subject of flying is far too big a subject for a short speech. You'll want to restrict your subject to what you can reasonably cover in the time available. You might state your specific purpose as follows: to inform the class about the principle of aerodynamics that allows a wing to "lift." Or you might talk about weapon and propeller synchronization in World War I Jennys. The more you can state exactly what it is you are trying to say or do, the more systematic and intelligent your preparation and communication will be. In some speeches to persuade, you may not wish to state your purpose to the audience. But when preparing and outlining your speech, you should always start with a precise statement of your specific purpose.

The Audience

Close on the heels of your specific purpose should be a careful consideration of your audience. In fact, if you know your audience, you should really be considering your specific purpose and audience at the same time. Most often, we know the general type of audience we will meet (for example, businessmen, teachers, housewives). In your classroom speeches you will know the specific audience. Introduction speeches give you a marvelous opportunity to gain insights into your specific audience.

Suppose your specific purpose were "to explain the five managerial functions of planning, organizing, controlling, coordinating, and communicating to an audience of management personnel." Your preparation and organization would be different if in checking on your specific management audience you discovered that they were executive vice-presidents rather than first-line foremen. Preparation and organization would apply in either case, but the application might vary widely. To continue the examples, you might revise your specific purpose as follows: "To explain the five managerial functions of planning, organizing, controlling, coordinating, and communicating to an audience of *executive-level* personnel."

Pertinent factors to be considered before you can collect speech materials most efficiently and intelligently are the *occasion*, the *environment*, and the *general descriptive measures of an audience* (size, age, education, and other factors—these are discussed in detail in chapter 2).

The speech subject, the language you use, the clothes you wear—these and many other matters are often directly related to the purpose of the gathering. In part, the question is, "Why have I been chosen to speak?" Are you a second or a third choice? Are you being paid? Is this a special meeting called for the specific purpose of hearing you? Did the audience pay for this experience? Were they forced to come? Is this one of a series of regular meetings in which they routinely ask interesting persons to speak to them? Are you the headline attraction, or are there other events or speakers on the program? If there are other speakers, when, in what order, and for how long will each person speak? All these questions must be answered by speakers as they prepare for and adapt to an audience.

If possible, speakers should know the special rules, habits, rituals, and practices they are likely to encounter. For example, organizations such as the Kiwanis, Rotary, Lions, Eagles, and Elks Clubs have relatively standard meeting formats. Many of these same organizations have certain "fun" rituals, which, though great sport if you are warned in advance, can be a nightmare if you are unaware. A speaker was once fined a dollar before saying his first word because he was wearing a red necktie! Know your occasion so well that you can predict these things and take them into account in your preparation.

Part of the occasion is the inevitable speech of introduction. (If you are the introducer, read chapter 9 now.) A bad speech of introduction can make life very difficult for the speaker. Seldom do introducers mean any harm, quite the contrary. If they give a lengthy speech, it is meant to be complimentary. They may even be so enthusiastic about your subject that they give part of your speech for you. The chairman or introducer almost always asks the speaker for help, and the novice or incautious speaker almost always answers with a blush and says, "Oh, it doesn't really matter." But it *does* matter, so *do* give them help. They will appreciate it, and you will reduce your risks at the same time. On one occasion, a speaker was asked to give a ten-minute critique of a championship debate held before a business audience. The university public relations department had sent a standard release to the chairman of the debate. This release consisted of about four pages of biographical material, including a careful listing of every award the speaker had received and publication with which he had been associated. You can guess what happened. The well-intentioned chairman read every word and took ten embarrassing minutes to do it, before introducing the speaker. This terrifying experience drew this somber comment from the critique speaker: "Make a careful study of the occasion and then expect the worst!"

Closely related to the occasion is the environment—the location and arrangement of the room or building in which the speech will be made. The same speech delivered in a church, a restaurant, or a fraternity house should change with the location. People expect different things in different types of buildings. Your distance from the audience is also a factor. If you are on an elevated platform that is far away from the first row of the audience, the style of your delivery should be qualitatively different than the style you would use if you were close to the group. The seating arrangement of the audience can make a difference.

Another environmental factor is the public-address (PA) system. If you'll be using a PA system, it may have an important effect on the way in which you use your visual aids. Most microphones fade if you move more than two feet away from them. It's a good idea to check such things *before* you speak.

The noise level of the room is often a problem, as are the lighting and ventilation. Many of these circumstances can be controlled (or at least adapted to better) if you merely consider them early enough.

The effectiveness of visual and audio aids is closely related to all these environmental factors. The size of the visual aid should be appropriate to the size of the room and the size of the audience. A chart big enough for a group of 25 may be hopelessly small for a group of 300. A series of slides may be useless if the room will not darken, and a tape recording may not be heard in a room filled with echoes.

The time for which the speech is scheduled is another environmental factor. Occasionally, A.M. and P.M. have been falsely assumed. The concept of "company time" versus "our time" often applies, and speakers might regulate not only the content but the length of their speech accordingly. It has been observed that industrial and business audiences are often more generous when they are listening on company time.

The message, of course, is most critical. The audience-message analysis discussed in chapter 2 is very important. Some practical questions that the speaker should answer are:

1 What is the significance of the subject for the audience?
2 What does the audience know about the subject?
3 What beliefs or prejudices does the audience have about the subject?

Some *general descriptive measures* that may aid you in analyzing your audience are age, sex, education, occupation, primary group membership, and special interests. (These are discussed in chapter 2.)

Finding Materials

Once you have thoroughly considered your specific purpose and related it to your analysis of the audience and the occasion, you are ready to start finding and collecting the materials that will make up the speech. The question now is, "Where do I find these materials?"

Your own knowledge and experience may give you a head start. Conversations with knowledgeable people can be very valuable. However, any serious interviewing or corresponding should usually follow some reading and observing. The purpose of starting your more formal research early is to help you understand better what the important questions are. If, for example, you were going to interview a professor of electrical engineering on the subject of information theory, you would be well advised to browse through one or two of the classic books or articles in the field in order to obtain maximum value from the interview. The same would be true if you were going to interview a speech professor on such subjects as semantics, psycholinguistics, or congruency. Your question right now is probably, "Where do I find these sources to browse through?"

THE LIBRARY   The simplest answer is your *library card catalogue*. This source is a vast treasure house of information, so take advantage of it. Almost every library has the *Reader's Guide to Periodical Literature*. This source lists magazine articles by author, title, and subject. It is bound into volumes by year and is found in the reference section of the library. You should use it much as you would the library card catalogue. You might also look through the *Cumulative Book Index* and its predecessor, *The United States Catalog;* these sources do for books about what the *Reader's Guide* does for magazines. The *Book Index* is arranged according to author, title, and subject. While you are in the library, see if it has *The New York Times Index.*

Photo credit: Stock, Boston.

This is the only complete newspaper index in the United States; it can be a real time saver. There is also an *Index to the Times* of London, England.

A good selection of general encyclopedias (such as *Britannica, Americana, New International*) and special ones (such as the *International Encyclopedia of the Social Sciences, The Catholic Encyclopedia, The Jewish Encyclopedia,* and the *Encyclopedia of Religion and Ethics*) is found in many libraries. Very often, these sources present the best short statement on a given subject to be found anywhere. These encyclopedias are usually kept current by annual supplements called yearbooks.

Do not overlook your dictionary. Good ones carry much more than a good vocabulary. Here are five quality desk dictionaries:

> *American Heritage Dictionary*
> *College Standard Dictionary*
> *Random House College Dictionary*
> *Webster's New Collegiate Dictionary*
> *Webster's New World Dictionary, Second Edition*

When you need statistics and short statements of factual data, see *The Statesman's Year-Book, The World Almanac and Book of Facts,* and the *Statistical Abstract of the United States.* Smaller general encyclopedias such as *Columbia* or *Everyman's* also contain compact statements and facts.

To learn more about the authority you may wish to discuss, interview, or quote in a speech, consult some of the better-known directories and biographical dictionaries, such as *Who's Who in America. Who's Who in American Education, Who's Who in Engineering, American Men of Science,* and the *Directory of American Scholars.* For information on prominent Americans of the past, see *Who Was Who in America,* the *Dictionary of American Biography, Lippincott's Biographical Dictionary,* and *The National Cyclopedia of American Biography.*

Most professional or trade associations publish journals of their own. Some of these organizations are the American Bar Association, the American Bankers' Association, the American Medical Association, the Speech Communication Association, the American Psychological Association, and the AFL–CIO. Many of the articles in the journals published by these organizations are indexed by special publications often available in your library (*Biological and Agricultural Index,* the *Art Index,* the *Index to Legal Periodicals, Index Medicus, Psychological Abstracts,* and many more).

In addition to the *Statistical Abstract of the United States,* mentioned earlier, other government publications can be excellent sources of speech materials. The *Commerce Yearbook* and the *Monthly Labor Review* provide much valuable information. The *Congressional Record* is an especially fruitful source for speech students. It includes a daily report of the House and Senate debates—indexed according to subject, name of bill, and representative or senator—and an appendix that lists related articles and speeches from outside of Congress.

Other sources of speech materials are the thousands of organizations that issue pamphlets and reports, often at no cost. You can write directly to these organizations for information and in some cases (for example, Planned Parenthood League, the World Peace Foundation, the American Institute of Banking, and the AFL–CIO) receive a speech outline or manuscript in return. If you would like to know the addresses of these or other organizations, refer to *The World Almanac* under the heading, "Associations and Societies in the United States."

If you cannot find enough information in all of these sources, or if you would like to *start out* with a printed bibliography on your subject, you may obtain in some libraries a bibliography on bibliographies—an index of bibliographies called the *Bibliographic Index*. Check with your librarian for this source.

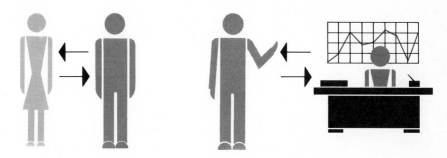

CONVERSATION AND INTERVIEW   Another way to gather materials is to talk with people about your topic, to "try it out" on somebody. If the somebody has first- or secondhand experience with your topic, you may be in luck. If on your campus or in your locality there are known experts on your topic who are available for consultation, you may be able to turn from conversation to a more formal interview. If you decide to interview someone, always do some preliminary research so you can ask clear and brief questions of your subject. Explain early in the conversation why you want this person's opinion or information. Avoid loaded or biased questions (even though you may have a bias), and try to be objective. Note any sources mentioned. Listen carefully, letting your subject do most of the talking.

Note Taking

While you are reading and absorbing all the materials discovered through the sources discussed above, you must consider how to select, sort, evaluate, and finally record the material. You will find that you need an almost mechanical system of taking notes in order not to be overwhelmed by the sheer amount of information available to you. The problem of not remembering exactly what you read or where you read it is frustrating, but if this failure of memory is serious enough to result in a return trip to the library, you have lost preparation time as well.

A very general "yes-no" selection of your potential major sources is usually possible after rapid browsing. After this preliminary sorting, you are ready to record the details that are most likely to support your specific purpose and audience analysis. One more suggestion, though, before you begin writing things down: you may wish to revise or add to your specific purpose as a result of your browsing, which may turn up important guidelines for choosing the materials you will use in your speech, selecting the issues you will discuss, or establishing the order in which you will present your topics. In other words, set up temporary categories of speech materials, issues to be discussed, and so forth. You can add, omit or subdivide later as your search becomes more specific. This categorizing will also give you a head start on the organizing and outlining of the speech itself.

Now you are ready to start taking systematic notes. The emphasis is on the word *system*. As long as you have done the rough sorting suggested above and are not taking notes without purpose, you may use any system that works for you. The most common system in library searches is the use of three-by-five or four-by-six file cards. You may have noticed debaters carrying small metal file cases filled with cards arranged either alphabetically or according to the issues that are relevant to their debate subject. You should write only one subject, source, classification, and note on each card. The big advantage of file cards over a notebook is that you can rearrange the file cards and thus reclassify or subclassify your material very easily. This shuffling of cards becomes very useful when you organize and outline your speech.

The next problem is what to write on the card. If you have found a general source that you "may or may not" wish to use later, a short summary in your own words may be in order. You will then be better able to decide at a later time whether you wish to reread the source. If you find a statement by an authority that you may wish to use, take it down word for word and put quotation marks around it. Be sure to record the name and qualifications of the authority. In taking down testimony or statistics, make sure you record the date; people change their minds and so may your sources. If you insert explanations or interpretations of your own, put brackets around these words so that later on you will not confuse your word with those of your sources.

In your English class you may have been taught a certain system of taking notes for a term paper. Whatever the system, it should be useful here. Whether you use classifications at the top of the card or footnotes at the bottom will depend in part upon your training and preference, as well as upon your specific purpose and subject. Some sample note-taking systems are illustrated in figures 7.1 through 7.4.

ORGANIZING THE SPEECH

Organization starts either with the specific ideas and speech details you have collected or with the general parts into which speeches can conveniently be divided. Let's look first at some useful methods for organizing the raw materials, and then we'll analyze ways of arranging the parts of a speech.

Methods of Organizing Ideas

CHRONOLOGICAL METHOD Materials are arranged according to the order in which a number of events took place. In speaking on "Life on Earth," we would probably discuss the following geologic periods chrono-

```
(Subject) Creativity      (Classification) Mental
                                            functions

1.  Absorptive-the ability to observe, and to
                apply attention.
2.  Retentive- the ability to memorize and to recall.
3.  Reasoning-the ability to analyze and to judge.
4.  Creative-the ability to visualize, to foresee,
                and to generate ideas.

SOURCE:  Alex F. Osborn, Applied Imagination,3rd ed.
         (New York:  Scribner's, 1963), p.1.
```

Figure 7.1

```
(Subject) Prehistoric man    (Classification)
                                            Dinosaurs

"...you will often see cartoons showing cave men being
chased by dinosaurs.  But this could never have happen-
ed.  The physical anthropologists tell us which bones
are the bones of the prehistoric men who lived in
caves.  The paleontologists tell us which bones are
the bones of giant reptiles.  The geologists tell us
that the human bones come from layers of earth that
are 50,000 years old, and the dinosaur bones come
from rocks 150,000,000 years old."

SOURCE:  Donald Barr, Primitive Man(New York:
         Wonder Books, 1961), p. 10.
```

Figure 7.2

logically: (1) Archeozoic, (2) Proterozoic, (3) Paleozoic, (4) Mesozoic, (5) Cenozoic, and (6) Present. Most historical subjects lend themselves readily to this method; so do processes of a sequential, 1–2–3 order, such as film developing. Remember, however, that these subjects may be handled in different ways. History is often more interesting and meaningful if discussed topically.

TOPICAL METHOD   Material is ordered according to general topics or classifications of knowledge. To continue the example of history, we might concentrate on the history of religion, war, government, education, or science. The importance of the topic may or may not be such that the presentation of the topic violates historical time. The topical method is a very useful way to start breaking down very broad topics. One can, for example, look at integration of the races in several topical ways—educationally, socially, militarily, economically, and so forth. A city may be described topically in terms of its industry, employment opportunities, recreational facilities, schools, climate, and so on.

LOGICAL METHOD   This method uses generally accepted or obvious cause-and-effect relationships, whether we are talking about the fall of the Japanese empire or the building of a house or a boat. When the order is naturally present in the subject or when the association of ideas is evident, it may be convenient to organize our speech materials accordingly. This method differs from the topical method in that subpoints almost always illustrate or explain to what they are subordinate, unless the audience already knows the logical relationship. You must analyze your audience thoroughly before using this method.

Figure 7.3

```
(Subject) Problem-solving      (Classification)
          Systems                        General
                                         Background

Chapter 2(Reasoning) of this book covers four special
readings, including some special problems.  Included
are the following: 1.  Reasoning in Humans;  2. An
Exper. Sty. of P. S.;   3.  The Sol. of Prac. Probs.;
4.  Prob. Sol. Proc. of Col. students. (Looks impress-
ive)

SOURCE:  T. L. Harris and W. E. Schwahn, The Learning
         Process(New York:  Oxford University Press,
         1961), pp. 29-79.
```

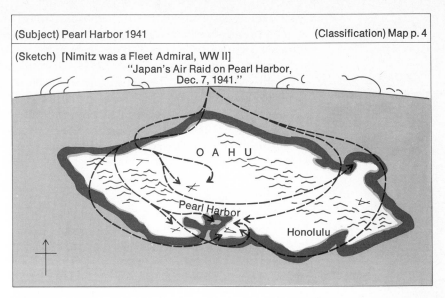

(Subject) Pearl Harbor 1941   (Classification) Map p. 4

(Sketch) [Nimitz was a Fleet Admiral, WW II]
"Japan's Air Raid on Pearl Harbor, Dec. 7, 1941."

OAHU

Pearl Harbor

Honolulu

Figure 7.4

DIFFICULTY METHOD For some subjects, particularly technical ones, it may help to organize your materials according to order of ease or difficulty, proceeding from the easiest aspect to the most difficult one. In discussing general principles of electricity, we might arrange a series of ideas as shown in figure 7.5.

Figure 7.5

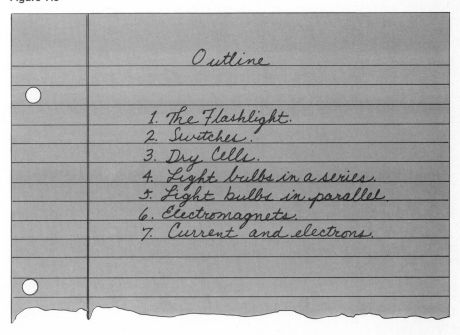

Outline

1. The Flashlight.
2. Switches.
3. Dry Cells.
4. Light bulbs in a series.
5. Light bulbs in parallel.
6. Electromagnets.
7. Current and electrons.

SPATIAL METHOD   This method is particularly useful for certain types of geographical or physical-order subjects. In a speech about the United Nations one might first describe each building, then discuss the offices in each building one floor at a time; the ideas are thereby organized spatially. This discussion could also be organized topically if the audience were familiar with the general political structure of the United Nations. In discussing "Nationalism in Africa," one might organize according to geographical space and simply divide the ideas from north to south and east to west. Chronological history might also be a useful method of organizing this speech.

NEED-PLAN METHOD   Materials are organized according to problems (needs) and solutions (plans). An affirmative debate team concerned with a resolution on government health programs usually will divide its material into these two general categories. The first speaker will concentrate on the various needs in our present programs. The second speaker will discuss the various plans and indicate why one is better than the others. The needs can be subdivided into many useful types, such as economic needs, health needs, and social needs.

Methods of Arranging the Parts

Various sets of terms refer to the *parts* of a speech: *beginning, middle,* and *end; introduction, body,* and *conclusion,* or in a more classical vein, *proem, statement, argument,* and *epilogue.* Other parts are the speech details and ideas you have already collected and perhaps partially organized into one or more of the sequences discussed in the last section.

Before analyzing these parts, let us look at three rhetorical principles important to arranging of the parts. These are *unity, coherence,* and *emphasis.*

UNITY   In discussing tragic drama, Aristotle once said that a play must be constructed so that the omission of any part damages the whole. He also noted that each part of the plot must contribute to making the purpose or end of the play unavoidable. By analogy, he said, a play must have a total unity in the same manner as a living organism. We still use the term *organic unity* to express this concept. With regard to a speech, organic unity means that the material should be unified to the point at which it can be summarized in a single statement of purpose. In some speeches this statement takes the form of a resolution or proposition that is openly announced. In other cases, such a proposition may be left unstated for purposes of strategy. But in all cases the speaker must understand his or her purpose if the speech is to have unity. This awareness of specific purpose helps the speaker evaluate the materials and ideas during preparation. The arrangement of the parts of a speech should be so unified that the purpose is clear to both the audience and speaker.

COHERENCE Coherence refers to the specific sequence of the parts of the speech; it therefore uses the various methods of ordering ideas and speech details that we considered above. To *cohere* is to be connected by a common principle or relationship. Coherence requires the logically consistent classification of ideas. The connection of the various parts and ideas of a speech is made with words or phrases. Unlike the writer, the speaker cannot go back and recheck the text to find a lost thread of meaning. Thus, we must be especially careful of our connectives, often repeating and clearly labeling them. Coherence must therefore always include the audience. In going from one point to another, we may lose our audience by assuming that it will see the relationship of ideas just because we do.

To achieve coherence, we must carefully consider our connecting words. Some of the types of connectives in our language are the following:[1]

1	*Indicating time:*	previously, formerly, at an earlier period, anterior, contemporary, at the same moment, in the same period, throughout this period, during this time, meanwhile, in the meantime, upon this, then, by that time, already, now, since then, after this, thereafter, in the end, at last, at length, at a later time, henceforth, now that.
2	*Making evident:*	thereof, thereby, thereto, therein, therefrom, in this case, in such a case, at such times, on such occasions, under these circumstances, in all this, in connection with this, together with this, here again.
3	*Returning to purpose:*	to continue, to return, to report, to resume, along with . . . , as I have said, then, now, again, once more, at any rate, at all events.
4	*Making reference:*	in point of, with respect to, as related to, concerning, as for.
5	*Citing:*	for instance, for example, to illustrate, by way of illustration, another case, a case in point is . . . , under this head.
6	*Excepting:*	with this exception, this exception made, except for this, waiving this question, leaving this out of account . . . , excluded, exclusive of . . . , irrespective of . . . , excluding this point.
7	*Summarizing:*	to sum up, to recapitulate, on the whole, briefly, in a word, in brief, in short, we have traced . . . , as we have seen, up to this point, yes, no.
8	*Concluding:*	to conclude, finally, lastly, in conclusion, last of all.
9	*Explaining:*	that is, to explain, in other words, this is as much as to say, that amounts to saying.
10	*Marking a change in tone or in point of view:*	at least, seriously, in all seriousness, jesting aside, to speak frankly, for my part, in another sense, as a matter of fact, in fact, to come to the point, in

[1] For a discussion of connectives, see Glen E. Mills, *Putting A Message Together,* 2nd ed. The following list is copyright © 1972 by The Bobbs-Merrill Co., Inc., and is reprinted by permission of the publisher.

		general, of course, you see, as the matter stands, as things are.
11	*Comparing:*	parallel with . . . , allied to . . . , comparable to . . . , from another point of view, in the same category, in like manner, in the same way, similarly, likewise, a similar view, yet more important, of less importance, next in importance, in contrast with this, conversely.
12	*Emphasizing:*	indeed, moreover, add to this, furthermore, besides, further, even without this, in addition to this, all the more, even more, into the bargain, especially, in particular, how much more, yet again, above all, best of all, most of all.
13	*Judging:*	so, therefore, consequently, accordingly, thus, hence, then, in consequence, as a result, the result is, we conclude, because of this, for this reason, this being true, such being the case, under these circumstances, what follows.
14	*Conceding:*	certainly, indeed, it is time, to be sure, it must be granted, I admit, true, granted, admitting the force of . . . , no doubt, doubtless.
15	*Opposing:*	yet, still, nevertheless, however, on the other hand, at the same time, none the less, only, even so, in spite of this, the fact is . . . , after all.
16	*Refuting:*	otherwise, else, were this not so, on no other supposition, on the contrary, no, never, hardly.

EMPHASIS Emphasis is based on the location, space, form, and order you give your most important ideas. Should you present your most important idea first, last, or as a climax? Does the amount of space you give the idea affect emphasis? Ordinarily, your main point should not be buried under some minor subpoint. Since a number of really important ideas may compete for attention, which idea should you emphasize the most? These questions can be answered best by your subject, your knowledge, your audience, and the occasion. Location, space, form, and order do make a difference and do affect emphasis. Successful emphasis requires the use of these devices in harmony with the relative importance assigned to each part or idea in your speech.

SYSTEMS OF ARRANGEMENT Aristotle used the Greek word *taxis,* which means division or arrangement, to explain what he thought was the most obvious and logical arrangement of the parts of a speech, particularly a persuasive or argumentative speech. He felt that the following elements were related most closely to the thinking habits of humans: proem (introduction), statement, argument, and epilogue (conclusion).[2] For Aristotle the proem and epilogue are used primarily as aids for memory and attention. The main *body* of the speech is the statement of purpose and the proofs or *argument.*

[2]See Lane Cooper, *The Rhetoric of Aristotle* (New York: Appleton-Century-Crofts, 1932), pp. 220–40.

H. L. Hollingworth listed the fundamental steps of a speech as being attention, interest, impression, conviction, and direction.[3] Just as Aristotle suggested that for some occasions the proem or attention step was less important than usual, Hollingworth explained that some speech elements are shortened or eliminated as the audience becomes more similar, focused, or polarized.

Alan H. Monroe, a speech psychologist, suggested that the fundamental elements of a speech are attention, need, satisfaction, visualization, and action.[4] Like Hollingworth, Monroe believed that the emphasis given each element depends upon the audience's mood and knowledge as well as the nature of the speech. A speech to inform might use only three elements, whereas a speech to persuade might call for all five.

These systems of arrangement and many more are very useful because they illustrate the complicated interaction of subject, audience, speaker, and arrangement. However, any system is undoubtedly an understatement or a dangerous generalization of unbelievably complex communication problems.

Other divisions of your speech are possible. The *general* purpose of your speech (to persuade, to inform, or to entertain) will dictate how much of a system you will need for the general divisions of introduction, body, and conclusion. In chapter 8 we recommend a special system of organizing that borrows not only from the systems above but also from learning theories; it includes the elements of attention, overview, information, and review. In chapter 11 several useful systems are discussed and illustrated, one of which is a combination of the elements of attention, need, plan, objections, reinforcement, and action. Let's view these elements in terms of the more common division of a speech into introduction, body, and conclusion.

More will be said about these specific organizational patterns in related chapters. Let's look now at the general requirements of a good introduction, body, and conclusion.

[3]H. L. Hollingworth, *The Psychology of the Audience* (New York: American Book Company, 1935, 1977), pp. 19–32.
[4]Alan H. Monroe, *Principles and Types of Speech* (New York: Scott, Foresman & Company, 1935).

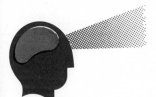

SOME GENERAL SYSTEMS OF ARRANGEMENT

				Attention Overview	
introduction	*Proem*	Attention	Attention		Attention
body	*Statement* *Argument*	Interest	Need	Information	Need
		Impression	Satisfaction		Plan
		Conviction	Visualization		Objections
conclusion	*Epilogue*	Direction	Action	Review	Reinforcement Action

INTRODUCTION The preceding analysis of systems of arrangement indicates that in all cases, gaining the listeners' attention is an important requirement of the beginning of a speech. We also learned in our discussions of emphasis and arrangement that the number of attention devices to be used depends on what attention level the audience has already achieved. In other words, if the listeners are on the edge of their seats and ready to hear what you have to say, a lengthy introduction designed to arouse their attention would be unnecessary. More will be said about attention in chapter 11.

Arousing attention is only one requirement of an introduction. Your introduction should also attempt to establish or strengthen good will among you, the group you represent, and the audience. In those rare cases in which good will is scarce (when you're facing a hostile audience), establishing an atmosphere for a fair hearing is perhaps the most for which you can hope. For example, Adlai Stevenson used humor to establish rapport with a tough Labor Day audience in 1952: "When I was a boy I never had much sympathy for a holiday speaker. He was just a kind of interruption between hot dogs, a fly in the lemonade."

Certain terms or language may be either vague or unknown, and *not* to define them is to confuse the audience (for example, cybernetics, carcinoma, data processing, method acting, and afram). In some situations, a function of the introduction is *orientation:* the speaker must sometimes supply certain background explanations or definitions to help the audience understand better the main body of the speech. A brief historical sketch often improves audience orientation. A good example is John F. Kennedy's opening address to a conference on African culture in New York City on June 28, 1959.

Some 2,500 years ago the Greek historian Herodotus described Africa south of the Sahara as a land of "horned asses, of dog-faced creatures, the creatures without heads, whom the Libyans declared to have eyes in their breasts, and many other far less fabulous beasts." Apparently when Herodotus found himself short on facts, he didn't hesitate to use imagination—which may be why he is called the first historian.

But we must not be too critical of Herodotus. Until very recently, for most Americans, Africa was Trader Horn, Tarzan, and tom-tom drums. We are only now beginning to discover that Africa, unlike our comic strip stereotypes, is a land of rich variety—of noble and ancient cultures, some primitive, some highly sophisticated; of vital and gifted people, who are only now crossing the threshold into the modern world.

The introduction seeks to *make your purpose clear;* it is often a kind of preview of what is to follow in the main body. This necessitates a certain amount of repetition, but remember that an *audience,* unlike a *reader,* cannot go back to a previous page. Therefore, more repetition is required.

In sum, the general functions of an introduction are (1) to secure *attention,* (2) to establish *good will,* (3) to assure a *fair hearing,* (4) to *orient* your audience to the subject, and (5) to make your *purpose* clear.

You can achieve good introductions in many different ways; however, any introduction should be related to both the subject and the situation. An unusual story describing your troubles in getting to the meeting is acceptable, especially if you can relate it to your subject. Humorous anecdotes also may be useful. Although research is uncertain on this point, most experts agree that if you are going to use jokes, they should be related in some way to the subject or situation.

The 1961 inaugural address of John F. Kennedy illustrates all the functions and requirements of a good introduction.

Attention   My fellow citizens:

> We observe today not a victory of party but a celebration of freedom—symbolizing an end as well as a beginning—signifying renewal as well as change. For I have sworn before you and Almighty God the same solemn oath our forebears prescribed nearly a century and three-quarters ago.

Orientation and Good Will   The world is very different now. For man holds in his mortal hands the power to abolish all forms of human poverty and to abolish all forms of human life. And, yet, the same revolutionary beliefs for which our forebears fought are still at issue around the globe—the belief that the rights of man come not from the generosity of the state but from the hand of God.

Fair Hearing   We dare not forget today that we are the heirs of that first revolution. Let the word go forth from this time and place, to friend and foe alike, that the torch has been passed to a new generation of Americans—born in this century, tempered by war, disciplined by a cold and bitter peace, proud of our ancient heritage—and unwilling to witness or permit the slow undoing of those human rights to which this nation has always been committed, and to which we are committed today.

Purpose   Let every nation know, whether it wish us well or ill, that we shall pay any price, bear any burden, meet any hardship, support any friend, or oppose any foe in order to assure the survival and success of liberty. This much we pledge—and more.

In still more specific terms, an introduction may utilize appreciation, personal reference, quotations, humor, and related stories or experiences. When the purpose of the speech is relatively obvious and the speaker and subject are well known, a related story, incident, or narrative with built-in attention often reinforces the purpose and gives the audience a fresh orientation. Booker T. Washington's introduction to his address at the Atlanta Exposition is a case in point.

Attention Mr. President and Gentlemen of the Board of Directors and Citizens: One-third of the population of the South is of the Negro race. No enterprise seeking the material, civil, or moral welfare of this section can disregard this element of our population and reach the highest success.

Good Will I but convey to you, Mr. President and Directors, the sentiment of the masses of my race when I say that in no way have the value and manhood of the American Negro been more fittingly and generously recognized than by the managers of this magnificent Exposition at every stage of its progress. It is a recognition that will do more to cement the friendship of the two races than any occurrence since the dawn of our freedom.

Fair Hearing Not only this, but the opportunity here afforded will awaken among us a new era of industrial progress. Ignorant and inexperienced, it is not strange that in the first years of our new life we began at the top instead of at the bottom; that a seat in Congress or the state legislature was more sought than real estate or industrial skill; that the political convention or stump speaking had more attractions than starting a dairy farm or truck garden.

Orientation A ship lost at sea for many days suddenly sighted a friendly vessel. From the mast of the unfortunate vessel was seen a signal, "Water, water; we die of thirst!" The answer from the friendly vessel at once came back, "Cast down your bucket where you are." And a third and fourth signal for water was answered, "Cast down your bucket where you are." The captain of the distressed vessel, at last heeding the injunction, cast down his bucket, and it came up full of fresh, sparkling water from the mouth of the Amazon River.

Purpose To those of my race who depend on bettering their condition in a foreign land or who underestimate the importance of cultivating friendly relations with the Southern white man, who is their next door neighbor, I would say: "Cast down your bucket where you are"—cast it down in making friends in every manly way of the people of all races by whom we are surrounded.[5]

During World War II, President Franklin D. Roosevelt also used a story in an introduction to one of the many appeals he made for the purchase of war bonds.

Once upon a time, a few years ago, there was a city in our Middle West which was threatened by a destructive flood in a great river. The waters had risen to the top of the banks. Every man, woman, and child in that city was called upon to fill sandbags in order to defend their homes against the rising waters. For many days and

[5]Quoted in A. Craig Baird, *American Public Addresses: 1740–1952* (New York: McGraw-Hill Book Company, 1956), p. 189.

nights destruction and death stared them in the face. As a result of the grim, determined community effort, that city still stands. Those people kept the levees above the peak of the flood. All of them joined together in the desperate job that had to be done—businessmen, workers, farmers, and doctors, and preachers—people of all races.

To me that town is a living symbol of what community cooperation can accomplish.[6]

BODY   The major discussion of the speech material takes place here. This is where the bulk of the information or argument is. All the previous discussions of organization, rhetorical principles, and arrangement come into focus here. Typical forms of the body will be explained and illustrated in the section entitled "Mechanics of Outlining" and in chapter 8. Some special systems of arrangement will be discussed in part 3.

CONCLUSION   The words from the arrangement chart on p. 157 are *direction, action, review,* and *reinforcement;* to these we could add *visualization, restatement,* and *summary.* These devices are all intended to rekindle attention and to assist the memory. Recall that Aristotle suggested that the major purpose of the conclusion is to help the memory.

The conclusion is generally shorter than either the introduction or the body. It may and generally should include a short summary that reinforces the message and makes it easier to understand. It may call for clearly stated directions if certain actions are part of the speaker's purpose. When your purpose has been inspiration, you may need a more impressive conclusion. Some of the devices suggested in the discussion on introductions (an impressive quotation, incident, or experience) apply here. A classic inspirational conclusion was provided by Martin Luther King, Jr. in his famous speech in support of civil rights legislation before an estimated 200,000 people.

So let freedom ring—from the prodigious hilltops of New Hampshire, let freedom ring; from the mighty mountains of New York, let freedom ring—from the heightening Alleghenies of Pennsylvania!
Let freedom ring from the snowcapped Rockies of Colorado!
Let freedom ring from the curvaceous slopes of California!
But not only that; let freedom ring from Stone Mountain of Georgia!
Let freedom ring from Lookout Mountain of Tennessee!
Let freedom ring from every hill and mole hill of Mississippi.
From every mountainside, let freedom ring, . . .
When we allow freedom to ring, when we let it ring from every village and every hamlet, from every state and every city, we will

[6]*Vital Speeches of the Day,* 9, no. 23 (1943), 703.

be able to speed up that day when all of God's children, black men and white men, Jews and Gentiles, Protestants and Catholics, will be able to join hands and sing in the words of the old Negro spiritual, "Free at last! thank God almighty, we are free at last!"[7]

Most important, make it clear when you are finished; consider your exit lines carefully. Speakers who do not know when they are going to finish, appear awkward and frustrate the audience. The never-ending conclusion, caused either by the ham in all of us or by improper preparation, leaves you with so many things to tie together that you cannot conclude your speech in any unified manner. The lesson is obvious: prepare your conclusion as carefully as the rest of your speech. Doing so serves as a good check on organic unity. And quit while you're ahead. Don't let an audience hypnotize you so much that you ruin a good speech by an overly long or overly dramatic conclusion.

Mechanics of Outlining

WHERE TO START You might start by rereading the chapter up to this point! The mechanics of outlining can be hollow indeed if they are not enriched by an understanding of (1) subject, audience, and occasion analysis; (2) methods of finding materials; and (3) methods of organization and arrangement.

The outline is to a speech what a blueprint is to a house. A good, clear outline can help you discover mistakes, weaknesses, and unnecessary information *before* you speak, just as the builder or architect often can save costly mistakes by taking a hard look at the plans before starting to build the house.

Begin by reviewing your specific purpose for speaking, which may turn into a proposition or a thesis. This review serves to narrow and unify the subject matter further, and should result in a precise summary statement of purpose. Your statement of purpose attempts to capture the gist of the entire speech in one sentence. It should not be confused with a title or a general subject area, although these may be closely related to your purpose.

Start your serious outlining with the body of the speech. The introduction and conclusion, though very important, only enrich, prepare, or reinforce the content-loaded main body. State your main points or ideas in terms of your purpose, and place your supporting material under the appropriate main points. After sketching the body of your speech, outline the introduction and conclusion.

Your rough outline should eventually become a *complete-sentence outline* (one in which all the major and minor points are written out as complete

---

[7]Quoted in Robert T. Oliver and Eugene E. White, *Selected Speeches from American History* (Boston: Allyn & Bacon, Inc., 1966), pp. 289–94.

sentences). This will force you to *think* your way through the material and help you avoid embarrassing moments on the platform. The sentence outline will also make it easier for your instructor to evaluate and help you with your speech planning. If you intend to use the speech again or if others may have to speak from it, a complete-sentence outline becomes valuable. After this kind of thorough outlining, you may prefer to redo the outline in a topical or key-word form for use on the platform. An outline is an aid to clear, orderly thinking. It is a blueprint of the speech.

PRINCIPLES OF OUTLINING   Mills suggests six principles that apply to all outlines.[8]

Simplicity means that each numbered or lettered statement should contain only one idea.

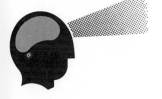

wrong ⓥ	right ⓒ

I I wish to cover the following major steps in music theory:
  A The kinds of notes and the musical staff.
  B Methods of counting and the relation of these to an instrument.
	I I wish to cover the following steps in music theory:
	  A The kinds of notes.
	  B The musical staff.
	  C Methods of counting the notes.
	  D The relation of these methods to an instrument.

Coordination means that a subordinate list of topics must have a common relationship.

wrong ⓥ	right ⓒ

A Manufacturing companies in Detroit.
  1 General Motors Corporation.
  2 Ford Motor Company.
  3 Chrysler Corporation.
  4 American Motors Corporation.
  5 Campbell Ewald Advertising Company.
  6 American Automobile Association.
  7 Benedict and Moore Insurance.
	A Manufacturing companies in Detroit.
	  1 General Motors Corporation.
	  2 Ford Motor Company.
	  3 Chrysler Corporation.
	  4 American Motors Corporation.
	B Service companies in Detroit.
	  1 Campbell Ewald Advertising Company.
	  2 American Automobile Association.
	  3 Benedict and Moore Insurance.

[8]Mills, *Putting a Message Together*, pp. 26–28.

Subordination means that related lesser points supporting a general category or statement should be grouped separately from the category, usually by means of indentation. Items of equal importance should be given equal billing.

wrong ⓥ	right ⓒ

A Learning to type.
  1 Preliminary preparation.
  2 Addressing the keyboard.
  3 Practice exercises.
  4 First-level maintenance.
    a Unsticking the strikers.
    b Cleaning the keys.
    c Replacing the ribbon.
  5 Selecting a typewriter.
    a Mechanical machines.
    b Electric machines.
    c Kinds of type.
	A Learning to type.
	  1 Preliminary preparation.
	  2 Addressing the keyboard.
	  3 Practice exercises.
	B First-level maintenance.
	  1 Unsticking the strikers.
	  2 Cleaning the keys.
	  3 Replacing the ribbon.
	C Selecting a typewriter.
	  1 Mechanical machines.
	  2 Electric machines.
	  3 Kinds of type.

Discreteness means that each item in an outline should be a distinct point and not overlap other items.

wrong ⓥ	right ⓒ

A Tennis strokes.
  1 The serve.
  2 The forehand.
  3 The backhand.
  4 Various shots.
	A Tennis strokes.
	  1 The serve.
	  2 The forehand.
	  3 The backhand.
	  4 The volley.
	  5 The approach shot.
	  6 The overhead.

Progression refers to the arrangement of related items in some sort of natural sequence, such as chronology, time, genre, or space. Keep the items in sequence and don't switch patterns. The following sequence, which is based on difficulty, is a good example.

wrong ⓥ	right ⓒ

A Principles of electricity.
  1 Current and electrons.
  2 Light bulbs in parallel.
  3 Light bulbs in a series.
  4 Dry cells.
  5 The flashlight.
  6 Switches.
	A Principles of electricity.
	  1 The flashlight.
	  2 Switches.
	  3 Dry cells.
	  4 Light bulbs in a series.
	  5 Light bulbs in parallel.
	  6 Current and electrons.

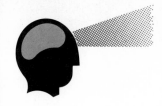

Symbolization means that similar symbols (I, 1, A, b, and so on) should represent items or points of equal importance. The symbol and its indentation should indicate the relative importance of the item that follows. Usually, main points are Roman numerals, major subpoints are capital letters, minor subpoints are Arabic numerals, and so on.

Logical outlining includes (1) divisions of ideas and (2) headings that make these divisions clear. If a topic is divided, there should be two or more parts. In other words, if you're going to have a *1,* you should also have a *2;* if you're going to have an *A,* you should also have a *B.* If your *2* or *B* is not important to your speech, the first point should be incorporated into its superior heading. For example,

A Wagon trains.
    1 Role in development of West.

becomes

A Wagon trains as factor in development of West.

The numbers and letters used as labels must be consistent. Let your symbols show clearly that the main ideas are relatively equal in importance, and that the subpoints are secondary to the main points.

The standard system of symbols and indentations is as follows:

Title
General End
Specific Purpose
Introduction
I.
A.
1.
a.
b.
(1)
(2)
2.
B.
II.

The number of *main points* you may have in a speech is debatable. If you use more than four or five, your listeners will have difficulty remembering the points and relating them to one another. Your main points, in order to be true main points and not subdivisions, should be of approximately equal importance. Each main point should be worded carefully and completely, and should contribute to the central purpose of the speech. The order in which you present your main points should aid the logical development of your speech and strengthen audience motivation, remembering, and understanding.

The system of arrangement in your outline may vary with your purpose and your instructor's preference. You may use the system of *introduction, body,* and *conclusion,* or some of the other systems discussed previously. In any case, you should probably capitalize, but not number, such words as *introduction, body,* and *conclusion,* and perhaps put words such as *attention, overview, need,* and *reinforcement* in the margins.

TYPES OF OUTLINES The *complete-sentence outline* is the most detailed and specific of all the forms. All main and minor points are written out as complete sentences so that their relationship to one another is clear. In all probability, however, your first try at outlining a speech will be in a topical, skeleton form. The phrases or groups of words that carry the

```
OUR FUTURE FIVE WONDERS
General End:        To inform.
Specific Purpose:   To inform the class of the future five wonders of the world, and to explain
                    their functions and how they differ from the old Seven Wonders.

                    Introduction

                    I. Let me briefly remind you of the Seven Wonders of the Ancient World.
                       (pictures)
                          A. The Great Pyramid of Cheops.
                          B. The hanging gardens of Babylon.
(Attention)               C. The tomb of Mausolus.
(Interest)                D. The temple of Diana at Ephesus.
                          E. The Colossus of Rhodes.
                          F. Phidias' Statue of Zeus.
                          G. The Pharos of Alexandria.

                   II. The future wonders that I will explain are as follows:
                          A. Australia's Snowy Mountains Scheme.
(Overview)                B. The United States' New York Narrows Bridge.
(Impression)              C. The Netherlands' Delta Plan.
                          D. The United States' Chesapeake Bay Bridge Tunnel.
                          E. The Mont Blanc Tunnel between France and Italy.

                    Body

                    I. Each of the future wonders will be of real benefit to man.
                          A. The Snowy Mountains Scheme will provide an additional 650 billion
                             gallons of water per year in the Australian desert.
                             1. This will be done by forcing the wasted water of the Snowy
                                River through the mountains in long tunnels.
                             2. This project will cost $1 billion.
```

(Information)

        3. This project will consist of many facilities.
          a. 9 major dams.
          b. 10 power stations.
          c. 100 miles of tunnels.
          d. 80 miles of aqueducts.
      B. The Chesapeake Bay Bridge Tunnel will connect Norfolk, Va. with the Delmarva Peninsula.
        1. Travel time will be 30 minutes.
        2. It will contain the world's longest span over exposed navigable water.
          a. Both tunnels and bridges are used. (diagram)
          b. It is 17.6 miles long.
          c. It will cost $140 million.
      C. The Netherlands' Delta Plan will prevent ocean storms from overrunning the land. (map)
        1. Prevent damage to property and life.
        2. Prevent salting of fertile land as in 1953.
        3. Five massive dams will cut off the sea arms.
          a. This is the first attempt to hold back this much sea.
          b. The cost will be $750 million.
      D. The United States' N.Y. Narrows Bridge will cross the narrows at the entrance to N.Y. harbor.
        1. The world's longest suspension span, 4260 feet.
        2. The world's largest and most expensive bridge.
          a. Will have 12 traffic lanes.

(Visualization)

          b. One granite block weighs 410,000 tons.
          c. Can be seen 20 miles at sea.
          d. Will cost $325 million.
      E. The French-Italian Mont Blanc Tunnel will permit travel under the Alps.
        1. The tunnel was a joint venture.
          a. French drilling company.
          b. Italian drilling company.
        2. The first all-year route from Paris to Rome.
          a. Cuts distance by 140 miles.
          b. Cuts time from a day of mountain roads 15 minutes' tunnel time.
        3. A brilliantly coordinated engineering feat.
    II. Modern wonders of the world are more incredible than the old.
      A. Modern wonders have beauty.
      B. Modern wonders have a utility the ancient wonders did not.

    Conclusion

    I. These new five wonders have useful purposes for man.
      A. Snowy Mountains Scheme will make Australia's desert lands places of lush vegetation.
      B. Chesapeake Bay Bridge Tunnel will enable people to travel more easily from Norfolk to the Delmarva Peninsula.
      C. The Netherlands' Delta Plan will secure the land from the damaging storms of the sea.
      D. The New York Narrows Bridge will allow traffic to cross the entrance of New York harbor.
      E. The Mont Blanc Tunnel will allow year-round travel through the Alps.
    II. These constructions are more wondrous than the ancient ones.
      A. Ancient wonders were noted primarily for art, size, and beauty.
      B. The modern wonders each have all of these plus unchallenged utility.

essential meanings are usually written as grammatically incomplete sentences. The disadvantage of the *topical outline* is that your memory may fail you, and the topics suddenly may be difficult to visualize as complete sentences or thoughts. Its advantages are fewer notes, more potential for extemporaneous speaking, and quick comprehension—*if* you are thoroughly familiar with the concepts. A key-word outline is an abbreviated topical outline. In terms of indentation and symbols it looks the same as the complete-sentence outline. The *key-word outline* is usually easier to remember, and it makes the extemporaneous reordering of ideas much easier when the situation calls for such adaptation.

Combinations of these forms are often advisable when you are speaking on a subject with which you are thoroughly familiar. The main points might be complete sentences, the subpoints phrases, and the sub-subpoints key words.

The examples given illustrate variations in outline form and show how symbols and indentations are used. The words in parentheses indicate other systems of arrangement. Different ways of arranging material are shown in Appendix B.

A shorter topical and key-word form of outline follows:

```
THE LEFT WING

General End:       To inform and entertain.
Specific Purpose:  To inform the audience about left-handed people, their problems,
                   theories as to why some people are left-handed, and what is being
                   done to help them.

                   INTRODUCTION

                   I.   Are you one of those people who have been described as
                        temperamental, unstable, unintelligent, pugnacious, or, in
                        a word, left-handed?
                   II.  Even if you are not, you should know some facts about this
                        persecuted group.
(Attention)             A.  Their number.
(Overview)              B.  Their difficulties.
                        C.  Assistance given.
                        D.  Theories as to why they are left-handed.

                   BODY

                   I.   Who are the southpaws?
                        A.  Number.
                            1.  ¼ North Americans originally left-handed.
(Information)               2.  Schools report an 8% increase.
                        B.  Some are famous.
                            1.  Present-day lefties.
                            2.  Historic lefties.
                   II.  Southpaw advantages and disadvantages.
                        A.  Advantages.
                            1.  Mirror writing.
                            2.  Sports.
```

```
                    B.  Disadvantages.
                        1.  Eating.
                        2.  Musical instruments.
                        3.  Knitting.
                        4.  Office machines.
              III.  Help for left-handers.
                    A.  The Association for the Protection of Rights of
                        Left-Handers.
                        1.  Oaths.
                        2.  Saluting.
                        3.  Fellowship.
(Visualization)      B.  Manufactured goods for lefties.
                        1.  Golf clubs.
                        2.  Musical instruments.
                        3.  Reversed turnstiles.
                    C.  Theories concerning southpaws.
                        1.  Cerebral dominance.
                        2.  Inherited.
                        3.  Present opinion.
                            a.  Surveys.
                            b.  Tests.


          CONCLUSION

            I.  If you are left-handed, be comforted in that:
                    A.  Though your numbers are small, you are not inferior.
                    B.  Your disadvantages are being reduced.
                    C.  The theories make you more interesting.
                    D.  Society is trying to help.
           II.  You righties should now have a right attitude about the left
                wing.
```

From a student speech by Robert Willard, Wayne State University.

7 SUMMING UP

One of the most important aspects of preparing, organizing, and outlining a speech is to achieve a clear understanding and statement of your *specific purpose*—the outcome, objective, or response that your speech is supposed to accomplish. Of almost equal importance is a careful consideration of the audience and the situation. The relationships between audience and subject as well as between audience and speaker are other critical factors in the preparation of a speech.

When you have considered your specific purpose thoroughly and have related it to an analysis of your audience and the occasion of your speech, you are ready to start finding and collecting the materials that will make up the speech itself. This chapter provides an extensive list of sources and procedures for making the task much easier than it may appear at first. Taking notes from your readings and sources should be done systematically; that way, you will have to do only a minimum of rereading and returning to the library. The use of file cards rather than a notebook will ease the eventual organizing and arranging of the various parts of the speech.

The principal ways of organizing ideas for speech purposes are the chronological, topical, spatial, logical, difficulty, and need-plan methods. The arrangement of the parts of a speech (beginning, middle, end; introduction, body, conclusion; and other variations) is related to your general end as well as to your specific purpose. Systems of arrangement are all closely interwoven and can usually be related by a simple introduction-body-conclusion system. The rhetorical principles of unity, coherence, and emphasis also have a strong bearing on the arrangement of the parts.

The general functions of a good introduction are (1) to secure attention, (2) to establish good will, (3) to assure a fair hearing, (4) to orient your audience to the subject, and (5) to make your purpose clear.

The conclusion is generally shorter than either the introduction or the body. It may, and generally should, include a short summary that reinforces the message and makes it easier to understand. It may call for clearly stated directions if certain actions are part of the speaker's purpose. It is important to make it clear when you are through; consider your exit lines carefully. Speakers who do not know when to finish appear awkward and frustrate the audience. Prepare your conclusion as carefully as the rest of your speech; doing so is a good check on organic unity. Remember to quit when you're ahead. Never ruin a good speech by an overly long or overly dramatic conclusion.

An outline is an aid to clear, orderly thinking. It is a blueprint of the speech. Useful principles that apply to all outlines are simplicity, coordination, subordination, discreteness, progression, and symbolization.

Start your serious outlining with the body of the speech. State your main points or ideas in terms of your purpose, and place your supporting material under the appropriate main points. After sketching the body of your speech, outline the introduction and conclusion. Your rough outline should eventually become a complete-sentence outline. After completing a thorough outline, you may then redo it in a topical or key-word form for use on the platform.

The numbers and letters you use as labels in your outline must be consistent. Let your symbols show clearly that the main ideas are relatively equal in importance, and that the subpoints are secondary to the main points. If a topic is to be divided, it should be divided into at least two parts. The number of main points in a speech should seldom go beyond four or five. Your main points should be of approximately equal importance. Each main point should be worded carefully and should contribute to the central purpose of the speech. The order in which you present your main points should aid the logical development of your speech and strengthen audience motivation, remembering, and understanding.

Speech Communication Principles

1 *Unity,* or a consciousness of specific purpose, helps us evaluate the materials and ideas of a message while we are preparing it. The arrangement of the parts of a speech should be so unified that the purpose is clear to both the audience and speaker.
2 *Coherence:* messages are transmitted more clearly when organized according to some practical natural order (for instance, chronologically, topically, spatially, logically, in order of difficulty).
3 *Emphasis:* arranging your message parts systematically (for instance, introduction, body, and conclusion) eases preparation and presentation and promotes better audience impact.
4 Speakers should consider, if possible, their specific purpose and audience analysis at the same time.

5 The style of your message and its delivery should be related to the location and arrangement of the setting, as well as to the content and the audience.

6 There is a commonly held set of mechanical rules for outlining messages that can improve preparation and evaluation measurably: simplicity, coordination, subordination, discreteness, progression, and symbolization.

Specific Learning Outcomes

1 We should learn how to use the basic resources of a library in message preparation; the *Readers' Guide to Periodical Literature,* the *Cumulative Book Index, The United States Catalog,* and related publications.

2 We should learn at least six methods of organizing materials: chronological, topical, logical, difficulty, spatial, and need-plan.

3 We should learn to prepare and test our messages in terms of unity of purpose, coherence and ordering of the parts, and the emphasis given to the most important ideas.

4 We should learn to arrange messages using the introduction-body-conclusion and attention-overview-information-review systems.

5 We should learn the functions and requirements of a good speech introduction: attention, good will, fair hearing, orientation, and purpose.

6 We should learn the six mechanical rules of outlining: simplicity, coordination, subordination, discreteness, progression, and symbolization.

Communication Competencies

1 We should be able to prepare an intelligent, two-to-three-page speech outline that passes the mechanical, organizational, and rhetorical tests discussed in this chapter.

2 We should be able to outline critically the oral messages of another for the purpose of evaluating that person's message strategy and preparation.

3 We should be able to deliver a two-to-four minute speech extemporaneously from an outline in such a way that an audience is not distracted by our use of notes.

4 By looking through standard library references, we should be able to find materials for a three-to-four-page speech outline.

Study Projects and Tasks

1 Prepare a detailed outline (see the models in this chapter) for a two-to-four-minute, one- or two-point speech. After your instructor has evaluated the outline, reduce it to a key-word form for use in delivering the speech to the class. In general, choose topics that are mainly explanatory or informative (rather than persuasive or entertaining).

2 Make simple one-page, main-point outlines of your classmates' speeches. Then give them to your instructor, who will feed them back to the speakers as a means of giving them insight into their organizational effectiveness.

3 Prepare only the *introduction* to a five-to-ten-minute speech that you might use later. Make your general and specific purposes clear, and try to achieve all of the functions of a good introduction (attention, good will, fair hearing, orientation, purpose). (See the model outlines in this chapter.)

4 Prepare an oral report or essay in which you attempt to prove or disprove any of the speech communication principles listed for this chapter.

5 Find a short speech manuscript or editorial.

a Using the introduction-body-conclusion system and Roman numerals for main points, outline the speech by using Arabic numerals (1, 2, 3. . .) only.

b Evaluate the introduction of the speech on the basis of the five functions discussed in this chapter (attention, good will, fair hearing, orientation of audience, clarity of purpose). Indicate by line number where each function is served.

c Evaluate the speech according to the method of organization used (chronological, topical, spatial, logical, difficulty, or need-plan). Justify your opinion.

d Evaluate the speech according to the rhetorical principles of unity, coherence, and emphasis.

e Find six types of connectives in the speech or editorial. See pages 155–56 for examples of connectives.

GENERAL LEARNING OUTCOMES

1 We should learn three basic learning principles and their relationship to message preparation.

2 We should learn the ways of increasing message clarity and audience interest in order to support a main point in an outline.

3 We should learn how to relate the choice and use of audio-visual aids to the cone of experience.

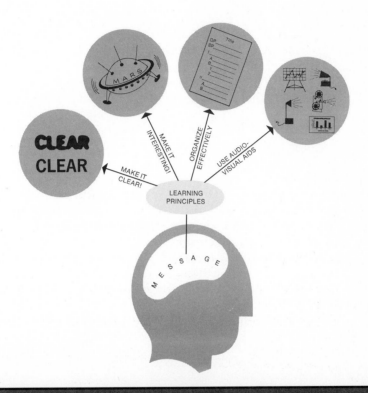

presenting information

HOW WE LEARN

One of the most frequent reasons for speaking or communicating is to inform people about something. In a sense you are a teacher: you must present your material in not only a clear and interesting way but also in a way that makes it easy for your audience to learn, remember, and apply the information. To achieve these goals, we need to know something of how humans learn.

From Known to Unknown

In chapter 1 we learned that people understand a message primarily by applying their previous experience and knowledge to it. It follows that teachers or speakers must select and arrange their material so that they best utilize the knowledge and experience the audience already has. In describing or explaining something, the rule might be stated as follows: *go from the known to the unknown*. For example, in trying to explain the relationship between wire size and electric current, an electrician compared the rule for selection of size to a garden hose (known) and the excess strain put upon the hose when someone restricts the opening with the nozzle. Having once burst a garden hose by turning the nozzle off, the writer understood his explanation. It was clear, interesting, and easy to apply.

Assuming that everybody knows the size of an English sparrow, a robin, and a crow, bird watchers typically relate the size of all unknown or unidentified birds to one of these three. This simple relating of known to unknown has made the communicating and sharing of much information far less frustrating for serious bird watchers.

Serial Learning

As we learned in previous chapters, people tend to learn more readily when things are arranged in some sequence or serial order, especially when they are aware of the order. We teach youngsters addition and subtraction before multiplication and division. Though we could start with algebra, we think it is more efficient to use a sequence based on difficulty. In history courses we often use a chronological order, but a sequence based on social issues might be used instead.

The particular ordering of the material to be learned is determined by the previous knowledge of the audience, the difficulty of the subject, and the specific information or skill the speaker wishes to deliver. The audience is said to be learning (serially) when it is able to connect each portion of the sequence to the one immediately following it. In learning to drive a car, we must learn a great many details, but we have not really learned to *drive* until we have connected clutching, braking, steering, and other operations in such a way that one action is followed automatically by the next appropriate action.

Reinforcement

Perhaps in an education or psychology course you have heard the expression SRX. In discussing the subject of learning, theorists use S to stand for stimulus, R for response, and X for reinforcement. This X may be a reward for responding in the desired way, a punishment, some form of known association, or perhaps some form of repetition. The exact nature and mode of operation of reinforcement is highly complex and is the subject of considerable academic debate. The teacher who "feeds back" criticism by a smile, a frown, or a high grade is practicing reinforcement. So is the drill sergeant with a really loud voice. This enhancement of a desired response is an application of reinforcement, whether it be by repetition, a loud voice, or some other form of emphasis.

A most interesting early communication experiment on the effectiveness of various forms of emphasis was conducted by Raymond Ehrensberger. A fifteen-minute speech containing a relatively neutral form of emphasis was delivered to various audiences. Experimental speeches on the same subject to similar audiences used many kinds of emphasis. All twenty-one audiences were tested on the material covered in the speeches in order to determine which kind of emphasis resulted in the greatest retention.

The results shown below are strong evidence of the value of emphasis, whether verbal, vocal, gestural, organizational, or some combination of the above. This evidence also contains some serious warnings for speakers. Note that although three repetitions were a significant factor in retention, four repetitions were much less of a factor, and two repetitions appeared to cause no effect. Although the results of one limited experiment in no way suggest that three repetitions are a magic number, they do imply that too much repetition is as bad as too little. All of us have grown weary of certain TV commercials that continually repeat a product name. On the other hand, you have probably learned to appreciate the teacher who repeats and reviews course work, making it easier to understand and recall the important items. It is also interesting to note that voice volume made a difference in this experiment. Although the results do not mean that we should never use a loud voice, they do demonstrate that in certain communication circumstances a loud voice may interfere with recall of information. In sum, take care not to overdo a good thing or to draw overly specific rules from limited experiences. Reinforcement in the form of verbal, vocal, gestural, and organizational emphasis can be a real asset to speakers presenting information—as long as they are careful to adapt the amount and kind of reinforcement to the particular subject, situation, and audience. "Now get this" might be a little strong for today's audiences!

THE EFFECTIVENESS OF VARIOUS MODES OF EMPHASIS COMPARED TO A NEUTRAL TREATMENT

Rank	Form of Emphasis	Experimental Mode % Right Answers	Neutral Mode % Right Answers	Statistical Analysis*
1	"Now get this" (verbal emphasis)	86	53.2	Very significant difference
2	Three distributed repetitions	78	51.4	Very significant difference
3	Repetition (early in speech)	72	50.7	Very significant difference
4	Speaking slowly	76	59.8	Very significant difference
5	Repetition (late in speech)	67	50.7	Very significant difference
6	Pause	69	55.4	Very significant difference
7	Gesture	66	53.2	Very significant difference
8	Four distributed repetitions	60	51.4	Significant difference
9	Two distributed repetitions	58	51.4	No real difference
10	Soft voice	56	55.4	No real difference
11	Loud voice	51	59.8	Significant negative difference

Adapted from R. Ehrensberger, "An Experimental Study of the Relative Effectiveness of Certain Forms of Emphasis in Public Speaking," *Speech Monographs*, 12, no. 2 (1945), 94–111.

PRIMARY OBJECTIVES

One of the primary objectives in presenting information is *clarity;* we utilize what we know about the psychology of learning to make understanding easier. Perhaps not quite so evident is the fact that an audience's *interest* in or motivation to learn may have an important effect on how much it remembers. The third primary principle of informative speaking is *organization.*

Achieving Clarity

The *scope* of your purpose (the amount of information you wish to cover in a given period of time) is a vital factor in clarity, as are the organization of the material and the choice of language. The use of audiovisual aids is still another method of improving clarity. These special factors will be discussed later; this section is concerned with verbal means of achieving clarity.

ILLUSTRATION OR EXAMPLE An education major who was also a student teacher had as her specific purpose "to inform the class of the basic principles of overcoming discipline problems in the fourth grade." She could have proceeded to discuss "projections of insecurity and overt cognitive intellectualization assistance from an interacting teacher." The class was fortunate because she elected instead to draw specific examples from her own experience to illustrate and clarify the complex problems of discipline, and this approach was much more interesting. She opened her speech by describing an experince with George Z. and his habit of putting gum in little girls' hair. She followed this with the story of Bernard B., who, though a gifted child, took special delight in swearing. Next she explained the psychological reasons for such behavior, the things for a teacher not to do, and the proper principles of discipline to apply. In a sense the whole speech was an extended example, and it helped make her point clear. The more detailed and the more vivid the incident, the more interesting it usually is. Very often, verbal illustration can be aided considerably by pictures or actual objects (perhaps a recording of Bernard B.'s language).

The confusing and often dull subject of taxes becomes more understandable through the following illustration.

What new state budget could cost each of us

The average Michigan resident might not fully comprehend $9,481,055,126—the proposed price tag for state government in the fiscal year starting Oct. 1.

Here's what it would do:
- Buy 189,621 houses costing $50,000 apiece or 2,370,263, 1979 Ford Pintos (average price $4,000.)
- Provide 3,495 bottles of Stroh's beer for every resident of the state—not including the deposit.
- Pave an 897,827-mile-long road of $1 bills placed end-to-end. That's 36 trips around the earth or slightly less than two round trips to the moon.

Viewed another way, $9.4 billion represents $1,041.42 for every man, woman and child in the state.

If Gov. William G. Milliken's budget is approved, state government will spend, $18,039 a minute, or nearly $301 a second.[1]

If your subject is one with which you have had no firsthand experience, you can often draw your examples from people who do have such experience. An excellent speech on aerial acrobatics was delivered by a student who had never been in an airplane but who used examples from the experiences of three veteran stunt pilots.

An illustration or example may be a hypothetical story (a made-up

[1]*Detroit News,* February, 1979.

story that is reasonable and fair to the facts). Such an example usually starts: "Suppose you were flying at 10,000 feet . . ." or, "Put yourself in this predicament. . . ." The hypothetical example does not carry the proof of a real or factual illustration, but it does have the advantage of adaptability to the point being made, since you may tell the story as you please. The major problem is an ethical one: make sure the hypothetical example is never taken for a factual one, and make sure it is consistent with known facts.

Illustration or example is a powerful, efficient way of clarifying and supporting a point. In choosing your illustrations, make sure that they are truly related to the point being made and that they represent the general rule. An example out of context or an example that is an exception to the general rule only confuses in the long run. In addition to being reasonable and fair, your illustrations and examples should contain enough details and excitement to add to the interest of the subject.

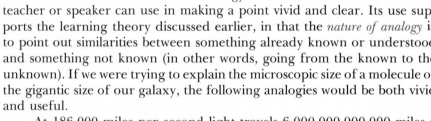

100,000,000 years

Figure 8.1
If *molecules* of water were poured into a drinking glass at the rate of one per second, it would take 100,000,000 years to fill it.

ANALOGY OR COMPARISON   Analogy is often the most useful device a teacher or speaker can use in making a point vivid and clear. Its use supports the learning theory discussed earlier, in that the *nature of analogy* is to point out similarities between something already known or understood and something not known (in other words, going from the known to the unknown). If we were trying to explain the microscopic size of a molecule or the gigantic size of our galaxy, the following analogies would be both vivid and useful.

At 186,000 miles per second light travels 6,000,000,000,000 miles a year, a distance equal to 240,000,000 trips around the earth. At this rate we

Figure 8.2   There is so much empty space inside an atom that if the atom could be magnified to a diameter of 100 yards, the nucleus would appear to be only the size of a billiard ball. *From Margaret Bevans, ed.,* The Golden Treasury of Knowledge *(New York: Golden Press, Inc., 1961), p. 1145.*

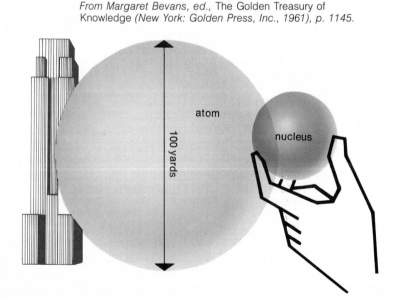

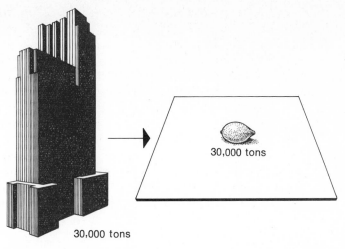

Figure 8.3 If all the nuclei and electrons that make up a skyscraper were squeezed together, they would be no longer than a cherry stone. But the cherry stone would weigh 30,000 tons, the same weight as the skyscraper. *From Margaret Bevans, ed.,* The Golden Treasury of Knowledge *(New York: Golden Press, Inc., 1961), p. 1145.*

could reach the sun in $8\frac{1}{2}$ minutes, the next nearest star in $4\frac{1}{2}$ years. If we started at age 20 and moved at the speed of light, we would be 80 before we reached the star Aldebaran. The really distant stars in our galaxy would take us thousands of years to reach!

Try these analogies—they explain the size of a molecule of water and the weight of an atom. They also are clever examples of visual aids. (Figures 8.1, 8.2, 8.3)

An interesting way to illustrate the scarcity of gold is illustrated in Figure 8.4.

Abraham Lincoln made good use of analogy and comparison not only for clarification but also for persuasion. During the Civil War there were those who loudly criticized his method of conducting the war. At that time, a tightrope walker named Blondin became famous for walking and for riding a two-wheel bicycle on a rope strung across Niagara Falls. In explaining the dangerous position of the nation, Lincoln directed the following analogy at his critics.

> Gentlemen, I want you to suppose a case for a moment. Suppose that all the property you were worth was in gold, and you had put it in the hands of Blondin, the famous rope-walker, to carry across the Niagara Falls on a tightrope. Would you shake the rope while he was passing over it, or keep shouting to him, "Blondin, stoop a little more! Go a little faster!" No, I am sure you would not. You would hold your breath as well as your tongue, and keep your hands off until he was safely over. Now the government is in the same situation. It is carrying an immense weight across a stormy

YOU'LL UNDERSTAND WHY GOLD IS SO PRECIOUS WHEN YOU KNOW HOW LITTLE EXISTS.

Beside the Washington Monument is an imaginary block of gold. The Monument is 555 feet, or 185 yards, in height—the block is 18 yards on each side, about one-tenth the Monument's mass.

This block represents not just the gold of America, but all the gold mankind owns. It is your watch, your ring, your necklace, as well as all the gold in all government reserves. It is all the gilding of churches, the solid gold museum artifacts, the dental fillings and even the gold plating on dime store doodads. It is all.

One should really reflect again on that dimension—an 18-yard-high cube—this is the gold of 6000 years. No wonder it is precious; no wonder man seeks more of it.

Figure 8.4 The Gold Information Center.

ocean. Untold treasures are in its hands. It is doing the best it can. Don't badger it! Just keep still, and it will get you safely over.[2]

STATISTICS The use of numbers to help make a point more clear or specific is not as simple as it may seem. Statistics are frequently used to support a point in a persuasive speech, but they are powerful evidence only if they are (1) meaningful to the audience and (2) related to the point under consideration. However, when statistics are overly precise and complicated, they may cloud rather than clarify an issue. Have you ever been given directions like these? "You go down Norfolk Street exactly 3.2 miles, turn left on Baker Street and go 2.4 miles to a Y intersection, turn right about 120° onto Charlie Street and go .3 miles, then turn right and go 150 yards and you're there." Some details are most helpful, but not these! Even if you *were* able to keep them straight, you would probably cause an accident by watching your odometer instead of the road. Of course, the other extreme ("You go up Norfolk quite a little piece and then a couple of miles or so on Baker to a kind of wide-angle left turn and then . . .") isn't any better. A "little" piece and a "fur" piece can vary by a good many miles.

[2]Quoted in *Town Meeting,* 11 (October 11, 1945), 24.

By themselves, statistics are abstract. Make them *concrete* by relating them to known things. To say that Latin America has serious economic problems because the average family income is $150 per year is reasonably clear; to compare this figure to the $13,263 of the United States or to show that $150 comes to only 41¢ a day is clearer.

The National Safety Council made their statistics clearer and more interesting in the following way:

WHILE YOU SPEAK!

While you make a 10-minute safety speech—2 persons will be killed and more than 200 will suffer a disabling injury. Costs will amount to $800,000.

On the average, there are 13 accidental deaths and about 1,300 disabling injuries every hour during the year. About one-half of the deaths occur in motor-vehicle accidents while more than one-third of the injuries occur in the home.

Accidents in the nation by class of accident and severity of injury occurred at the following rates in 1973:

Class of Accident	Severity	One Every—	No. per Hour	No. per Day	No. per Week	Total 1973
All Accidents	Deaths	4 minutes	13	320	2,250	117,000
	Injuries	3 seconds	1,310	31,500	220,000	11,500,000
Motor-Vehicle	Deaths	9 minutes	6	153	1,070	55,800
	Injuries	16 seconds	230	5,500	38,500	2,000,000
Work	Deaths	37 minutes	2	39	270	14,200
	Injuries	13 seconds	290	6,800	48,100	2,500,000
Workers Off-Job	Deaths	12 minutes	5	121	850	44,100
	Injuries	10 seconds	380	9,000	63,500	3,300,000
Home	Deaths	20 minutes	3	71	500	26,000
	Injuries	8 seconds	470	11,200	78,800	4,100,000
Public Non-Motor-Vehicle	Deaths	21 minutes	3	68	480	25,000
	Injuries	11 seconds	340	8,200	57,700	3,000,000

From *Partnership for Health,* 4, no. 1 (1975), 2. The figures are National Safety Council estimates.

We live more and more by statistics that predict things. From Univac's vote predictions to insurance rates, from the number of cancer-causing things in a carton of cigarettes to the average number of cavities in a given group of children, we are in an age of specific, predictive statistics. We have learned to combine statistics with analogies or comparisons to make sense out of the astronomical numbers of outer space. We express speed as Mach 1, 2, or 3 instead of miles per hour, and we speak of distance in terms of light-years.

Statistics can give a speech a sense of precision if we remember to relate the statistics to known things and to make them meaningful to the audience.

TESTIMONY   Like statistics, testimony has great use in speeches to persuade but is also valuable for its ability to clarify. In a speech to inform, it may add considerable *interest* to what might otherwise be straight explanation.

In describing the course of events on D-Day in Europe, one might express the story more vividly by using a series of datelines and statements from a dozen GIs who hit the beaches:

> *0400,* Pvt. Johnson: "There were ships and little boats and men all tangled up in one maze of confusion."
> *0430,* Pvt. Sandrin: "The men coming down the cargo nets to the LCIs (Landing Craft Infantry) seemed to be 20 feet from the deck one minute and a step away the next."
> *0500,* Pvt. Brown: "The LCI to our left just seemed to evaporate."
> *0600,* Sgt. Glover: "Where the hell is the air cover?"
> *2300,* Lt. Rucks: "This has been the longest day of my life."

The explanation of events is often clearer and more impressive as a result of the use of testimony. More will be said on this subject in chapter 12.

RESTATEMENT   Restatement is more than simple repetition. It is saying the same thing in a different and reinforcing way. This is particularly useful if the material is complex or the vocabulary specialized. The value of reinforcement in terms of learning theory was demonstrated earlier in this chapter.

If you were to reread chapter 1 of this book, you would find many different definitions of the process of communication, all trying to say the same thing. One descriptive definition was a long paragraph, another consisted of a short paragraph, another reduced the definition to encoding and decoding. This is an example of restatement for clarification. If the meaning were not clear in one definition because of sentence structure or in

Figure 8.5 Animal Crackers. *Reprinted by permission of the Chicago Tribune-New York News Syndicate, Inc. All rights reserved.*

another because of vocabulary, you were given still more choices. If you understood all the definitions at first glance, fine. Assuming that it was not too extended, this repetition should have reinforced the learning. To restate the value of restatement: it is more than simple repetition, it is saying the same thing in different ways in order to reinforce learning, and it is particularly useful if the subject is complex or if the vocabulary is specialized or strange to the audience.

Developing Interest

Interest, the second of the three primary principles in presenting a speech to inform, refers to the motivation of the audience to want to listen or learn. The problem is to hold the attention of your audience while you are practicing all the suggestions for clarity just discussed. What are the categories of things that tend to interest all of us? How can they be applied to your subject in such a way as to motivate the audience to pay attention and want to learn? Much of a speaker's *interest* is, of course, dependent upon the speaker's style of delivery and use of vocal variety; however, we are concerned here mainly with speech content. Here are some of the more useful qualities of speech content that stimulate interest.

SPECIFICITY   When a speaker says, "Let me give you an example of what I mean by dog-tired," you probably pay closer attention than if he or she were simply to give you some general, academic explanation. Suppose the speaker used this example:

> The men of Hurricane Camille's Red Cross rescue group thought after two days of forced march through wreckage-strewn coastal areas that they were dog-tired. Then they saw the remote victims of the storm, who seemed to be moving on sheer instinct and determination alone. They staggered through their broken homes with drooping shoulders, so physically drained that it seemed to take every last ounce of strength to put one foot in front of the other.

Specificity, reality, or *concreteness* are more interesting than vague generalities or abstractions. Instead of saying, "A boy was run over," be specific: call him by name; indicate his age; identify the car. "Mark Scott, age 6, dashed into the street to greet his mother approaching from the other side and was dashed to the pavement by a 1979 Thunderbird traveling at the 30-mile speed limit." The safety statistics cited on p. 183 are also a good example of specificity used to develop interest.

CONFLICT   TV stories always seem to pit "bad guys" against "good guys." This conflict and fighting pay off in viewer interest. Can you imagine a *Rockford Files, Kojak,* or even a *As the World Turns* story without conflict or uncertainty? Sports contests, even when you know that Ohio State will surely beat Otterbein College, create interest for most people. Disagreement and opposition have elected and destroyed many a politician, but almost always in an interesting way! If in your examples, illustrations, and explanation, you can use conflict without seeming to set up nonexistent battles, your speech should have added interest for the audience.

NOVELTY Something that is *novel is different, unusual, contrasting, or strange.* Of course, if the subject is so exotic that listeners cannot relate it to their previous knowledge and experience, interest may be lost rather than gained.

Novelty is not limited to exoticness. Relatively average things become novel if the world about them is in contrast. At one time a bikini would have been a novelty, mostly because of its contrast to more conservative swimsuits. In our time a woman would probably gain more attention wearing one of the old-fashioned neck-to-ankle suits of the early 1900s or an ultramodern "topless." Of course, as one student put it, "It depends on the woman." New Yorkers find nothing unusual or novel about their skyscrapers, but a visitor might become a novelty to the natives by staring trancelike into the low clouds that hide the Empire State Building or World Trade Towers from view.

The unusual, the contrasting, the exotic, the strange, the rare, and the generally different things in life are more interesting than the run-of-the-mill. Let your examples, analogies, and explanations be novel for added audience interest.

CURIOSITY One of the more marvelous and exasperating aspects of young children is the seemingly endless series of questions they ask about countless subjects. Grown children (men and women) are not really much different, except that they may become a little more precise about the subjects they want to know about and the questions they ask. Humans seem to have to find out what lies around the corner or beyond the stars. Each new discovery in space leads to added suspense about what the universe is really like and to the big question, "Is there life out there?"

Unanswered questions, uncertainty, suspense—these are the ingredients of curiosity that may be used effectively by speakers to arouse interest.

IMMEDIACY By immediacy we mean the use of *issues of the moment* or of the specific occasion that will quickly arouse and maintain attention and interest when related to a speaker's subject. A company training director has the rare ability to memorize names of individuals along with other relevant facts after just one informal meeting. Such a person once startled a group of forty executives on the second day of a course by randomly calling them by name throughout a two-hour period: "Mr. William Sandy, what do you think of. . . ?" Needless to say, interest was high. You never knew when he would call your name, cite your job description, or ask your opinion.

A reference to a previous speaker or a recent incident that is known to the audience may also heighten interest. In a speech to a business audience in Grand Rapids, Michigan, a speaker noticed several members of his audience staring out the window at the falling snow, probably more from apprehension than a lack of interest. In any event, he too looked toward the window, paused, and commented, "Misery loves company. We have 18 inches of snow in Detroit and you have 42 inches. The weatherman is predicting clearing skies in the next few hours." The audience seemed more interested after that. Not only had a distraction been acknowledged, but the audience felt closer to the speaker.

Learning about the speech occasion, the audience, last-minute headlines, and all other matters of the moment is time well spent in trying to make your speech interesting.

HUMOR   If you feel you do not tell a joke well or if you find it difficult to be a humorous speaker, perhaps you need not be too concerned. The limited speech research on the impact of humor on an audience seems to indicate that at least in *persuasive* speeches it makes no difference. A study by P. E. Lull[3] found that audiences listening to humorous and nonhumorous speeches on socialized medicine were equally persuaded by both speeches. Donald Kilpela obtained the same results in a more recent study which used government health insurance as the topic.[4] Both methods were effective, but they did not vary significantly in effectiveness. A series of studies by Charles Gruner produced similar results, except that humor seemed to improve the character ratings of the speaker.[5] A study by Allan Kennedy found that "subjects viewed the humorous introductory speech as significantly more effective, enjoyable, and interesting."[6] A study by J. Douglas Gibb comparing humorous and nonhumorous *information* lectures did show significantly better student *retention* of the humorous lecture.[7] Lull and Kilpela were quick to point out, however, that the type of humor in their studies may not have been very professional. In other words, a Don Rickles or a Bill Cosby might have produced significant persuasive results. In any event, funny anecdotes (if told well and in good taste) have probably helped many an otherwise dull speaker, subject, or audience.

[3] P. E. Lull, "The Effectiveness of Humor in Persuasive Speeches," *Speech Monographs,* 7 (1940), 26–40.

[4] Donald Kilpela, "An Experimental Study of the Effects of Humor on Persuasion" (unpublished Master's thesis, Wayne State University, 1961).

[5] C. Gruner, "Effect of Humor on Speaker Ethos and Audience Information Gain," *Journal of Communication,* 17, no. 3 (1967), 228–33.

[6] Allan J. Kennedy, "The Effect of Humor upon Source Credibility," *Speech Communication Association Abstracts,* 1972, p. 10.

[7] J. Douglas Gibb, "An Experimental Comparison of the Humorous Lecture and the Non-humorous Lecture in Informative Speaking" (unpublished Master's thesis, University of Utah, 1964).

The professional writers of humorous lines certainly think so. They received $300 per minute of delivery time for the following:

(Roast of a successful clothing manufacturer)
Well, Tom, we managed to get all your friends together under one roof . . . they're outside in the car.
The reason for Tom's success is that with every dress he sells, he includes free installation.
Actually Tom adores his wife and four children. He always wanted a big family . . . it saves on manikins.

(Introduction of a famous plastic surgeon)
Dr. Stevens has integrity. In fact, he's so honest he returns your old parts.[8]

The head of this agency (Comedy Unlimited) describes how he goes about his work and it makes for good advice.

A lot of research goes behind just one line. We do a thorough analysis of the client's needs before sitting down to the typewriter.
Some business comes from public relations people who are called on to write sparkling material for an executive's speech.
They suddenly realize the skill it takes to create comedy and they come to us, confidentially.

When taking a job, he finds out the type of audience being addressed, their education, the time of day of the talk, seating arrangements, if drinks are being served, and what interests those present.

We look for lines that are perfectly appropriate for both the client and the audience. What might be hilariously funny and quite effective for a sales manager might be disastrous for the chairman of the board.
It's important to be able to take a raw idea and convert it into a form which is perfectly balanced—not one syllable in the sentence that doesn't belong—with the impact at the end.
The balance is critical and this is where most, including some very humorous people, as well as performers, as well as writers, fall down—the polishing.[9]

If you do decide to try humor in the form of anecdotes in order to create interest, make the humor as professional as possible. There is no feeling quite as desperate as the one that results from viewing a poker-faced audience after you have told your best joke. Make sure that the anecdote is related to either the subject or the occasion; make sure you can tell it fluently; make sure you remember the punch line; and make sure that it will

[8]*Detroit Free Press,* July 26, 1978, p. 3C.
[9]*Ibid.*

not offend your audience. The best advice of all—try it out on a small group of friends first. In other words, *practice* and *polish!*

Vital Factors   If, while reading this book you had the FM radio playing and the announcer suddenly broke in to say, "Alert! Alert! Please turn to your Conelrad frequencies at the civilian-defense white triangles on your radio dial," you would undoubtedly stop reading and turn the dial as instructed. The reason is obvious. Staying alive, protecting your loved ones, defending your home—all these are *vital concerns* to you, and you are interested because you have to be.

Vital factors, if truly vital, will gain attention because of personal involvement. Those things that affect our self-preservation, reputation, property, sources of livelihood, and freedoms are truly vital factors. More will be said about the role of these factors in part 3.

Organizing Effectively

The learning theory discussed at the beginning of this chapter also should have given you the theory for organizing information effectively. What does it tell us? It tells us of the need to grab the listeners' attention early and motivate them to continue listening; it tells us of the value of serially ordered material; and it tells us of the need for reinforcement and for preparing states of readiness to learn or listen.

One durable and effective method of organizing informative material that roughly meets these requirements was voiced by the gifted speaker Chauncey Depew, a state senator from New York: first, tell them what you are going to tell them; second, tell them; and third, tell them you have told them.

1. Tell 'em what you're going to tell 'em.

2. Tell 'em.

3. Tell 'em you've told 'em.

Let's revise this language to suit our purposes better. We also shall add a fourth step designed to motivate the audience to listen. Here is what we end up with: *attention, overview, information,* and *review.*

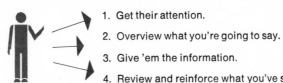

1. Get their attention.

2. Overview what you're going to say.

3. Give 'em the information.

4. Review and reinforce what you've said.

The interest factors discussed earlier are all excellent means of gaining attention. Your immediate purpose is to create a desire in the listeners to hear more about the information you have to offer. If the audience is already highly motivated, your attention step becomes proportionately less important.

In a student speech "to inform the class about some of the sociological problems facing India," the speaker opened with the following *(attention* and *interest):* "Did you know that half of the world's population is illiterate and that one-third of this half lives in India? Did you know that over three hundred languages are spoken in India? That fourteen thousand babies a day are born in India?" He then discussed each of these three points in order. He gave us the detailed *information.* At the close of the speech, he repeated the three points, but in addition he briefly summarized some of the important details from the *information* step. In other words, he *reviewed* the speech, or "told 'em what he told 'em." The completeness or amount of detail you put into your summary or *review* will depend upon the complexity of the subject, the time allotted, and your purpose. In some speeches you may prefer to deliver a brief synthesis of the points you have tried to make, in others, perhaps detailed conclusions that sum up your speech.

The *reinforcement value* of this four-part development is obvious. Once more, remember that a listener cannot go back and reread or review. Speakers must therefore be sure that their information is being communicated to the audience. Toward this end, an occasional internal summary, review, or preview in the *information* step may help. A study by Fred Miller clearly shows that, other things being equal, audiences listening to well-organized speeches score higher on retention tests than audiences hearing poorly organized speeches.[10]

Organization, the third primary principle of presenting information, may thus be aided by following the four-part development scheme based upon learning theory: *attention, overview, information,* and *review.* A model outline showing this type of organization follows on page 191. After that, a second version on page 192 illustrates a slightly more detailed outline of the same material using *introduction, body,* and *conclusion* as its method of organization. Other outlines demonstrating these two recommended ways of organizing the same informative material are shown in Appendix B.

AUDIO-VISUAL AIDS

Teaching or learning aids are used to help make a subject clear, to build interest, and to reinforce the message. On all counts they are valuable to the speaker, although they are not without some hazards and problems. The question of what kind of aid to use in what situation is critical. The role of

[10] Fred Miller, "An Experiment to Determine the Effect Organization Has on the Immediate and Delayed Recall of Information" (unpublished Master's thesis, Miami University, Ohio, 1966); see also E. C. Thompson, Jr., "An Experimental Investigation of the Relative Effectiveness of Organizational Structure in Oral Communication," *Southern Speech Journal,* 26 (1960), 59–69.

INTRODUCTION TO MUSIC

General End: To inform.
Specific Purpose: To state and explain the fundamental concepts of music theory.

Attention

A {
  I. Play a few bars of music on the violin. (demonstration)
  II. Poke fun at the music majors in the class.

Overview

  I.   The kinds of notes.
  II. The musical staff.
  III. Methods of counting the notes.
  IV. Relation of these three points to an instrument.
}

Information

B {
  I.   The kinds of notes.
       A. Neutral notes: A, B, C, D, E, F, G.
       B. Sharp notes: a halftone up.
       C. Flat notes: a halftone down.
  II. Explanation of the musical staff.
       A. The treble clef and melody.
           1. Contains 5 lines; E, G, B, D, F.
           2. Contains 4 spaces: F, A, C, E.
       B. The bass clef and rhythm.
           1. Contains 5 lines: G, B, D, F, A.
           2. Contains 4 spaces: A, C, E, G.
  III. Methods of counting the notes.
       A. Whole note gets 4 beats.
       B. Half note gets 2 beats.
       C. Quarter note gets 1 beat.
       D. Eighth note gets half a beat.
  IV. Relation of these points to a musical keyboard.
       A. The notes (whether neutral, sharp, or flat) correspond to the lines
           and spaces in the staff.
       B. The position of the notes on the staff determines what note or key
           is to be played on the musical instrument.
       C. The number of beats the note receives tells how long the note is to
           be played on the instrument.
}

Review

C {
  I. I have tried to make clear the following four factors of musical theory:
      A. The kinds of notes.
      B. The musical staff.
      C. Methods of counting the notes.
      D. Relating the theory to an instrument.
  II. Now you can start writing your own music or at least sneer at the music
      majors.
}

A = INTRODUCTION

B = BODY

C = CONCLUSION

INTRODUCTION TO MUSIC

General End: To inform.
Specific Purpose: To state and explain the fundamental concepts of musical theory.

Introduction
    I. Play a few bars of music on a violin. (demonstration)
        A. I wish I really was good at this.
        B. I can't teach you to play an instrument in this short speech, but perhaps I can
           review music theory so that you'll feel superior to the three music majors in
           this class.
    II. I would like to cover the following major steps in music theory:
        A. The kinds of notes.
        B. The musical staff.
        C. Methods of counting the notes.
        D. Relation of these three points to an instrument.

Body
    I. The kinds of notes.
        A. Neutral notes: A,B,C,D,E,F,G.
        B. Sharp notes: a half tone up.
        C. Flat notes: a half tone down.
        (A demonstration and a piano keyboard were introduced here.)
    II. Explanation of the musical staff.
        A. The treble clef and melody.
           1. Contains 5 lines: E,G,B,D,F.
           2. Contains 4 spaces: F,A,C,E.
           (A visual aid was shown here.)
        B. The bass clef and rhythm.
           1. Contains 5 lines: G,B,D,F,A.
           2. Contains 4 spaces: A,C,E,G.
           (A visual aid was shown here.)
  III. Methods of counting the notes.
        A. Whole note gets 4 beats.
        B. Half note gets 2 beats.
        C. Quarter note gets 1 beat.
        D. Eighth note gets half a beat.
        (A blackboard sketch and demonstration were used here.)
  IV. Relation of these points to a musical keyboard.
      (The piano keyboard was displayed here.)
        A. The notes (whether neutral, sharp, or flat) correspond to the lines and spaces
           in the staff.
        B. The position of the notes on the staff determines what note or key is to be
           played on the musical instrument.
        C. The number of beats the note receives tells how long the note is to be played on
           the instrument.
        (A short demonstration here.)

```
Conclusion

  I. I have tried to make clear the following four factors of musical theory:
      A. The kinds of notes.
      B. The musical staff.
      C. Methods of counting the notes.
      D. Relating the theory to an instrument.
 II. Now you can start writing your own music or at least sneer at the music majors.
```

Adapted from a student speech by Gary Carotta, Wayne State University.

demonstration as an aid is especially important to beginning speakers. Teachers almost always ask for a demonstration speech, in part because it causes you to move and thereby work off excess tension. In this section we'll relate the use of audio-visual aids to audience involvement and discuss the special role of demonstration.

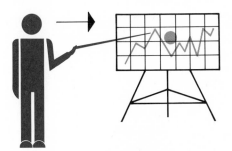

The Cone of Experience and Types of Aids

Edgar Dale, an expert on the use of teaching aids, has given us a model that classifies these aids in terms of telling, showing, and doing, and grades audience involvement according to the degree of abstractness of the aid. Those aids that allow the audience to "do" or experience something are more concrete than those aids that simply "show" something; "telling" is the most abstract of the three types of aids. Hollingworth thinks of this ladder of abstraction as being ordered in terms of "interestingness"—that is, the direct, purposeful experience would be the most interesting.[11] Dale is quick to point out the danger of too absolute an order based on either interestingness or learning, since the other aspects of a speech situation are so variable. Audience response is affected by the previous experience of the audience, the subject of the speech and whether teaching aids can be used to illustrate it, the ability of the speaker to visualize the topic by using word pictures, the real purpose of the speaker, and the interest level of the audience.

[11] H. L. Hollingworth, *The Psychology of the Audience* (New York: American Book Company, 1935, 1977), p. 73.

The specific aids in Dale's Model are shown in figure 8.6. The top of the cone (the "telling" area) contains visual symbols that aid the audience—graphs, charts, cartoons, diagrams, flat pictures, blackboard sketches, and so on. Typical forms of graphs that a speaker might use include pictograms (figures 8.7 and 8.8), bar graphs (figures 8.9 and 8.10), area diagrams (figures 8.11 and 8.12), and line graphs (figure 8.13). Some typical forms of charts include organization charts (figure 8.14), stream or tree charts (figures 8.15 and 8.16), and tabular charts (figures 8.17 and 8.18).

All the items in the middle of the cone (the "showing" area) are self-explanatory (except for demonstrations, about which more will be said in the next section). These devices bring the audience closer to reality than mere telling, but still not to the real personal involvement found in "doing."

The bottom of the cone (the "doing" part) contains contrived (artificial) experiences and dramatic participation. These would include LINK

Figure 8.6 The cone of experience. *From* Audio-Visual Methods in Teaching, Third Edition, *by Edgar Dale. Copyright* © *1946, 1954, 1969, by Holt, Rinehart, Winston. Reprinted by permission of Holt, Rinehart & Winston.*

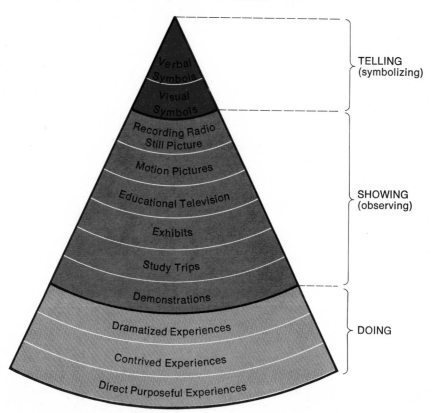

Black Workers' Earnings As a Percentage of White Workers'

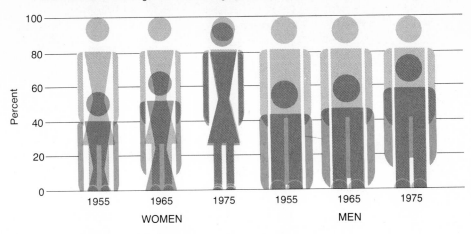

Figure 8.7 Pictogram depicting earnings. *Adapted from and reprinted by permission from* TIME, *The Weekly Newsmagazine; Copyright Time Inc., 1978.*

trainers for pilots, artificial weightlessness chambers for astronauts, and other mock-ups, as well as the personal involvement experienced in role playing or working on case-study problems. Perhaps in grade school you played a Pilgrim landing at Plymouth Rock, an angel at Bethlehem, or Paul Revere. In management training programs today, some of our top executives once again play roles except that now they are of an irate foreman, a shop steward, or an unhappy manager. Why? Because it is

Figure 8.8 Pictogram.

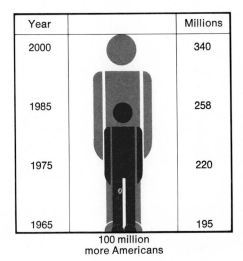

Year		Millions
2000		340
1985		258
1975		220
1965		195

100 million
more Americans

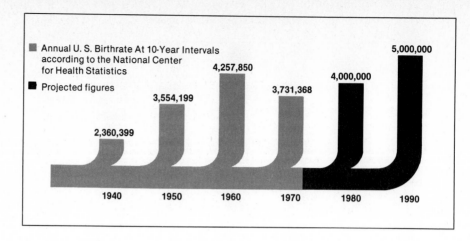

Figure 8.9   Modified Bar graph, *By permission of* Passages,
April, 1978. The Magazine of Northwest Orient Airlines.

Figure 8.10   Bar graphs, 1978 *Reprinted by permission from* TIME, *The
Weekly Newsmagazine; Copyright Time Inc., 1978.*

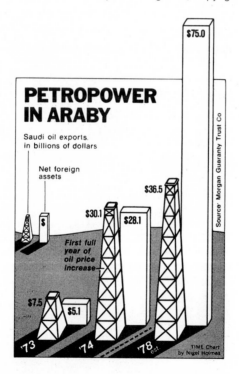

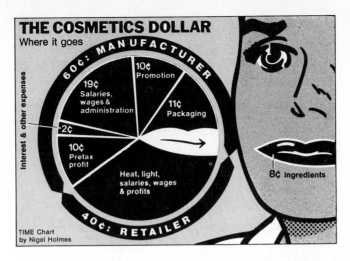

Figure 8.11 Area Diagram or Pie Chart. *Reprinted by permission from TIME, The Weekly Newsmagazine; Copyright Time Inc., 1978.*

Figure 8.12 Area diagram showing the four zones of the earth's interior. *Special permission granted by My Weekly Reader, No. 5, published by Xerox Education Publications © Xerox Corporation, 1964.*

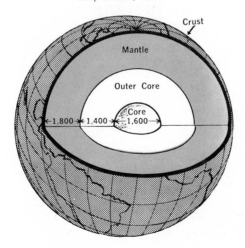

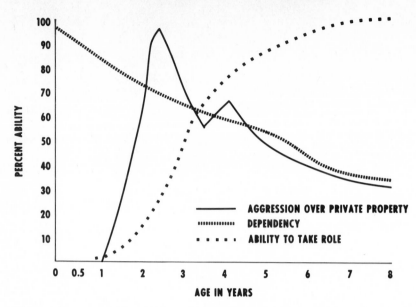

SOCIALIZATION IN CHILDREN

AGGRESSION OVER PRIVATE PROPERTY
DEPENDENCY
ABILITY TO TAKE ROLE

Figure 8.13 Line graph: Child growth and development. *From* Audio-Visual Products Catalog for 1974–75, *p. 26.*

Figure 8.14 Organization chart: Functional organization—typical department store. *From* Audio-Visual Products Catalogue for 1974–75, *p. 42.*

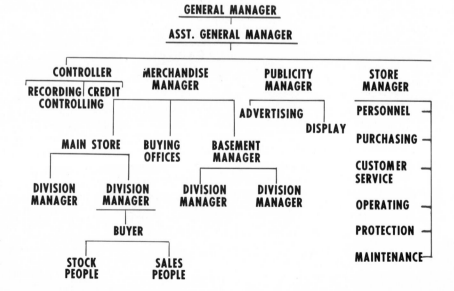

FUNCTIONAL ORGANIZATION-TYPICAL DEPARTMENT STORE

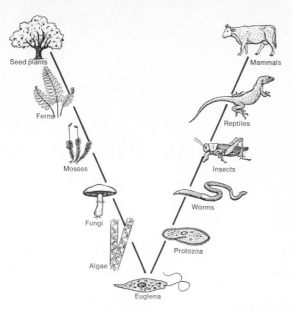

Figure 8.15 Stream or tree chart (plant life is represented on the left side of the "V," animal life on the right). *From Truman J. Moon, Paul B. Mann, and James H. Otto,* Modern Biology *(New York: Henry Holt and Company, 1947), p. 249. Reproduced by special permission of Holt, Rinehart & Winston.*

Figure 8.16 Tree chart.

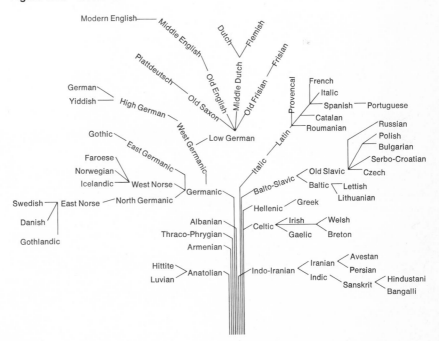

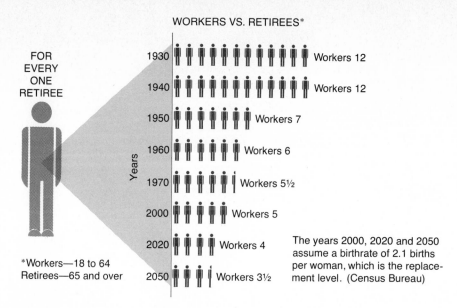

WORKERS VS. RETIREES*

FOR EVERY ONE RETIREE

1930   Workers 12
1940   Workers 12
1950   Workers 7
1960   Workers 6
1970   Workers 5½
2000   Workers 5
2020   Workers 4
2050   Workers 3½

Years

The years 2000, 2020 and 2050 assume a birthrate of 2.1 births per woman, which is the replacement level. (Census Bureau)

*Workers—18 to 64
Retirees—65 and over

Figure 8.17 Tabular Chart, *From* John B. Walters of *The Detroit News.*

Figure 8.18 Tabular Chart Showing Noise in Decibels. *Adapted from Glamour. Copyright © 1978 by The Condé Nast Publications Inc.*

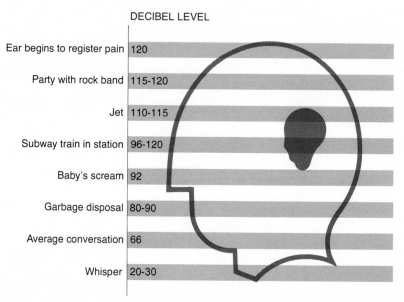

DECIBEL LEVEL

Ear begins to register pain	120
Party with rock band	115-120
Jet	110-115
Subway train in station	96-120
Baby's scream	92
Garbage disposal	80-90
Average conversation	66
Whisper	20-30

thought that this contrived slice of life involves the person more in the lesson and approaches real experience more closely.

The Special Role of Demonstration

The demonstration aspect of teaching aids is especially important to a speech class because a demonstration speech is often an early assigned exercise or informative speech. A demonstration speech reduces anxiety and at the same time helps in the presentation of information. The purpose of a demonstration is to show how a skill, a procedure, a process, or a device is used so that the audience will find it easier to learn the skill or acquire the knowledge. A demonstration combines *showing with telling*. Many grade schools have sessions called "show and tell." These are essentially demonstrations and are excellent early speech-training exercises if conducted by teachers who have some basic speech experience.

The value of demonstration is that the audience can learn by seeing what is demonstrated. Demonstration helps speakers remember their material; it appeals to several senses of the listener; it reinforces the message; it saves time; and finally, it has dramatic appeal and is more concrete than just telling

However, *demonstrations don't always work as planned*. A few years ago many commercials were not taped, as they are now. In a Westinghouse commercial Betty Furness, while swishing gracefully between refrigerator doors that were rhythmically opening and closing, had a door close on part of her lovely, full-skirted dress. Ms. Furness finished the commercial without the bottom half of her dress! The point is she finished the speech. We can draw a lesson from this, but first let's recall another fiasco. Do you remember when an announcer tied a Timex watch to the propeller of an outboard motor, lowered the propeller into a fifty-gallon drum full of water, and started the engine? When the motor was withdrawn, the watch was gone. The camera panned down into the drum and there before millions of viewers was a very dead watch badly in need of reassembly! What would you have done? (Due to a poised handling of this difficult situation, Timex sales actually went up, not down.) Sometimes, demonstrations can be dangerous. In another TV commercial a man added water to a bottle of pills being advertised, and then shook the bottle to liven up the demonstration. It blew up only moments after it was out of his hand!

Classroom demonstrations are just as much fun and can often be just as hazardous. A student once demonstrated a tear-gas pencil in an overheated, poorly ventilated classroom with the temperature outside about zero. Talk about audience involvement! Another student, demonstrating the toughness of unbreakable, bulletproof glass, dropped it on a concrete floor. It did not break—it exploded! This produced one badly shaken speaker. (A glass company spokesman informed us later that the chances of the angle of impact, the temperature, the force, and other factors being perfectly coordinated—which caused the shattering—were about 1 in 10,000.)

The obvious questions are "What can I do to reduce the probability of things going wrong?" and "If something does go wrong in spite of careful planning, what do I do at that moment of truth?"

The answer to the first question is careful *planning*. Plan exactly *how* you will perform the demonstration. Make sure you have *all* your equipment and have it in the right sequence. Be sure the demonstration *works* in your practice sessions. Emphasize safety precautions. Check for conditions that may vary from the practice session (for example, electric current). Finally, be sure *you* can do the demonstration. A flight instructor was teaching cadets the principles of airfoil and how an airplane develops lift. To demonstrate, he put a piece of 8½-by-11 paper between his lower lip and his chin. He then blew over it, creating a partial vacuum on top of the paper, which caused the paper to lift. A new instructor who had observed this demonstration rushed to the next class with no time for practice. Confident that he could do it, he proceeded to blow—with no movement from the paper and with an audience of well-disciplined cadets trying not to explode with laughter. There are some moments when defeat is very evident.

The answer to the second question, "What if it happens anyway?" is again to be found in planning. More specifically, calculate the extent and nature of the risk and then plan emergency alternative procedures for every disaster you can think of. This is a must. You have no time to protect yourself when something does go wrong, and the shock and confusion may cause you to react emotionally rather than rationally.

Pilots of high-speed aircraft have long talked of calculated risk and alternate procedures. There are preplanned procedures to meet pre-classified emergencies. If two engines go out, what do you do? Talk it over? NO; you go to alternate plan two on a prearranged signal, thereby cutting confusion and perhaps saving your life. There simply isn't time to respond in any other way.

The student with the "unbreakable" glass had a calculated risk of 1 in 10,000. One can hardly blame him for not being thorough in planning alternate procedures. These are probably better odds than a pedestrian has on the Los Angeles Freeway. Nevertheless, this student could have had two pieces of glass, just as you should always have two bulbs for your slide or movie projector. Extra equipment or spare parts are only part of the answer. The real problem is what you will say. Plan your communication strategy very carefully. *When and if the glass breaks I will say, "The odds on that happening were 1 in 10,000. Let me prove it by beating the next piece of glass with this hammer."* If the next piece breaks, you may have to resort to an alternate plan using prayer. You can't win them all!

Some Practical Rules

using aids

---

1 Never obstruct the vision of your audience: make sure the lectern or stand is out of the way; try not to stand in front of your materials.

2 Use your aids to reinforce, not to distract; introduce them when pertinent, not before (unless for attention).

3 Talk to the audience; "talk" to your visual aid only when you wish the audience to look at it.

4 Make sure you understand thoroughly how and when you intend to use your visual aid. Orient your audience to the aid (for example, "This is a top view").

preparing aids

1 Relate your choice of aids to the cone of experience (figure 8.6), a careful audience analysis, your subject, and your specific purpose.

2 Make a visual aid readily visible. Is it big enough? Are the lines heavy and dark enough (one-eighth to one-half inch thick)?

3 Make each visual aid understandable. Do not put too much detail or too many ideas on one aid. Label all the significant parts clearly. Let the aid be simple enough so that you will be able to orient the audience to it easily and quickly.

4 Organize the aid systematically so that it is easier for you to recall your speech material when using the aid.

8 SUMMING UP

Presenting information orally to an audience is a task similar to that of a teacher. Teaching is a science as well as an art and includes the serious evaluation and application of learning theory. This same learning theory is therefore useful to any speaker who would attempt to inform. Three critical principles in communicating information are (1) relating new information to what an audience already knows; (2) ordering the material in some serial progression that makes it easier for people to follow and relate the significant points; and (3) reinforcing the message and the response through a sensible amount of repetition, verbal emphasis, organization, and voice—all of which communicate importance, reward, punishment, or some other meaning. The final lesson to be gained from learning theory is that there appears to be a point of diminishing returns with all these devices; too much repetition can be as harmful as too little. This point of diminishing returns depends upon the specific and total communication circumstance.

The primary principles in informative speaking are clarity, interest, and organization. Methods of achieving clarity include illustration or example, analogy or comparison, statistics, testimony, and restatement. The factors that create or add interest are specificity, conflict, novelty, curiosity, immediacy, humor, and things of vital importance to the audience. Achieving psychologically sound organization requires (1) gaining *attention;* (2) preparing the audience through a preview or *overview;* (3) presenting the detailed *information;* and (4) *reviewing* the significant points for added reinforcement.

Teaching aids are a vital part of public speaking, particularly when the goal is clarity. Edgar Dale's cone of experience is a good model for classifying these aids in terms of *telling, showing,* and *doing,* and on the basis of audience involvement. The model helps us make decisions about our selection and use of audio-visual aids by grading them according to abstractness.

Some typical forms of graphs that a speaker might use are pictograms, bar graphs, area diagrams, and line graphs. Some typical forms of charts are organization charts, stream or tree charts, and tabular charts.

Demonstration is a special form of teaching aid for the speech student. The purpose of a demonstration is to show how a skill, procedure, process, or device is used so that the audience will find it easier to learn the skill or acquire the knowledge. A demonstration combines showing with telling. It appeals to several senses of the listener, reinforces the message, saves time, is more concrete than just telling, has dramatic appeal, and helps speakers remember their material and burn off nervous energy.

The practical rules for reducing the hazards of demonstrations all include planning in advance: (1) calculate the risks; (2) devise alternate procedures, including what you will say if something does go wrong; and (3) make practice runs to ensure that you can perform the demonstration.

The general rules for using all teaching aids are: (1) make sure your audience can see your aids, and (2) select the proper aids to meet the specific requirements of your subject, purpose, and audience.

Speech Communication Principles

1 Message senders are most effective when they arrange and select their material so as to utilize the knowledge and experience of their receivers. We learn by relating the known to the unknown.

2 People tend to understand and learn more readily when messages are arranged in some serial order.

3 Message reinforcement in the form of verbal, vocal, gesticulative, and organizational emphasis aids audience understanding.

4 An audience's *interest* or motivation to learn may significantly affect how much they remember.

5 The cone of experience (telling, showing, doing) allows us to select and evaluate audio-visual aids according to their level of abstractness.

6 A psychologically sound organization of an informative message should include (1) gaining *attention,* (2) preparing the audience through a preview or *overview,* (3) presenting the detailed *information,* and (4) *reviewing* the significant points for added reinforcement.

Specific Learning Outcomes

1 We should learn to make informative messages *clear* by relating new information to an audience's previous knowledge and experience (in other words, relating the known to the unknown).

2 We should learn to make informative messages *clear* by arranging messages in some serial order.

3 We should learn to make informative messages *clear* through the use of organization repetition, restatement, and reinforcement.

4 We should learn to make informative messages *clear* and more *interesting* through the use of illustration, analogy, statistics, and testimony.

5 We should learn to make informative messages *interesting* through the use of specificity, conflict, novelty, curiosity, immediacy, humor, factors vital to the audience, and figures of speech.

6 We should learn to make informative messages *clear* and *interesting* through the use of visual aids, specifically graphs and charts.

7 We should learn the purposes, planning, and special hazards of the demonstration speech.

8 We should learn to organize informational messages according to the learning sequence of *attention, overview, information,* and *review* (see model outlines in this chapter).

Communication Competencies

1 We should be able to prepare an intelligent, detailed two-to-three-page outline for a five-to-eight-minute speech to inform that meets the message preparation tests of chapters 6, 7, and 8.

2 In a speech to inform we should be able to prepare and effectively utilize visual aids of the graph and chart variety so that they meet the practical rules listed at the end of chapter 8.

3 We should be able to give a two-to-four-minute demonstration speech that is both clear and interesting to the audience and to the instructor.

4 We should be able to evaluate critically other students' use of forms of support for purposes of clarity and interest.

Study Projects and Tasks

1 Prepare a detailed two-to-three-page outline for a four-to-six-minute speech to inform that meets the message preparation tests of chapters 6, 7, and 8 (see model outlines in chapters 7 and 8).

2 Prepare visual aids to accompany a four-to-six-minute speech to inform that are designed to increase clarity and interest.

3 Prepare a three-to-four-minute speech to teach through demonstration that includes some audience participation and/or performance (for example, demonstrating knot tying, basic tennis shots, a dance step, crewel, basic golf, reading aloud, working a calculator, working a slide rule, timing an engine, sketching a landscape, a card trick, shooting dice, solving a puzzle, tying a bow tie, folding a flag, walking like a model). Offer a careful demonstration for your listeners to follow. Help them personally with any difficulties they may be having. Be specific about the items or steps of the process you want them to remember the most.

4 Prepare a one-to-two-minute demonstration of a simple but interesting process. The demonstration need not use audience performance, as does project 3.

5 Prepare an informative talk on your favorite hobby. Use visual aids and/or demonstration.

6 Practice evaluating your classmates critically by using the criteria suggested on the classroom rating scale in figure 8.19. Your instructor may wish to collect the forms, remove the evaluators' names, and feed back the information to the speakers.

7 Prepare an oral report or essay in which you attempt to prove or disprove any of the speech communication principles listed in this chapter.

8 Analyze speech manuscripts or editorials and find, if possible, one example of each of the following types of support: illustration, analogy, statistics, and testimony.

9 Analyze speech manuscripts or editorials and find, if possible, one example of each of the following ways of increasing interest: specificity, conflict, novelty, curiosity, immediacy, humor, vital factors, figures of speech.

10 Analyze speech manuscripts or editorials and find attempts at clarity through reinforcement.

11 Analyze speech manuscripts or editorials and discuss how the speaker or writer used the basic learning principles of (1) going from the known to the unknown, (2) serial order, and (3) reinforcement.

12 Design a visual aid for one of the speech outlines in Appendix B, and explain your reasons according to the principles discussed in this chapter.

Figure 8.19

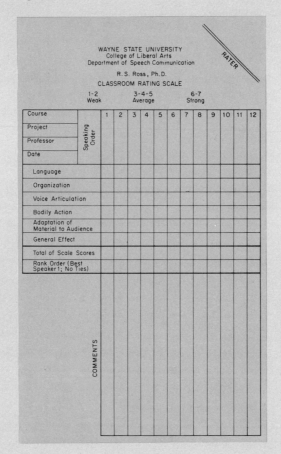

GENERAL LEARNING OUTCOMES

1 We should learn that every speech communication situation is a potential open forum and may include audience participation.

2 We should learn of our all-important responsibilities to the audience, the material covered, and the time requirements–responsibilities that apply despite interruptions.

3 We should learn how to deal with questions and interruptions in audience-participation situations.

4 We should learn the basic principles that apply to four standard special-occasion speeches.

5 We should learn the special preparation and techniques of speech adaptation necessary for the radio and television media.

an advanced course in algebra, which makes more sense if the teacher in the previous course covers *all* the preliminary material and does the job thoroughly. Our man pleaded sincerely for interruptions and he *got* them —some good, some bad, some ridiculous. He tried to react, answer, or comment on each equally. The result was that he was unfair to his audience collectively. The audience's evaluation of him reflected this. He covered only one-fourth of his material, and even this part was confused because of the virtual free-for-all participation. Imagine the problem faced by the next speaker!

Another situation in which you may find yourself is the more typical *open forum* after a speech. The problems indicated above all apply here—but perhaps to a lesser degree, because you have much better control of your time and you have probably covered the points you set out to cover. Whatever time is left is controlled by simply cutting off the questions. Life can be miserable, however, when you are given three hours and have only one hour's material. The situation is just as bad when you have no time for a promised question period.

The third typical audience situation is the *symposium forum*. Any discussion situation obviously requires one to participate with the *other* members of the group. However, a symposium forum usually allows one-third of the total time for questions from the general audience. Many convention programs are run this way. Once again, the rules and problems are similar to the two situations discussed above, except that a decision must often be made as to which participant should respond. The respondent must now consider both the audience and his or her fellow panel members. The size of the audience is again a key factor. If the audience is larger than was expected (say, 100 instead of 35), the moderator might have the panelists ask one another questions first, thereby assuring some intelligent questions. Furthermore, audience size alone may discourage members of the audience from asking questions.

General Principles

The *first* principle obviously ought to be,

> "Know your subject and audience."

If you know your subject and audience, you are in a position to apply the *second* principle,

> "Second-guess the situation."

Try to guess what areas of your subject are most vulnerable to questions, and try to predict what questions this particular audience will ask. *Third,*

> "Try sincerely to answer or at least react to all questions."

Consider and react courteously to even the irrelevant questions, and attempt, if necessary, to clarify or postpone the question. The *fourth* principle, and one that is very easy to overlook in your eagerness to meet the question asked, is

> "Consider carefully the rest of the audience."

You must try to satisfy not only the person asking the question, but the total audience as well. Otherwise, you might satisfy the statistician, for example, while thoroughly confusing everybody else. *Fifth,*

> "Do not feel or act as if you have to know everything or win every argument."

Finally,

> "Attempt to encourage good questions and audience participation."

It is very easy to discourage questions with even a slightly overbearing attitude. (However, it is possible to be so overbearing that the audience decides to interrogate you.)

People who assume leadership constantly have to be on guard not to intimidate others simply because of their position or rank. The colonel who follows the manual's advice and asks the cadets, "Are there any dumb questions?" is not apt to get many. But he knew that; that was why he said it! When such an attitude is *not* intended, it is even more tragic. A training director for a large corporation sincerely asked the trainees to comment on the meals during their three-week session. Before he made this request, however, he told some funny stories about the "idiot club" that had registered all kinds of silly complaints during the last session. Most of the complaints *were* silly and even funny. The training director did not mean to intimidate anyone, and the trainees did think the anecdotes were funny. Nevertheless, because of these remarks not a word was said about the meals, despite numerous private, bitter complaints about the food and the preselected menus! The tragic part is that not only did the director fail to receive accurate feedback, but also the lack of response by the trainees was taken as an indication of their satisfaction. This is a good example of how you can be 100 percent wrong. Worse, this unfortunate lack of communication can be reinforced and may become habit.

Rules for Answering Questions

Years ago at Purdue University, an audience of about four hundred students was listening to a famous philosopher speak. He did a creditable job for a person who came from a school whose catalogue did not list speech communication. At the close of the speech the chairman asked for questions from the audience. Most of the raised hands were in the first row, where the

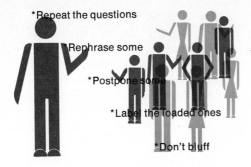

*Repeat the questions

*Rephrase some

*Postpone some

*Label the loaded ones

*Don't bluff

philosophy club had gathered. The speaker pointed to a hand in the first row, a mouth opened, and to those near the middle of the audience the question souded like this: "I should zzum ug ask hrump zud Hegel?" The speaker moved to the lectern, stroked his chin, and said, "A very good question." He then proceeded to give what was probably a very good answer. The problem was that most of the audience did not know the question because they had not *heard* it. The speaker handled three or four more questions in the same manner, the audience becoming frustrated, then restless, and finally rude in some cases as they started to leave.

repeat   *Repeat the question* is the first rule. This is a good idea even with smaller audiences, for although the members are in a position to hear, they may not be listening. Another serious aspect of the all-too-common error illustrated above is that people will attempt to reconstruct what the question must have been in terms of the answer. You can immediately see this as an invitation to confused communication. Counter-questions based on inaccurately reconstructed questions can really raise confusion to a high level.

You may hear a question that is asked in a loud, clear voice, but the wording is awkward or unclear. A famous army general was giving a speech at Ohio State University during the time of the Suez crisis. In the large audience were foreign students from all of the countries involved, including Eqypt, France, England, and Israel. One of these students took the general to task in perfectly clear and audible English, except that the question was long and complicated. The general said, "I know what you're getting at," and proceeded to answer for about ten minutes. As the general completed his answer, the foreign student leaped to his feet and proceeded to give another short speech, which said in effect, "But that's not what I asked." The general tried again, for five minutes this time, but still with no success. After one more unsuccessful attempt, a desperate general finally held up his hand and said, "Let's see if we can agree on what the question is." Sometimes it

rephrase   is necessary not only to repeat but also to *rephrase the question*. Along with rephrasing, one should always gain the approval of the questioner. Some ways of checking the adequacy of your restatement of the question are to ask the questioner if your phrasing is a fair statement of the question, to see if the person objects verbally. You do not always have to rephrase questions; do so only when it is necessary for clarity, and then always seek approval.

Some of the long, complicated questions discussed above deserve careful attention if they are relevant to the issue and if you are capable of giving some kind of answer or reaction in the time available. When, however, you receive questions that, long or short, are irrelevant, demand a highly technical or complex answer, or would consume all the open-forum time, you have a different kind of problem. Such questions can ruin an otherwise good speech. Though in principle you do not want to avoid questions, you also owe it to the rest of your audience to stay on the subject and to give more than one person a chance to ask a question. Let us **postpone** therefore formulate our third rule: *postpone the irrelevant, overly technical, or time-consuming questions.* Postpone these questions until after the official open-forum period or until the end of the period if you have time remaining. For interruptions this rule becomes more complex, for a person may ask a question that you had intended to cover later in the speech. In this situation you should most often delay the answer until you arrive at that point (for example, "Could I hold the answer to that for a few minutes? I will cover the issue a little later.") The problem is trying to remember the questions you may have postponed. One solution is to suggest that the person ask the question again, but after you have covered the point at hand.

The loaded question (see p. 315) is dangerous. People will sometimes deliberately ask the "Are you still beating your dog?" kind of question, but far more difficult are the questions that are unintentionally loaded. These are difficult to detect because they are often subtle and naive at the same time and are frequently asked by people who are not troublemakers by reputation. "Why is it that textbook writers have such insatiable egos?" an author was once asked. If you are a writer, try to answer that without **label loaded** condemning yourself! Thus, rule four is, *label a loaded question.* There are **questions** several ways to do this if you are lucky enough to detect such a question in time. The most effective way is to pause long enough for the audience to label it for you. An audience is often quick to chuckle if they see the speaker faced with a "heads I win, tails you lose" situation. Or the speaker could say frankly, "That's a loaded question." A more tactful way might be, "It looks like I'm in trouble no matter how I answer this." Another method is to ask the questioner to repeat the question. The audience will listen more closely and may label the loaded question for you, or the questioner may "unload" it. After you have successfully labeled or unloaded the question as courteously as possible, you should then attempt to answer. With the proper labels applied, the audience is not apt to be prejudiced by the question.

The surest way to get in trouble in an open-forum period is to try to **don't bluff** bluff your way through a question for which you honestly do not have a satisfactory answer. Once an audience senses that you are bluffing, you can expect them to ask more questions specifically on this bluff point. The solution is to know your subject thoroughly—but if you do not have an answer, say so right away and save yourself the embarrassment of being trapped later on. No speaker is expected to have all the answers to all the questions in the world. This rule, then, might simply be called the *"I don't know"* rule.

A graduate student once learned the preceding advice the hard way. The occasion was her final oral examination. The committee of examining professors was seated in a circle, ready to fire questions for the next two hours. The very first question was a highly theoretical and complex one that not even the members of the committee could answer adequately (if indeed it was answerable at all). The candidate, who was under great emotional pressure, felt that she simply had to answer the first question. She stumbled and fumbled for ten minutes, and a narrow-eyed committee then proceeded to ask increasingly specific questions on the same point. After another twenty minutes of torture, the candidate finally blurted, "I guess I just don't know the answer." The rejoinder from the chairman of the examining committee is worthy of a piece of marble: "We didn't expect you to answer the question, but we expected you to *know when you didn't know.* It is a wise person who knows when and what she doesn't know." The candidate was promptly failed.

However, you cannot escape the hard facts of life by simply saying, "I don't know." In some question-answer situations you may wish to say, "I don't know, but I have an opinion," or "I don't know, but I can answer in terms of my specialty." The point is that you should answer any question you are capable of answering and yet be honest enough to admit it when you cannot supply an answer.

GENERATING PARTICIPATION

In the general principles discussed earlier, the last suggestion was to encourage feedback and questions. We illustrated the dangers of letting an audience run off with your speech, as well as the dangers of unintentionally intimidating an audience to the point of no participation.

Your total speech personality affects the kind of communication climate in which you find yourself. In some cases, audiences just seem to spring into action. In other cases, even with very skilled and audience-sensitive speakers, they must be given the proper stimulus for participation. Here are several speakers' techniques that might be useful to you.

The Overhead Question

This is a direct question from the speaker or discussion leader to the entire audience. If no questions arise from the audience (or even if they do), you might say, "Let me ask this question in order to get a reaction from an intelligent Midwestern audience." The immediate problem is to make sure you choose a question that will cause a reaction, for if there is silence you may be worse off than before. Sometimes you can react to your own question in such a way as to promote participation. Consider carefully the wording of a few general overhead questions and expected reactions as a method of fostering participation.

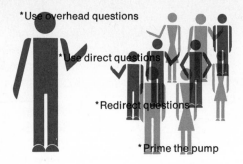

*Use overhead questions

*Use direct questions

*Redirect questions

*Prime the pump

The Direct Question

This technique is choosing a specific member of the audience and asking that person a direct question. This is often very effective if this individual is known to the rest of the audience or is in some special way qualified to answer. The size of your audience may present a problem, in that the audience may have difficulty seeing or otherwise determining who has been singled out. Classroom-size audiences or larger groups, if they meet regularly, respond well to this technique. You probably know many good teachers who make excellent use of the direct-question technique. Social and civic groups such as the Lions, Elks, Kiwanis, Knights of Columbus, and Rotary, whose members know one another, often make good use of direct questions.

Try not to call on the same person all the time, but do pick those individuals who are most apt to get participation started. Try to tailor the question directly to the individual chosen. The question should be relatively short and clear and should demand more than a simple yes or no answer—but if the situation is really desperate, you may have to settle for yes or no.

Suessmuth and Stengels suggest three types of questions:

Convergent—a question that brings together facts to form a fact or theory.
Divergent—a question that evokes interpretation, explanation, and translation.
Evaluative—a question that requires the listener to make judgments about the facts presented.[1]

The Redirected Question

This technique may also be called the reverse method or the relay method. In using the reverse technique you simply redirect a question to the person who asked it: "That's a very good question—how would you answer

[1]Patrick Suessmuth and Marit Stengels, "The Art of Asking Questions," *Training*, October 1974, pp. 46–50.

it?" In using the relay method you redirect the question to some other person: "A good question; let's see how Mrs. Wright would answer it." A third approach is to overhead the question to the whole audience.

As a general rule, do not redirect a question unless you yourself know at least a partial answer to it; an exception to this rule is a simple question of fact upon which you can freely admit ignorance. The story of the beginning teacher who redirected a tough question (to which he did not have the answer) to each individual of the class, only to find that it came right back to embarrass him, is not without foundation. A second suggestion is not to redirect so freely that you lose control of the situation.

Priming the Pump

This is the all-important technique of building questions into your speech. In the main, your questions or implied questions should develop your point, stimulate audience thinking, and, in general, attract interest and attention.

SPECIAL-OCCASION SPEECHES

All communication occasions are in a sense special, yet many occasions call for speeches that are surprisingly similar in form and style, if not in content. Speeches of introduction, for example, occur often enough, usually are governed by the same principles, and are so frequently unsuccessful that a further and more specific application of the speech and communication theory discussed previously is helpful. In addition to speeches of introduction, we will discuss the following special-occasion speeches: speeches of presentation, speeches of tribute and commemoration, after-dinner speeches, and adaptations of speech material to radio and television.

Speeches of Introduction

"I just now met our speaker, who is a friend of our chairman and a speaker on human relations. He teaches speech communication and should

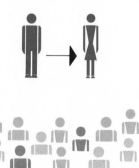

be a good example for all of you to follow. It gives me great pleasure to introduce Mr. James E. Mason."

How would you like to speak to a strange audience after that introduction? Attention was called to the speaker's oratory instead of his subject. It sounded as if the speaker were being foisted upon the group by a buddy in the organization. It was evident that the introducer in this case did not know anything about the speaker and was not particularly interested in "human relations." The only good point about the introduction was its briefness!

Even more devastating as a speech of introduction is a twenty-minute nightmare of poor jokes, trite language, and overly dramatic praise of the speaker's virtues. This is especially cruel when the speaker intends to speak for only thirty minutes. What makes the situation really unfortunate is that the introducer is usually a well-intentioned, sincere, and genuinely nice person who is simply unskilled at introducing people.

It is very difficult for speakers in this situation to recover their poise, because ordinarily they cannot lash back as they might like to do. However, on one occasion a speaker evened the score. A young instructor was introducing a distinguished professor to a group of university personnel who knew the professor. The instructor proceeded to give a speech that explained every accomplishment of the professor and every entry on his bibliography. It was embarrassing to everyone and almost began to sound like satire because of the sheer volume of detail. His final remark was, "Professor, have I overlooked anything?" The obviously irritated professor rose to his feet, glowered at the introducer, and said, "I caught a big fish once!"

What, then, are some principles and rules of introduction that you can apply in order to avoid making life intolerable for the speaker? Remember that the major purpose of a speech of introduction is to create harmony between the speaker and the audience, which in turn creates a desire for the audience to want to hear the speaker's subject. You want the audience to like and respect the speaker, and to be inclined to listen attentively. Toward this end, follow these principles:

1 *Make sure you know something about the speaker and the subject.* If you can, consult the speaker before the meeting; see if there are some things the speaker prefers to be said or not said.
2 *Be brief but adequate.* Make sure that enough is said about the speaker and the subject to achieve a harmony and advance the speaker's credibility. Do not overplay *your* role, for you are not the main speaker. Remember that your job is to focus attention on the speaker and the subject. The length of the speech of introduction is also related to how well the speaker is known to the audience. You might introduce our president simply and adequately with, "Ladies and gentlemen: the President of the United States." Seldom should a speech of introduction run more than three or four minutes.
3 *Stress the importance and appropriateness of the speaker's subject.* However, take care not to give the main speech! Do not explain the speaker's qualifications

to the point of neglecting to create curiosity and attention for the subject.

4 *Speak with sincerity and enthusiasm.* If you are not familiar with the speaker or the subject or are simply not interested, have someone else make the introduction. Do not affect enthusiasm; do not overpraise; do not stress the speaker's "oratorical" skills; do not use trite language. In general, speak about accomplishments rather than about virtues.

5 *Pay attention to the speaker.* After you have finished your speech of introduction, making sure that you announced the speaker's name and subject clearly and correctly, be a model listener. This suggests that the audience also be good listeners. A gabby or hyperactive introducer can ruin the audience's attention and speaker-audience harmony. Mark Twain lost his patience with awkward introductions, and for a while he insisted that he not be introduced at all.

An excellent example of a speech of introduction is this speech by Professor Glenn R. Capp, in which he introduced Dr. A. Q. Sartain to the Baylor University chapter of the American Association of University Professors.

"If a man be endowed with a generous mind, this is the best kind of nobility." This statement by Plato characterizes our speaker for tonight. During the more than twenty years that I have known Dr. Sartain, I have become increasingly impressed not only with his generous and penetrating mind, but with his kindly spirit.

A risk that one runs in introducing a cherished friend is that he may deal in extravagant statements. I find myself in somewhat of a paradoxical situation this evening because a simple factual recital of the training, accomplishment, and contributions of Dr. Sartain appears to be overstatement. I am tempted to dwell at length on such matters as these:

(1) His writings, which include co-authorship of a recent textbook, *Human Behavior in Industry,* his forthcoming textbook to be published by Prentice-Hall, and numerous articles in professional journals.

(2) His important positions, which he has held at Southern Methodist University, where he was first the Director of Forensics, later Professor of Psychology, and now is chairman of the Department of Personnel Administration. He also has more than a passing interest in Baylor University, having taught recently as visiting professor in our summer session.

(3) His membership in important organizations. For example, he served recently as president of the Southern Methodist University chapter of the American Association of University Professors. He is president of the Southwestern Psychological Association, a fellow of the American Psychological Association, and a member of the Association for the Advancement of Science.

Rather than dwelling on these matters, may I say simply that I congratulate you for securing Dr. Sartain for this occasion. I have been impressed with the excellence of his forensic teams, but even more with him as a man—his pleasant disposition, his sense of fair play, his high ethical standards, and his ability as a scholar. I present to you my friend and the friend of all teachers—Dr. A. Q. Sartain.[2]

Speeches of Presentation and Acceptance

"Thanks for holding down the other end of the log" was engraved on a simple brass plaque and signed by four outstanding graduate students. The students presented this award by simply placing it on the center of a professor's desk before he retired from a major university. With this close little group, a speech, a banquet, even a meeting between professor and students was unnecessary. The recipient was honored and felt that his efforts were appreciated and recognized. Most often, however, a speech is called for when an award is given. The major purpose of such a speech should be to show honor, appreciation, and recognition.

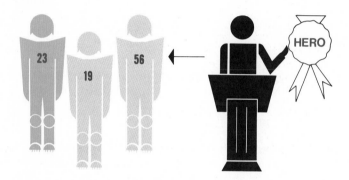

Good will and appreciation can be transmitted under considerably different circumstances. A five-minute formal speech read from a manuscript before a banquet audience of 300 people concluded: "For these and his many other achievements, it was unanimously agreed by the Executive Faculty of the Marquette University School of Speech that Dr. James W. Cleary was richly deserving of our Distinguished Alumni Award in the field of Speech Education." The point is that presentations vary widely. The size of the group, the nature of the award, and the occasion all determine how much is said and how formally it is said.

Here are two general principles for most speeches of presentation:

1 *The speech should sincerely communicate honor, appreciation, and recognition.* It should not stray from the facts; if it does, it becomes insincere. Do not overpraise, overstate, or overemotionalize. Review the recipient's accomplishments honestly.

[2]Glenn R. Capp, *How to Communicate Orally,* 2nd ed. (Englewood Cliffs, N.J.: Prentice-Hall, Inc., 1966), p. 351.

2 *Adapt your speech to the occasion and the award.* For annual and routine service awards, only a short, straightforward word of congratulation may be necessary, even on a formal occasion. When many similar awards are given, as with forensic-contest winners, one short speech can often show honor and recognition for the entire group, each of whom might then step forward individually to receive a medal. This is not to say that a brief speech should be a less sincere speech. Make sure the speaker selected to present an award is thoroughly familiar with the kind of effort and achievement involved.

On some award occasions, the speaker may also have to consider the donor of the gift. A university giving an honorary degree or a distinguished alumni award deserves some recognition and reflected glory. This is also true of business and industrial concerns who honor long-time employees. In situations in which the award may have a history or be unusual in some other way, a short description of these facts may be in order.

An acceptance speech should measure up to the total communication situation, and especially to the expectations of those making the award. If you are representing a group or organization, make this clear and explain briefly why the award is appreciated by the others as well as yourself. If appropriate, you may wish to mention individuals and their specific efforts or merits related to the award. If the award is a personal gift, your response might vary from a simple but sincere "thank you" to a short statement of gratitude. So much depends on the nature of the award, the expectations of those honoring you, the total communication climate—and, of course, your own feelings.

As an example of a speech of presentation, consider this volume of tributes paid to Dr. J. W. Crabtree, Secretary Emeritus and founder of the National Education Association, by W. E. Givens.

Dr. Crabtree's record speaks more eloquently than any speaker could. He came to Washington in 1917 and started the office of the National Education Association in one room of his house, with one secretary. On January 1, 1935, when he became Secretary Emeritus, he left a modern, seven-story building on the "Street of the Presidents" six squares from the White House in our nation's capital, and he left there a loyal office force of one hundred and forty-five people, all of whom love and respect him.

He started in 1922 the life membership movement that put up that great building, and that has grown from that time until tonight our great national Association has some 5400 life members scattered throughout this great nation.

Miss Hale read you a few of the letters that he has received. It is my pleasure on behalf of his friends throughout the nation to present to him from you a beautiful volume of some seven hundred letters from his friends, bound in a beautiful binding presented by the publishers of our *Journal* as a compliment to Mr. Crabtree. It is a great pleasure to present this volume to Mr.

Crabtree tonight and to assure you all that it is a great honor to be the successor of such a man.[3]

Speeches of Tribute and Commemoration

This form of special-occasion speaking includes eulogies, anniversary addresses, dedicatory speeches, and some nominating speeches. The *eulogy* is typically a speech of tribute upon the death of a person or shortly thereafter. It may also apply to the anniversary of the birth or great moments in the life of a historical figure such as Lincoln or Washington. *Anniversary* speeches celebrate an event, a person, or an institution. *Dedicatory* speeches are usually tributes; buildings, monuments, ships, libraries, and other things are generally dedicated to the honor of some outstanding personality, institution, or group of people. In some *nominating* speeches, it is the practice to pay tribute to the nominee as a way of proving his or her qualifications for office. Since most organizations now use nominating committees, nominations are made with less oral flourish.

All commemorative speeches are tributes to men or women, their ideals, and their achievements. Their purpose is to gain or increase respect, emulation, and appreciation for the people being honored and their impact upon society and its institutions.

You can organize your speech according to the history of the person or institution being commemorated. Or if time is short and the history is generally well known, you can concentrate on selected aspects of personality, achievement, or impact on society.

Here are three general rules for most tributes and commemorative speeches:

1 *Develop a sensitive understanding about the subject.* To deliver a funeral oration about a stranger would be awkward and embarrassing, if not disrespectful. Make sure you have *more* than just the immediate facts about the person, occasion, memorial, or building being commemorated. Try to capture the personality of the subject in both large and small incidents that

[3] W. Hayes Yeager, *Effective Speaking for Every Occasion* (Englewood Cliffs, N.J.: Prentice-Hall, Inc., 1940), p. 159.

typify the person's virtues or outlook on life. Know the outstanding achievements well, but do not lose sight of the personality.

2 *Be objective and fair to the facts.* Perhaps we should not speak ill of the dead, but neither should we be totally dishonest. To eulogize a lazy, intemperate, hardheaded old lady as "this kind, generous model of moral simplicity" is apt to incite outright laughter and do a disservice to whatever virtues and respect the woman did have. No person is perfect in every way. Washington was not a model tactician at Valley Forge; young Lincoln was defeated so many times at the polls that his political future was in real danger. You will want to magnify and concentrate on the subject's virtues and achievements, but let the person be human.

3 *Use a style of language and delivery that is in keeping with the occasion.* Commemorative occasions often demand a style that is slightly more elevated than the style generally prescribed in this book. The expectations audiences have of a speaker in a church or cemetery are somehow special. In paying tribute to someone tragically killed, one can hardly escape the effects of voice and the measured cadence that help express the grief, reverence, and solemnity of the occasion. There are many happy anniversaries, dedications, and tributes, on the other hand, and these call for a different style. Most commemorative speeches demand an element of elevated style at some point during the speech.

The abridged model that follows helps illustrate this point. It was delivered on the floor of the United States Senate by Senator Everett Dirksen after President Kennedy's assassination. A formal resolution was read, and Senator Dirksen was then recognized.

MR. DIRKSEN: Mr. President, the memory of John Fitzgerald Kennedy lingers in this forum of the people. Here we knew his vigorous tread, his flashing smile, his ready wit, his keen mind, his zest for adventure. Here with quiet grief we mourn his departure. Here we shall remember him best as a colleague whose star of public service is indelibly inscribed on the roll of the U.S. Senate.

And here the eternal question confronts and confounds us. Why must it be? Why must the life of an amiable, friendly, aggressive young man, moved only by high motives, lighted on his way by high hopes, guided by broad plans, impelled by understanding and vision, be brought to an untimely end with his labors unfinished? And why, in a free land, untouched by the heel of dictatorship and oppression, where the humblest citizen may freely utter his grievances, must that life be cut short by an evil instrument, moved by malice, frustration, and hate? This is the incredible thing which leaves us bewildered and perplexed.

On the tables of memory, we who knew him well as a friend and colleague can well inscribe this sentiment:

"Senator John Fitzgerald Kennedy, who became the 35th President of the United States—young, vigorous, aggressive, and scholarly—one who estimated the need of his country and the world and sought to fulfill that need—one who was wedded to peace and vigorously sought this greatest of all goals of mankind—one who sensed how catastrophic nuclear conflict could be and sought a realistic course to avert it—one who sensed the danger that lurked in a continuing inequality in our land and sought a rational and durable solution—one to whom the phrase 'the national interest' was more than a string of words—one who could disagree without vindictiveness—one who believed that the expansion of the enjoyment of living by all people was an achievable goal—one who believed that each generation must contribute its best to the fulfillment of the American dream."

The *te deums* which will be sung this day may be wafted away by the evening breeze which caresses the last resting place of those who served the Republic, but here in this Chamber where he served and prepared for higher responsibility, the memory of John Fitzgerald Kennedy will long linger to nourish the faith of all who serve that same great land.[4]

The combination of appreciation and eulogy is illustrated by the touching speech that Tom Hughes gave in tribute to his brother, football player Chuck Hughes, who died of a heart attack while playing for the Detroit Lions. All of the Lions were at the funeral in San Antonio. Tom gathered the Lions around him and spoke.

Words cannot express the gratitude for you that I now hold in my heart. Sunday you were names. Today you are and always will be in my heart and the hearts of all of those that I hold dear. The love we have for Chuck, I now feel, was shown by you, the Detroit Lions.

This to me is the finest tribute you could ever bestow on him. I have on numerous occasions heard that the Lions are a team of class. These past three days you have shown it. Please try to continue this. You strike me, an outsider really, as being a tightly knit family. My personal family is this way too.

Please don't let this tragedy spoil the things that make you stand out so prominently. Chuck died doing the one thing he wanted to do for such a long time. It was his life.

I'd prefer it, and so would he, that he died on the field, rather than in some other tragic way. Forget the tragedy of Sunday and remember him as the man you knew personally. He'd like that. He gave his all and I know that if he had to die he would tell you, losing is the tragedy. Play it to win.[5]

After-dinner Speeches

Today's after-dinner speeches are not what they invariably used to be. In our day, a banquet may be the setting for a very serious and profound speech to persuade or inform. All the lessons discussed previously apply to these speeches, as they would to any other. There is, however, a tradition of

[4]*Congressional Record,* 1964, pp. 21, 596–97.
[5]Quoted by Jerry Green in the *Detroit News,* October 28, 1971, p. 5D.

after-dinner speaking that is rather special in our society. This is the good-humored, lighthearted, genial situation whose major purpose is a sociable dinner and relaxed enjoyment. This is the type of speech situation with which we are concerned here. The audience has been made content with good food and is tolerant and benevolent. It is not in a mood for argumentation, moral reevaluation, or complex issues. The speeches with which we are concerned here are typically brief, light, and humorous. They are not easy speeches to deliver; for some, they appear almost impossible. You need not be a professional jokester; indeed, unless you tell a good, relevant joke especially well, you are better advised to use your humor in another vein. Some general principles to guide you are as follows:

1 *Select suitable topics.* "Great Snafus of the Civil War" was a delightful after-dinner speech at a history buff's banquet recently. The group was, of course, interested in the deeper aspects of the war, but not at this particular moment. Look on the lighter side of issues for your subjects. If you are going to talk about teachers, concentrate on their eccentricities, for example.
2 *Be good-humored.* The diners are full of food and full of good will. Heighten the fellowship. Avoid bitter argument.
3 *Adapt to the audience.* A joke or a story is often funny to one group and not to another. More important, it may be offensive. Make sure you know the audience, the occasion, and the program for the evening. Capitalize on this information; tie your good humor appropriately and directly to your specific audience. A speech for all occasions is seldom successful.
4 *Be clear and brief.* Avoid complex organization; stick to one or two obvious main points. Do not use complicated forms of support. Use examples and humorous illustrations. Above all, be brief. Attention spans are often short after a long day and a pleasant dinner. Plan several cutoff points in your speech to be used should the whole program take more time than expected or should the audience seem unusually restless or quiet (asleep).

ADAPTING MATERIAL TO RADIO AND TELEVISION

Over 95 percent of our households have television sets today. Seventy million Americans heard and saw the first Kennedy-Nixon debate in 1960. The space shots and President Nixon's visit to China attracted over 100

million viewers. In 1863 only 20,000 Americans heard Lincoln at Gettysburg. In 1978, over 75 million Americans and countless foreign fight fans saw or heard Muhammed Ali regain the heavyweight boxing crown. Never before has a speaker had access to such a potentially vast audience. Never before could a speaker be ignored more easily.

Big business has taken the media adaptation problem seriously. Here is an example:

> The chief executive of a Detroit corporation is being grilled in a Chicago TV studio. He's used to asking tough questions and watching subordinates squirm. Now the hot lights and cameras are on him and an obnoxious reporter is asking the probing questions. About his company's energy policies. Live.
>
> The beleaguered executive answers a question and blunders into a trap. The questions don't let him tell his side of the story. He's beginning to sweat.
>
> He slumps in his chair, then cranes his neck to peer at the camera behind him. Where is that red light they told him about? Oh, there it is. Why is the stage manager making those weird hand signals? What is the fool reporter saying now?
>
> He grimly answers the final question, knowing he has not excelled.
>
> The interview is over and he stumbles off the set to look at the videotape of this fiasco. It could have been a bitter moment; it wasn't. But the interview was a setup. It was arranged by a major ad agency in its own TV studio to prepare the client for an appearance on a national public-affairs TV show.[6]

Much of this training is obviously related to other chapters in this book, but red lights, hot lights, and weird hand signals are the gist of this short passage. General Motors Corporation has 680 people receiving similar training. One oil company has eighteen different groups in class. Public utilities are interested in helping their representatives look and sound good on the media.

[6] Yvonne Petrie, *Detroit News,* October 16, 1977, p. 1G.

Although it is the point of view of this book that the same basic oral speech and communication processes and skills apply in principle to all media and situations, there are some practical differences when dealing with the mass media, whether in the modern classroom or in your local radio or television station. Radio and TV are part of the modern speech communication scene.

Apart from the special interview problems described earlier and the adaptation problems to be discussed shortly, the radio and TV media have marvelous advantages. In addition to potentially giant audiences, a speaker may be free of live audience interruptions such as questions, heckling, movement, falling chairs, side conversations, and the like. Through close-up TV camera work, one can show small objects and visual aids that would be impossible to present in regular speech situations. Emphasis and mood can be varied with dramatic effect as the various cameras take close-up shots and then more distant ones. The viewing screen can be divided so that you can simultaneously and selectively compare or emphasize various objects or concepts relevant to your message. Audio or video-taping for future use gives you the very important advantage of seeing how you appear to the audience; you have the opportunity to make changes, based on this appearance. The mass media can create an intimacy that is often overlooked—the kind of person-to-person communication that is so very difficult with really large audiences in typical platform speech situations. We are only now learning how to make use of the many instructional and educational advantages of radio and TV.

It is not the purpose of this section to explain the engineering, the production, and the more complicated techniques of radio and television performance. Instead, we shall explain some of the essential differences between platform speaking and the use of microphones and cameras, and suggest methods of adapting your communication to these differences.

Probably the most difficult problem for a good platform speaker on radio or television is the *lack of feedback* from the audience; except for occasional studio audiences, the listeners are unseen and unheard. Truly sensitive platform speakers constantly check their audience for signs of fatigue, misunderstanding, confusion, or approval, and they pace their rate, volume, and vocabulary accordingly. A radio studio can be a lonely place. A television studio has a few more technicians and a monitor, which allows you to see yourself, but still no important listener feedback.

The next important difference for a good platform speaker is the great number of mechanical and technical *distractions and limitations.* This is much more of a problem on television than on the radio because cameras and lights, as well as microphones, call for more cues, more technicians, and more prearranged signals.

If you are the courageous type who moves a great deal on the platform, you will quickly find yourself in trouble with the producer, the director, and just about everyone else working a TV show; your movement will cause you to be off camera, off mike, or both. The microphones of today are versatile and are more adaptable to movement than the microphones of a few years ago, but the camera is still an enemy to the amateur. Often, two or more cameras are operating, and you talk to the camera that has its little red tally light on. TV cameras move quickly and silently, and a momentary glance at your notes or time cues is long enough for the evil eye to appear suddenly right in front of you, so close that you can see yourself reflected in the lens—that is, if the flood lights have not blinded you. Even more frightening is the modern zoom lens that enables a camera to secretly inspect your ear, or whatever, at a distance! These mechanical headaches are mentioned here merely to convince you to inspect the scene and take advantage of any preshow rehearsals. These actions will help acquaint you with some of these problems and prevent you from being caught flat-footed or open-mouthed while on the air.

If this is not enough to chill the bones of a speaker, there is one more critical operating difference. Despite the large and diverse broadcast audiences available, they are not assembled in large halls in the manner of a great audience listening to a famed orator. They are seated individually, sometimes within a few feet of your face. They are subject to numerous distractions and are free from the restraints of a large hall. A few moments of boredom may cause them to be less attentive.

In addition, sensitive microphones may increase "normal" projection, force, and volume to such an extent that they detract from your oral style. A teacher once had a radio announcer in class who had difficulty adjusting to a regular classroom audience. He spoke in a beautiful, intimate voice as if he were on mike; consequently, many in the room could not hear him. He explained that if he projected and used the suggested platform manner while on microphone, he would soon be out of a job. And he was right. What, then, are some guidelines for adapting your speeches and general communications to the special characteristics of the radio and television media?

Guidelines

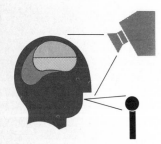

1 *Consider the advantages of microphone and camera*. Utilize the variety of camera shots available for presentation of visual aids, for emphasis, or for mood. Let the producer and director help you improve your presentation. Use the monitor to see how you appear to others.

2 *Prepare yourself for a lack of audience feedback*. Determine your most likely audience in advance, and adapt to them. Try your speech on live audiences of one or two individuals so that you have a basis for imagining realistic feedback during air time.

3 *Accept the differences and limitations of the microphone and camera*. Limit your movements and body action to the range of the equipment. Visualize a small conversational audience rather than a vast multitude assembled in one location. Limit your use of voice and style accordingly. Check your dress and your grooming, particularly for television close-ups.

4 *Learn to expect and live with mechanical distractions*. Observe a show. Re-

hearse on the set and learn the cues. Watch the producer, director, or engineer for cues. If you are not sure who is who, ask. If you are on television, follow the camera with the red tally light on. Look right into the camera. Check the monitor occasionally for feedback on yourself. Are you inanimate, leaning to one side, grinning? Wear cool clothes; the lights are hot.

5 *Prepare your speech material carefully.* Time is a major concern. Time your material until it is exactly the right length. Write time cues for yourself in the margins of your script. Prepare time fillers in advance; select portions that you can cut in order to save time. Organize simply so that these time adjustments can be made without completely baffling the audience. Remember that despite all the headaches and crises discussed in this section, it is your message that really counts. In the final analysis, this is true in all communication situations. Do not let the medium become the message!

9 SUMMING UP

One of the most elementary mistakes a speaker can make is to assume that everyone has heard and understood the question asked. Listening to answers without knowing the question is the height of frustration. Every speech has potential audience participation, most often in the form of questions, comments, or objections. You should calculate the risk of being interrupted or even heckled. Unreasonable questions and interruptions have ruined some speeches. The speaker has to control audience participation so as to do justice to the audience, the material to be covered, and the time restrictions. Typical audience-participation situations include open forums, symposium forums, instructing situations, and group discussion before an audience.

Some general principles of speaking in an audience-participation situation are:

1 Know your subject and audience.
2 Second-guess the situation.
3 Try to answer or at least react to all questions.
4 Consider the total audience.
5 Do not grant opposing arguments reluctantly.
6 Generally encourage questions.

Specific rules for answering questions are as follows:

1 Repeat the question.
2 When necessary, rephrase the question.
3 Postpone irrelevant or overly complicated questions.
4 Label loaded questions.
5 Don't bluff, instead, say "I don't know."

To help generate audience participation, you may use the *overhead technique*—a question from the speaker to the total audience. You may ask a *direct question* of a specific member of the audience. You may use the *redirect* technique, which is reversing or relaying the question. In reversing, you redirect the question to the person who asked it; in relaying, you redirect it to some other person. You are also counseled to *prime the pump*—to build questions into the formal part of your speech.

In the participation part of your speech, try not to call on the same person all the time; try to tailor your questions directly to the audience or to the individual you choose; keep your overhead or direct questions short, clear, and free of yes-or-no answers. In the main, your questions or implied questions should develop your point, stimulate audience thinking, and, in general, obtain attention and interest.

All communication is in a sense special, yet many occasions call for speeches that are surprisingly similar in form and style. Special-occasion speaking is mainly introductions, presentations, tributes and commemorations, after-dinner speeches, and adaptations of speech material to radio and television.

The major purpose of a speech of introduction is to create harmony between speaker and audience, which makes the audience want to hear about the speaker's subject. Toward this end, (1) make sure that you know something about the speaker and the subject; (2) be brief but adequate; (3) stress the importance and appropriateness of the speaker's subject; (4) speak with sincerity and enthusiasm; and (5) pay attention to the speaker after he or she starts to speak.

The two general principles for most speeches of presentation are: (1) the speech should sincerely communicate honor, appreciation, and recognition; (2) the speech should be adapted to the specific occasion and to the award. An acceptance speech should measure up to the total communication situation and especially to the expectations of those making the award.

Speeches of tribute and commemoration include eulogies, anniversary addresses, dedicatory speeches, and some nominating speeches. The purpose of all commemorative speeches is to gain or increase respect, emulation, and appreciation for the people being honored and their impact upon society and its institutions. The key topics on which to concentrate are the subject's personality, achievement, and impact on society. Three general rules are to (1) develop a sensitive understanding of the subject; (2) be objective and fair to the facts; and (3) utilize a style of language and delivery in keeping with the occasion.

The after-dinner speeches with which we are concerned are made in a good-humored, lighthearted, genial situation whose major purpose is a sociable dinner and relaxed enjoyment. These speeches should be brief, light, and humorous. Some principles to follow are: (1) select suitable topics; (2) be genuinely good-humored; (3) adapt to the specific audience; and (4) be clear and brief.

Some guidelines for adapting your speeches and general communications to the special characteristics of the radio and television media are as follows: (1) consider the advantages of the microphone and camera; (2) prepare yourself for a lack of audience feedback; (3) accept the differences and limitations of the microphone and camera; (4) learn to expect and live with technical distractions; and (5) prepare and carefully time your speech material in order to aid your adaptation of it to the medium involved. Remember, the message is still the most important part of any speech.

Speech Communication Principles

1 Attempting to evaluate an answer without knowing the question is the height of frustration for most listeners.

2 A speaker must control audience participation in such a way as to do justice to the audience, the material to be covered, and the time restrictions.

3 Audience size alone may discourage members from asking questions.

4 "Priming the pump"—building questions into your speech—will help generate audience participation.

5 We are better equipped to generate and deal with questions and interruptions if we know the subject and audience, second-guess the situation, try to react to all questions, consider the whole audience, grant points readily when necessary, and encourage participation.

6 We are apt to be more successful in audience-participation situations if we repeat the questions; when necessary, rephrase the questions; postpone irrelevant or overly complicated questions; label loaded questions; and say "I don't know" instead of trying to bluff.

7 The successful speech of introduction creates harmony between the speaker and the audience, which in turn creates a desire for the audience to want to hear about the subject.

8 A good speech of introduction is a form of pragmatic, ethical proof, which advances the speaker's credibility.

9 Successful speeches of presentation communicate honor, appreciation, and recognition, and are closely adapted to the occasion and the award.

10 Successful commemorative speeches pay tribute to persons (or institutions), their

ideals, and their achievements to increase emulation of, and respect and appreciation for the recipient.

11 The traditional after-dinner speech is brief, light, and humorous. It avoids argumentation, moral reevaluation, and complex issues.

12 Except for practical differences, basic oral speech and communication processes, skills, and principles apply to radio and television.

13 Successful adaptation to radio and television includes preparing yourself for mechanical distractions, an absence of or a different kind of feedback, and rigid time limits.

Specific Learning Outcomes

1 We should learn the principles of general preparation for audience-participation situations.

2 We should learn the specific rules for answering questions originating from the audience.

3 We should learn the general techniques for generating audience participation.

4 We should learn that special accommodations are necessary for participation by really large audiences (roughly 100 persons or more).

5 We should learn the major purpose, general principles, and specific rules of speeches of introduction, speeches of presentation, speeches of tribute or commemoration, and after-dinner speeches.

6 We should learn the specific guidelines for adapting speeches and general communication to the special characteristics of microphone and camera (especially to television).

Communication Competencies

1 As speakers, we should be able to stay in control of an audience-participation situation when under fire from a group of twenty or more during the course of a five-to-eight-minute, open-forum speech.

2 We should be able to stay in control and help generate audience participation in a five-to-eight-minute, interrupted speech.

3 We should be able to apply the five basic rules for handling questions in any audience-participation situation.

4 We should be able to anticipate both obvious and subtle questions about our messages.

5 We should be able to write and deliver a successful one-to-two-minute speech of introduction that follows all the principles and rules presented in this chapter.

6 We should be able to write and deliver a successful one-to-two-minute speech of presentation (or acceptance) that follows all the principles and rules presented in this chapter.

7 We should be able to write and deliver a successful one-to-two-minute speech of tribute or commemoration that follows all the principles and rules described in this chapter.

8 We should be able to write and deliver a two-to-four-minute, after-dinner speech that follows the suggestions in this chapter.

9 We should be able to deliver a one-to-three-minute speech or participate in a discussion while on microphone and camera, without panic or confusion.

Study Projects and Tasks

1 Prepare a four-to-five-minute persuasive speech that will be followed by a three-to-four-minute open forum. Remember to stay in control by following the principles, rules, and suggestions in this chapter.

2 Prepare a six-to-eight-minute, persuasive speech in which you invite interruptions. Control the interruptions in such a way that you cover the material in your outline and stay absolutely within your time limit (eight minutes).

3 Observe an open forum or interrupted speech episode in person or on radio or television. Evaluate how well the participants follow the principles and rules described in this chapter. Be especially alert to the five rules for answering questions.

4 Prepare an informative or instructional four-to-six-minute speech in which you attempt to generate audience participation. Use the overhead, direct, and redirect questions. Make sure you cover your material and stay within the minimum and maximum time limits.

5 Assume you have just spoken to your classmates on a topic that is currently in the news. Now prepare for a two-to-three-minute open forum. Anticipate the key questions, and give some thought to their answers. Remember to follow the five basic rules for answering questions.

6 Prepare a one-to-two-minute speech of introduction for a student speaker from your class. Interview the person thoroughly and follow the rules suggested in this chapter.

7 Prepare a one-to-two-minute speech of introduction (in written form) for some well-known celebrity. Assume the audience is your class. You may make up some of the details for the purposes of the exercise.

8 Prepare a one-to-two-minute speech of presentation to a real or hypothetical person of your choice. The gift or award may also be hypothetical (athlete of the year, dad of the year, most valuable player, recipient of an honorary degree, and so forth).

9 Prepare a one-to-two-minute speech of tribute or commemoration to an institution, organization, or person of your choice. Make it sensitive and sincere. See the illustrations in this chapter for ideas, and consider the various types of tributes and commemorative speeches (eulogies, anniversary addresses, dedicatory speeches, and nominating speeches).

10 Prepare a two-to-four-minute, after-dinner speech that is truly good-humored, relaxed, and fun. Try your hand at a joke or two.

11 Prepare to do project 1, 2, or 3 above on radio or television. Check with your instructor about trying it out in whatever laboratory or studio facilities are available.

12 Prepare for a five-to-ten-minute, problem-solving discussion (see the study projects in chapter 14) that will be radio- or television-recorded. Prepare as for project 5 above.

13 Watch a live television show and try to guess what kind of technical distractions, signals, and cues are being used and what effect they are having upon the message of the sender.

14 If possible, observe a live television show from behind the camera (in the studio) and write a two-page report on the influence of technology on the participants and their messages. What advice would you give a person about to go on camera for the first time?

GENERAL LEARNING OUTCOMES

1 We should learn about the nature of human emotion and its relation to confidence.

2 We should learn the basic principles of reducing and controlling speech fright.

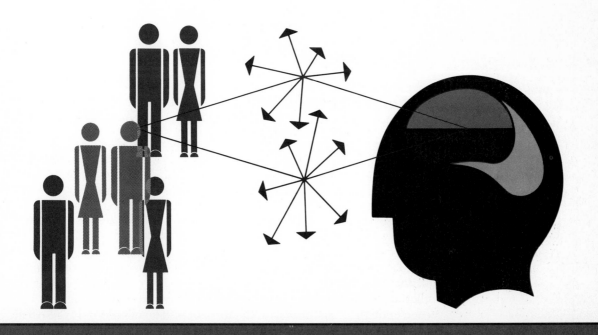

emotion
and confidence

Americans have some degree of fear of many different things. A sample of 2,543 adults rank ordered a list of fears as follows:

1	Speaking before a group	40.6%
2	Height	32.0
3	Insects and bugs	22.1
4	Financial problems	22.0
5	Deep water	21.5
6	Sickness	18.8
7	Death	18.7
8	Flying	18.3
9	Loneliness	13.6
10	Dogs	11.2
11	Driving or riding in a car	8.8
12	Darkness	7.9
13	Elevators	7.6
14	Escalators	4.8[1]

It is interesting that 40.6 percent had "some degree of fear" about "speaking before a group." The researchers comment on this as follows:

> About 46% of women have this fear, while 36% of men indicate some concern. There is little difference by age, but people in the $15,000 plus income group seem somewhat less concerned about public speaking. The more education a person has, the less likely he is to fear addressing a group. People living in the southern part of the United States seem to have the greatest fear while those in the northeast seem less concerned.[2]

Beginning speech-communication students also consider this a problem. Surveys indicate that 60 to 75 percent of a class may admit that they are bothered by "nervousness in speaking." Twenty-five percent may be concerned enough to ask for help in the form of instructor conferences, specific reading assignments, or desensitization (exercises that help ease speech fright). Most of this is typical, if not always normal. Much of it is temporary and based upon one's expectations of anxiety in speaking situations.[3] Most of you will find, other things being equal, that the more formal the audience or the situation the more speech fright there is (or what has been called stage fright).

[1] "What Are Americans Afraid Of?" *The Bruskin Report* (New Brunswick, N.J.: R. H. Bruskin Associates, July 1973), p. 1.

[2] *Ibid.*

[3] William T. Page, "The Development of a Test to Measure Anticipated Communicative Anxiety," in *Bibliographic Annual in Speech Communication,* ed. Ned A. Shearer (New York: Speech Communication Association, 1971), p. 99.

Psychologists and speech communication scholars stress the difference between a general proneness to anxiety and a kind of particular anxiety of the moment.[4] We are most interested in the latter type in public speaking and in small-group communication. The level of anxiety and the kinds of experience that cause it may vary in conversation, small groups, and public-speaking situations. When a pattern of fear extends across all or nearly all interpersonal relationships involving oral communication, it may be called *reticence*. According to research at the Pennsylvania State University, reticence may affect as much as five percent of a class.[5] McCroskey calls this phenomenon "communication apprehension.[6]

One conclusion of all the surveys and much of the research is that many of you will suffer some form of speech fright of varying intensity in different communication situations.

If it is true that misery loves company or that there is safety in numbers, then it will be reassuring to know that you are certainly not alone. Even professional performers report startling emotional reactions before some public performances. Consider these reports.[7]

> It's really not fun, acting. Always that tremendous fear. . . . Do you know that before a performance sometimes Laurence Olivier goes back to the foyer and, to release his tension, swears at the audience? Some actors even stick pins in themselves.
>
> *Jane Fonda*

> Acting is a way to overcome your shyness every night. The writer creates a strong, confident person, and that's what you become—unfortunately, only for the moment.
>
> *Shirley Booth*

> Acting scares me senseless. I hate everything I do. Even if it's a crummy radio show with a script, I throw up, I tell ya—it's the equivalent of going voluntarily to hell.
>
> *Judy Holliday*

[4] Douglas H. Lamb designates the first "A-Trait" and the second "A-State" in "Speech Anxiety: Towards a Theoretical Conceptualization and Preliminary Scale Development," *Speech Monographs*, 39, no. 1 (March 1972), 62–67; see also Ralph R. Behnke, Larry W. Carlile, and Douglas H. Lamb, "A Psychophysiological Study of State and Trait Anxiety in Public Speaking," *Central States Speech Journal*, 25, no. 4 (1974), 249–53.

[5] G. M. Phillips, "Reticence: Pathology of the Normal Speaker," *Speech Monographs*, 25, no. 1 (March 1968), 44.

[6] J. C. McCroskey, "Oral Communication: A Summary of Recent Theory and Research," *Human Communication Research*, 4, no. 1 (Fall 1977), 78.

[7] Phyllis Battelle, "Stars Give Their Views On Acting as a Career," *Detroit News*, December 6, 1961; Cleveland Amory, "Daddy's Last 'Hamlet' Just the Start for Lynn," *Detroit News*, March 21, 1976.

> Acting really comes from being shy. You don't particularly like who you are, but on stage you can be somebody else. I used to be absolutely tongue-tied in any face-to-face conversation, but I suddenly realized that I wasn't like that on a stage. And as I got confidence there, some of it came back to me in real life.
>
> *Lynn Redgrave*

That audiences do not view your fright as seriously as you do indicates that you do not appear and sound as bad as you feel; this should be reassuring. But whether or not your fear is readily apparent, the result may be the same: as in other frightening situations, you may feel a dryness in the mouth, a rapid heartbeat, a sinking feeling in the stomach, and even difficulty with abdominal control. Mulac and Sherman found four main elements in speech fright: *rigidity, inhibition, dysfluency,* and *agitation.*[8] The following behaviors characterize fright and should be expected in various degrees.

behaviors

Voice	1	Quivering or tense voice
	2	Too fast
	3	Too slow
	4	Monotonous: lack of emphasis
Verbal Fluency	5	Nonfluencies: stammering; halting speech
	6	Vocalized pauses
	7	Hunts for words: speech blocks
Mouth and Throat	8	Swallows
	9	Clears throat
	10	Breathes heavily
Facial Expression	11	Lack of eye contact; extraneous eye movements
	12	Tense face muscles; grimaces; twitches
	13	Deadpan facial expression
Arms and Hands	14	Rigid or tense
	15	Fidgeting; extraneous movement
	16	Motionless; lack of appropriate gestures
Gross Bodily Movement	17	Sways; paces; shuffles feet

[8] Anthony Mulac and Robert A. Sherman, "Behavioral Assessment of Speech Anxiety," *Quarterly Journal of Speech,* 60, no. 2 (April 1974), 134–43; also, see Theodore Clevenger, Jr. and Thomas R. King, "A Factor Analysis of the Visible Symptoms of Stage Fright," *Speech Monographs,* 28, no. 4 (November 1961), 296.

For the most part, people with much speech fright do not vary from others in general intelligence, reasoning ability, or most important aspects of personality. They may vary, however, in education, experience, linguistic ability, self-concept, and even social attraction.[9]

While you are pondering these symptoms and aspects of fright, you should realize that speech courses do help with this all-too-commom problem. Mulac and Sherman found that after eight weeks and four speeches, observable anxiety was significantly reduced.[10] Actual speaking experience appears to help gain confidence.

In most studies of specific techniques for helping students with anxiety problems, all forms of counseling, group therapy, and group desensitization have been found helpful.[11] A general state of anxiousness (such as reticence) which extends beyond the normal speech communication contexts discussed here (but including these) seems most treatable by a form of "insight" counseling and group therapy. Some interpersonal instruction has also had positive effects.[12]

The *desensitization* approach has proved effective with the typical temporary public-speaking form of fright.[13] Desensitization has been defined as a form of emotional reeducation using deep relaxation.[14] Some speech communication departments have developed desensitization laboratories and other programs of help. One such program is described by Gordon Paul:

> During the first treatment hour, a maximum of 10 minutes was spent exploring the history and current status of the subject's problem. Five to 10 minutes were spent explaining the rationale and course of treatment. Each subject was told that his emotional reactions were the result of previous experiences with persons and situations, and that these inappropriate emotional reactions could be unlearned by first determining the situations in which he becomes progressively more anxious, building a hierarchy from the least to the most anxious situations associated with giving a speech, and then repeatedly visualizing these situations while deeply relaxed. The subject was also told that relaxation was

[9]*The Bruskin Report,* p. 1; see also Gordon M. Law and Boyd V. Sheets, "The Relations of Psychometric Factors to Stage Fright," *Speech Monographs,* 18, no. 4 (November 1951), 266–71; J. C. McCroskey and V. P. Richmond, "The Effects of Communication Apprehension on the Perception of Peers," *Journal of the Western Speech Communication Association,* 11, no. 1 (Winter 1976), 14–21.

[10] "Behavioral Assessment of Speech Anxiety," p. 140.

[11] Donald H. Meichenbaum, J. Barnard Gilmore, and Al Fedoravious, "Group Insight Versus Group Desensitization in Treating Speech Anxiety," *Journal of Consulting and Clinical Psychology,* 36, no. 3 (June 1971), 410–21; see also J. C. McCroskey, D. C. Ralph, and J. E. Barrick, "The Effect of Systematic Desensitization on Speech Anxiety," *Speech Teacher,* 19, no. 1 (January 1970), 32–36.

[12] R. E. Barnes, "Interpersonal Communication Approaches to Reducing Speech Anxiety." Paper delivered at the Central States Speech Convention, Chicago, Ill., 1976.

[13] Meichenbaum and others, "Group Insight," p. 419.

[14] J. Wolpe, *Psychotherapy by Reciprocal Inhibition* (Stanford, Calif.: Stanford University Press, 1958).

beneficial because the muscle systems of the body could not be both tense and relaxed at the same time, and that by proceeding gradually up the hierarchy, the previous anxiety-provoking situations would become associated with relaxation, thus desensitizing the anxiety.[15]

In the subsequent four or five sessions, time was spent constructing speech communication situations ranging from reading alone to giving a speech before an audience. Subjects also received training and practice in "progressive relaxation," a technique using muscle relaxation exercises in modern laboratories equipped with soft lights and appropriate relaxation music. In the later sessions, two to eleven of the disturbing situations were presented to a relaxed subject. The items might be presented from two to ten times for a period of three to thirty seconds. The subjects were then aroused from their deep relaxation and asked to discuss their reactions and images.

An important question you may ask is, "Even if I overcome speech fright in this class, using whatever help I can get (perhaps just reading the rest of this chapter), will my speech communication training carry over and help me in another situation?" Several researchers have explored this question, and their findings are reassuring. This question is on the psychological and learning problem referred to as *transfer*. In a study by S. F. Paulson, speakers were taken from their regular class and made to speak before a strange class audience. The results of an adjustment inventory test indicated no decrease in confidence scores; it was concluded that a transfer of training did take place.[16] It is also encouraging to note that even three-fourths of a group of students at Penn State defined as reticent indicated noticeable improvement in their out-of-class oral behavior after ten weeks of speech training.[17]

To a great extent humans are afraid of what they do not understand. Young children may be paralyzed with fear during a severe elecrical storm until their mother or father explains what causes the thunder and lightning. Even afterwards, the child will experience fear, but not of a paralyzing nature. Loud noises make all of us jump, but knowledge and understanding of what causes the loud noises make it possible for us to stop jumping *between* noises.

Because we are dealing with the symptoms and causes of an emotional reaction, we will be better able to control emotion if we know in some detail what it is and how it operates.

---

[15] Gordon L. Paul, *Insight vs. Desensitization in Psychotherapy* (Stanford, Calif.: Stanford University Press, 1966), p. 20.

[16] Stanley F. Paulson, "Changes in Confidence during a Period of Speech Training: Transfer of Training and Comparison of Improved and Nonimproved Groups on the Bell Adjustment Inventory," *Speech Monographs*, 18, no. 4 (November 1951), 260–65.

[17] Phillips, "Reticence," p. 49.

In 1884 the famous philosopher and psychologist William James presented a relatively simple and extremely useful theory of emotion. One year later, Carl Lange, who had worked independently of James, derived a strikingly similar thesis. The theory is now refered to as the *James-Lange theory of emotion*. Although there is controversy over this theory in some academic circles, the theory has great practical value for speakers.

> Our natural way of thinking about . . . emotions is that the mental perception of some fact excites the mental affection called the emotion [for example, fear] and that this later state of mind gives rise to the bodily expression. My thesis on the contrary is that the bodily changes follow directly the perception of the exciting fact [stimulus] and that our feeling [awareness] of the same changes as they occur *is* the emotion.[18]

The gist of these words is that our awareness of our *reactions* to a frightening situation is the *real* emotion. James's favorite illustration of this theory was that of a man coming upon a bear in the woods. In a nonscientific way, we might say the bear triggers the emotion of fear in us. Not so, for according to James our body reacts almost automatically to the bear. Our natural survival devices take over to prepare us for an emergency. Our muscles tense for better agility, our heartbeat and breathing quicken to provide larger supplies of fuel, our glands secrete fluids to sharpen our senses and give us emergency energy. All of this happens in an instant. Then we become aware of our bodily reactions. We sense our heavy breathing, our muscles tense to the point of trembling, perhaps even adrenalin surges into our system. It is this *awareness* of our reactions that frightens us; in other words, the awareness is the emotion. Of course, the bear still has a lot to do with our condition! It would be ridiculous to tell you that if you understand clearly all the physiological reactions described above, you have eliminated the bear. However, this knowledge and understanding, other things being equal, *will* help you better control what action you take and thereby improve your chance for survival. This is what we mean by emotional or speech fright control, and this is why we use the term *control* rather than *eliminate* when speaking of fear.

In the same manner that our fear of the bear is caused not by the bear itself but our *awareness* of our bodily reactions to the bear, in speech fright it is our *awareness* of our internal and external reactions that provides us with the emotion—or at least heightens the emotion—and that may therefore cause a large part of our trouble. The speech situation, though obviously less dangerous than the bear, poses a more difficult problem. Nature prepares

[18] William James and Carl Lange, *The Emotions,* vol. 1 (Baltimore: Williams & Wilkins, 1922), p. 12 (emphasis added).

us for flight or fight, so we either flee from the bear or attack it. The speech situation rules out the utilization of survival tactics, for you can neither attack the audience nor run for the woods. The problem is to drain some of your excess energy while holding your ground and facing a fear-provoking stimulus (the audience). In your favor, however, there are no recorded instances of an audience eating a speaker!

The point of the bear story is to help you better understand the nature of emotion, for understanding and knowledge almost always promote emotional adjustment. There is a second lesson, closely related to the first, that may be of even more use to you. This is the principle of *objectification*. That is, an intellectualization or objective explanation of what is happening to you which may destroy or take the edge off emotions. Imagine a great lover who, when kissing his beloved, decided to analyze exactly what he was doing. A former student, reporting on one of his own objectification experiments, reported, "You know, Doc, it takes all the kick out of it!" By the same reasoning, detailed intellectualization of speech-fright experiences should help take some of the "kick" out of them.

Have you ever asked yourself, "Why do my arms and hands tremble? Why do I have that sinking feeling in my stomach?" The issue is not *whether* you experience these things, but rather *why?* If you do ask why and answer, "Because I'm scared to death," you probably only add to the emotion. This is the time to apply both the James-Lange theory of emotion and the principle of objectification. Remember that the emotion is largely the result of your *awareness* of your own bodily reactions and that an objective explanation of these reactions will take the edge off of your awareness.

Let's take the case of the *trembling* arms and hands. Skeletal muscles are usually arranged in *antagonistic* groups—one group opposes the other. The muscles on the inside (anterior) surface of the arm and forearm are called *flexors;* those on the back or outside (posterior) surface are called *extensors.* The flexors bend or draw up your arm, the extensors extend or straighten the arm. When either set of muscles contracts, the opposing set relaxes—but not completely, for there is a *tone* to skeletal muscles, which gives them a certain firmness and maintains a slight, steady pull upon their attachments. Suppose you *will* your forearm to rise as in figure 10.1—try it. Your flexor muscles contract and the extensor muscles on the other side of your arm are forced to relax. If you will your arm to straighten itself, the antagonistic muscles simply will reverse functions. Now try something more interesting. Put your arm in about the position shown in figure 10.1; will it to stay there, and at the same time will both sets of muscles to contract at the same time. If you are really working at it, you will notice a tremble in your arm. If you extend your fingers, the tremble usually will be quite evident in your hands. You have just produced a state very similar to the trembling that takes place in speech fright.[19] Fright increases the natural tension of your

[19] Ralph R. Behnke, Michael J. Beatty, and James T. Kitchens, "Cognitively-experienced Speech Anxiety as a Predictor of Trembling," *Western Journal of Speech Communication,* 42, no. 4 (Fall 1978), 270–5.

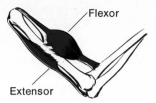

Figure 10.1 Antagonistic muscles of the arm and forearm.

antagonistic muscles and causes the same kind of trembling. You will still experience some trembling, and you will still be aware of it, but—theoretically, at least—not in exactly the same way as before. You have now increased your knowledge of why your arms and hands tremble. Other things being equal, you are better equipped both consciously and subconsciously to adjust to this event when it occurs. Some of the "kick" has been taken out of it. Although the lightning still startles you, you're somewhat more comfortable because science has explained *what* it is. Most important, your behavior may change qualitatively in a direction more acceptable to social custom.

A detailed and vivid description of the bodily reaction to threatening situations is provided by W. B. Cannon. These were his conclusions, based upon experiments with animals.

> The adrenalin in the blood is increased . . . which causes strong, rapid heartbeat, suspended activity of the stomach and intestines, wide opening of the air passages in the lungs, release of sugar from the liver, delay of muscle fatigue, free perspiration, dilation of the pupils of the eyes, more red corpuscles to carry oxygen, faster blood coagulation, and increased blood pressure.[20]

The sinking feeling in the stomach that we experience under stress can be explained in great detail. When faced with a fear-provoking situation, the body calls upon its glandular secretions, notably adrenalin, for emergency energy. These secretions chemically interfere with and halt the digestive system. This process tends to make the stomach contract and produces the sensation typically referred to as a sinking feeling. At the same time, we also become aware of many lesser reactions, such as a rapidly beating heart (for added circulation) and heavier breathing (for extra oxygen), that help prepare the body for survival. These rational explanations should help you maintain perspective and psychological equilibrium. We are often afraid of things simply because we do not understand them.

Most individuals cannot experience two opposite or different types of emotional reactions at the same time. For example, at the instant when you are boiling mad you are probably not afraid. This is not to suggest that you

[20]W. B. Cannon, *Bodily Changes in Pain, Hunger, Fear, and Rage* (Boston: Charles T. Branford, 1953), p. 368; see also Ralph R. Behnke and Larry W. Carlile, "Heart Rate as an Index of Speech Anxiety," *Speech Monographs*, 38, no. 1 (March 1971), 65–69.

Figure 10.2   The Wizard of Id. THE WIZARD OF ID *by permission of Johnny Hart and Field Enterprises, Inc.*

freely substitute anger for your fright, but you may already have observed that when a speaker is really involved in a subject, he or she will tend to be less frightened by the platform situation. This in part helps explain our almost instinctive actions to ward off fright situations. It explains why, for example, we whistle while walking through a dark alley. We are acting "as if" we are unafraid—perhaps happy, indignant, or angry. Acting "as if" has helped all of us through emotionally charged situations. It is healthy to whistle in the dark; it is often the difference between poise and panic. Your choice of a speech topic may therefore be important to you emotionally as well as rhetorically. If you are excited or can become excited about your subject, you will make theory work for you—a kind of natural and intelligent whistling in the dark.

DEVELOPING CONFIDENCE

In the preceding section we discussed some of the principles useful in controlling speech fright. Let's talk now about some specific actions you can take to make further use of the theory of emotion.

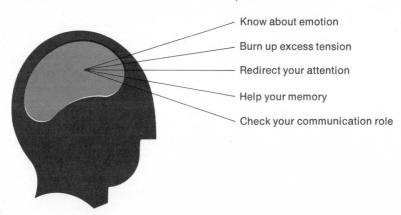

Know about Emotion

Remember that emotion is mainly the result of *your awareness* of your own bodily reactions. Analyzing these reactions should help you control fright. Emotion loses its intensity under examination and objectification. Face up to your problems and get the facts straight. It is healthy to talk objectively about your fright. Instructors are good listeners. Let yours help you talk out your fright. In these ways you will meet your fright on a conscious level, at which you have the most control. If your mouth feels dry, find out why. If your knees shake, find out why. If you feel faint, find out why. The *why* is usually rather mundane and unexciting, but it is extremely logical and objective. Should inordinate speech fright persist, you may find it useful to review this entire chapter at a later date.

Burn up Excess Tension

It should be clear from the previous discussion, particularly from the bear story, that we direct our actions most usefully once we break the wall of tension with the first step. Physical motion—either away from the bear at full speed or toward him in Davy Crockett style—bursts the dam of tension. In your speech situation you are in no real danger. Your first problem is to release some of the extra energy that your body dutifully provides. Once again, the *first* step is very important. *Bodily activity* will help you utilize your extra energy or tension. This is evidenced by expectant fathers who pace the floor rather than staying seated.

In a speaking situation you might be concerned about how your activity looks and what it communicates to the audience. The strategy here is very simple: plan and direct some of your gross bodily movement in advance—not in a stereotyped way, but nevertheless systematically, complete with options. For example, at the close of your introduction or perhaps at a transition between points, you might plan on moving a step to the side or raising a book or card for emphasis. You have the option of selecting the precise time and action, depending upon how natural it seems and how tense you are. Another very natural kind of activity is that associated with visual aids. The communication values of visual aids are almost self-evident, but their value as emotion-controlling devices may not be as obvious. If you comment on a picture, demonstrate an object, or write on a blackboard, you have to make perfectly natural movements in the process. This is an excellent way to utilize excess energy, and it is why you will probably be asked to give a demonstration or visual-aid-speech early in the semester. The lesson is obvious: use planned and directed activity freely as a means of utilizing excess tension and energy.

Prespeech physical actions can help you reduce your tension and relax. A brisk walk has helped many an athlete unwind. Even moderate exercises are in order. Of course, you cannot do push-ups in the classroom, but deep breathing is possible. Lifting or pressing your chair has been prescribed successfully by speech teachers. Isometric exercises are inconspicuous and should help. A yawn is a natural outlet as long as you do not look *too* relaxed! A certain amount of repetition may also be a useful prespeech exercise. If the journey from your chair to the speaker's platform is a real torture, rehearse this activity in an empty classroom or in measured distances at home. Keep rehearsing it until you sense a monotony in the repetition. Often college debaters inadvertently repeat cerain strategies and argument patterns so zealously in practice that they risk becoming stale when presenting the same ideas in debate. Football teams have had similar experiences. The point is that monotonous repetition may help us drain that keyed-up feeling.

Good health and a reasonable amount of rest are necessary for sound emotional adjustment. Speech and communication demand both because so much energy is required. Assuming an understanding of and a willingness to utilize the suggestions above, a moderate amount of repression of external behavior may also be in order to help you get started. By *repression* we mean a form of mental discipline in which you force yourself to get on with the business at hand. This is by no means a form of final adjustment, because continued repression would resuit in extreme fatigue and possible emotional disintegration. However, it is neither unusual nor abnormal to use moderate repression of external behavior as a first step in adjusting to the speaking situation.

Redirect your Attention

Let your emotions work for you when you can. In moments of strain, redirect your attention to other things and bring more tolerable emotions into focus. Try to become so involved in one thing that you are less aware of the other. Psychologists call this *compensation*. In a speech situation, one very obvious and natural avenue of distraction from your fright is an absorbing interest in your subject. If you can become excited about your subject or develop a positive desire to communicate it, you will often find your fright diminishing. If you can find humor in your task or in your reactions to it, you may have found a very healthy distraction.

You can redirect your attention by concentrating on the smiling and pleasant faces in the audience for moral support. Most of your audiences are, after all, supportive. Research indicates that at least in persuasive speeches, unfavorable feedback may result in some deterioration of the speaker's adequate bodily movement, fluency, and the like.[21] One professor reported that he started to overcome his speech fright when he began concentrating on the sleeping faces. He may have been substituting anger in this instance, or he may have decided his fear was a little ridiculous if he were talking only to himself.

[21] Philip P. Amato and Terry H. Ostermeier, "The Effect of Audience Feedback on the Beginning Public Speaker," *Speech Teacher,* 16, no. 1 (January 1967), 56–60.

One can overdo this form of compensation. Take care not to concentrate so much on redirecting your attention that you lose sight of the purpose of your total effort—communication.

Help your Memory

Our memory, like our perceptions, may become less dependable under severe forms of emotional strain.[22] Beginning speakers are often frightened, or the initial cause of their fright is reinforced, by just the thought of forgetting their speech. Apparently, speech fright becomes a cause of forgetting, and the thought of forgetting causes or reinforces speech fright—a vicious circle.

As in redirecting attention, your topic may be important to helping your memory. The more you know about a subject and the more enthusiastic you are about it, the less likely you are to forget your material. Your attitude toward your subject, your involvement in it, and your eagerness to communicate it are all related to your ability to remember it.

In preparing your speech, the key word for memory protection is *system*. We remember better, we learn better, and we speak better if the material with which we are dealing is arranged systematically. Your organization of material can significantly affect your ability to remember it. More will be said about rhetorical organization in later chapters. The point here is simply that it is easier to remember a list of twenty automobile names grouped according to some system (that is, according to manufacturer, size, horsepower, and so on) than one in a random order. Have you ever noticed how rapidly you can learn the names of baseball players? Obviously, it is because of the system of positions they play; if you do not know the positions, you will be slower at learning the names. Find a natural and constructive way (for you) of ordering your speech materials, and you will find it much easier to remember what comes next. Your audience, incidentally, will probably find your material easier to follow as a result.

One of the most effective memory aids is a *visual aid*. If you are explaining how an internal combustion engine works, it is obviously easier to remember functions and parts if you have the engine before you as an illustration. If your speech uses numbers and statistics, a large card with the numbers listed and identified considerably eases the pressure on your memory. Tucked in your pocket as a precaution, a note containing testimony, statistics, or other details is also helpful, even if it is not used. Just the knowledge that you have such a backstop is often worth more than the material on the cards. Some of the best speeches are delivered from a visual outline. All the major points and supporting statements are put on large cardboard visual aids in much the same way that one might put notes on three-by-five file cards. These aids serve much the same function, except

---

[22] James T. Freeman, "Set versus Perceptual Defense: A Confirmation," *Journal of Abnormal and Social Psychology*, 51 (1955), 710–12.

that now you are credited for using visual aids instead of criticized for depending too much upon your notes. A visual-outline speech or a chalk talk, in which you use the blackboard, is an exercise your instructor may wish to prescribe to help you learn the value of visual aids both as memory aids and as agents for clarity.

Despite all the protection you can give your memory, all speakers occasionally experience the frustration of "blanking out," or momentarily forgetting. A good question is, "What do I do now?" If you have ever watched youngsters delivering memorized poems or salutations at an elementary school convocation, you have heard them forget their materials on occasion. You have probably also noticed that they almost instinctively keep repeating the last line they *do* remember in a frantic effort to rerail their memory. This effort may help, but often the prompter also has a busy day. Word-for-word memorization is really not a very intelligent "system," because the memory cannot relate so many small, unrelated parts. However, the principle of repeating the last thing you do remember is still useful. The practical application is to *review* the material you have just covered. If your memory fails toward the end of your speech, you can *summarize* the key points you have made. Practical experience indicates that such a technique does help you reawaken your memory. One student who found this suggestion useful formulated her own rule: "When in doubt, summarize." If you blank out before you have really said anything, however, your summary had better not start, "In summary," or "In review"!

Check your Communication Role

We have talked earlier of a professor who felt less speech fright when he discovered that most of his class was asleep. With all due respect to student audiences, an honest appraisal of them is that they are not eagerly leaning forward, straining with every muscle to record for all time the wisdom you are about to deliver. Professors know this and so should you. Audiences may on occasion be lively, but more often than not this is due to the efforts of the speaker. Experienced speakers and teachers live for such moments. Be objective about your audience. An analysis of speech-rating charts, particularly the added comments, indicates that the audience sympathizes with the speaker. This means that if your audience is listening at all, it is rooting for you.

However important your speech message, it will probably not be recorded for the future. If every speaker in a class of twenty-five gives 10 speeches, any particular speech is 1 out of 250. If it is reasuring to be part of the crowd, then relax. Be realistic about your speech goals and their effect upon your audience.

Think of your speech in terms of the communication process discussed in chapter 1, and realize the worthy purpose of speech training. Instead of worrying about the damage your ego may suffer, be afraid of *not* being able to motivate an audience to listen.

Finally, *evaluate your communication role* completely. Your speeches will be lost among hundreds of other speeches; your audience is generally sympathetic; your instructor is trained to be alert to your problems; and the rhetorical and psychological research in speech has given us reliable methods and knowledge to help you learn. Have faith in hard-earned experience and knowledge; have faith in the goodness of people; and have faith in yourself.

10 SUMMING UP

Most beginning speech students admit that they are bothered by nervousness. Professional performers report similar feelings of tension. Significantly, though, reports indicate that you do not *appear* and *sound* as bad as you *feel*. Research also indicates that frightened people do not differ from the confident minority in very basic ways such as intelligence and the important aspects of personality. Research reveals, further, that most students do gain confidence during a course in speech and are able to transfer this learning to other situations.

Understanding the nature of emotion is useful because it helps us objectify our feelings and reactions. The James-Lange theory of emotion suggests that our awareness of our *reactions* to a frightening situation is the *real* emotion. Emotion is a good and necessary phenomenon. The problem is one of control. An understanding of our bodily reactions to frightening situations helps us control our emotions. The objectification of emotional reactions tends to take the edge off emotion, making it easier to control. An increase in intellectual activity helps reduce emotional intensity. We are afraid of what we do not understand.

Most individuals cannot experience two different types of emotional reaction at the same time. If you are excited or can become excited about your subject, you are making theory work for you—a kind of natural and intelligent whistling in the dark.

Here are some specific suggestions for controlling emotion:

1 Understand emotion and the principle that objectification and intellectualization reduce tension.
2 Utilize excess tension by planning some of your gross bodily activity before you begin the speech.
3 Redirect your attention to more pleasant emotions in order to let your emotions work for you.
4 Protect your memory through logical systems of organization, visual aids, and preset psychological options.

5 Evaluate your communication role and situation honestly, and have faith in knowledge, in the goodness of people, and in yourself.
6 Concentrate on the message more than on yourself.

Last, when at your wit's end, remember that there is no recorded experience of an audience having eaten a speaker!

Speech Communication Principles

1 Most beginning speech students admit that they are bothered by nervousness.
2 The speaker's nervousness is not as apparent to the audience as it is to the speaker.
3 Nervous student speakers do not differ from the confident minority in intelligence and other important personality traits.
4 Generally observable behavior patterns in cases of acute speech fright include rigidity, inhibition, dysfluency, and agitation.
5 It is our awareness of our *reactions* to a frightening situation that is the *real* emotion.
6 Understanding our bodily reactions to frightening situations helps us control emotion.
7 Objectification of emotional reactions tends to reduce their intensity.
8 An increase in intellectual activity helps reduce emotional intensity.
9 Most individuals cannot experience two different types of emotional reaction at the same time.

Specific Learning Outcomes

1 We should learn that nervousness is a common problem among beginning speakers.
2 We should learn that frightened individuals do not differ from the confident in intelligence and other important personality characteristics.
3 We should learn that most students do gain confidence during a course in speech.

Communication Competencies

1 We should be able to give a five-minute extemporaneous speech before an audience of twelve to thirty-five in such a manner that our anxiety does not seriously interfere with our sense of communication, as far as the *audience* is concerned.
2 We should learn to be sympathetic and emotionally reinforcing listeners for obviously frightened speakers through an appreciation of the material in this chapter.

Study Projects and Tasks

1 Prepare a five-minute extemporaneous speech in which you explain or demonstrate how to do something (driving a golf ball, serving a tennis ball, swinging a bat, casting a

fly, lifting a weight, skiing, and so forth). Make sure you can do it; practice before coming to class.

2   Prepare a five-minute extemporaneous speech describing some exciting event you witnessed or participated in (a race you won, an accident, the big game, a close call, a big fish, a fight, a surprise present, your lucky day, and so forth). Make sure you really were excited about or involved in the event, so that your enthusiasm will help you look forward to telling the story.

3   Assess your speech-anxiety level according to the following inventory.[23] If you check twelve or more items and feel nervous, it would probably be a good idea to confer with your instructor. You're probably not the only one.

Check only those statements that you feel apply to you to an abnormal or extraordinary degree.

1   Audiences seem bored when I speak.

2   I feel dazed when speaking.

3   I am continually afraid of making some embarrassing or silly slip of the tongue.

4   My face feels frozen while I am speaking.

5   I have a deep sense of personal worthlessness while facing an audience.

6   Owing to fear, I cannot think clearly on my feet.

7   While preparing my speech I am in a constant state of anxiety.

8   I feel exhausted after addressing a group.

9   My hands tremble when I try to handle objects on the platform.

10 I am almost overwhelmed by a desire to escape.

11 I am in constant fear of forgetting my speech.

12 I dislike using my body and voice expressively.

13 I feel disgusted with myself after trying to address a group of people.

14 I feel tense and stiff while speaking.

15 I am so frightened I scarcely know what I'm saying.

16 I hurry while speaking in order to finish and get out of sight.

17 I prefer to have notes on the platform in case I forget what I'm saying.

18 My mind becomes blank before an audience and I am scarcely able to continue.

19 I particularly dread speaking before a group that opposes my point of view.

20 It is difficult for me to search my mind calmly for the right word to express my thoughts.

[23] Adapted from the research of H. Gilkenson by R. S. Ross and W. J. Osborne, Wayne State University.

- [ ] 21 My voice sounds strange to me when I address a group.
- [ ] 22 My thoughts become confused and jumbled when I speak before an audience.
- [ ] 23 I am completely demoralized when suddenly called upon to speak.
- [ ] 24 I find it extremely difficult to look at my audience while speaking.
- [ ] 25 I am terrified at the thought of speaking before a group of people.
- [ ] 26 I become so confused at times that I lose the thread of my thinking.
- [ ] 27 My posture feels strained and unnatural.
- [ ] 28 Fear of forgetting causes me to jumble my speech at times.
- [ ] 29 I am fearful and tense throughout the time I am speaking before a group of people.
- [ ] 30 I feel awkward.
- [ ] 31 I am afraid the audience will discover my self-consciousness.
- [ ] 32 I am afraid my thoughts will leave me.
- [ ] 33 I feel confused while speaking.
- [ ] 34 I never feel I have anything worth saying to an audience.
- [ ] 35 I feel that I am not making a favorable impression when I speak.
- [ ] 36 I feel depressed after addressing a group.
- [ ] 37 I always avoid speaking in public if possible.
- [ ] 38 I become flustered when something unexpected occurs.
- [ ] 39 Although I talk fluently with friends, I am at a loss for words on the platform.
- [ ] 40 My voice sounds as though it belongs to someone else.
- [ ] 41 At the conclusion of the speech I feel that I have failed.

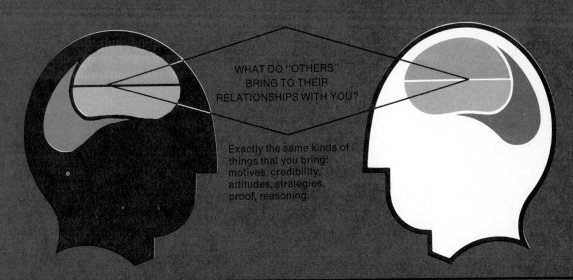

WHAT DO "OTHERS"
BRING TO THEIR
RELATIONSHIPS WITH YOU?

Exactly the same kinds of
things that you bring:
motives, credibility,
attitudes, strategies,
proof, reasoning.

part three

THE PSYCHOLOGY
OF PERSUASION

Persuasion is the study of human motives. If we are to live in a democracy, we must understand how people are influenced. Persuasion is the major means of settling problems, selling ideas and products, and changing people's attitudes. Persuasion is the heart of advertising and political campaigns. Persuasion is central to leadership and interpersonal relations.

As receivers, we hear and see numerous appeals on radio, television, and in the print media. Rarely are these "one-time" persuasion efforts. They usually can stand alone but are almost always part of a larger plan or *campaign* of persuasion.

One division of a major automobile manufacturer spends over $75 million dollars a year on advertising! You had better believe there is a master plan or campaign. This plan tries to persuasively schedule and coordinate all of the commercials, the car shows, the news releases—even "punt-pass and kick" contests. Persuasion *is* the business of advertising and marketing. There is clearly a consumer appreciation and protection function in the study of persuasion.

In a democracy, hard-fought, persuasive political campaigns replace revolution and force. Political campaigns sell candidates, programs, and promises. Candidates' speeches are carefully prepared to address the main issues at the right time. Even the time at which a candidacy is announced is part of the campaign strategy. There is also a citizen protection function for persuasion students here!

In persuading people, we are concerned with altering their attitudes. Does oral argument (speech) affect attitudes? For centuries we have answered yes, based on our subjective observations.

Many teachers, after a particularly exasperating day, may conclude that nothing happened to the minds of their students. We do have scientific evidence that some teaching appears to have little effect on student attitudes. As early as 1927, Donald Young found, after measuring class attitudes, that his course, "American Race Problems," had no effect upon the racial prejudices of his students at the University of Pennsylvania.[1] If Young's lectures and assignments were considered oral argument and persuasion, and if he measured the right attitudes at the right time, then we had better take a closer look at oral persuasion and its effects.

In 1935, F. H. Knower reported specific insights into this question in a study that has become a classic in speech research. This study was done in 1931, during Prohibition. The issue was prohibition but the study was completed before anti-Prohibition feeling reached its height.

Knower constructed four carefully tested speeches. Two favored maintaining Prohibition (dry speeches) and two opposed it (wet speeches). One wet and

---

[1] "Some Effects of a Course in American Race Problems on the Race Prejudices of 450 Undergraduates," *Journal of Abnormal and Social Psychology*, 22 (1927), 235–42.

one dry speech were predominantly factual and logical; the other speech on each side of the issue was an emotional appeal.[2]

Of all the carefully drawn conclusions, the most important for our purposes is that 60 percent of the experimental group made a positive change in attitude, demonstrating that oral argument does affect attitude! Of almost equal importance was Knower's discovery that logical and emotional speeches were equally effective in producing changes in attitude.

In chapter 1 we discovered that in the decoding part of the communication process, people attach meaning to symbols by reaching into their storehouse of knowledge and experience. In chapter 8 we discussed the learning process in order to gain the necessary theoretical background for the speech to inform. The learning process is also a concern of ours in part three. Learning includes habitual behavior. Once a form of behavior (including attitudes) becomes habitual in a listener, the persuader has difficulty altering it, because the listener finds it less necessary to select from her storehouse of experience in order to interpret the message. When we are faced with a specific or attention-getting argument, our hostile attitude and our habits may simply cause us to rehearse arguments against the persuader's general position and not really perceive her argument. For these reasons, a wide range of dimensions of human motivation are discussed in chapter 11. We are motivated by our biological needs as well as our social and psychological needs.

Our personality is thought to affect the way we decode persuasive messages. The various theories of persuasion are also discussed in chapter 11.

The logical supports of persuasion are a large part of successful communication. Evidence, proof, reasoning, and the four basic fallacies are explained in chapter 12.

[2]F. H. Knower, "Experimental Studies of Changes in Attitudes: I. A Study of the Effect of Oral Argument on Changes of Attitude," *Journal of Social Psychology,* 6 (1935), 315–47. See also John E. Baird, Jr., "Sex Differences in Group Communication: A Review of Relevant Research," *Quarterly Journal of Speech,* 62, no. 2 (1976), 179–92.

GENERAL LEARNING OUTCOMES

1 We should understand the concepts of persuasion, motivation, and attitude.

2 We should learn the basic elements of ethical persuasion.

3 We should learn how our biological and social needs affect persuasion.

4 We should learn A. H. Maslow's theory of dynamic human needs and how it relates to motivation.

5 We should learn the importance of credibility and ethical proof to persuasion.

6 We should learn about such theories of persuasion as classical rhetoric, attitude functions, social judgment, and consistency.

7 We should learn how to relate the psychological order and psychological sequences to persuasive messages.

8 We should learn of the nature and applications of both-sides persuasion to antagonistic receivers.

9 As receivers of persuasion, we should be able to detect the strategies, theories, and devices being directed at us and learn to sort out the rational from the emotional.

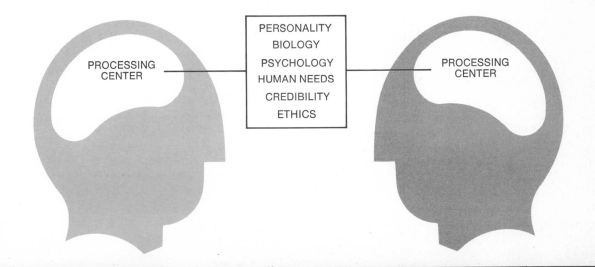

PERSONALITY
BIOLOGY
PSYCHOLOGY
HUMAN NEEDS
CREDIBILITY
ETHICS

PROCESSING CENTER

PROCESSING CENTER

dimensions of human motivation

DEFINITIONS AND CONCEPTS

Persuasion and Motivation

Persuasion is the ability to (1) assess the causes of motivation in human affairs and (2) assess the available means of influencing attitudes and behavior.[1]

Where *motivation* refers to specific deficiency and abundancy needs in the human experience.

Where *attitudes* refer to the thinking, feeling, and behavioral intentions which govern one's predispositions toward people, situations, and things.

Seldom are we persuaded by only one thing. Success and satisfaction foster motivation. So do failure and dissatisfaction. We are *motivated by need and by plenty* We are often persuaded through social compliance and laws. We have avoidance needs as well as growth needs. Our human motives have been defined by Krech and Crutchfield as *survival, security, satisfaction,* and *stimulation.*[2] These are grouped into *deficiency* motives (survival and security) and *abundancy* motives (satisfaction and stimulation). Deficiency motivation is characterized by needs to avoid danger, threat, disruption, and discomfort. Abundancy motivation is characterized by desires to grow, discover, create, enjoy, and achieve.

We also are persuaded by *logical appeals* as well as by *emotional appeals* When we are persuaded to buy a product, take a position, join a cause, how much of our behavior is based on reasoned discourse? How much on

[1] With apologies to Aristotle who defined rhetoric as "the faculty of observing in any given case the available means of persuasion." Aristotle, *Rhetoric and Poetics,* trans. W. Rhys Roberts (New York: Modern Library, 1954), p. 24.
[2] D. Krech and R. S. Crutchfield, *Elements of Psychology* (New York: Alfred A. Knopf, Inc., 1958), p. 279.

Figure 11.1 THE WIZARD OF ID *by permission of Johnny Hart and Field Enterprises, Inc.*

appeals to our emotions? This is more evidence that humanity is multi-motivated!

The *psycho-environment,* our work or study surroundings, also motivates and persuades us. Particularly influential are the leadership we deal with, the attitudes we cope with, and the communication climate we find. Since most of us deal with organizations, these kinds of environmental persuaders surely affect specific appeals to persuade us.

Sometimes it is not the sender that influences us but the *people* between the sender and us. Upon hearing of a hot issue from a political candidate, we might suspend judgment until we check it out with others. Friends, family, and other people we respect often are *intermediary* persuaders. These intermediaries are opinion leaders who screen and shape the attitudes of all of us. There may be several *significant others* between us and a persuasion source. In complex campaigns and social issues, it is probably a multistep rather than a two-step flow of persuasion. Mass media research suggests that this is a major source of their influence, that these intermediaries interpret the original messages for others. Social relationships have great influence on how all of us are affected by persuasion.

The various motivations discussed above are both *verbal* and *nonverbal.*

In sum, all of us are *multimotivated.* Although one particular appeal may be the trigger, these other factors are part of the total persuasive effect.

Despite our multimotivation, it does appear that we all prefer a kind of *psychological comfort* We want consistency in our attitudes and in our behavior. We want comfort in what we feel and in what we think. We seek an agreeable, balanced set of relationships in our notions of the world and in our latest perception of it. As observers, we assign or attribute reasons to the actions of others—it's more comfortable that way. We attribute causes for internal reasons: "She winked because she likes me," or external reasons, "She winked because of dirt in her eye." We probably infer attitudes on the basis of these attributions.[3] It is thought to work as follows: we observe others' actions and their effects; we then infer their intentions from this information; and finally, we make attributions about the individuals or their attitudes.[4]

The Concept of Attitude

Persuasive efforts are directed in large part at changing or maintaining the attitudes of others. These attitude efforts are usually directed at some related behavior: a vote, the sale of a product, some compliant action.

[3] H. H. Kelley, "Attribution Theory in Social Psychology," in *Nebraska Symposium on Motivation,* Vol. 15, ed. D. Levine, (Lincoln, Nebraska: University of Nebraska Press, 1967), pp. 192–238.

[4] E. E. Jones and K. E. Davis, "From Acts to Dispositions: The Attribution Process in Person Perception," in *Advances in Experimental Social Psychology,* Vol. 2, ed. L. Berkowitz, (New York: Academic Press, 1965), pp. 219–66; also see (for comparison of dissonance theory to attribution theory), C. A. Keisler and P. A. Munson, "Attitudes and Opinions," *Annual Review of Psychology,* 26 (1975), pp. 415–56.

Attitude refers to the thinking, feeling, and behavioral intentions which govern one's predispositions toward people, situations, and things.[5]

An attitude has also been defined as a *tendency* to respond in a given way.[6] This response may be *cognitive* (how one thinks), *affective* (how one feels), or *behavioral* (how one *behaves*, or *intends* to behave).

Some experts reserve the word attitude for the affective aspects. The cognitive aspects they call beliefs.[7] *Beliefs* are related to our thinking. We think (or believe) a thing is true or false. Pigs are dirty. Cats are sneaky. Attitudes, on the other hand, pertain more to favorable-unfavorable evaluations. I don't like pigs. I love cats. We develop our attitudes, in part, according to what we believe. The behavioral aspects in this view also include "intent" to behave. An opinion is a more lightly held judgment than an attitude or belief. It is usually more cognitive than affective.[8]

Value is a broad life goal or standard usually made up of many attitudes, beliefs, opinions, and behavioral intentions. Values are not always logical. They are formed from experience, the environment, perhaps even from frustration. Money has become a controlling value for many. It may not always be logical, but it affects how we think, feel, and behave. The value assigned to civil liberties is another example. Values are systems which hold attitudes together. Knowing a person's value system often predicts attitudes toward smaller issues. A strong, positive value about women's liberation might predict that person's attitude toward the Equal Rights Amendment.

Attitudes, in the larger sense, are also thought to serve different functions. We can examine our attitudes as receivers in terms of what function they're serving. As senders, our success may depend on how we assess an audience's reason for holding a specific attitude.

Some reasons for attitudes are quite *practical*. We form favorable attitudes toward those who feed and stroke us. We form favorable attitudes toward things that reward us—high grades, money, and special privileges. The practical function could also extend to unfavorable attitudes. For example, we form very practical attitudes toward punishment or low grades. These practical attitudes supply *reference* points for assessing new information.

---

[5] For an interesting synthesis of attitude definitions, see Stephen W. Littlejohn, *Theories of Human Communication* (Columbus, Ohio: Charles E. Merrill Publishing Company, 1978), and William J. McGuire, "The Nature of Attitude and Attitude Change," in *Handbook of Social Psychology,* vol. 3, G. Lindzey and E. Aronson, eds. (Reading, Mass.: Addison-Wesley Publishing Co., 1969), pp. 136–314.

[6] G. W. Allport, "Attitudes," C. Murchison ed., *Handbook of Social Psychology* (Worcester, Mass.: Clark University Press, 1935), 795–884.

[7] M. Fishbein and I. Ajzen, "Attitudes and Opinions," *Annual Review of Psychology,* 23 (1972), 487–544; also see M. Fishbein and I. Ajzen, *Belief, Attitude, Intention, and Behavior: An Introduction to Theory and Research* (Reading, Mass.: Addison-Wesley Publishing Co., 1975).

[8] Stuart Oskamp, *Attitudes and Opinions* (Englewood Cliffs, N.J.: Prentice-Hall, Inc., 1977), p., 12.

Many of our attitudes are expressions of our *values*. These maintain and promote our value systems and our *self-identity*. If we value clean air highly, we will have unfavorable attitudes toward smoking and fluorocarbons. We feel more consistent, more comfortable that way.

All of us are somewhat directed by our own self-interest. It is thought by some to be a major motivator of all human conduct (egoism). We defend our own egos, our own welfare and advancement above all else. Take care of number one! This self-interest attitude has been called an *ego defensive* function. It most often is difficult to change and frequently is destructive. Attitudes have various functions. Among them are referencing, self-identity, and ego defensive.[9]

Our attitudes are seldom simple and seldom unrelated to other attitudes. Larger attitudes may be considered as a cluster of related notions. Some of these notions are more important than others. Some clusters contain more notions than others do. For example, consider an attitude toward the use of marijuana. It resembles a flower or leaf with + and − petals (notions) whose sizes are based on importance.

[9] Katz, "The Functional Approach to the Study of Attitudes," *Public Opinion Quarterly,* 24 (1960), pp. 163–204. (Katz also considers knowledge to be a function of attitude.)

Figure 11.2

The prevailing attitude is negative (22−, 15+) and we have a measure of strength. We shall have more to say later about how we resolve these uncomfortable differences. For now it helps us see the complex nature of attitudes.

Measuring attitudes is difficult because we cannot see them. We infer attitudes from what people do or what they tell us. Try this statement of attitude:

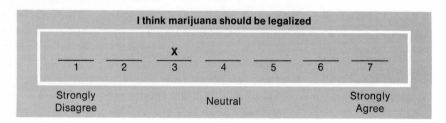

Figure 11.3

Our leaf cluster would appear to fall in #3. However, we are not really sure. Although illegality greatly affected (9−) this person's attitude toward *use*—he or she might lean toward legalization!? Suppose this person did check #3 above. It sounds as though he or she would be difficult to persuade. This might be the case if that were really the only position favored. Suppose, however, there was a range of numbers that fit his or her attitude. Perhaps this person could also live with #2 and #4. These we can label acceptable positions. Perhaps #5, 6, 7, and 1 were unacceptable. We have more attitude information now.

I think marijuana should be legalized

Unacceptable	Acceptable			Unacceptable		
1	2	3	4	5	6	7
	X	**X**	X			

Strongly Disagree   Neutral   Strongly Agree

Figure 11.4

Although #3 is the *most* acceptable, this person's range does include the neutral position. Persuasion looks more promising now.

Suppose this person had a large range or latitude of *noncommitment* on the following scale.

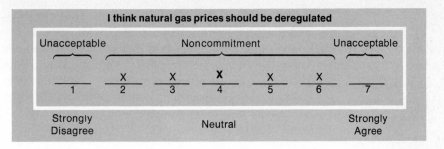

Figure 11.5

If she or he had enough interest or ego involvement to tolerate persuasion, we could assume he or she would be easy to persuade (either way). However, if the range were very narrow, and the most acceptable position were still #4, he or she might be very difficult to persuade. This person has rejected all the other positions! See below.

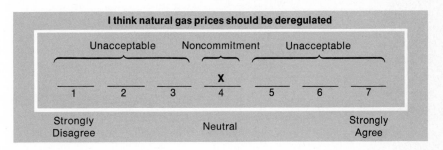

Figure 11.6

In general, the larger the range of rejection (unacceptable positions), the more ego defensive this person becomes and the more difficult to persuade. The larger the range of acceptance or noncommitment, the less one's ego is involved and the easier it is for one to change one's attitude.

These three positions have been called *latitudes of acceptance, rejection, and noncommitment* [10] They also have been referred to as ego-involvement theory.

The Concept of Ethics

An ethical persuader has a moral responsibility for the strategies employed and for their social consequences. Techniques and strategies are

[10] From assimilation-contrast theory. See M. Sherif and C. Hovland, *Social Judgment* (New Haven: Yale University Press, 1961).

not unethical unless they are dishonest, unfair to the facts, or so subtle that they give no clue to the receiver. The clue is important. It protects the receiver's fundamental right of some *choice*. Even in social compliance, one usually has *some* choice. When it is minimal, there at least are some alternatives (the courts when necessary). The ultimate decision of how to behave, act, or believe must in some way be left to the receiver. These are difficult ethical questions when faced with social dilemmas like "compulsory schooling" versus "parental rights." Some religious groups refuse to send their children to school. We do not always perceive choice. Perhaps in very special cases it is small. Nevertheless, *choice* is a very special, ethical consideration for all sources of persuasion.

Honesty and being fair to the facts are obvious moral obligations. We must play by the game's rules and the law. Outright lies, manufactured facts, and "dirty tricks" are clearly unethical persuasion. Even here we have some problems. Prudence is a virtue. It does not call for us to be dishonest, but it does call for us to be cautious. One can be both prudent and forthright.

Let us not forget our ethical responsibilities as receivers of persuasion. As receivers we have a moral obligation to give a *fair hearing*, once we have committed ourselves to some legitimate interest in the issue. A fair hearing is an effort to understand the position of the sender. It means a *tolerance* and understanding of persuasive strategy. It is the substitute for force in a free society! A fair hearing also includes a close analysis of your own *range of acceptance*. Are you really stuck on the end of a seven-point scale? Might you dare to consider a six or even a five? Fair hearing also means giving the sender some chance to be heard. It does not outlaw heckling, demonstrations, or protests. Ethical receiving demands, however, that you give the sender some chance to make and explain his or her point.

As ethical receivers, we also have a moral obligation to comply with the persuasion by legitimate authority and law. This is not to say that we must like it. This is not to say that we shouldn't try to change things. This *is* to say that *compliance persuasion* from legitimate authority in a democracy gives us a chance to make changes through nonviolent, persuasive means. Strikes are, by definition, nonviolent. Grievance procedures are clearly opportunities for persuasive changes. Laws can and have been changed. Petition campaigns, recall campaigns, protests, demonstrations—all are part of ethical persuasion—so long as they comply with the legitimate authority governing them.

There is no lasting persuasion without honesty, pressure free of violence, receiver choice, tolerance for strategy, fair hearing, and a willingness to comply with persuasion from legitimate authority. In a democracy, ethical persuasion is the major means of social influence.

Persuasion in this context is a nonviolent means of ethically influencing the thinking, feeling, intentions and/or behavior of others. The rest of the chapter will discuss the means.

SPRINGBOARDS OF MOTIVATION

Let's start by considering the basic springboards of human motivation: our biological and social nature, and our human needs.

Our Biological Nature

To some philosophers the proper study of humankind begins with a single person. The most remarkable thing about our biological nature is the striking similarity of all people. All doctors use the same anatomical chart, and all search for your heart in about the same place.

BIOLOGICAL NEEDS To survive, a person needs *oxygen, food, water, rest, elimination of wastes,* and *exercise.* Although these needs originate within the body, they must be met from outside the body. Needs, even at the basic level of food and water, allow us choices and behavior over which we have some control. But whether we choose water, milk, or beer, we must satisfy our basic need for fluids.

In our culture, it is only in times of great stress, ill health, or drug abuse that a biological imbalance may have serious consequences. Nevertheless, the motivations resulting from such imbalances are constantly with us, affecting our behavior and the intensity with which we attempt to satisfy our needs.

Studies show that people become increasingly less interested in the finer aspects of culture as they are systematically starved. Such findings indicate that some needs may become more important than others. When the biological needs of oxygen, food, water, rest, elimination, and exercise are not being adequately met, even humankind's complex and important social needs may become secondary.

Our Social-psychological Nature

Our biological nature, however primary, is overlaid by a variety of social-psychological motives, usually learned needs and goals. We learn to seek these social satisfactions almost as intensely as we seek survival.

Prescientific explanations of personality attempted to predict human behavior and a person's reactions to patterns of persuasion. Personality should be thought of as the sum of a person's motives, whatever their source.

One of the earliest *typological theories* (judging people by type) is credited to Hippocrates, the father of medicine, in 460 B.C. Some six hundred years later, the medical philosopher Galen related Hippocrates' classification of "humors" and biles to temperaments and personality.[11]

[11] Galen, "On the Natural Faculties," trans. A. J. Brock, in *Great Books of the Western World*, vol. 10, ed. R. M. Hutchins (Chicago: Encyclopedia Britannica, 1952), pp. 163–215.

There were four basic biles. If the *blood* bile predominated, according to Galen, your personality was sanguine—cheery, optimistic, and warm-hearted. If the *black* bile predominated, your temperament was melancholy or gloomy. If the *yellow* bile was foremost, you were hot-tempered. If *phlegm* predominated, your temperament was characterized by a lack of energy and alertness.

To a great extent, the sources of persuasion are found in an understanding of human nature and behavior. Since ancient times, humankind has tried to find simple explanations of what motivates people to do what they do. If one could find these explanations and determine universal systems of human motivation, one theoretically could control the behavior of others in many ways. To some philosophers, most notably Aristotle, "the proper study of man is man himself." The assumption is that all humans, at least in a general sense, are much alike. At the physiological level this assumption presents few problems, for despite obvious individual differences in height, weight, color, and other physical attributes, all people exhibit a striking physical similarity. We could hardly have a science of medicine were this not true. In the nonphysiological realm the problem is more complicated. Plato argued that to study man one must investigate his environment; for Plato, man was a reflection of his society. Today, we say that one must understand both man himself and his environment in order to understand human behavior.

There have been many theories for classifying people, including those with psychological and sociological foundations. Among *psychological theories,* perhaps you are most familiar with Jung's *introvert-extrovert* classification.[12] Even this useful system illustrates the danger of typing people too hastily. Jung himself regretted the either/or system that seems to follow necessarily from his classification. He thought, rather, of all people having tendencies toward both introversion and extroversion, with one or the other appearing to dominate in a given area. The introvert in a speech class may be a tigerlike extrovert on the football field.

Instinct theory is still with us, and like other theories it is useful in our attempts to explain human behavior as long as we recognize its limitations. It is to some extent a distortion of Aristotle's theory of inborn human nature. If we had a long list of urges that were in no way learned and that were present in all people, we could select our systems of persuasion much more scientifically than we do now. From the realm of psychology, William McDougall gave us a list that is considered useful today, even though the instinct theory has been discredited rather thoroughly. McDougall's list of urges, which he called "native propensities," include the following:

1 To desire food periodically (hunger).
2 To reject certain substances (disgust).
3 To explore new places and things (curiosity).

[12]C. G. Jung, *Psychological Types* (New York: Harcourt, Brace, 1922).

4 To try to escape from danger (fear).
5 To fight when frustrated (anger).
6 To have sex desire (mating).
7 To care tenderly for the young (mothering).
8 To seek company (gregariousness).
9 To seek to dominate (self-assertiveness).
10 To accept obvious inferiority (submissiveness).
11 To make things (construction).
12 To collect things (acquisitiveness).[13]

Many people in a given culture seem to react similarly to similar stimulations. However, to suggest that learning plays only a minor role in such reactions, or that a person has absolutely no choice, which the word *instinct* implies, seems unrealistic and unobjective.

Classifying Human Needs

Though modern social scientists doubt that any of these so-called wants, appeals, and propensities exist in everyone, lists of *motive appeals* are thought to be useful to advertisers in particular and to persuaders in general. When properly related and evaluated in terms of the needs, personality, and communication processes of a specific listener or audience, they can be most helpful.

In speech education, one of the older and more durable of these lists includes self-preservation, property, power, reputation, affections, sentiments, and tastes.[14] Keeping in mind the dangers of overgeneralizing for nonspecific audiences, let's look at the explanation of two of these motives or needs.

> *Affections:* "Affections as an Impelling Motive" means the desire for the welfare of others—kindly concern for the interests of mother, father, wife, son, daughter, sweetheart, friends, any being, human or divine. Also it includes desire for the welfare of our town, country, state, and nation, in so far as this desire is altruistic and not selfish.
> *Sentiments:* "The Impelling Motive of Sentiments" includes the desire to be and to do what is right, fair, honorable, noble, true—desires associated with intellectual and moral culture. It embraces duty, liberty, independence, and also patriotism considered as a moral obligation.[15]

Advertising studies supply us with a variety of terms that, like those of an earlier day, are useful to the persuader who is careful to relate them first to a specific audience. Here is a random collection of these terms.

[13] William McDougall, *An Introduction to Social Psychology* (London: Methuen, 1908), p. 106.
[14] A. E. Phillips, *Effective Speaking* (Chicago: Newton, 1931), p. 48.
[15] *Ibid.,* pp. 53–54.

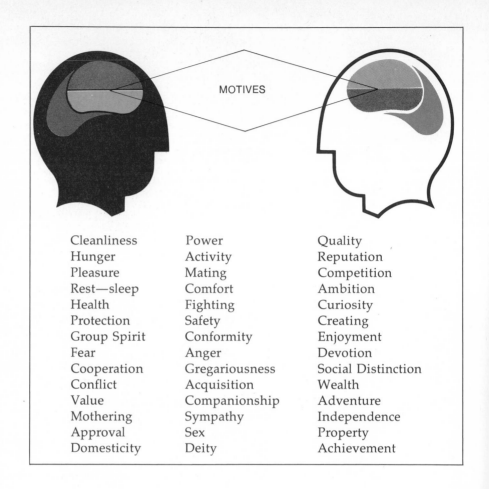

Cleanliness	Power	Quality
Hunger	Activity	Reputation
Pleasure	Mating	Competition
Rest—sleep	Comfort	Ambition
Health	Fighting	Curiosity
Protection	Safety	Creating
Group Spirit	Conformity	Enjoyment
Fear	Anger	Devotion
Cooperation	Gregariousness	Social Distinction
Conflict	Acquisition	Wealth
Value	Companionship	Adventure
Mothering	Sympathy	Independence
Approval	Sex	Property
Domesticity	Deity	Achievement

The Maslow Priority of Human Needs

Any attempt to classify human needs must begin with biological needs. Such a system has been supplied by A. H. Maslow,[16] one particularly useful to the psychology of persuasion. Maslow's five general categories of needs, in the order of their importance, are *physiological, safety, love, esteem,* and *self-actualization*

Maslow believes that most behavior is the result of several motives. One act could be a response to all the needs. Maslow's theory is a general-dynamic one based on the integrated wholeness of the human organism.

PHYSIOLOGICAL NEEDS These are the biological needs referred to previously. They are related directly to self-preservation. Although they are generally rated first in importance, their importance diminishes if they are satisfied. A starving person may be dominated by thoughts and visions of

[16]A. H. Maslow, "A Theory of Human Motivation," *Psychological Review,* 50 (1943), 370–96.

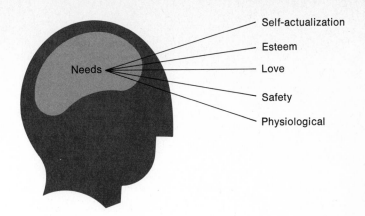

food, but physiological needs do not dominate the behavior of most of us. The primary physiological needs are (1) oxygen, (2) food, (3) water, (4) rest, (5) exercise, (6) avoidance of bodily damage, and (7) excretion.

SAFETY NEEDS   These reflect our desire for a sense of security and our dislike for personal violence, harm, or disease. Most often, we prefer a safe, predictable environment to one plagued by unknown and unpredictable events. This protective desire may prompt us to be concerned with insurance and with jobs that offer security first and high wages second. We are concerned here with psychological safety rather than the physiological safety discussed previously.

Like physiological needs, our safety needs do not dominate our lives except in times of emergency or danger. Nevertheless, many people are seriously concerned with threats to their security. A change in a work routine, even when carefully explained, often causes visible anxiety. The change in environment experienced by college freshmen is often an extreme threat to their safety needs; the individuals affected in this way may be quite open to persuasion that promises more security through campus organizations, housing, trips home, and friends. The first year of military service presents a similar experience. The desire for psychological safety is a strong need in all of us.

LOVE NEEDS   Some social scientists use the term *belonging* to designate this group of needs. People must be loved and in turn must express their love. Sharing our life with others is important to us, and we often react quickly to even the possibility that this need of ours will be denied. We find satisfaction for love needs most often through our family and close friends, but the category extends beyond this. We desire the approval and acceptance of our classmates, our fellow workers, and the many groups of people with whom we associate and with whom we tend to identify ourselves. We alter our behavior and perhaps even our standards in order to be accepted, to belong, to be loved by our chosen friends and groups.

The most significant aspect of this set of changing needs is the realization that its satisfaction involves both giving and receiving. To be well adjusted, we must give as well as receive love. Our lonely-hearts clubs owe their existence to this powerful need to give and to share love. Dishonest persuaders have often taken advantage of this need with campaigns that pretend to help suffering people.

ESTEEM NEEDS When our physiological, safety, and love needs are satisfied, our esteem needs theoretically become most important. These needs go beyond the more passive belonging or love needs into a more active desire for recognition and self-respect. Esteem needs include evaluation of oneself. According to Maslow they are of two slightly different types, or *sets:*

> [One is] the desire for strength, for achievement, for adequacy, for confidence in the face of the world and for independence and freedom. Secondly, we have what we may call the desire for reputation or prestige (defining it as respect or esteem from other people), recognition, attention, importance, or appreciation.[17]

In our culture esteem needs are very important. Americans are often accused of being self-centered. A threat to our ego or self-esteem, whether real or fancied, often prompts swift reaction. Our radio and television commercials appeal to our esteem needs by emphasizing the prestige of a certain expensive car or by suggesting that our status in a group is threatened if we are offensive or only "half-safe."

The satisfaction or partial satisfaction of esteem needs leads to self-confidence and a feeling of personal worth. Esteem needs are often accompanied by many frustrations and personal conflicts, for people desire not only the recognition and attention of their chosen groups but also the self-respect and status that their moral, social, and religious standards require. When the chosen groups call for behavior that conflicts with a person's standards, that person must often make heroic choices in order to remain well adjusted. People play many roles in order to satisfy some of the different groups to which they belong.

The problem of explaining the precise extent of one's esteem needs is complicated by one's entire system of needs. The esteem needs of some poorly adjusted individuals are so great that they will seek achievement (or what they consider achievement) at the great price of their own self-respect, morals, and ideals. This is not to say that the so-called achievement motive is abnormal. Much has been written about the need for achievement as a motivating force.[18]

---

[17]*Ibid.,* p. 382.

[18]See D. C. McClelland, *The Achieving Society* (Princeton, N.J.: D. Van Nostrand Company, 1976); and S. W. Gellerman, *Motivation and Productivity* (American Management Association, 1963), chap. 12.

SELF-ACTUALIZATION NEEDS This term, first used by Kurt Goldstein, refers to what might be called *self-fulfillment*—or *self-realization*—our desire to reach the height of our personal abilities and talents. In Maslow's words, "What a man *can* be, he *must* be." This need becomes increasingly important as the previous four needs are satisfied, and in our culture it is a very important aspect of human behavior and motivation. The large number of retired or established people who return to college or take adult courses in art, writing, or drama in order to satisfy creative urges is one response to self-actualization needs. At Detroit's Wayne State University (a large metropolitan institution), the *average* age of the student body is twenty-six, and many students have full-time jobs. One part-time student is eighty-seven; the oldest full-time student is only eighty-two.

Maslow talked of "trends to self-actualization."[19] He spoke of *growth needs* when referring to young people "growing well" on their way to self-actualization. Just before his death, Maslow suggested an extra or half step up the needs ladder between esteem and self-actualization. What Frank Goble diagrams as *growth needs,* Maslow called *being-values* or *metaneeds.*

Figure 11.7 is my attempt to relate the psycho-environmental prerequisites to the basic-needs system of Goldstein and Maslow.[20] The rank and the practical importance of these needs depend on the degree to which each need is satisfied. Because this degree of satisfaction is constantly changing (dynamic), even among our physiological needs, communicators are advised to know their audience. In chapter 1 we pointed out that receivers decode according to *their* past experiences, emotions, and attitudes. More specifically, they decode in terms of their interacting needs. At one time our need for *love* may predominate, coloring the meaning we attach to a communication; at another time our need for esteem may be foremost, and our openness to persuasion is altered accordingly. The degree of satisfaction of these five needs for an average person is hard to pin down, especially if we presume that it is constant. Nevertheless, an estimate, even an old one, gives us a benchmark from which to start. Maslow suggests that the average person achieves the following degrees of satisfaction:[21]

1 Physiological needs 85%
2 Safety needs 70%
3 Love needs 50%
4 Esteem needs 40%
5 Self-actualization needs 10%

Since a satisfied need is not a strong motivator, the smaller figures should indicate the areas in which we are most open to persuasion.

[19] A. H. Maslow, *Toward a Psychology of Being* (New York: Van Nostrand Reinhold Company, 1968), p. 25.
[20] For another attempt, see Frank Goble, *The Third Force* (New York: Grossman, 1970), p. 50.
[21] Maslow, "A Theory of Human Motivation," p. 389.

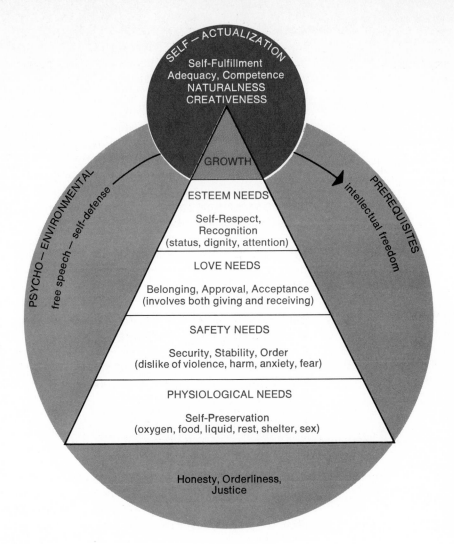

Figure 11.7

The prerequisites (see figure 11.7) are so important to the Maslow explanation of human needs and motivations that they themselves become strong motivators when denied or endangered. These environmental prerequisites include such things as free speech, intellectual freedom, the right to self-defense, and a desire for justice, honesty, and orderliness.

The lists of specific terms called needs, motives, appeals, and so forth can be roughly sorted under the five basic needs in the Maslow system (page 277).

Human motivation is terribly complex; we should be wary of sure-fire persuasive appeals.

MOTIVE TERMS AND THE MASLOW NEEDS

Physiological Needs	Safety Needs	Love Needs	Self-esteem Needs	Self-Actualization Needs
1. Bodily comfort	1. Fear	1. Loyalty	1. Pride	1. Creativeness
2. Sex attraction	2. Conformity	2. Family affection	2. Reputation	2. Curiosity
3. Physical enjoyment	3. Companionship	3. Sympathy	3. Power	3. Constructiveness
4. Hunger	4. Saving	4. Mothering	4. Achievement	4. Ambition
5. Activity	5. Conflict	5. Respect for Deity	5. Social distinction	5. Independence
6. Rest and sleep	6. Cleanliness	6. Sentiments	6. Appearance	6. Freedom from restraint

Credibility and Ethical Proof

It may be more fact than fiction that "what you are speaks so loudly I can't hear what you're saying."

Figure 11.8 The closed mind and source credibility. © 1970 United Features Syndicate, Inc.

Credibility refers to the receiver's acceptance of or disposition toward the source. Aristotle used the term *ethos* to designate the audience's perception of the speaker. In regard to ethical proof, Aristotle set forth the general rule that "there is no proof so effective as that of the character."[22]

Source credibility is related to Aristotle's notions of *good will, good moral character,* and *good sense,* as these are perceived by receivers. In modern times, source credibility has been discussed as *good intentions, trustworthiness,* and *competence* or *expertness.* Our source credibility includes our perceptions and attitudes of trust and confidence, which are based in part on our beliefs about the intent, position in society, knowledge, and sincerity of the speaker. High source credibility generally produces more attitude change in the receiver. Both reason and research tell us that an untrustworthy speaker, regardless of his or her other qualities, will be viewed as a questionable message source.[23]

[22] Aristotle, *Rhetoric,* 1377b21–1378a19.
[23] Raymond G. Smith, "Source Credibility Context Effects," *Speech Monographs,* 40, no. 4 (1973), pp. 303–9.

Sears Roebuck, in its 1908 catalogue, used the credibility of its bankers to persuade the customer that it was a respectable and responsible company (figure 11.9).

Ethical proof is the practical credibility that is established or reinforced by the speaker's ethical characteristics (as perceived by the audience) and behavior during the sending of the message. In its most general sense, it refers to the audience's impressions of the honesty, character, wisdom, and good will of the speaker.[24]

Other dimensions of ethical proof include the perceived (by the receiver) similarity of attitudes held by speaker and audience, and the speaker's use of voice and language, humor, and evidence. Other things being equal, persuaders may be influential when they are perceived by receivers as having attitudes similar to their own.

The social status of a speaker may be detected from the language segments and vocal signals that he or she uses. Studies of excess verbalizations and signals indicating disorganization have found that an absence of these behaviors aided a speaker's credibility.[25]

The use of humor may enhance speakers' pragmatic ethical proof, if not their persuasion, as measured by attitude shifts among the audience. Humor and satire, when used with a professional touch, can affect audience interest and attention and thereby retention. That it can boomerang when not used in this way is very clear from research[26] and common experience.

Even sources who enjoy high credibility lose some of their ethical proof over time. The use of evidence may help a speaker regain lost credibility. The variable of source credibilty perceived by an audience is critical to any research project or communication episode. A speaker's use of evidence may significantly increase immediate attitude change and source credibility when the message is delivered well, particularly when the audience has little or no prior familiarity with the evidence.[27] The channel of communication used by the speaker does not appear to affect the impact of evidence upon the audience. Evidence appears to make one less easily persuaded by counter-argument. Assuming a message has some essential worth, the delivery of it and its accompanying ethical proof are important to how we perceive its source.

[24] Lester Thonssen and A. Craig Baird, *Speech Criticism* (New York: Ronald Press, 1948, 1970), p. 387.

[25] Eldon E. Baker, "The Immediate Effects of Perceived Speaker Disorganization on Speaker Credibility and Audience-Attitude Change in Persuasive Speaking," *Western Speech,* 29 (1965), pp. 148–61; also see James J. Bradac, Catherine W. Konsky, and Robert A. Davies, "Two Studies of the Effects of Linguistic Diversity upon the Judgments of Communicator Attributes and Message Effectiveness," *Communication Monographs,* 43 (March 1976), pp. 70–79.

[26] D. K. Berlo and H. Kumata, "The Investigator: The Impact of a Satirical Radio Drama," *Journalism Quarterly,* 33 (1956), pp. 287–98.

[27] J. C. McCroskey, "The Effects of Evidence as an Inhibitor of Counterpersuasion," *Speech Monographs,* 37 (1970), pp. 188–94.

JAMES B. FORGAN,
President.
CHARLES N. GILLETT,
Cashier.
WM. H. MONROE,
Assistant Cashier

CAPITAL $8,000,000
SURPLUS $6,000,000

First National Bank OF CHICAGO.

Chicago, October 23, 1907.

TO WHOM IT MAY CONCERN:
      It is with pleasure that we testify to our own good opinion
of the integrity, responsibility and business ability of Sears,
Roebuck & Company. They are one of the largest mercantile institutions in the United States.
      Anyone can, in our judgment, feel perfectly secure in sending
money to them with their orders, as we understand they ship their
goods agreeing that anything not proving entirely satisfactory when
received can be returned to them, and the money paid will immediately
be returned to the purchaser.
      The officers of the company are well and favorably known to
us, command our full confidence, and we believe can be relied upon to
do exactly as they agree.   Yours very truly,

In writing to the above bank as to our reliability, be sure to enclose a 2-cent stamp for reply.

ERNEST A. HAMILL, PRESIDENT
CHARLES L. HUTCHINSON, VICE PRESIDENT
CHAUNCEY J. BLAIR, VICE PRESIDENT
D. A. MOULTON, VICE PRESIDENT

JOHN C. NEELY, SECRETARY
FRANK W. SMITH, CASHIER
B. G. SAMMONS, ASS'T CASHIER
J. EDWARD MAASS, ASS'T CASHIER

No. 5106

THE CORN EXCHANGE NATIONAL BANK
OF CHICAGO
CAPITAL $3,000,000
SURPLUS $3,000,000

CHICAGO, October 22, 1907.

TO WHOM IT MAY CONCERN:
      We are pleased to testify to the responsibility of Sears,
Roebuck & Company. The company enjoys the highest credit with their
Chicago banks, of which this bank is one.
      We believe anyone who has dealings with this company will be
treated in the fairest manner possible. We confidently assure anyone
who is thinking of placing an order with them, that, in our judgment,
there is absolutely no risk in sending the money with the order.
                  Yours very truly,

Cashier.

In writing to the above bank as to our reliability, be sure to enclose a 2-cent stamp for reply.

Figure 11.9 *From Joseph J. Schroeder, Jr., ed., 1908 Sears, Roebuck
Catalogue, no. 117 (Northfield, Ill.: DBI Books, Inc.), p. 18.*

THEORIES OF PERSUASION

Classical Rhetoric

Rhetoric is primarily a strategy of persuasion. Aristotle defined rhetoric as "the faculty of observing in any given case the available means of persuasion."[28] Aristotle's rhetoric is based on four fundamental assumptions:[29]

1 Rhetoric is a useful art—it is an instrument of social adaptation.
2 Rhetoric can be taught.
3 Rhetorical theory is based on the doctrine of the mean—that is, it is free from extremes.
4 It is the method of giving effect to truth.

The five basic tasks in preparing and sending persuasive messages are referred to as *canons* in classical rhetoric. Let us consider each of them.

INVENTION   This is the task of investigating the message and the audience in order to discover the available means of persuasion. Invention includes narrowing the purpose of the speech and gathering and analyzing facts and evidence on the issues that are found in it, particularly as they relate to the receiver's needs. Goods considered to be desired by all people include happiness, justice, courage, temperance, health, wealth, friendship, reputation, and life itself, among others. Aristotle defined three modes or means of persuasion that, when used to investigate a specific message and audience, became sources of persuasion:

> Of the modes of persuasion furnished by the spoken word there are three kinds. The first kind depends on the personal characteristics of the speaker, ETHOS; the second on putting the audience into a certain frame of mind, PATHOS; the third on the proof or apparent proof provided by the words of the speech itself, LOGOS.[30]

Other tools that aid the invention process are provided by Aristotle in his *Rhetoric and Poetics.* These tools include (1) the *enthymeme,* "a kind of imperfect syllogism which produces, not the conclusive demonstration that we get in science and logic, but belief or persuasion, and (2) the *example,* a specific verifiable phenomenon used as the basis for inductive reasoning."[31] More will be said of the enthymeme and reasoning (logos) in chapter 12.

---

[28] Aristotle, *Rhetoric and Poetics,* p. 24.
[29] Thonssen and Baird, *Speech Criticism,* pp. 70–71.
[30] Aristotle, *Rhetoric and Poetics,* pp. 24–25.
[31] Edward P. J. Corbett, *Classical Rhetoric for the Modern Student* (New York: Oxford University Press, Inc., 1965, 1971), p. 68.

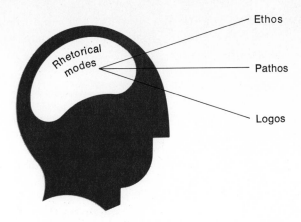

Ethos has been discussed earlier in this chapter in the section entitled "Credibility and Ethical Proof."

ARRANGEMENT   This canon concerns the process of organizing the speech or message. Aristotle used the Greek word *taxis*, meaning "division" or "arrangement," to explain what he thought was the most obvious and logical arrangement of the parts of a speech. He felt that the following elements were related most closely to the thinking habits of humans: proem (introduction), statement, argument, and epilogue (conclusion).[32] Much has already been said of this canon in part 2; more will be said of special persuasion sequences later in this chapter.

STYLE   This canon refers to the kinds of language in which you clothe your message. Try to use acceptable, correct, appropriate language; make your language clear and direct; make it polished, noble, and vivid; adjust it to your message, audience, and personality. Style involves selecting words that arouse the appropriate emotional response in the audience and help establish the proper image of the speaker.

MEMORY   This canon refers to a speaker's ability to remember his or her content in some kind of sequence. Of the five canons, Aristotle had the least to say about memory. Some good advice on protecting your memory was presented on pp. 249–250.

DELIVERY   This canon refers to the art of sending the oral message. Its main elements are voice and body action. The ancients warned of vocal monotony, improper rate of speech, bad posture, and too many random gestures and movements. They were much concerned with nonverbal communication.

[32] Lane Cooper, *The Rhetoric of Aristotle* (New York: Appleton-Century-Crofts, 1932), p. 220.

There was a strong ethical character to ancient rhetoric. Quintilian's definition of a persuasive orator as a "good man" skilled in speaking sums up this point.

Attitude Functions

One theory is that attitudes have different functions for our different personalities.[33] If we understand why people have the attitudes they do, then we are better prepared to predict how and when they might change. People may hold similar attitudes but for quite different reasons. One person's attitude toward liberalizing marijuana penalties might be based on the practical problems of enforcing the current law; anothers on a difference in life style. The same attitude might serve an ego-defensive function for a user. Another person might arrive at the same attitude for some combination of the above reasons. Here are three general functions[34] of attitudes:

1 A *referencing* function. "People need standards or frames of reference for understanding their world, and attitudes help to supply such standards."[35] We derive prepackaged norms and attitudes from our larger values systems and culture. These supply reference points for better comprehension of a very complex world. When we are exposed to new knowledge which affects us, we often find our attitudes a handy frame of reference for categorizing and understanding it.

We also use pleasure and pain, good and bad, reward and punishment as references. These are very practical attitudes. We adjust and modify this referencing function in very practical ways. We tend to classify high grades, money, special privilege, and so forth as favorable and their opposites as unfavorable. We also acquire some of our attitudes completely or partly because of this practical, referencing function.

2 A *self-identification* function. Our attitudes help us define and know who we are. Some attitudes express our value systems positively. We gain identity as well as satisfaction from the expression of some cherished attitudes. Our prayers in church, our oath of office or allegiance, even the clothes we wear—all help us assert and identify ourselves. When our feelings do not agree with our beliefs, we sometimes have trouble with this function.

3 An *ego-defensive* function. We often develop attitudes thought to protect our egos from conflict and frustration. These attitudes help us reduce anxieties and adjust to threats. They can help us survive temporarily difficult times by removing the heat from conflict, the pain from frustration. When totally unrealistic and persistent, they can hurt us by delaying objective solutions to problems and delaying our social adjustment to the real world.

[33] D. Katz, "The Functional Approach to the Study of Attitudes," *Public Opinion Quarterly*, 24 (1960), 163.

[34] With apologies and appreciation to D. Katz who identified four functions: adjustment, ego-defensive, value-expressive, and knowledge. *Ibid.*, pp. 163–204.

[35] Katz refers to this as the *knowledge* function.

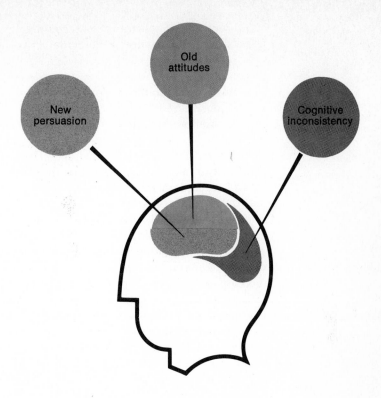

Consistency Theory

Consistency here refers to a kind of mental agreement between a person's notions about some object or event and some *new* information about that same object or event. *Cognition* is the mental process by which knowledge is both acquired and known, usually through perception, reasoning, and decoding. However, cognition is more than a search for meaning. It also involves the attitudes and images we hold of the world. The assumption is that when new information is contradictory to or inconsistent with a person's notions and attitudes, it will lead to some confusion and tension. This tension motivates people to adjust their attitudes or behavior. Our cognitive system seeks a harmonious, agreeable, balanced, *consistent* set of relationships between our notions of the world and our latest perceptions of it. The cognitive consistency theories do provide us with many practical principles of persuasion.

CONGRUITY THEORY   Congruity refers to agreement, similarity, or harmony. According to the authors of this theory, we seek somehow to keep our attitudes in harmony or consistent with the world around us.[36] When

[36] Charles E. Osgood and Percy H. Tannenbaum, "The Principle of Congruity in the Prediction of Attitude Change," *Psychological Review,* 62, no. 1 (1955), p. 43.

faced with differing attitudes, we tend to average them out according to their strength or power. Persuasion is then the result of this pressure to reduce incongruity. However, when incongruence is so great as to be unbelievable, it inhibits persuasion and attitude change. During World War II, our shipbuilding production rate was so high that American propagandists reduced the actual figures for fear the enemy would not believe them and therefore be less likely to surrender.

BALANCE THEORY   According to balance theory, when two persons interact with an event or object of mutual concern, the interaction—both individual and interpersonal—is, cognitively, either balanced or unbalanced. When it is balanced, no persuasion is possible. When it is unbalanced, tension is produced, which generates a motivation to restore balance.

Despite some old sayings, balance theory suggests that similar personalities attract, and that familiarity, other things being equal, breeds attraction, not contempt. In Heider's words, "With similar attitudes proximity will increase the degree of positive sentiment; with slight dissimilarity of attitudes a mutual assimilation might be produced, and with it an increase in friendliness; with strong dissimilarites the hostility will be increased."[37]

A more interpersonal orientation to balance theory is provided by Newcomb's *strain toward symmetry*,[38] a tendency to communicate which reduces tension or imbalance. The individual respect and trust people have for one another in their interpersonal relations do influence the success of communication in reducing strain.

Rosenberg and Abelson build on the balance model in their affective-cognitive consistency theory.[39] According to this theory, attitude consists of two elements, feelings and beliefs. People seek balance between them. Persuasion may then be achieved by modifying either the affective (feelings) or cognitive (belief) element of an attitude.

COGNITIVE DISSONANCE   In this theory, *cognitive* means "any knowledge, opinion, or belief about the environment, about oneself, or about one's behavior."[40] The word *dissonance* replaces the previously used *inconsistency; consonance* refers to consistency. The basic hypotheses of this highly regarded theory, according to Leon Festinger, its chief architect, are:

[37] F. Heider, *Psychology of Interpersonal Relations* (New York: John Wiley & Sons, Inc., 1958), p. 190.
[38] T. M. Newcomb, "An Approach to the Study of Communication Acts," *Psychological Review*, 60 (1953), 393–404; see also T. M. Newcomb, "Individual Systems of Orientation," in *Psychology: A Study of a Science*, vol. 3, ed. S. Koch (New York: McGraw-Hill Book Company, 1959), pp. 384–422.
[39] M. Rosenberg and R. Abelson, "An Analysis of Cognitive Balancing," in *Attitude Organization and Change*, ed. C. Hovland and M. Rosenberg (New Haven: Yale University Press, 1960), pp. 112–63; see also M. Rosenberg, "An Analysis of Affective-Cognitive Consistency," in *Attitude Organization and Change*, pp. 15–64.
[40] Leon Festinger, *A Theory of Cognitive Dissonance* (Stanford, Calif.: Stanford University Press, 1957), p. 3.

1 The existence of dissonance, being psychologically uncomfortable, will motivate the person to try to reduce the dissonance and achieve consonance.
2 When dissonance is present, in addition to trying to reduce it, the person will actively avoid situations and information which would likely increase the dissonance.[41]

Festinger points out that we could substitute the words *frustration* and *disequilibrium* among others, for *dissonance*. Whatever the label, the word refers to ill-fitting relations among beliefs, a practically unavoidable condition in a wide variety of situations. Festinger suggests the following as typical sources of dissonance between two beliefs: *logical inconsistency, cultural mores, past experience,* and *when one specific opinion is included by definition in a more general opinion* (for instance, Democrats are not supposed to favor a Republican candidate for office).[42]

The theory of cognitive dissonance states clearly that behavior can cause persuasion. Many very creative research projects support this point and provide suggestions for involvement and self-persuasion. For example in a study of *oral counter-attitudinal advocacy*—that is, arguing against one's own point of view, as college dabaters must often do—Janis and King found that the speakers changed their attitudes more than the listeners did. This kind of advocacy apparently creates dissonance and, as a result, self-persuasion. It also indicates the possible influence of role playing on opinion change.[43]

Hundreds of pieces of evidence confirm the theory that our cognitive system seeks a harmonious, agreeable, balanced, consistent set of relationships between our notions of the world and our latest perceptions of it.

Social Involvement Theory

A superficial opinion of the number of beans in a jar doesn't represent much personal involvement. A lightly held belief or attitude, such as a preference for one brand of coffee over another, suggests only a modest personal involvement. A commitment to one's religion, family, country, or life style is quite another matter. We are dealing with values. Values were defined earlier as *systems which hold attitudes together*. These value type attitudes involve us very personally. They help define our self-concept. They are ego-centered. As was said earlier, attitudes cannot be represented adequately by a single point on a scale. They represent different strengths and different ranges of acceptance. The marijuana example on page 266 helps explain this point.

Research on how humans make judgments about physical objects also

---

[41]*Ibid.*
[42]*Ibid.,* p. 14.
[43]I. Janis and B. King, "The Influence of Role Playing on Opinion Change," *Journal of Abnormal and Social Psychology,* 49 (1954), pp. 211–18.

gives us insights into our social judgments.[44] One classic experiment is to put your hand in a pail of hot water for a minute or so and then put it in a pail of lukewarm water. You tend to judge it *colder* than it is. If you went from cold to a pail of warm water, you tend to judge it *warmer* than it is. The hot pail (or cold) serves as a referent point or anchor for your succeeding judgments. When the temperature sharply contrasted from that of the anchor, you tended to perceive it as farther from the anchor than it really was. When temperatures were close to that of the anchor, you tended to assimilate it, to perceive it as closer than it really was. Similar experiments in judging weights in which one first is given a one-pound object to anchor one's judgments produce similar results.

This tendency for assimilation and contrast has been applied to attitude change. A receiver's initial attitude toward the persuasion serves as a referent point or anchor for making judgments about the message. In general, the more extreme the initial attitude (anchor), the less attitude change one can expect. The less extreme the anchor, the more change one can expect.

After much creative research, the authors of this theory make the following predictions of our attitude assimilation and contrast tendencies.

> If a message or communication does not fall appreciably beyond the range of acceptances, the discrepancy will be minimized in placing the communication. Hence, the communication is likely to be *assimilated* into his range of acceptances.
>
> If the message falls well beyond the range of acceptances, the individual will appraise it as more discrepant than it actually is. Its position will be displaced away from his acceptable range, and the extent of the *contrast effect* will be in proportion to the divergence of the communication from his acceptable range.
>
> The greater the commitment or dedication of an individual to his stand on an issue, the greater the displacement of a discrepant message away from the bounds of his acceptance.[45]

MESSAGE ORGANIZATION AND CONTENT

The Natural Order

The apparent similarities between motivation patterns on the one hand, and thinking-learning rules on the other, offer many suggestions for organizing persuasive material. Probably the most famous normal or natural thought system is what John Dewey called the reflective thinking pattern.

---

[44] H. Helson, *Adaptation Level Theory* (New York: Harper & Row, Publishers, Inc., 1964).
[45] C. Sherif, M. Sherif, and R. Nebergall, *Attitude and Attitude Change* (Philadelphia: W. B. Saunders Company, 1963), p. 226.

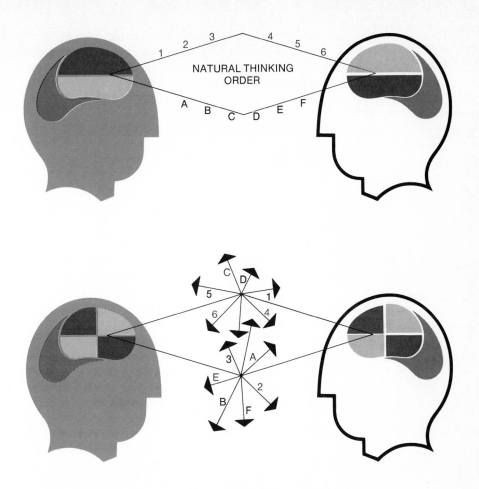

This system is also used frequently in problem-solving and group-discussion courses and is discussed further in chapter 14.[46] It includes:

1 Attention and awareness of felt difficulty.
2 Recognition of a problem or need.
3 Sorting of objections and counter-plans in search of the best solution.
4 Working out and visualizing the proposed solution.
5 Evaluation of the solution, leading to its acceptance or rejection.

Persuaders and speech scholars have made many adaptations similar to this one. Hollingworth suggests that the fundamental tasks of a speaker are attention, interest, impression, conviction, and direction.[47]

Alan H. Monroe calls his system the *motivated sequence*, "the sequence of ideas which by following the normal process of thinking, motivates the

[46] John Dewey, *How We Think* (Boston: D. C. Heath & Company, 1933), p. 107.
[47] H. L. Hollingworth, *The Psychology of the Audience* (New York: American Book Company, 1935, 1977), pp. 19–32.

audience to respond to the speaker's purpose."[48] The key steps in this natural order are (1) attention, (2) need, (3) satisfaction, (4) visualization, and (5) action. This system argues that, first, our attention must be caught; second, we must be made to feel a definite need; third, we must be shown a way to satisfy this need; fourth, we must be made to see how the proposal applies to us personally; finally, we must be shown how we should act. This system is really a need-plan or need-solution system, as we explained in chapter 7.

In making generalizations from empirical evidence, Carl Hovland also supports a need-plan natural order: "Presentation of information relevant to the satisfaction of needs after these needs have been aroused brings about greater acceptance than an order which presents the information first and the need-arousal second."[49]

Natural-order systems for organizing persuasion all make much of the *attention concept.* William James once said, "What holds attention determines action. . . . The impelling idea is simply the one which possesses the attention. . . . What checks our impulses is the mere thinking of reasons to the contrary. . . ."[50] Attention may be considered as a focus of perception that leads to a readiness to respond.

In chapter 8, we found the forms of emphasis useful in transferring information to the audience. Audiences were better able to recall and remember things that they had been told with emphasis. This is an example of how a speaker can make good use of audience attention in informative speeches. Granted, an improvement in an audience's remembering or interest does not necessarily prove that their attitudes have been changed or even that they are more open to change. However, *if* attention and interest *do* help determine action and a readiness to respond, as James says, then the suggestions for presenting information fit here also.

Our attention, like all perception, is selective. Because of this, the persuasive speaker must concentrate on keeping the audience interested in his or her subject. Other factors are constantly competing for the listener's attention—sounds, sights, people, conflicting ideas, and so on.

Whatever specific organization adaptation you decide upon, the following *psychological order* is used, at least theoretically, in all persuasion speeches:

1 Creation of attention and location or establishment of need.
2 Arousal of interest and problem awareness by relating the need to the specific audience.
3 Explanation of the solution in terms of the problem, need, previous experience, knowledge, and personality of the audience.

---

[48] Alan H. Monroe, *Principles and Types of Speech* (Chicago: Scott, Foresman & Company, 1949), pp. 308–9; see also Alan H. Monroe and Douglas Ehninger, *Principles of Speech Communication* (Glenview, Ill.: Scott, Foresman & Company, 1969), p. 261.
[49] Carl Hovland, *The Order of Presentation in Persuasion* (New Haven: Yale University Press, 1957), p. 135.
[50] William James, *Psychology: Briefer Course* (New York: Holt, Rinehart & Winston, 1892), p. 448.

4 Evaluation, when necessary, of all important objections, counter-arguments, or alternative solutions.

5 Reinforcement of your message throughout your speech, particularly toward the end of it, through verbal reminders, reviews, summaries, and visualizations.

Antagonistic Receivers

Apart from the question of antagonism, or opposition to one's point of view, the question of where to put your best argument is an old one. Answers from research are confusing and in need of interpretation. The elusive variable of initial audience attitudes is most important. When such attitudes are unstructured, it may be that subsequent audience attitudes are affected most by first-position arguments.[51] Perhaps it is also true of retention or remembering but until we do more research in which the initial-attitude variable is better accounted for, it's still guesswork. The effects of *argument arrangement* on antagonistic receivers—particularly when their initial attitudes are known—can, however, be stated quite generally.

A classic study done for the U.S. War Department by Hovland, Lumsdaine, and Sheffield[52] contains many insights into and suggestions for the psychology of persuasion, particularly for antagonistic receivers. The

[51] See Irving L. Janis and Rosalind L. Feierabend, "Effects of Alternative Ways of Ordering Pro and Con Arguments in Persuasive Communications," in *The Order of Presentation in Persuasion,* ed. Carl I. Hovland (New Haven: Yale University Press, 1957), pp. 115–28; and Norman Miller and D. T. Campbell, "Recency and Primacy in Persuasion as a Function of the Timing of Speeches and Measurements," *Journal of Abnormal and Social Psychology,* 59 (1959), pp. 1–9. See also N. H. Anderson and A. A. Barrios, "Primacy Effects in Personality Impression Formation," *Journal of Abnormal and Social Psychology,* 63 (1963), pp. 346–50.

[52] Information and Education Division, U.S. War Department, "The Effects of Presenting 'One Side' versus 'Both Sides' in Changing Opinions on a Controversial Subject," in T. M. Newcomb and others, *Readings in Social Psychology* (New York: Holt, Rinehart & Winston, 1947), pp. 566–77; see also C. I. Hovland A. A. Lumsdaine, and F. D. Sheffield, *Experiments on Mass Communication* (Princeton, N.J.: Princeton University Press, 1949), pp. 201–27.

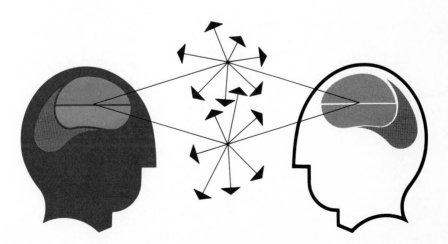

experiment involved the issue of a long war (WWII) and overoptimism. The subjects were 625 army personnel. The War Department felt that the weight of evidence indicated at least two more years of war in the Pacific. The specific question the experimenter wished to answer was this: When the weight of evidence supports the main thesis being presented, is it more effective to present only the arguments supporting the point being made, or to introduce also the arguments opposed to the point being made?

The persuasion was transmitted by two prerecorded radio broadcasts. Both speeches were in the form of a commentator's analysis of the Pacific war. The commentator's conclusion was that the job of finishing the war would be tough and that it would take at least two years after V–E (Victory in Europe) Day. The first program (A—one side) presented only those arguments indicating the war would be a long one, arguments relating mainly to problems of distance and of the moving, supplying, and quartering of troops. The second program (B—both sides) presented all the same arguments, but in addition it briefly considered arguments for a short war. Two of these arguments were our naval victories and superiority, and our previous progress despite a two-front war.

A preliminary survey of estimates of the length of the war was used to determine initial opinions. To register a change in attitude, a man had to revise by at least six months or more his estimate of how long the war would continue. An added analysis compared the scores of high-school graduates with the scores of men who did not graduate from high school.

Here are the researchers' conclusions:[53]

1 In the case of individuals who were initially opposed to the point of view being presented, presenting the arguments on both sides of the issue was more effective than giving only the arguments supporting the point being made.
2 For men who were already convinced of the point of view being presented, however, including arguments on both sides was less effective for the group as a whole than presenting only the arguments favoring the general position being advocated.
3 Better-educated men were affected more favorably by the presentation of both sides; poorly educated men were affected more by the communication that used only supporting arguments.
4 The presentation of both sides was least effective for the group of poorly educated men who were already convinced of the point of view being advocated.
5 An important incidental finding was that the omission of a relevant argument was more noticeable and detracted more from effectiveness in the both-sides presentation than in the one-side presentation.

[53] Also, see Ralph L. Rosnow, "One-Sided versus Two-Sided Communication under Indirect Awareness of Persuasive Intent," *Public Opinion Quarterly*, 32 (Spring 1968), pp. 95–101; Glen Hass and Darwyn Linder, "Counterargument Availability and the Effects of Message Structure on Persuasion," *Journal of Personality and Social Psychology*, 23 (August 1972), pp. 219–33; and Edmond Winston Jordan Faisen, "Effectiveness of One-Sided and Two-Sided Mass Communications in Advertising," *Public Opinion Quarterly*, 25 (1961), pp. 468—69.

The most important of these findings for our purposes is the first. Though it was less important to the issue in this study, the second finding also is interesting. However, if we knew that the convinced group would be exposed to counterpropaganda at a later date, then what kind of communication decision should we have made?

Fortunately, a similar study has thrown light specifically on the issue of counter-propaganda.[54] They compared the resistance produced by a one-sided versus a two-sided propaganda presentation. Once again, the experimental design used prerecorded radio programs. A one-sided speech (Program A) and a two-sided speech (Program B) were drafted. As before, these were directed at a kind of overoptimism. The main difference between this study and the one previously described is that here, half of the subjects (half who heard Program A and half who heard Program B) were exposed to counterpropaganda one week after the speeches.

The researchers found that the groups who were previously persuaded with "both-sides" argumentation were more resistant to counterpropaganda than those persuaded with one-sided argumentation. Only two percent of the latter groups maintained the desired attitudes when subjected to counterpropaganda, whereas sixty-one percent of the former groups resisted the counterpropaganda and maintained the desired opinion. The researchers concluded that a two-sided presentation is *more* effective in the long run than a one-sided one (a) when, regardless of initial opinion, the audience is *exposed* to subsequent counterpropaganda, or (b) when, regardless of subsequent exposure to counterpropaganda, the audience initially disagrees with the commentator's position.

It is readily apparent that this study supports the War Department's study. It shows that we must consider the use of both-sides persuasion because of the possibility that an audience may be exposed to counterargument later.

Many speech studies have in part measured the effects of *both-sides persuasion* Often such studies indicate the "other" factors are so important that they make generalization dangerous. For example, the speaker's prestige or ethos may seriously offset any advantage that he or she is predicted to have.[55] There is evidence that in full-blown, emotional, political oratory, a straightforward argumentative approach may be more effective than a both-sides presentation.[56]

Both-sides persuasion nevertheless has the appeal of objective, rational evaluation. It is a subtle and honest call for fair play. Opposing arguments are not omitted, and, therefore, opposed listeners are not antagonized. Listening should be more favorable because the listener will not be re-

---

[54] Arthur A. Lumsdaine and Irving L. Janis, "Resistance to Counter Propaganda Produced by a One-Sided versus a Two-Sided Propaganda Presentation," *Public Opinion Quarterly,* 17 (1953), pp. 311–18.

[55] Stanley F. Paulson, "The Effects of the Prestige of the Speaker and Acknowledgment of Opposing Arguments on Audience Retention and Shift of Opinion," *Speech Monographs,* 21 (November 1954), pp. 267–71.

[56] Thomas Ludlum, "Effects of Certain Techniques of Credibility upon Audience Attitudes," *Speech Monographs,* 25 (November 1958), pp. 278—84.

hearsing counterarguments during your positive (pro-side) persuasion. Both-sides persuasion not only helps insulate audiences against counterarguments but also forces speakers to be more audience-oriented. Both-sides speakers must be more sensitive to their audience's attitudes and to all the arguments and issues pertaining to their subject. One student speaker, after much research on both sides of his speech subject, reported that he was now convinced of the "other" side of the subject. Both-sides persuasion is, then, (1) a most effective form of motivation and (2) a most scientific and rational form of preparation—a new rationalistic persuasion!

Both-sides persuasion almost always employs some kind of concession. The advertisements in figures 11.10 and 11.11 are good examples. Mon-

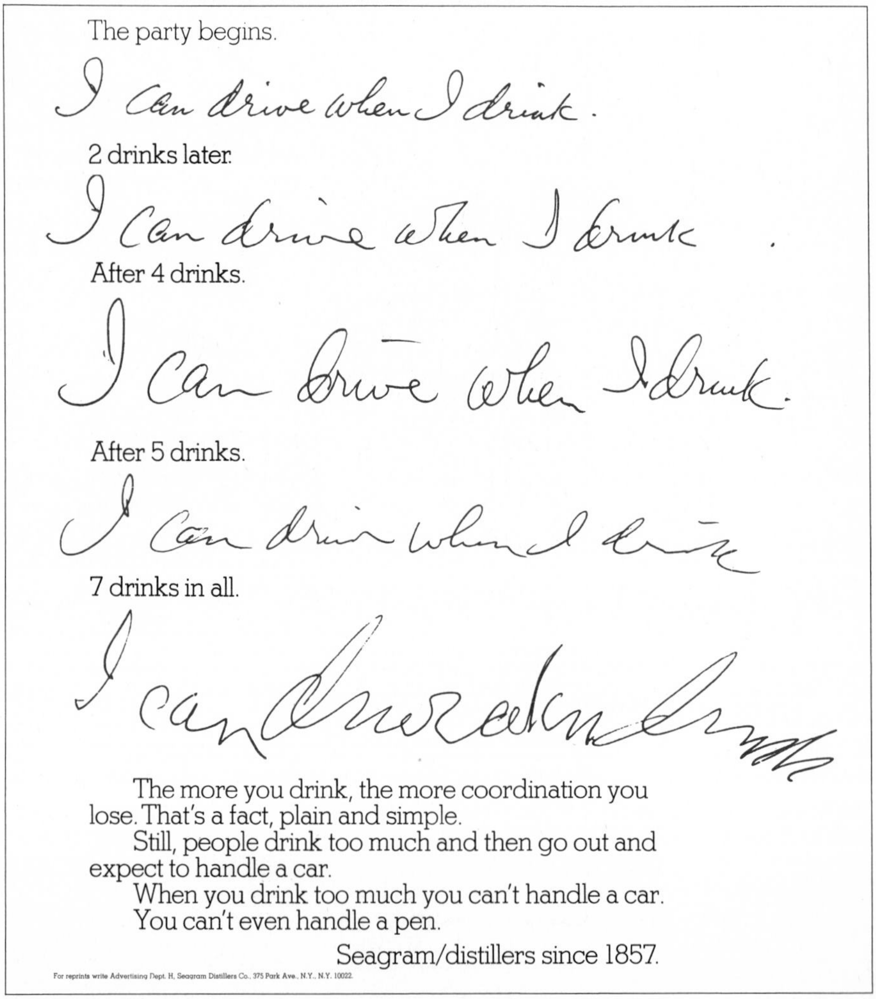

Figure 11.10 "Moderation Messages," *(New York: Seagram Distillers Co., 1975).*

The party begins.

I can drive when I drink.

2 drinks later.

I can drive when I drunk.

After 4 drinks.

I can drive when I drunk.

After 5 drinks.

I can drive when I drink

7 drinks in all.

I can drive when I drink

The more you drink, the more coordination you lose. That's a fact, plain and simple.

Still, people drink too much and then go out and expect to handle a car.

When you drink too much you can't handle a car. You can't even handle a pen.

Seagram/distillers since 1857.

For reprints write Advertising Dept. H, Seagram Distillers Co., 375 Park Ave., N.Y., N.Y. 10022.

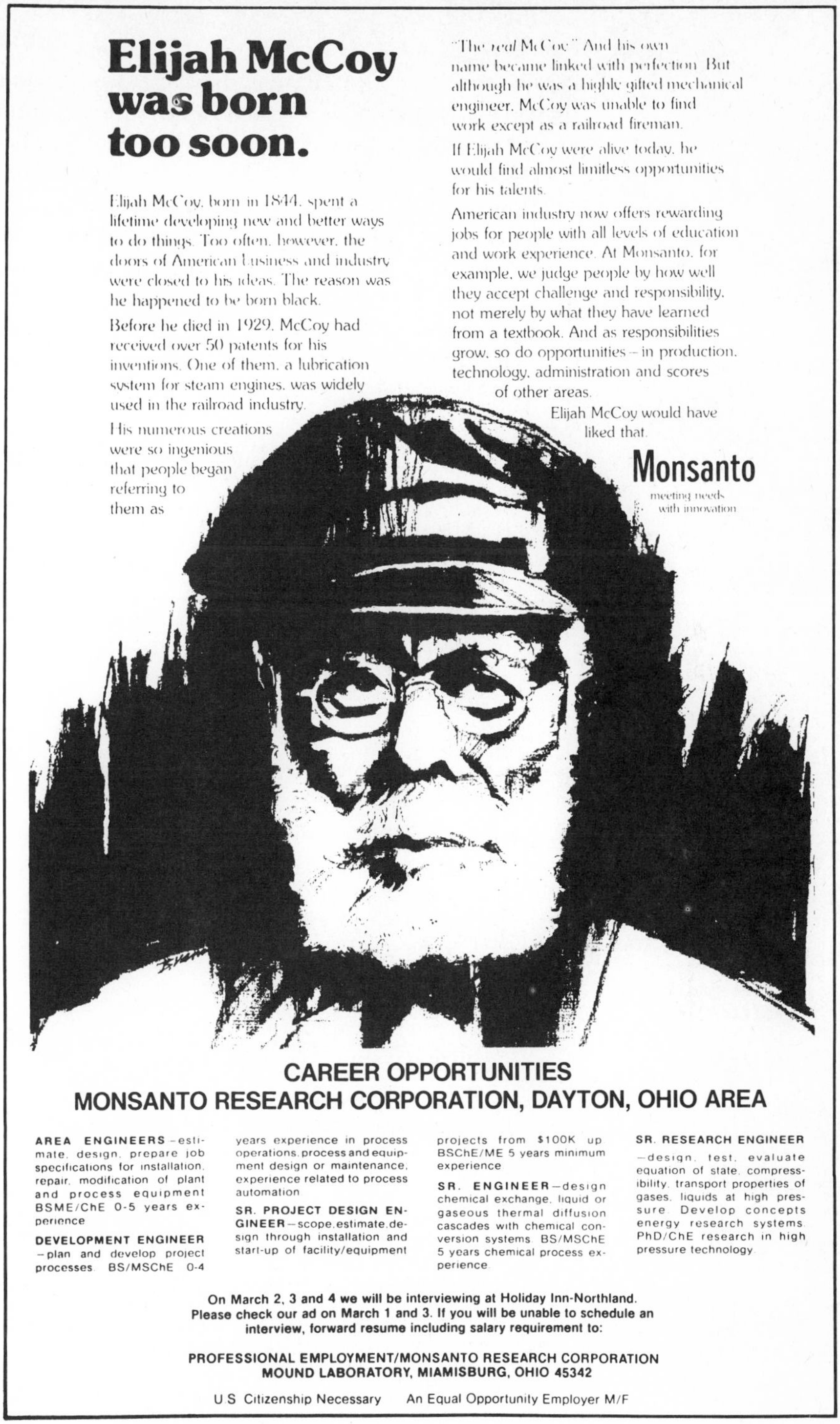

Figure 11.11 *From Monsanto Research Corp., (Miamisburg, Ohio), 1975.*

santo concedes that it may have been negligent in the past. Seagram concedes the disrupting effects of too much alcohol. The handwriting in the Seagram ad is also a clear and interesting use of the logical supports of persuasion.

Here are some specific characteristics of a both-sides persuasive speaker:

1 *Objectivity:* fair, honest, bias based on evidence.
2 *Suspended judgment:* avoids superpositive statements; creates doubt; frequently uses the hypothesis form.
3 *Nonspecific opponents:* does not identify audience as the opposition; suggests audience is undecided; creates a common ground.
4 *Critical willingness:* arouses audience reevaluation; motivates audience to reconsider the "other" side.
5 *Qualified language:* does not overstate the position and the evidence; is careful of overgeneralized statements.
6 *Audience-sensitive:* adapts the presentation to feedback signs; considers alternative actions before making the speech.
7 *Ethical:* above all, honest; presents significant opposing arguments in an objective manner; in addition, believes honesty is the best practical policy.

"He who knows only his side of the story doesn't know that—"

J. S. Mill

Two model outlines illustrating various organizational patterns follow. Additional persuasive outlines may be found in Appendix B.

BUCKLE UP AND STAY ALIVE

General End: To persuade.
Specific Purpose: To persuade the audience to always use the seat belts in their cars.

Introduction

I. A cure for cancer or heart disease! What excitement would be generated if medical authorities made this announcement. Mortality would be reduced to less than one fifth of the present rate.

(Attention)   II. For the third leading cause of death, namely, auto accidents, there already exists a lifesaving device that relatively few people use.
        A. An investigation of the accidents of last July 4.
            1. 442 victims, with no belts engaged.
            2. Belts would have prevented exactly one half the deaths.

(Physiological and Safety Needs)   B. These statistics are very meaningful to me because last summer I was involved in an accident in which a person without a belt was killed.

Body

I. No medical miracle short of a cure for cancer or heart disease can save so many lives.

(Safety Need)   A. Auto accidents are the leading cause of death between the ages of fifteen and twenty-four.

                              B. The risk of death is cut by 80 percent when safety belts are used.

                    II. Most drivers don't know the facts.

A. Ejection of an occupant is the most frequent factor in serious injury. Investigations by twenty-two states indicate that you are five times more likely to be killed if ejected.

B. The typical victim is not a speed demon on a strange road.

    1. The National Safety Council found that three out of five fatal crashes occur on roads familiar to the driver.

    2. My accident was on a road I've been traveling all my life.

(Interest)   3. The victim is more typically a young homeowner, a wife picking up her husband, or a teenager backing out of a driveway.

    4. Fifty percent of all fatalities occur at less than 40 mph.

    5. There is no guarantee against getting struck from behind or sideswiped.

C. Common misconceptions set straight.

    1. You are not safer if thrown out of your car.

    2. Careful drivers are not immune to accidents.

    3. Local drivers are not immune to accidents.

    4. Driving slowly is no protection.

(Meeting Objections)   D. Some objections set straight.

    1. Don't seat belts often cause injuries?

       a. Hip bruises - my friend would have traded her fractured skull for a dozen hip bruises.

       b. Submerged in water or on fire.

(Visualization)   (1) With a seat belt you are more apt to remain conscious.

           (2) Seat belts can be released with one hand in two seconds.

    2. I don't drive often, far or fast; why bother?

       a. Three of five fatal crashes are on local and familiar roads, within 25 miles of home.

(Reinforcement)   b. Fifty percent of all fatalities are under 40 mph.

       c. It takes <u>two</u> to tango.

Conclusion

    I. Safety belts have been publicized and made mandatory in cars.

       A. All car manufacturers.

       B. United States Health Service.

       C. American Medical Association.

       D. Insurance companies.

    II. Always buckle up for safety to save lives and prevent serious accidents.

       A. Have everyone buckle up no matter how short the ride.

       B. It takes only six seconds to cut the risk of death by 80 percent.

Adapted from a speech by Darlene Uten, Wayne State University.

```
OVER SIXTY-FIVE
General End:        To persuade.
Specific Purpose:   To persuade people to change their attitudes and/or behavior toward
                    senior citizens.
```

Introduction

(Attention)

    I. The Los Angeles Times recently received a letter from an eighty-four-year-old widow. Mrs. Brown's letter began, "I'm so lonely I could die. I see no human beings. My phone never rings. The people here say, 'Pay your rent and go back to your room.'" She enclosed one dollar and six stamps. "Will someone please call or write?" she asked. In a city of almost three million people, Mrs. Brown didn't have one person with whom she could talk.

    II. Now I'm going to tell you another true story. Every single one of us is going to grow old someday! There is no fountain of youth! You may end up like Mrs. Brown, unless you help change society's attitudes and behavior toward our senior citizens.

(Overview)

I am going to tell you what it means to be over sixty-five in America: it typically means inadequate income, poor health care, and near isolation.

Body

    I. People over sixty-five are inordinately poor.
        A. One out of every four of the twenty million Americans over sixty-five lives below the poverty level.
        B. One-third are foced to go on welfare for the first time.
        C. The majority of older citizens are hit by inflation and fixed income.
        D. Pension plans are deceptive.
            1. A U.S. Senate study revealed only 5 to 15 percent of workers covered since 1950 have ever received any pension money.
           2. Layoffs, plant shutdowns, company mergers, and employer bankruptcies have altered originally sound pension plans.
           3. The average American couple gets only $3,252 in social security a year; the poverty level is approximately $3,000 a year.

    II. People over sixty-five are inordiately ill.
        A. Eighty-six percent of men and women over sixty-five have serious chronic illnesses.

(Physiological Needs)

        B. Medical bills of average elderly couple are $1,700 a year, three times those of younger people.
        C. Medicare does not alleviate the medical bill problem.
            1. Astonishingly, the elderly pay the same with Medicare as they did without it. One third can't pay their bills.
           2. Medicaid doesn't pay for drugs, eyeglasses, or dentures.
        D. It is estimated that one third to one half of all health problems of the elderly are related to malnutrition.

    III. People over sixty-five are inordinately isolated.
        A. The elderly are troubled by a sense of alienation from human companionship.

(Love Needs)

        B. Nursing homes are impersonal. People are sent there simply because they have nowhere else to go.
        C. Men and women over sixty-five commit suicide at a rate 20 percent higher than the national average.

Conclusion

(Reinforcement)
I. How ironic it seems that a nation that has advanced so far in one century to stretch the life expectancy of its citizens from forty-seven to seventy cannot make these additional years worthwhile.

II. This is the terrible plight of those citizens over sixty-five. They are victims of inadequate income, poor health care, and isolation. Everyone should try to help improve these conditions.

(Review)
Let's change our attitude toward older people. How much can we tolerate the abuse and neglect of older, vulnerable people for the sake of avoiding the inconvenience and cost of properly caring for them. Let's make the "golden years" the best years.

Adapted from a speech by Darlene Glowgower, Wayne State University.

11 SUMMING UP

Persuasion is the ability to (1) assess the causes of motivation in human affairs and (2) assess the available means of influencing attitudes and behavior.

Motivation refers to specific deficiency and abundancy needs in the human experience. We are motivated by both *need* and by *plenty: survival* and *security* but also *satisfaction* and *stimulation.* We desire consistency in our attitudes and our behavior, in what we feel and what we think. Discomfort is a motivating force.

Attitudes refer to the thinking, feeling, and behavioral intentions which govern one's predispositions toward people, situations, and things.

An attitude may also be defined as a readiness to respond. The dimensions of attitude have been described as cognitive, affective, and behavioral.

An opinion is a more lightly held judgment than an attitude or belief. Value is a broad concept usually made up of many attitudes and beliefs. Attitudes have different functions such as *practical, value expressive,* and *ego-defensive.* We infer and attribute attitudes, beliefs, and intentions from what people do or what they tell us. Attitudes have latitudes of *acceptance* as well as of *rejection* and *noncommitment.*

A persuader has a moral responsibility for the strategies employed. Strategy is *not* unethical unless it is dishonest, unfair to the facts, or so subtle that it gives *no* clue to the receiver. Receivers must be afforded some choice.

Force is not an ethical persuasive strategy. As receivers of persuasion, we have an ethical obligation to give a fair hearing and to comply with the persuasion from legitimate authorities and laws.

Persuasion is a means of influencing others through ethical, nonviolent techniques. Persuasion is seldom a one-shot matter. It is almost always part of a larger plan or campaign.

The systems of the body and the maintenance of a constant internal bodily environment provide some of our most basic motivations. To survive, humans need *oxygen, food, water, rest, elimination of wastes,* and *exercise.* In our culture, it is only in situations of great stress, ill health, or drug abuse that a biological imbalance may have serious consequences. Nevertheless, these basic imbalances are constantly with us, affecting our behavior and the intensity with which we attempt to satisfy our needs.

Our biological nature, however important, is overlaid by a variety of social-psychological motives. Prescientific explanations of personality attempted to predict human behavior and a person's reactions to patterns of persuasion. Personality may be considered as the sum of human motives, whatever their source. Early typological theories believed humors and body biles to be related to personality. Among psychological theories, Jung's introvert-extrovert classification is the best known. To a great extent, the sources of persuasion are found in an understanding of human nature and behavior. Instinct theory has given us many useful concepts for theorizing about persuasion. McDougall's "native propensities," such as hunger, disgust, curiosity, fear, anger, and mating, are still popular.

Maslow provided us with a useful classification of human dynamic needs. In the order of their importance, these needs are physiological, safety, love, esteem, and self-actualization. A satisfied need is no longer a motivator, according to this theory. Motive appeals are useful triggers of human needs.

Credibility, or *ethos,* refers to the receiver's or audience's acceptance of or disposition toward the source. It is related to Aristotle's notions of *good will, good moral character,* and *good sense.* In modern times, source credibility is discussed in terms of *good intentions, trustworthiness,* and *competence* or *expertness.* High source credibility generally produces more attitude change in the receiver.

Ethical proof includes practical factors like attitude similarity, language, humor, voice, and evidence.

In the theory of classical rhetoric, the five basic tasks in preparing and sending persuasive messages are called *canons.* These include *invention* (investigating the message and audience), *arrangement* (message organization), *style* (selecting language that arouses the appropriate emotional response), *memory,* and *delivery.* According to classical theory, a persuasive orator is a good *person* skilled in speaking.

In functional attitude theory, attitudes may be said to serve (1) a *referencing* function, (2) a *self-identification* function, and (3) an *ego-defensive* function. People may hold similar attitudes but for different reasons.

Theories of *consistency* offer many practical principles of persuasion. They refer to a kind of mental agreement between a person's notions of some object or event and some new information about that same object or event. Congruity theory, balance theory, and cognitive dissonance theory are three major theories of cognitive consistency. These theories assume that when the new information is contradictory to or inconsistent with a person's notions and attitudes, some psychological confusion and tension will result. This tension motivates people to adjust their attitudes or behavior in order to reduce this inconsistency. Persuasive communications tend to be effective when they reduce inconsistency or dissonance and to be ineffective when they increase dissonance.

In social judgment or involvement theory, one's initial attitude serves as an anchor for making judgments. If a message does not fall too far outside one's range of acceptance, it is likely to be assimilated. If it falls well beyond the range of acceptance, it will be judged more discrepant than it actually is (a contrast effect).

A natural thinking order suggests the following for organizing persuasive messages:

1 Creation of attention and location or establishment of need.
2 Arousal of interest and problem awareness by relating the need to the specific audience.
3 Explanation of the solution in terms of the problem, need, previous experience, knowledge, and personality of the audience.
4 Evaluation, when necessary, of all important objections, counter-arguments, or alternative solutions.
5 Reinforcement of your message throughout the speech, particularly toward the end of it, through verbal reminders, reviews, summaries, and visualizations.

There are many adaptations similar to this one. Hollingworth suggests that the fundamental tasks of a speaker are attention, interest, impression, conviction, and direction.

Alan H. Monroe calls his system the *motivated sequence*, "the sequence of ideas which by following the normal process of thinking, motivates the audience to respond to the speaker's purpose." The key steps are (1) attention, (2) need, (3) satisfaction, (4) visualization, and (5) action.

Both-sides persuasion has been shown by experiments to be superior to one-sided persuasion when the audience is initially opposed to the point of view being presented or when, regardless of initial attitude, the audience is exposed to counterargument. A rational form of persuasion, the both-sides approach is characterized by objectivity, suspended judgment, nonspecific opponents, critical willingness, qualified language, audience sensitivity, and ethical conduct.

Attention is vital to persuasion because so many other factors may distract the listener.

Human motivation is a highly complex phenomenon, the dynamic interaction of all of our previous perceptions of the world. The dangers of oversimplified, overstructured, or other sure-fire systems of persuasion are considerable.

1 Oral communication and argument affect attitudes, beliefs, and behavioral intent.

2 A persuader has a moral responsibility for the strategies employed and the social consequences resulting.

3 A receiver has a fundamental right of *some* choice.

4 Honesty and fairness to the facts are ethical obligations.

5 Receivers have ethical obligations for a fair hearing, and to comply with persuasion from a legitimate authority.

6 Persuasion is a nonviolent means of ethically influencing the thinking, feelings, and/or behavior of others.

7 Humankind's basic biological needs are oxygen, food, water, rest, elimination of wastes, and exercise. When these needs are not met, our social needs may become secondary.

8 In our culture, we seek psychological-social satisfaction almost as intensely as we seek survival.

9 Understanding a receiver's personality (the sum of one's motives), especially his or her self-image, value system, assumed role, and life experience, is critical to a theory of persuasion.

10 The basic needs of all humans are essentially the same: physiological wants, safety, love and belonging, esteem, and self-actualization.

11 The order and the practical importance of our dynamic needs depend on the degree to which we satisfy each need.

12 Several needs may be motivating us at the same time.

13 Source credibility includes our perceptions and attitudes of trust and confidence, which are based in part on our beliefs about the intent, position in society, knowledge, and sincerity of the speaker.

14 High source credibility generally produces more attitude change in the receiver.

15 Attitudes serve different functions: referencing, self-identification, and ego-defense.

16 People may hold similar attitudes but for quite different reasons.

17 When new information is contradictory to or inconsistent with a person's notions and attitudes, it leads to psychological confusion and tension. Persuasion is the result of pressure to reduce incongruity.

18 When one runs into a lack of agreement attitudinally between two attitude objects, there is a tendency for compromise toward a point on a scale reflecting the various strengths.

19 When incongruence is so gross as to be unbelievable, then it inhibits persuasion and attitude change.

20 Attitudes have affective and cognitive elements, and people seek consistency between them.

21 Cognitive dissonance, being psychologically uncomfortable, will motivate a person to reduce dissonance and achieve consonance.

22 People will actively avoid situations and information which increase dissonance.

23 Behavior itself can cause persuasion.

24 Most attitudes have a range of latitude (acceptance, rejection, noncommitment).

25 The larger the range of rejection, the more difficult the persuasion becomes.

26 The larger the range of acceptance or noncommitment, the less difficult the persuasion becomes.

27 If persuasion falls within or close to a receiver's range of acceptance, the discrepancy will be minimized and the persuasion *assimilated*.

28 If persuasion falls well beyond a receiver's range of acceptance, it will be appraised as more discrepant than it actually is and *contrasted*.

29 The most persuasive arrangement of speech material is an arrangement similar to people's normal thinking habits.

30 Both-sides persuasion is superior to one-sided persuasion when the audience is initially opposed to the point of view being presented; one-sided persuasion is more effective when an audience is already convinced of the view being presented.

31 People persuaded with both-sides argumentation, regardless of their initial attitudes, are more resistant to counterpropaganda than those persuaded with one-sided argumentation.

32 In a both-sides presentation, a hostile audience is persuaded more readily by a con-pro order than a pro-con order. When an audience initially agrees with the position taken by a credible source, the pro-con order of presentation is superior.

Specific Learning Outcomes

1 We should learn definitions of persuasion, motivation, and attitude.

2 We should learn the moral and ethical responsibilities of both the senders and the receivers of persuasion.

3 We should learn about the essential human biological needs: oxygen, food, water, rest, elimination of wastes, and exercise.

4 We should be aware of the importance of personality to persuasion.

5 We should learn a system for classifying human needs (physiological, safety, love, esteem, and self-actualization).

6 We should learn the basic elements of source credibility: intention, trustworthiness, and expertness.

7 We should learn the meaning of ethical proof as it relates to persuasion.

8 We should learn about the canons of classical rhetoric: invention, arrangement, style, memory, and delivery.

9 We should learn the functions of attitudes: referencing, self-identification, and ego-defense.

10 We should learn about cognitive consistency, especially congruity theory, balance theory, and cognitive dissonance theory.

11 We should learn that most attitudes have a range or latitude of acceptance, rejection, and noncommitment.

12 We should learn specific arrangement systems for persuasive messages.

13 We should learn the specific characteristics of both-sides persuasion.

Communication Competencies

1 We should be able to prepare an intelligent, ethical, two-to-three-page outline for a five-to-eight-minute speech to persuade which applies the psychology of arrangement and follows one of the outline formats suggested by the models in this chapter.

2 We should learn to apply the basic needs proposed by A. H. Maslow to a persuasion strategy.

3 We should learn to apply the psychology of cognitive inconsistency, attitude function, and social judgment to a persuasion strategy.

4 We should learn how to select a high-credibility source as a form of support for persuasion.

5 We should be able to apply both-sides persuasion in a persuasive message to antagonistic receivers.

6 We should be able to apply a natural, motivated sequence in a persuasive message (for instance, the sequence of attention, need, satisfaction, visualization, and action).

7 We should become more critical and more objective receivers of persuasive messages.

Study Projects and Tasks

1 Prepare a three-to-five minute talk in which you attempt to persuade the audience to belief or action on any subject. You must effectively use the primary needs and motive appeals discussed previously. This is an exercise, and therefore you need not use the both-sides approach or have an elaborate outline. Simply demonstrate that you know how to apply the theory of persuasion to a speaking situation. Indicate on your outline the main theories, appeals, and other devices you are using.

2 Prepare a detailed two-to-three-page outline for a four-to-six-minute persuasive speech which follows any of the formats of the model outlines in this chapter. Indicate in the margins of your outline those needs, theories, or appeals that you are stressing (safety, love, esteem, self-actualization, dissonance, and so forth).

3 Prepare a detailed outline for a five-to-seven-minute persuasive speech based on a motivated sequence. The five major divisions of the outline could be labeled:

I Attention		I Attention	
II Need		II Problem	
III Satisfaction	or	III Solution	
IV Visualization		IV Visualization	
V Action		V Action	

Indicate the motives, appeals, and other devices on which you are relying in your outline (safety, esteem, self-preservation, and so on).

4 Clip three newspaper or magazine advertisements and evaluate them in terms of the sequence in project 3. Create an ad of your own.

5 Report and illustrate a radio or television commercial or other appeal (whether for antagonistic groups or not) that made use of both-sides persuasion. Create one of your own.

6 Prepare an eight-to-ten-minute persuasive speech on a topic to which your class audience is relatively hostile (for example, pick the more unpopular side of a social issue). Meet the significant opposition arguments first and make concessions where you must before turning to the other side of the question. Make use of the best aspects of both-sides persuasion by utilizing the specific characteristics listed on page 294. See project 7 for further assistance.

7 Use the following criteria in building your own both-sides persuasive speech; use them also in judging and critiquing the speeches of your classmates.

a Did the speaker impress the audience with his or her objectivity, open-mindedness, and bias based only on evidence? Could any of the following methods be identified?

    (1) Presented the significant opposing arguments.

    (2) Did not try to hide his or her own stand on the issue.

    (3) Did not grant opposing arguments reluctantly.

b Did the speaker develop a rapport with the audience and prevent the audience from identifying itself as the opposition? Could any of the following methods be identified?

    (1) Avoided "I"; used "we" and "you and I."

    (2) Was nonspecific about opposition; identified people other than the audience as opponents.

    (3) Suggested audience was an undecided group; created a common ground.

c Did the speaker develop suspended judgment in the audience and arouse a critical willingness to consider both sides? Could any of the following methods be identified?

    (1) Avoided superpositive statements; created doubt; frequently used hypothesis form.

    (2) Created doubt rather than certainty; did not overstate the position and evidence; was careful about making overgeneralized statements.

    (3) Was above all ethical; presented significant opposing arguments in an objective, honest manner.

8 The following topics were found to have an antagonism or controversy rate (attitude disagreement) of 25 percent or more for 348 college students.[57] They might suggest topics for projects 6 and 7.

    a U.S. Olympic athletes should be subsidized by the federal government.

    b Sex education should be required in all public schools.

    c College students should hold a part-time job while in school.

    d America should train women astronauts for future space flights.

    e High school dropouts should be drafted into the armed forces.

    f The federal government should enact a law to require the sterilization of the feebleminded and the insane.

    g College social fraternities and sororities should be banned.

    h Most college students drink too much.

    i The population explosion should be curbed by a federal law limiting families to two children.

    j Movies should be taxed according to their movie code ratings.

    k Gambling should be legalized in our state.

    l The honors system for taking exams should be adopted at this school.

    m Marijuana should be legalized.

    n Cigarettes should be taxed more heavily.

    o A conviction for drunk driving should be automatically penalized by loss of license.

    p Men are unduly discriminated against in divorce proceedings.

    q Further manned exploration of space is worth the expense.

    r The choice of abortion should rest solely with the pregnant female.

    s Men are better suited for high political office than women.

  t Aid to Dependent Children should be eliminated.

  u Premarital sexual relations should be encouraged.

  v The NAACP is relevant to all black Americans.

9 Analyze a speech manuscript, editorial, or advertisement, and find the following natural-order steps: attention, need, satisfaction, visualization and action.

10 In a speech manuscript, editorial, or advertisement, find appeals to any of the following human needs: physiological, safety, love, esteem, self-actualization. Take the specific audience into account.

11 Write a two-to-three-page report of three of your attitudes that are referencing, self-identification, and ego-defense.

GENERAL LEARNING OUTCOMES

1 We should learn about evidence and proof through reasoning.

2 We should learn to be better receivers of persuasion through our knowledge of fallacious reasoning.

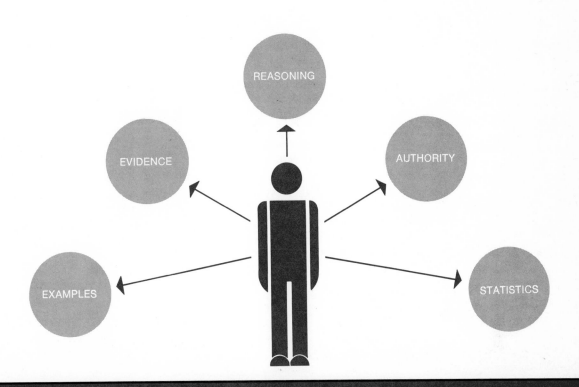

logical supports of persuasion

Pathos versus Logos

In chapter 11 we were concerned with the dimensions of human motivation—the psychological supports of persuasion. In this chapter we shall be concerned with evidence, formal reasoning, and argument—the logical supports of persuasion. The ancient Greek rhetoricians used the words *pathos* and *logos* to make this distinction, and debates about the nature and advisability of using each approach continue to this day. For our purposes as communication-conscious individuals, we need to know about both *pathos* and *logos*.

Evidence

Aristotle was one of the first to distinguish between extrinsic and intrinsic proof.[1] *Extrinsic* proof used facts in the world about us or statements based upon such facts—self-evident, observable phenomena. If you were to go to Baldwin School and count 525 students, that number would be a fact that you had observed. It would still be a fact if a document written by the principal said there were 525 students in Baldwin School. *Intrinsic* proof depends upon reasoned effort on our part, upon the application of rhetoric and logic.

Essentially, the sources of evidence are objects or things that are observable or reports about things that are observable. The most useful forms of support, or sources of evidence for our purposes are (1) statements by authorities, (2) examples, and (3) statistics.

FORMS OF SUPPORT

Authority

This evidence is usually in the form of quoted *testimony* from a person better qualified than the speaker to give a considered opinion about something. However, the value of an authority depends on how expert the person is. Perhaps the testimony simply supports the observations of the speaker. In chapter 11 authority was discussed briefly under the heading, "Credibility and Ethical Proof," and was translated into intent, trustworthiness, and competence.

The idea or statement being supported determines in part who the experts are. If you are trying to prove that the man who crashed into your car ran a red light, the expert is the lone person who was standing on the

---

[1] *Intrinsic* and *extrinsic* also are frequently called *artistic* and *nonartistic*. See L. Cooper, *The Rhetoric of Aristotle* (New York: Appleton-Century-Crofts, 1932), p. 8.

corner and saw the whole thing. With this kind of nonprofessional testimony, you often need more than one witness. If you are trying to prove that you have observed a bird considered extinct, such as the passenger pigeon, you will need the testimony of a qualified ornithologist. This expert will insist on firsthand observation of a captured bird in this exceptional case.

Authorities are qualified to give expert testimony by their closeness to a firsthand observation or experience and by their training in observing the phenomenon in question. The authority should be an expert *on the topic under discussion*. You would not ask a doctor of medicine to diagnose a problem in an airplane engine.

Other problems of authority are your audience's knowledge and opinion of the person quoted. The bias the audience assigns your expert may be very troublesome. When the audience simply does not know who John Doe is, then you must explain why his testimony is authoritative (for example, "John Doe is professor of economics at Cornell University and a member of the U.S. Tax Commission").

Examples

An example is a *specific illustration, incident, or instance* that supports a point you are trying to make. A hypothetical example (as discussed in chapter 8) may be a real aid to clearness and is often very persuasive, but it is *not* proof as we are discussing it in this chapter. We are concerned here with real, factual examples.

To prove that a person can operate normally in a state of weightlessness, we can cite one example of an astronaut who has done so successfully. However, in some situations *one* factual example, though proving its own case, may be so exceptional that it does not truly support a generalization. If you were arguing that Volkswagens were assembled poorly and carelessly, and you supported this statement with only *one* example of a car that was indeed assembled poorly, then your proof would become suspect. The question in the latter case becomes, "How many specific examples do I need?" This involves the question of inductive proof, which we'll discuss shortly.

Statistics

A joker once said, "First comes lies, then big lies, then statistics." (Or was it, "Figures don't lie, but liars figure?") Despite the jokes and despite fraudulent uses of statistics, the truth is that we live by statistics. We accept data on births, deaths, and accidents as facts. However, using statistics as a method bewilders many people. You do not have to be a statistician to realize that a *mean* (an average) is not always the most representative measure. Let's take eleven hypothetical educators and their yearly incomes:

	Salary		Salary
Educator A (Administrator)	$26,000	Educator G	$10,000
Educator B (Administrator)	25,400	Educator H	8,950
Educator C	15,000	Educator I	8,600
Educator D	14,200	Educator J	8,300
Educator E	12,000	Educator K	8,000
Educator F	10,500		

The mean income of these eleven educators is $13,359. The problem is obvious: two educators (the administrators) make the figure unrepresentative, particularly if you are concerned more with "teachers" than with administrators. Counting halfway down, we find $10,500. This is the *median,* which in this case is a much more meaningful and representative figure. If we take away the two administrators, the average income of the teachers is $10,617 and the median is $10,000. You then could figure the amount by which each income differs from the average; the average of these differences is the *average deviation.* If you were to translate these deviations from the average onto a so-called normal distribution, you could then determine the *standard deviation* or *sigma.*

Our national divorce statistics are frequently distorted. The dramatic statistics, often as high as "one in four," are generated by a one-year sample. For example, if your city showed records of 100,000 marriages and 33,000 divorces, you might say that the divorce rate was 33 ⅓ percent or "one in three." However, if you judge the statistics *over time,* perhaps there will be one million marriages in the city. The divorce rate then becomes 3 percent! The statistics on the average duration of marriage are something like 6.9 years; however, the median duration is 43 years.

It should now be evident that statistics can very quickly become complicated, capable of many applications, and (if we are not careful)

Figure 12.1 "Which to Use?"

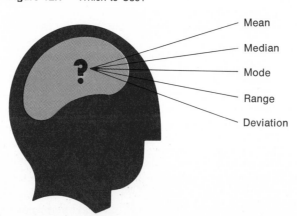

meaningless. The lessons are (1) to select the most appropriate statistics for your point or proposition and (2) to make sure your audience will understand them. Statistics (figures) do not lie, but liars *do* have the opportunity to "figure"!

REASONING AND PROOF

Inductive and Deductive Proof

Induction is the process of reasoning by which we arrive at a conclusion or generalization through observing specific cases or instances. "Properly conceived (it) may be thought of as the synthetic process used in moving from particulars to probable conclusions."[2] If you were to observe 500,000 spiders, and if each one had eight legs, it would be reasonable to conclude that spiders have eight legs. The induction is perfect for the 500,000 cases, since there were no exceptions. To be intolerably scientific, however, our induction is merely a prediction (although a highly probable one) when applied to all the spiders in the world. Assuming we are happy with the generalization, "All spiders have eight legs," we can then conclude *deductively* that this particular eight-legged thing in our garden is a spider. In sum, inductive proof starts with particular cases and proceeds to a generalization, whereas deductive proof starts with a generally accepted law or principle and applies it to a particular case. Formal deduction uses syllogistic reasoning, which we shall discuss shortly. Here are some requirements for safe inductive reasoning:

1 Is the example relevant?
2 Are there a reasonable number of examples?
3 Do the examples cover a critical period of time?
4 Are the examples typical?
5 Are the negative examples noncritical?[3]

Causal Relations

If we were to see a man accidentally shoot a live man and then see the victim fall dead with a bullet in his heart, we could say the *effect* was death, and the *cause* was the bullet or the man with the gun. Even this simple, observed, cause-to-effect relationship is full of problems. If the shooting were deliberate, would it in any way change the relationship? Let us suppose you found a dead man (the effect of something) with a bullet in his heart. Can we conclude absolutely that the bullet is the cause? This is reasoning

[2] George W. Ziegelmueller and Charles A. Dause, *Argumentation: Inquiry and Advocacy* (Englewood Cliffs, N.J.: Prentice-Hall, Inc., 1975), p. 88.
[3] Austin J. Freeley, *Argumentation and Debate* (Belmont, Calif.: Wadsworth Publishing Co., Inc., 1971, 1976), pp. 118–19.

from *effect to cause—a posteriori reasoning.* The bullet is certainly a possible cause, but as any *Columbo* fan knows, the man might have been killed by arsenic poisoning and then shot after his death to hide the real cause!

One more example: suppose a man dashes into your classroom, shoots a gun at your professor, and dashes out; your professor falls to the floor and everyone runs out screaming. You observed the cause and concluded that the effect was murder or attempted murder. (A roleplay?)

Your car battery is weak, you observe that it's 10° below zero, and you conclude that your car isn't going to start. This is before the fact, or *a priori, reasoning;* the conclusion is based upon circumstances you observed before the disputed fact. You are reasoning from *cause to effect.*

If, when you get up tomorrow morning you say, "It's 10° below zero; my car won't start; I'll be late for school," you are reasoning from *effect to effect.* Both your faltering battery and your tardiness (and the thermometer reading too) are the effects of a common cause—low temperature. In arguing from effect to effect, you must first sort out the effect-to-cause and cause-to-effect elements and then apply the general requirements for arguments based on causal relations. These requirements are as follows:

effect to cause[4]

1 Is the attributed cause able to generate the particular effect?
2 Is the claimed cause the only possible cause of the effect?
3 Has coincidence been mistaken for cause?
4 The alleged cause must not have been prevented from operating.

cause to effect[5]

1 Is the alleged cause relevant to the effect described?
2 Is this the sole or distinguishing causal factor?
3 Is there reasonable probability that no undesirable effect may result from this particular cause?
4 Is there a counteracting cause?
5 Is the cause capable of producing the effect?

FALLACIES

Aristotle devised a *classification of fallacies* that has been the springboard for all classification systems to this day. He divided fallacies into two principal types: those in the language of the argument and those in the content or matter of the argument. Fallacies of language were discussed in chapter 3. There are seven fallacies of matter, or "beyond the language." Aristotle

---

[4]The first three items of this list are taken from Craig R. Smith and David M. Hunsaker, *The Bases of Argument* (Indianapolis and New York: The Bobbs-Merrill Co., Inc., 1972), pp. 88–89.

[5]This list is taken from Freely, *Argumentation and Debate,* pp. 123–27.

himself admitted that there were problems in his system, so we may presume to rearrange his list. For our purposes we shall examine four major types of fallacies, together with their respective subtypes. The four are *overgeneralization, false cause, begging the question,* and *ignoring or ducking the issue*

"They're all dumb."

"The dance caused the rain."

"Still cheating?"

"What discrimination?"

1. Overgeneralization

Snap judgments or generalizations based on insufficient evidence or experience belong in the category of overgeneralization. We are not talking here about language and the dangers of the word *all,* but rather the concept of *allness* itself. This fallacy results in going from the general case to a specific case or vice versa. It is similar to the problems of induction and deduction.

It is in the exceptions to generally accepted rules that overgeneralization causes the most trouble. We would all agree that it is wrong to kill a person. However, a specific case of killing in self-defense is for most of us an exception to this rule. To take another example, there could be several exceptions to the rule, "Alcohol is harmful."

SAMPLING   A group of star high-school football players was being oriented to a certain Big Ten campus when they observed a dozen, devastatingly chic females coming out of a campus building. To a man, the generalization was "Wow! What coeds this place has!" The coach did not bother to tell them that these women were all professional fashion models who had just come from a faculty wives' program. Consider the size and representativeness of your sample before generalizing. A rash of teen-age delinquencies may cause some to conclude that all teen-agers are juvenile delinquents, but this would be an unfair generalization.

The most treacherous part of this fallacy is that it does start with facts. There *were* twelve stylish females on a given campus; teen-age delinquency *has been* recorded. It is our lack of objective analysis of our sample of experiences or subjects that gets us into trouble.

EXTRAPOLATION   Stuart Chase refers to this fallacy as the "thin entering wedge."[6] It is also known as the "camel's nose in the tent." It is a form of sampling trouble (as are all overgeneralizations), except that this one is keyed to prediction and probability.

[6] Stuart Chase, *Guides to Straight Thinking* (New York: Harper & Row, Publishers, Inc., 1956), p. 6. This book is an excellent supplement to your reading on fallacies.

Chase put it well: "You chart two or three points, draw a curve through them, and then extend it indefinitely!"[7] Space scientists extrapolate or they do not predict at all. This is also true of the economist and the weatherperson. Scientists usually know the dangers of extrapolation; to offset these dangers, they generally phrase their predictions in terms of statistical chance or confidence. Scientists draw predictive curves only when they have found enough points to make a qualified prediction. We are well advised to do the same.

2. False Cause

This is the fallacy of assigning a wrong or false cause to a certain happening or effect. It also is refutation with irrelevant arguments. Superstitions belong here. If you blow on the dice and win, was it the blowing that brought you luck? We still sell rabbits' feet, and most hotels still have no thirteenth floor. Debaters call it *non sequitur.*

AFTER THIS, THEREFORE BECAUSE OF THIS   Superstitions fit here. In our saner moments we are not really unaware of the fallacy. It is the more subtle misuse of time sequence that hurts us. If a new city government comes into power after a particularly rough winter and is faced with badly damaged roads, it may indeed be easier than not to hold them responsible as you survey one ruined $70 tire: "We didn't have roads like this until after their election." After this, therefore because of this. The great Roman Empire fell after the introduction of Christianity—care to try that one? You will hear it in Latin as *post hoc ergo propter hoc.*

THOU ALSO   This fallacy consists of making a similar, but essentially irrelevant, attack upon one's accuser. A discussion between a Brazilian student and several Americans about Communist infiltration in Latin America became quite heated. Suddenly, the Brazilian said, "Communists? How about segregation in your country?" The retort was equally brilliant: "How about Nazis in Argentina?" A classic instance of this fallacy occurred in an army basic-training mess line a few years ago. The mess steward put a perfectly good salad right in the middle of a soldier's mashed potatoes. When told what an ignoramus he was, the steward retorted in a most effective (if illogical) way, "Yeah, what about those poor guys in Vietnam?" or how about "Tell it to the Marines!"

CONSEQUENT   This fallacy simply is the corruption of the reasoning or inferential process used in conditional syllogisms. The problem is with possible, partial, or even probable truths. If he lies, he will be expelled from school; he was expelled; therefore, he lied. (In actuality, he may have been expelled for poor grades.)

[7]*Ibid.*

When we use a conditional syllogism and argue from the truth of the consequent (he was expelled) to the truth of the antecedent (he lied), or when we argue from the falsity of the antecedent to the falsity of the consequent, we are committing the fallacy of the *consequent.*

EITHER-OR   Certainly, there are things in this world that are either one way or another. You are either living or dead; the lake is frozen or it is not. There is no such thing as being partially pregnant. However, when a statement or problem with more than two possible solutions is put in an either-or context, we have a fallacy. "The fight is either Jan's or Jim's fault." It may be neither's fault, or it may be the fault of both. There are shades of gray in most things. All too often, we hear either-or arguments that only slow real solutions: science versus religion, capitalism versus socialism, suburban versus city living, and so forth.

LOADED QUESTION   This trick usually asks two questions as if they were one. You're in trouble no matter how you answer. In a speech it may take the form of a great many questions, the combination of answers leading to fallacious reasoning. The answers sought are *yes* or *no.* "Have you stopped cheating? *Yes* or *no?*" If you answer *no,* you are an admitted cheater. If you answer *yes,* you are an admitted former cheater. Either way, the loaded question stacks the deck against you. "Heads I win, tails you lose."

3. Begging the Question

This fallacy assumes the truth or falsity of a statement without proof. A common form is the use of two or more unproved propositions to establish the validity of one another. Other forms are simple, unwarranted assumptions or statements. It is related to "loaded questions" above.

ARGUING IN A CIRCLE   This is the classic form of using two or more unproved propositions to prove one another. Professional boxing should be outlawed for it is inhumane; we know it is inhumane because it is a practice that should be outlawed. Take the course, "Speech and Communication Theory," at Northwestern University because it is the best in the country. Why is it the best in the country? Because it is taught at Northwestern University.

DIRECT ASSUMPTION   In this form of question begging, language is carefully selected to help conceal bald assumptions. Many statements may be used, or perhaps just a word or two is subtly inserted. In a discussion of big-time college football, an opposition speaker started with the words, "It is my purpose to show that buying professional players is not in the best interest of college football." This statement begged the whole proposition by assuming at the outset that colleges buy professional players. Unless the statement is proved, it remains an assertion.

4. Ignoring or Ducking the Issue

This fallacy can be a subtle, treacherous and often vicious process. It almost always uses apparently relevant but objectively irrelevant arguments to cloud or duck the real issue or argument. This fallacy has several types, and each is worthy of a word of warning to the listener and unsophisticated speaker.

ATTACKING PERSONALITIES   Also known as *ad hominem*. When a speaker attacks the personal character of an opponent rather than the issue at hand, that person is guilty of *ad hominem* argument. If intended, the purpose of *ad hominem* is to change the issue from an argument on the proposition to one of personalities. To argue the stage and screen abilities of Frank Sinatra by referring to him as "that self-centered, woman-chasing louse" is a good example of *ad hominem*. Mr. Sinatra's alleged stage and screen *abilities* have no direct logical connection to his off-stage pursuits. This is not to say that every personal attack is unfair or illogical. If Mr. Sinatra were being evaluated on his public relations abilities, it might be a different matter.

APPEALS TO PREJUDICE   This is an appeal to the people through their biases and passions. The symbols of motherhood, the flag, race, and sin are typical themes. Vicious and often unsupported attacks have been made against liberal Americans in the name of "un-Americanism." "Romanism" was tried again in the presidential campaign of 1960. Hopefully, bald-faced *ad populum* appeals will become less successful as the general population becomes better educated and more sophisticated.

FALSE APPEAL TO AUTHORITY   This type of fallacy is an appeal to authority and dignity. When the authority is legitimately connected to the subject, as Aristotle is to logic, we have no problem. However, if in our reverence of Aristotle we use him to oppose modern probability theory, we are guilty of false appeal. Roger Staubach and Johnny Bench are highly paid experts in their specialized fields. They are probably not authorities on laser theory or even shoes or shaving cream. If you are impressed because Dr. Whosis says that alcohol causes cancer, find out if Whosis is an M.D. or an English professor!

APPEALS TO IGNORANCE   This is a mean trick, such as hiding one's weak arguments by overwhelming an audience with impressive materials about which they know little. A twelve-cylinder vocabulary can screen many a feeble argument. An improper use of statistics (or even a proper one) for people ignorant of the theory or the numbers involved is a good example of appeals to ignorance. This is not to say that vocabulary and statistics are the problem. It is the intent with which the speaker adapts them to the audience.

12 SUMMING UP

In this chapter we were concerned most with the nature, source, and types of evidence, formal reasoning, and argument—the logical supports of persuasion.

Extrinsic proof deals with facts in the world about us or statements based upon facts—self-evident, observable phenomena. *Intrinsic* proof depends upon reasoned effort on our part—upon the application of rhetoric and logic.

The most useful sources of evidence are authorities, examples, and statistics.

Induction is that process of reasoning by which we arrive at a conclusion or generalization through observing specific cases or instances. *Deduction,* on the other hand, starts with a generally accepted law or principle and applies it to a particular case.

Causal reasoning may proceed from cause to effect, effect to cause, or effect to effect. The requirements for legitimate argument from effect to cause and cause to effect follow. In arguing from *effect* to *cause:*

1 Is the attributed cause able to generate the particular effect?
2 Is the claimed cause the only possible cause of the effect?
3 Has coincidence been mistaken for cause?
4 The alleged cause must not have been prevented from operating.

In arguing from *cause to effect:*

1 Is the alleged cause relevant to the effect described?
2 Is this the sole or distinguishing causal factor?
3 Is there a reasonable probability that no undesirable effect may result from this particular cause?
4 Is there a counteracting cause?
5 Is the cause capable of producing the effect?

There are four major types of fallacies: (1) overgeneralization; (2) false cause; (3) begging the question; and (4) ignoring or ducking the issue. Specific cases of the last type attack the personal character of an opponent rather than the issue, appeal to popular prejudices and passions, appeal to authority and dignity for inappropriate subjects, and appeal to or misuse audience ignorance.

Speech Communication Principles

1 Evidence aids persuasion and source credibility when the message is delivered well, and the evidence is relatively new to the audience. (A highly credible source has less need of evidence.)
2 *Sources* of evidence (such as authority, examples, and statistics) are objects or things that are observable, or reports about things that are observable.
3 *Extrinsic* proof supports persuasive efforts and deals with facts in the world about us or statements based on such facts, self-evident, observable phenomena.
4 *Intrinsic* proof supports persuasive efforts and depends upon reasoned effort—upon the application of rhetoric and logic.
5 Authority as evidence depends upon the intent, trustworthiness, and competence of the source.
6 *Induction* supports persuasive effort and is the process of reasoning by which we arrive at a concluson or generalization through observing specific cases or instances.
7 *Deduction* supports persuasive effort and is the process of reasoning that starts with a generally accepted law or principle and applies it to a particular case.
8 *Causal reasoning* is a logical support of persuasion; there are generally accepted requirements for legitimate argument from effect to cause and cause to effect.
9 The intelligent receiver of persuasive messages needs to know and to recognize the major types of fallacious reasoning.

Specific Learning Outcomes

1 We should learn the differences between extrinsic and intrinsic proof.
2 We should learn the characteristics of evidence derived from authority, examples, and statistical data.
3 We should learn the differences between inductive and deductive proof.
4 We should learn the requirements of the several types of causal reasoning (cause to effect, effect to cause, and effect to effect).
5 We should learn the four major types of fallacies and their respective subtypes.

Communication Competencies

1 We should be able to prepare an intelligent outline for a two-to-three-minute, persuasive, one-point speech that uses the logical supports of persuasion.
2 We should learn to apply the principal tests of evidence to the one-point speeches of others, thereby becoming more able critics.

3 We should be able to find and define examples of fallacious reasoning from daily print media (or audio-video media).

Study Projects and Tasks

1 Prepare a detailed two-to-three-page outline for a two-to-three minute, persuasive, one-point speech using the logical supports of persuasion (authority, examples, statistics, causal reasoning, syllogistic reasoning, and so forth).

2 Critically evaluate the logical support of your classmates' speeches; especially watch for fallacious reasoning. Write out your critique and be prepared to cross-examine the speaker.

3 Search the daily print media and find two examples of fallacious reasoning; define and explain the fallacies according to the material in this chapter.

4 Prepare a two-to-three-minute oral exercise in which you attempt to use as many fallacies as possible. See if you can fool your classmates, but be prepared to explain your sophistry should you prove too successful at deceiving them.

5 Check your thinking habits on the following items:

    a An archeologist found a coin marked 45 B.C. How old was it?

    b If you divided 30 by $\frac{1}{2}$ plus 10, how much would you have?

    c Which side of a horse has more hair?

    d How far can a dog walk into the woods?

    e If you went to bed at 8:00 and set the alarm to ring at 9:00 in the morning, how many hours of sleep would you get?

    f Does England have a Fourth of July?

6 What is the Wizard of Id guilty of in figure 12.2?

7 Apply the various tests of reasoning to the following thought by R. L. Evans,[8] and be prepared to discuss your observations and conclusions in class (page 321).

[8] Copyright 1969 by Atesons. Used by permission.

Figure 12.2 By permission of Johnny Hart and Field Enterprises, Inc.

"chance could not have done it. . ."

As men move farther out from the magnificent earth and look back on its awesome beauty, its movement, its precision and proportion, upon the wondrous working, and magnificent majesty of it all, we come to the quiet conviction of these simple words: "In the beginning God created heaven and the earth. . . ." Chance could not have done it." And God saw everything that he had made, and, behold it was very good."[*]

Well, man has done much with his marvelous God-given mind, in the discovery and use of natural law. But much as man has done, he has scarcely touched the surface of all this majesty of meaning, and of infinite understanding.

Think a moment of the organizing and engineering and operation of it all—of keeping a world within a livable range of temperature; of air and water renewing themselves; of insect, animal and bacterial balance in infinite variety. And the creation is evidence of a Creator, design is evidence of the Designer, and law is evidence of its Maker and Administrator.

"When a load of bricks, dumped on a corner lot, can arrange themselves into a house;" wrote Bruce Barton, "when a handful of springs and screws and wheels, emptied onto a desk, can gather themselves into a watch, then and not until then will it seem sensible, to some of us at least, to believe that all . . . [this] could have been created . . . without any directing intelligence at all."[**] Then and only then will I believe that this was done by chance—or without eternal plan and purpose.

"Behind everything stands God. . . ." said Phillips Brooks. "Do not avoid, but seek the great, deep, simple things of faith."[†]

"And God saw everything that he had made, and, behold it was very good."

---

*Genesis 1:1.
**Bruce Barton, *If a Man Dies, Shall He Live Again?*
†Phillips Brooks, *The Light of the World and Other Sermons: The Seriousness of Life.*

part four

INTERPERSONAL AND GROUP COMMUNICATION

We discuss and interact for social and emotional reasons as well as to direct the logical work of society. Humans are social animals and may on occasion seek out others for the sheer joy of their presence or may affiliate with others in order to overcome their loneliness or misery. Although our interest in chapter 14 is directed at group interactions with some kind of purpose or goal, we are reminded in chapter 13 that the more casual interaction is a potent communication force. This force is capable of releasing the same tensions and emotions that often emanate from the more structured, goal-seeking groups.

The feelings and attitudes we bring to a communication interaction are based to a large extent on our experience with events and persons important to us. We reveal ourselves and judge others interpersonally through several critical judgments or evaluations that we make. These are (1) our self-concepts, roles, and notions about others, (2) interpersonal attraction, (3) our assessment of settings and power relationships, and (4) the empathy or response we receive from others. Much of chapter 13 explores these matters.

More and more, we find ourselves interacting informally and formally in small groups. It is a sign of the times to participate in study groups, workshops, committees, boards, councils, buzz groups, case conferences, and many other such groups. Our modern teaching methods call for subgroups of larger groupings, such as task forces, research groups, and role-playing groups. Our jobs often place us in very specialized work groups. Then, of course, there are the countless social and recreational groups that help occupy the time and efforts of us all. We are asked to interact and to discuss cooperatively, sometimes systematically, sometimes for the vaguest reasons. It has been estimated that there are more than 50,000 meetings each *day* in New York, 35,000 in Los Angeles, 20,000 in Atlanta, and so on.[1]

The discussion groups and discussion-group procedures described in chapter 14 are to be viewed as engaging in a democratic process. Assigned or emerging leaders may vary in style, but the decision process is essentially democratic—it could hardly be otherwise. "To discuss means to behave democratically."[2] In the broadest sense, we can say that small-group discussion is essential to the success of our society.

We will learn of the contemporary forms of discussion, agenda systems, problem solving, leadership, climate setting, and participant responsibilities in chapter 14. It is useful to think of the small group as a type of audience. We will see that in some respects it is a more threatening audience, since the feedback is usually so immediate, and differences of opinion cannot be generalized as easily as with a larger audience. Each member of a small group may have a different opinion.

[1]Carl R. Terzian, "PR for the Firm that Can't Afford It," *SKY* Magazine, March, 1974, p. 18.

[2]Dean C. Barnlund and Franklyn S. Haiman, *Dynamics of Discussion* (Boston: Houghton Mifflin Company, 1960), p. 5.

In part 4 we will be concerned with interpersonal relations generally and with communication dimensions specifically. We will examine a model of human interaction on the theoretical side and prescriptions for small-group problem solving on the pragmatic side.

1   We should understand better the enormous complexity of human interaction.

2   We should understand the effect of self-concept on human interaction.

3   We should learn the factors of interpersonal attraction so that we may improve our human interaction.

4   We should learn the important influence of setting on human interaction.

5   We should learn the important influence of psychological climate on human interaction.

13

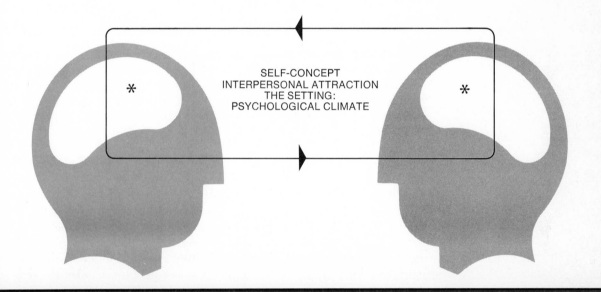

SELF-CONCEPT
INTERPERSONAL ATTRACTION
THE SETTING:
PSYCHOLOGICAL CLIMATE

human interaction

AN INTERACTION MODEL

All interpersonal communication is concerned with what might be called *relationship* communication, since the meanings grow to a large extent from the notions we form about others while actively interacting with them.[1] There is, of course, a *content* aspect also, and both are ever present. Watzlawick and Beavin capture this distinction in the following:

> "If woman A points to woman B's necklace and asks, 'Are those real pearls?', the content of her question is a request for information about an object. But at the same time she also gives—indeed, cannot *not* give—her definition of their relationship. How she asks (especially, in this case, the tone and stress of voice, facial expression, and context) would indicate comfortable friendliness, competitiveness, formal business relations, etc. B can accept, reject or redefine, but cannot under any circumstances—even by silence—not respond to A's message. A's definition may, for instance, be a catty, condescending one; B, on the other hand, may react to it with aplomb or defensiveness. It should be noticed that this part of their interaction has nothing to do with the genuineness of pearls or with pearls at all, but with respective definitions of the nature of their relationship, although they may continue to talk about pearls."[2]

We can define human *interaction* as content and relationship communication directed toward another person when that person's self-concept and reactions are taken into account. Oliver Wendell Holmes explained the problems of human interaction as the perceptions and notions two individuals might have of each other's, and their own, personalities.[3] He labeled the personalities John and Thomas, and suggested that there are *three* Johns: (1) the real John, known only to his maker; (2) John's ideal John, never the real one, and often very unlike him; and (3) Thomas's ideal John, never the real John, nor John's John, but often very unlike either. There are, of course, three equivalent Toms. To Holmes's three categories we can add a *fourth,* "John's Tom's John"—that is, John's notion of what Tom's notion is of him. See figure 13.1.

Let's analyze the model in more detail. The real John (or real Tom)

[1] John Stewart, "An Interpersonal Approach to the Basic Course," *The Speech Teacher,* 21, no. 1 (1972), 7–14; also, see John Stewart, *Bridges Not Walls,* 2nd ed. (Reading, Mass.: Addison-Wesley Publishing Co., Inc., 1977), chap. 1.

[2] Paul Watzlawick and Janet Beavin, "Some Formal Aspects of Communication," in *The Interactional View,* P. Watzlawick and J. H. Weakland, eds., (New York: W. W. Norton and Company, Inc., 1977), p. 61.

[3] Oliver Wendell Holmes, *The Autocrat of the Breakfast Table* (Boston: Phillips, Simpson, 1858), p. 59.

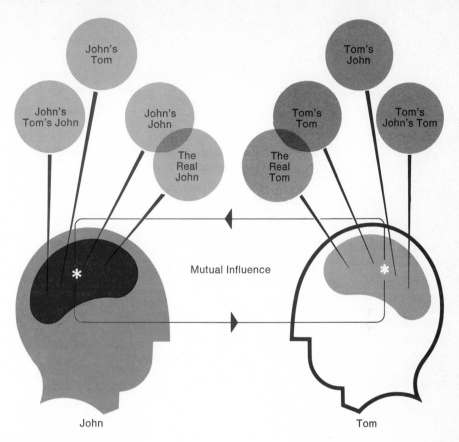

Figure 13.1 An interaction model.

becomes an important philosophical concept if John feels that John's John is his own reality. If John's John is John's notion of himself, his self-concept, and if self-concepts can be incorrect, then John's John can also be incorrect. The model is useful in making this point clear: the real John and John's John do not overlap completely. That the circles overlap at all indicates that John's notion of himself is, at least in part, fair to the facts. We could argue about how much the two circles should overlap for the average person. If the circles did not overlap at all, the model would suggest that John's self-concept was in no way related to reality, and psychologists would probably label John schizoid. This is not to say that all of us do not lose touch at some time with some topic or with some person. That brings us to John's Tom (or Tom's John), which is John's notion of Tom. John's notion may or may not be accurate, depending upon how well he knows Tom and how objective he is. If he does not know him very well, he had better pay close attention to him and seek feedback to improve his evaluation. If John did not know Tom at all, he would normally proceed with a very tentative, general, or stereotyped notion. The danger of stereotypes is now obvious! Our notions of each other certainly affect our interaction with each other.

Now let's consider what the participants *think* the other person thinks of them. As will be discussed shortly, that is an important part of how one's self-concept develops. John's Tom's John is John's notion of what Tom's notion is of him—what John thinks Tom thinks of him. From Tom's point of view, it is what Tom thinks John thinks of him (Tom's notion of what John's notion is of him). If either of these notions is much in error, Tom and John may have some very unusual, confusing, perhaps even unfortunate interaction ahead of them. With this much complexity, is it any wonder that we have misunderstandings with one another?

Feedback, both verbal and nonverbal, is very important to John and to Tom's attempts to communicate and interact in an objective, prudent, and nonthreatening way. It is important that we be our best *self*—yet an honest and realistic best self, or we may quickly offend people. If a phony self is momentarily successful, it will almost always catch up with us in future interactions. We can also see in the model that John's John is also affected by Tom's John—or at least by John's Tom's John (John's notion of what Tom's notion is of him)—and vice versa.

SELF-CONCEPT

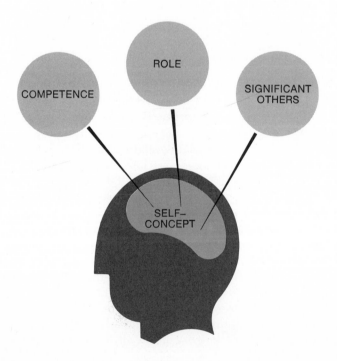

The model illustrated on page 329 suggests the importance of a person's self-image to human relations. We use words such as *self-percept, self-concept,* and *self-identity* to talk about one's notion of oneself.[4] However, words such as *self-esteem, self-valuation,* and *self-regard* are of a slightly different order. We tend to think of these as positive or negative traits. A related term is *self-acceptance.* A person with high self-acceptance exhibits a willingness to accept both positive and negative notions as a part of his or her total self-concept.

A large portion of our self-concept is shaped by interactions with individuals whom we consider significant to us. We develop concepts of our physical, emotional, and social selves, and tend to perceive, respond, act, and communicate to a considerable extent using this complex self-image. For the most part we try to be consistent in our self-image: when we are extremely frustrated, perhaps by too positive or too negative a self-image, we may resort to various unrelated behaviors to compensate for our frustration. (For example, we may become overtalkative when insecure.) A realistic self-image can be a critical part of communication and perception as well as of motivation generally. Every person is the center of his or her own field of experience, and the way one perceives and responds to that field is one's own reality.

Research suggests that an unreasonable or unrealistic self-concept, particularly one low in self-esteem, may contribute to failure, thereby acting as a kind of self-fulfilling prophecy. The student who will not even discuss a math course because his self-concept tells him he is mathematically illiterate is not apt to do well in a math course. This is tragic when *only* a student's poor opinion of himself stands in the way of success. However, suppose a student really has little or no math aptitude. Were he to develop an unrealistically positive conception of his mathematical ability, he would obviously be headed for frustration and ultimately an even poorer self-concept than his original one.

The point is that your self-concept, whether good or bad, high or low, should be within the realm of physical or social reality. Knowing what is *realistic* as well as what is exceptional is, of course, the eternal problem.

Your sense of *competence* also is related to your self-concept. "Competence means capacity, fitness, or ability. The competence of a living organism means its fitness or ability to carry on those transactions with the environment which result in its maintaining itself, growing and flourishing."[5] A self-concept that includes a feeling of incompetence may leave you in a state of helplessness and inertia and promote a sense of inferiority. You must build realistic confidence as well as competence into your self-concept. A persistent challenge to your sense of personal competence is a prime mover toward frustration and, not infrequently, aggression. Your sense of

[4] John J. Sherwood, "Self Identity and Referent Others," *Sociometry,* 28 (1965), 66–81.
[5] Robert W. White assisted by Katherine F. Bruner, eds., *The Study of Lives* (New York: Atherton, 1966), p. 74.

competence is important to your interaction and communication with others.

Now let us discuss how we develop our general self-concept. *Other* human beings who are significant to us form no small part of our self-concept. *Group memberships* are an important influence on us. Our self-concept reflects the society in which we live. Our family, school, and church are all thought to influence greatly our self-concept and personality in general. This is not to suggest that we all are carbon copies of those having a background similar to our own. Even the culture in which we live determines only what we learn as a member of a group, not what we learn as an individual. This explains in part why humans alter their behavior in what seem to be most inconsistent ways. Living in a society requires one to meet certain standards or to fit into certain patterns roughly agreed on by the members of that group. Much nonstandard individual behavior is *sublimated,* expressed in constructive, socially acceptable forms in deference to these group codes. The *valuation, regard,* and *acceptance* individuals have of their total group—and their conceptions of the group's valuation, regard, and acceptance of them—are critical to the development of their self-concept.

Role pertains, in part, to a more specific aspect of group membership and is also thought to have a strong influence on our self-concept. Some roles are cast upon us by society because of our age, our sex, even our size, and, unfortunately, sometimes our race. Some roles we assign ourselves on the basis of our life goals, and some are really disguises of our private personalities, disguises that we create in order to be accepted by certain groups. In its most important sense a role is that part we cast for ourselves on the stage of life. We may portray many roles to the world, but each of us determines, with the aid of society and its subgroups, what our particular role will be. Our self-concept is influenced by that decision.

The *situational* influences upon our self-concept and our total personality include those exceptional, unpredictable, and often accidental events that happen to all of us. These are events that can alter our lives, casting us into roles that may profoundly affect our self-concept—a jail sentence, a lost love, a scholarship, a riot, an insight or perspective suddenly and never

Figure 13.2   Peanuts. © 1958 United Feature Syndicate, Inc.

Figure 13.3 Peanuts. © 1959 United Feature Syndicate, Inc.

before achieved. A really good teacher probably alters the lives and careers of many unsuspecting students. An unexpected failing grade or a hard-won A from such a teacher can be a self-concept shaker and/or maker!

How others feel about us, or at least how we think they feel about us—particularly if they are significant "others," whether reference groups, respected friends, or even those whose roles are ill defined—is probably the most important part of self-concept. What these others expect of us, how they react to us, and how socially realistic we are in evaluating these expectations and reactions form a large part of our self-concept.

Self-concept is a major part of one's personality. We may consider personality to be the sum of a person's knowledge, motives, values, beliefs, and goal-seeking patterns.

Human communication is affected by self-concept in several interesting ways. In general, we can expect others to perceive and react to us and the rest of the world in ways that are as consistent with their self-concept as possible. Trying to "see" and understand others by understanding what their self-concepts are thus becomes a characteristic of sensitive human communication. We all should occasionally reevaluate our *own* self-concept in terms of physical and social reality. Sometimes we downgrade or take ourselves too seriously. If the *self-regard* part of our self-concept is unusually negative, we might very well become difficult, negative, or even sullen communicators. An unrealistically positive *self-valuation* can, of course, make us different but equally painful communicators. A healthy, reality-centered, positive self-concept should, other things being equal, make us better and more confident communicators. Most important, it should include some willingness to accommodate change.

In review, a good self-concept is objective, realistic, positive, and yet self-accepting; it can live with negative notions too. A healthy self-concept should include some willingness to change, a tolerance for confusion, patience with disagreement, and empathy for other self-concepts. If you are a "significant other" for someone, if only for a moment, you have a special communication responsibility, for we are reasonably sure that such individuals are a key to the development of one's self-concept.

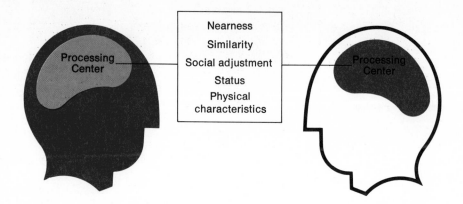

Our need to create and sustain relationships is one of the great stimulations of human interaction. We talk to some individuals and nothing really significant or important happens. With others we may form positive first impressions, and then after a few months or perhaps even days we sense the relationship is going sour. Another possibility, of course, is that a very negative first impression may not remain negative. These possibilities are all aspects of *interpersonal attraction.*

Before discussing the *factors of interpersonal attraction,* we should remind ourselves that our perceptions—the way we see the world—are essential to each factor and that these perceptions include both our feelings and our beliefs. In other words, what we know and how we feel about things will lead us to infer the unknown from the known. Our beliefs about a person usually relate to obvious physical observations—good-looking, overweight, dark-complexioned; our feelings usually affect our inferences about the individual's personality—nervous, peculiar, warm. Recall, however, that our perceptions are often inaccurate, as was demonstrated in chapter 1.

How accurate are our interpersonal perceptions? What factors are part of these perceptions? There are some answers.[6] *Age.* We get better as we get older—generally. *Intelligence.* Smarter people are usually more accurate. *Sex.* No hard evidence, but there is a tendency for women to be more accurate than men. Beyond these, very few personality characteristics stand out. Good and bad interpersonal judges are found among a wide variety of personalities. That some people are better judges of people than others (most of the time) seems obvious. Some behavior extremes, found to be blocks to happy perceptions of social adjustment, will be discussed shortly.

[6]See Mark Cook, *Interpersonal Perception* (Baltimore: Penguin Books, 1971).

WOMEN TALK

but men cut in

Wanda: Did you see here that two sociologists have just proved that men interrupt women all the time? They—
Ralph: Who says?
Wanda: Candace West of Florida State and Don Zimmerman of the University of California at Santa Barbara. They taped a bunch of private conversations, and guess what they found. When two men or two women are talking, interruptions are about equal. But when a man talks to a woman, he makes 96% of the interruptions. They think it's a dominance trick men aren't even aware of. But—
Ralph: These people have nothing better to do than eavesdrop on interruptions?
Wanda: —but women make "retrievals" about one-third of the time. You know, they pick up where they left off after the man—
Ralph: Surely not all men are like that, Wanda.
Wanda: —cuts in on what they were saying. Doesn't that—
Ralph: Speaking as a staunch supporter of feminism, I deplore it, Wanda.
Wanda: (sigh) I know, dear.

Reprinted by permission from TIME, The Weekly News Magazine, September 25, 1978. Copyright, Time, Inc. 1978.

Numerous experiments have attempted to discover whether there are any systematic bases for our attraction to others. These studies have attempted to analyze the results of communication encounters. They suggest that our attraction to others is not haphazard, but rather is shaped and strengthened by at least five factors: *(1) nearness, (2) similarity, (3) social adjustment, (4) status and recognition, and (5) physical characteristics.* The explanation breaks down a bit when two or more conflicting factors are operating at the same time. For instance, forced nearness to someone of widely dissimilar attitudes does not typically lead to attraction—perhaps better understanding if we are lucky.

Nearness

The first factor is the most obvious. Other things being equal, we tend to develop ties to those who live near us, work with us, go to church with us, or are in some way physically near us. After initial attraction has been established, separation or a lack of proximity will usually weaken the relationship unless other factors are strong and positive.

Persons who are both active as communicators and physically near the action—a student government scene, a political convention, or whatever—appear to have a potential advantage in terms of attraction.[7] Unless

[7]See Mark Abrahamson, *Interpersonal Accommodation* (Princeton, N.J.: D. Van Nostrand Company, 1966).

the person is a real boor, this is not surprising. This finding does suggest that we form attractions more readily to those near us, providing the other factors are not in gross conflict and providing there is opportunity for communication.

Similarity

We speak here not so much of physical similarities, but similarities of attitudes toward questions and issues important to us. Momentary feelings of anxiety that are perceived as similar, even among total strangers, often trigger a fellowship tendency. We find it attractive to seek company, especially company of like mind or like situation. Misery not only likes company, it likes miserable company. Similar personalities as well as attitudes—exceptions and old sayings to the contrary—do attract, and familiarity, other things being equal, breeds attraction, not contempt.

We tend to find others more attractive when we perceive them as holding attitudes similar to our own. This presents an opportunity for deceit: unscrupulous persuaders may lead us to believe they hold attitudes similar to ours (when in fact they do not) for the purpose of selling an object or gaining a vote. This interesting fact of interpersonal attraction also suggests that each of us should be more open and objective when we listen to individuals who have attitudes differing from our own; such an occasion may be a good time for us to reexamine our own attitudes and the reasons behind them.

The point is that if you have really strong opinions about controversial issues such as abortion, aid to parochial schools, and God, then the attitudes you perceive in others toward these issues will affect their attractiveness to you (and your attractiveness to them). Our personal attraction, even to an old friend, may be strained if the friend suddenly discovers an attitude we hold toward race, cheating, or drugs that is quite different from her own. This is often true of lighter topics and attitudes as well. If you like sports trivia, movies, Chinese food, or skiing, you may be attracted to someone who has those same preferences.

Although there is some evidence that racial similarity leads to attraction, it is more accurate to say that the amount of perceived prejudice leads a person to like or dislike another.[8]

Social Adjustment

There is good evidence that we find well-adjusted people, those with healthy self-concepts, more attractive than those who are poorly adjusted and have negative self-concepts. Interestingly, people with superpositive self-concepts, people who exhibit an inconsistency in what they really are and what they *think* they are, are not perceived as attractive.

[8]G. Lindzey and E. Aronson, eds., *The Handbook of Social Psychology,* 2nd ed., vol. 2 (Reading, Mass.: Addison-Wesley Publishing Co., Inc., 1968), pp. 498–500.

In judging social adjustment, we must take care to consider the setting. Behavior is often adapted to special situations and may not be representative of a person's normal social adjustment. We all lose our tempers once in a while. More will be said of settings shortly.

Behaviors thought to improve another's perceptions of a person's social adjustment, and therefore attraction, include establishing rapport easily and quickly; fairness; and showing anger rarely and when doing so, usually toward those who "should know better." People who exhibit these traits are sociable and interested individuals.

Behaviors or traits found to be blocks to perceptions of good social adjustment are the personality extremes: on the one hand, superiority and egoism, as exhibited by aggression, overconfidence, sarcasm, boastfulness, and a domineering attitude; on the other hand, excessive inferiority, as shown by dependence, depression, withdrawal, listlessness, and excessive timidity. Either extreme can lead to defensive communication behavior by the receiver.

Social adjustment is a most significant factor in interpersonal attraction.

Status and Recognition

Status and recognition are anticipated rewards—not in a monetary sense necessarily, but in terms of, "He makes me happy, she makes me laugh, he is very helpful, she has all the answers." We tend to enjoy being with people who provide us with status, praise, and recognition—the teacher who laughs at our jokes, the person who begs us to tell a certain story, the friend who flatters us for some quality. Because of the anticipated or expected rewards they contain, all of these events contribute to the attraction we may feel toward someone. This category of attraction is mainly a result of verbal communication, although nonverbal messages obviously may help.

Those who would play games with this factor of interpersonal attraction can fail miserably if their praise or flattery is found to be unwarranted or phony. Honesty with a measure of prudence is still the best policy. The status of the person praising or blaming us also influences this dimension of attraction. As was indicated in the interaction model, a person's self-concept is also in this complex equation.

Sometimes, status and recognition can be translated better as a person offering a helping or supportive relationship. An anticipated reward of a sympathetic ear is often a strong reason for interpersonal attraction. Good listeners are attractive people, perhaps because they are so rare.

Physical Characteristics

When we first see another person, we are affected by what we see, even before we communicate orally. Large, fat, sloppy, handsome, cool, or whatever—each characteristic will attract or repel us. Physical characteristics are more than just physical attractiveness, although in an initial meeting we often have little else to judge.

By *physical characteristics* we mean the total physical makeup of an individual. This includes environmental causes of appearance, such as diet, drugs, and climate, as well as hereditary factors. People vary physically in their reaction time, energy level, and rate of learning. They also vary in hearing, sight, color, size, shape, and so on—all of which add up to and influence total personality as well as physical attractiveness. After all, beauty is skin deep only in the superficial sense. The feedback we decode from society about our physical makeup and the way we accommodate that feedback probably affect our attractiveness more than our superficial physical characteristics do.

Other things being equal, well-adjusted, smart young people are perceived as more attractive then those not as smart. There is some evidence that physical attractiveness is more important between than within the sexes. That is, girls tend to care more about what their boyfriends look like than what their girlfriends look like (and vice versa). The role of clothing, cosmetics, calorie counting, surgery, and other possible means of improving our appearance becomes critical when added to what nature gave us.

SETTINGS

Communication and interaction always occur somewhere, in some context or setting. The place in which a communication and its *ritual* occurs is important for it affects both senders and receivers of messages. In the following pages the importance of the setting will be discussed. First, we'll talk about the impact of place and ritual. Second, we'll consider the influence of purpose and agenda, almost as if they were separate from place. We may not always like or approve of certain settings, but sensitive human interaction demands that we take them into account. We should take the setting into special account when we evaluate a person's social adjustment. A "nut" may not be a "nut" when he is out of the special setting you are observing. The berserk football fan may be Mr. Cool when we find him in church.

Place and Ritual

Our communication, whether public speaking, group discussion, or informal interaction, is often limited by where we are. Some settings may restrict communication, whereas others may aid it. In addition, settings may have a ritualistic aspect. Much of our communication is dictated by the place and ritual alone. Observe the impact on communication of a church, an elevator, a commuter bus, a 300-seat Boeing 747; study their rituals.

Now let's illustrate the often awesome impact of place. Visualize an impressive church complete with stained-glass windows, exquisite statues, and a high-arched ceiling. In it we feel close to our creator. There is a temptation to whisper—a rock group would surely be out of place here. The speakers seem to alter their voices, their language, and their dress to meet the communication requirements of this powerful setting. The ritual associated with this setting also dictates much of the verbal as well as the nonverbal communication. Even an empty church is a powerful communication setting, and we adjust our signals accordingly.

Ceremonial settings such as weddings, funerals, initiations, and graduations are important influences on interpersonal communication wherever they are held. Weddings are held in gardens, living rooms, and woods, as well as in churches. Graduations may take place inside, outside, in a gym, in an auditorium, and so on. Part of the influence of such an occasion comes from its obvious purpose, but much of the influence is also tradition and ritual, which seem to go beyond the obvious. Human communication in such settings is somehow different.

Think about the last wedding you attended and consider your total verbal exchange. It probably concerned the bride and groom, their families, their apparel, and the wedding arrangements. Being present at the wedding had a strong impact on what you said. The same holds true to an even greater extent at funerals. However, once you are out of the setting, the controlling aspect of place and ritual disappears.

Even the dinner hour is a rather formal setting for some families. It is a time for prayer and thanksgiving and not a time for deep conversation or heated argument. Test the wind of this setting when you are a dinner guest, or you may very easily break the ritual and therefore much of the communication that otherwise might have been possible.

Visualize yourself at a football game. We live in a spectator world, often finding ourselves jammed into a stadium watching our favorite team. In this interaction context we may find ourselves talking to total strangers, but not about dress styles, war, or elections. Our communication usually takes the form of amazement at some super play, disgust at the end of a rally, or second-guessing the management on some trade or maneuver. Our nonverbal communication is often affected by the press of the crowd, our empathy with a goal-line stand, or our ecstasy over a circus catch. Once we leave the setting, however, the effect of the place and ritual ends. We may no longer even exchange pleasantries and observations: the influences of the sports-arena setting are removed, and we usually adjust our interpersonal communication with strangers accordingly.

The lesson is clear. Time, place, and ritual have a tremendous influence upon human communication, and we are well advised to take them into account when we speak.

Purpose

In some settings the *purpose* or the agenda is so important that it has a greater impact on interpersonal communication than the place has. If the purpose is strictly social, the political advocate may find himself poorly received. If a person's communication purpose is to obtain reassuring messages from you, all the jokes in the world are not apt to be received very well. A few of the many general purposes of communication interactions are illustrated below.

SOCIAL Many times, we get together for sheer joy, fellowship, and fun. Perhaps the setting is a party. In this instance we get together primarily to have a good time. (However, a party could be a disguise for another purpose.) After the party, we usually evaluate the time spent in terms of fun. "Did you enjoy yourself?" "Was it fun?" "Why don't we get together more often?" "That was a dull party." "Those two loud men were arguing about politics." Party topics are predictably uncontroversial: sports, weather, or current gossip. The communication pattern is without clear direction or agenda; many discussions may occur at the same time. If we tire of one subject, person, or group, we may move on to another if the gathering is large enough. If it's a smaller group, we may not have as many communication options or as many people with whom to talk. However, watch for some ritual even in principally social communication settings.

VENTILATION Another reason we interact is to unload gripes and generally express pent-up feelings—to unwind. In this situation we are usually looking for a sympathetic ear. We are not interested in having our statement and viewpoint challenged, at least critically.

Have you ever been misunderstood by parents or friends when your purpose was really simple ventilation? You're trying to blow off some steam, but your listener misinterprets the situation and proceeds to give you point-by-point arguments on all the gross generalizations you've blurted out. All you really wanted was a quiet, sympathetic listener and now you've committed yourself to an emotional argument you really didn't need or want! Responsibilities run both ways in these ventilation situations. Take care when ventilating; hear your friend out to discover his or her *real* purpose.

SEEKING HELP AND INFORMATION In the previous category we were seeking a listener who did not interfere continually as we griped, vented our emotions, and otherwise used him or her as a release for accumulated strong feelings. This category leads us to a more specific call for help—a call for a response, for information, support, and reinforcement. There are many such situations, ranging from the simple request for time, date, or directions to asking a person to assume a more emotionally complex, supportive role. Once again, the *why* is the influencing factor. Some call these types of purposes therapeutic, in that we are seeking a cure or answer for a difficulty. It is quite important and sometimes difficult for a receiver to really know when someone wishes help and support or prefers only a sympathetic ear.

Have you ever asked one of your classmates a simple question, only to receive a lecture on transcendental ontology? Your classmate may honestly have misunderstood the intent and scope of your question, or he may have found a victim on which to try out his new learning! That's not all bad either—communication most often *is* a compromise of purposes and intentions.

Sometimes the real help we seek is a nonverbal presence, not talk at all. When the play is a bomb, the team has fumbled near the goal line, your speech was a mess, or you've flunked the exam, you may just prefer silent, miserable company, unless you're ventilating. Misery does love company, especially people with the same problem.

BARGAINING   Still another purpose that greatly affects interpersonal communication is bargaining, working out differences together. This purpose is sometimes evident, as with known, honest differences of opinion. However, it may also operate quite subtly, sometimes by design and sometimes quite by accident. In bargaining, the response to a statement often determines the next response. A statement may contain a specific intent unknown to the receiver. This intent may be concealed in some code or message intended to have persuasive effect on the receiver. Notice the bargaining influence in the communication when you're buying a used car or a motorcycle. The seller may suggest $800 as an asking price. You're interested in determining just how low the seller is really willing to go in price. In this special kind of setting there is often a hidden motive and a payoff (which we expect as part of the game). The setting is sometimes called a game because of this payoff aspect. Unless you recognize this purpose and adjust accordingly, you may come off second best in the negotiation without really having played the game.

Bargaining among unions and employers is a similar communication interchange, except that it is much more formal. Most of these bargaining situations are worked out cooperatively. We usually hear about the few that are deadlocked as if they are typical!

Sometimes we bargain without knowing it. Asking to use big brother's car may really be more bargaining than a simple request for help. If this is so, your initial purpose may be to seek information. You may then shift to an expression of feelings as you attempt to establish common ground. You may then prepare to move into the bargaining stance. Whatever your line will be, you must be aware that in this type of context the receiver may not always give you the specific answer you want. (That's part of the game, too.) If after several exchanges you sense that your goal is not likely to be achieved, you may decide to offer more in exchange, modify your time requirement, or do whatever is possible to work out the bargaining together. That bargaining is often unsuccessful is another fact of life! Most bargaining would probably be more successful if the participants knew more about the process and recognized a bargaining situation when they were in one.

EVALUATION   Even in feeding back something relatively trivial, such as spelling errors (which would not be trivial in the setting of an English class) or minor arithmetic mistakes, one may be surprised at how threatening this purpose and setting is to some people. If you are in a position giving negative feedback—such as an umpire, referee, traffic officer, or teacher—and everyone expects this kind of discipline or feedback from you, it is one thing. When you offer such advice freely, in a different setting, and with a less specific purpose, it is quite another thing!

The evaluative or negative feedback setting is never easy, even for professional counselors and skilled teachers. When our purpose is to direct negative feedback at someone else, we must work especially hard at being our best self, our most sensitive self. When you *ask* for evaluation or feedback, prepare yourself for some blunt remarks: most people will be quite honest, but not always objective, and rarely as kind as you think they should be.

Do not be too eager to evaluate others. The great counselor and psychologist Carl Rogers was known to say, "The older and wiser I get, the less eager I am to rush in to fix things."[9] Objectivity is critical to sensitive feedback situations, but so is tact.

PSYCHOLOGICAL CLIMATE

Psychological climate refers to *all* of the influences that affect the communication between John and Tom in the interaction model or in any of the settings discussed above. It includes all of the *environmental dimensions*, both physical and psychological, and particularly those human aspects of climate variously described as *accepting, understanding, facilitating*, and so on. These aspects could also be negative—that is, strongly *judgmental, evaluative, defensive, dogmatic*, and the like.

A healthy communication climate might be described as a *cohesive* environment in which the discussants, through *interaction*, achieve a mental state of relative psychological safety and freedom. According to Shepherd,[10] *cohesion* refers to the forces that bind members of a group, the degree of closeness and warmth they feel for one another, their pride as members, their willingness to be frank and honest in their expression of ideas and feelings, and their ability to meet the emergencies and crises that may confront them.

Interaction, you will recall, is communication behavior directed toward another person or persons when their reactions or mutual behavior are taken into account. It pertains directly to one's interpersonal responsibilities in communication.

What is being discussed is obviously a large part of the psychological

[9] Carl Rogers, *On Becoming a Person* (Boston: Houghton Mifflin, 1961), p. 21.
[10] Clovis R. Shepherd, *Small Groups: Some Sociological Perspectives* (San Francisco: Chandler, 1964), p. 26.

climate. If one is faced with bad news, deserved criticism, necessary evaluation, or generally unhappy feedback, some cold or even defensive psychological climate is perhaps unavoidable. This is precisely the time when we must be our very best communicative selves, or we may make an already difficult psychological climate really impossible.

If you remember your driver training, you probably recall at least a few bad days during which criticism of your driving behavior seemed harsh (to you) or threatening, however necessary it may have been in the name of highway safety and your own driving skill. The way in which such criticism is given as well as taken is what is known as psychological climate.

If your English professor objectively criticizes a bad essay of yours line by line (as she is paid to do), it is easy to become defensive in a subsequent, one-to-one encounter. The climate and both persons' assessment of and contribution to it are truly essential to how each learns, communicates, and grows.

We can also think of psychological climate as feelings of safety or freedom. We probably feel less safe psychologically in communication settings pertaining to evaluation than in a social conversation or a loving relationship. When there is good rapport and basic respect for one another, a person may achieve a kind of *psychological freedom,* a happy climate in which one's status is not unreasonably threatened, in which he or she feels accepted as a person, in which he or she has the freedom to be wrong and to become involved. Both psychological safety and freedom involve being accepted as an individual of some worth in a climate in which one is not persistently evaluated as a person.

Human interaction is, of course, a knife that cuts both ways. One may lack *sensitivity* as a message sender, but one may be too sensitive as a receiver. If, on a given day John is feeling superdefensive about his race, national origin, or some other large dimension of his personality, his friend Tom may find communication very difficult indeed. At this point, Tom has a considerable communication obligation to avoid being overly sensitive in his role as a receiver and to strive to reestablish a healthier communication climate. It is as if we must have both thick and thin skins at exactly the same time. We need to develop a tolerance for conflicting information, beliefs, and perceptions, as well as a general tolerance for doubt and uncertainty.

When the setting is tense and angry, emotional voices are heard, and we are put to a real communication test. When our feelings (our affective states) are out of balance or inconsistent with our beliefs (our cognitive states), we are apt to ruin the psychological climate. Our emotions may affect the way we think in a given situation or communication episode, but the reverse is also true: the way we think affects the way we feel. If John *thinks* Tom is going to ridicule or insult him, he is probably going to *feel* angry or defensive. If Tom *thinks* John really intends to threaten their relationship, wouldn't he *feel* fear and apprehension?

We cannot stop people from being human, which means John or Tom may occasionally let anger get the best of them. The advice of a great communication teacher, Irving Lee, was to "stay angry—but look again at what you are responding to." Don't just count to ten or turn the other cheek, but look again objectively to see if your anger is justified. According to Lee, three out of every four times a person becomes angry, a second look will show that he or she is overreacting or is not justified in feeling angry. "When angry look again."[11]

During a long, hot summer a young police officer, weary and angry over innumerable car thefts in his precinct, saw a person removing a wheel from a car. His blood boiled as he reached for his gun. He called upon all of his training and experience to pause and look again; he knew the man, it was his own car, and he was replacing a flat tire! A possible tragedy was avoided because a young police officer fought his emotions long enough to "look again." Before you blow your cool, run it through one more time! Is it what it appears to be? Is it really worth the extent of your anger?

[11] Irving J. Lee, *How to Talk with People* (New York: Harper & Row, Publishers, Inc., 1952), pp. 113–20.

13 SUMMING UP

Human interaction is a process involving both content and relationship communication. It also involves mutual influence. What looks like a simple two-part interaction is not simple after all! You bring at least three other "you's" with you to every interaction: who you think you are (your self-concept), who you think the other person is, and what you think that person thinks of you. To confuse things, that other person brings along the same kinds of notions, all with varying degrees of accuracy. It is important that we be our realistic, best self, or we may quickly offend people.

The study of self-concept and perception gives us much insight into speech and communication. A healthy, realistic, positive self-concept should make one a better communicator.

Our tendency to create and sustain relationships is one of the great stimulations of human communication. Studies of interpersonal attraction have sought to analyze the results of people communicating together. They suggest that our attraction to others is not haphazard, but rather is shaped and strengthened by at least five factors: (1) *nearness,* (2) *similarity,* or attitude and mood agreement, (3) *social adjustment,* (4) *status* and *recognition,* or how much social reward we anticipate, and (5) *physical characteristics,* or how we are perceived physically. These factors are interpreted through human perceptions, which are often in error.

Persons who are active communicators and who are in the midst of the action appear to have an advantage.

People are usually evaluated as more attractive when they are perceived as having attitudes similar to our own. Momentary feelings of anxiety often trigger tendencies to seek company of like minds. Similar and familiar personalities usually breed attraction, not contempt.

There is good evidence that we find well-adjusted people with healthy self-concepts more attractive than people with poor social adjustment and negative self-concepts.

The factors of status and recognition are related to anticipated social reward and a supportive relationship. A sympathetic ear is often a strong reason for interpersonal attraction.

Feedback that concerns our personality and the way in which we respond to the world probably affects our attractiveness to others more than the plain facts of our physical appearance.

The setting is critical to human interaction. The place and ritual of the setting influences the amount and kind of communication. The purpose of the setting is also critical to human interaction.

Some general purposes that tend to have a substantial impact on human communication and interaction are (1) *social*—fun and fellowship; (2) *ventilation*—releasing feelings; (3) *seeking help and information;* (4) *bargaining*—working it out together; and (5) *evaluation*—necessary feedback.

Psychological climate is all of the influences that affect communication in the interpersonal model and in any setting in which communication takes place. This climate is important to how a person learns, communicates, and grows. Both psychological safety and freedom include being accepted as an individual of some worth in a climate in which one is not persistently evaluated as a person. To build a healthy, realistic psychological climate, we need to develop a tolerance for conflicting information, beliefs, and perceptions as well as a general tolerance for doubt and uncertainty.

Speech Communication Principles

1 Successful interaction is the style, kind, and amount of communication directed toward another person or persons when their self-concepts and reactions are taken into account.

2 Interaction is a process of *mutual* influence, involving both content and relationship aspects.

3 Interpersonal communication is a process of common experience and mutual influence.

4 A large portion of our self-concept is shaped by interactions with individuals whom we consider significant to us.

5 Active communicators in the midst of the action tend to be more attractive to others (other things being equal).

6 People are usually evaluated as more attractive when they are perceived as having attitudes similar to our own.

7 Feedback that concerns our personality and the way in which we respond to the world probably affects our attractiveness to others more than the facts of our physical appearance. (Obviously, however, appearance can stimulate attraction.)

8 Status and recognition given us by others breed attraction because of our anticipation of rewards and a supportive relationship.

9 A sympathetic ear (a good listener) is often a strong reason for interpersonal attraction.

10 Well-adjusted people with healthy self-concepts are more attractive than people with poor social adjustment and negative self-concepts.

11 The place and ritual of the setting influence the amount and kind of communication that takes place.

12 The purpose and setting influences the amount and kind of communication that takes place.

13 Psychological climate affects how a person communicates, learns, and grows.

Specific Learning Outcomes

1 We should be able to illustrate in an oral or written report the complexity of human interaction.

2 We should be able to discuss in a two-page report five factors of interpersonal attraction.

3 We should be able to explain orally or in a short essay the influence of place and ritual on human communication.

4 We should be able to explain orally or in a short essay the influence of purpose on human communication.

5 We should be able to explain how emotion affects psychological climate.

6 We should be able to relate the foregoing general and specific learning outcomes to the speech communication principles listed in this chapter.

Communication Competencies

1 We should be able to evaluate a real or hypothetical interpersonal interaction according to the principles above.

2 We should be able to exhibit a sensitivity to the notions of others in our interpersonal interaction.

3 We should develop a sensitivity to self-image as it affects both the sending and receiving of signals in the process of communication.

4 We should be able to become more objective in our evaluations of the attractiveness of others.

5 We should be able to adapt our interpersonal communication behavior to the specific setting in which we find ourselves.

6 We should be able to help create a healthier psychological climate for our interpersonal interaction.

Study Projects and Tasks

1 Observe several two-person interactions until you find a really good or a really bad one. Describe the interaction and defend your evaluation in two pages or less. Be prepared to report in class.

2 Select a person who attracts you, and assess your evaluation of that person in terms of the factors of attraction discussed in this chapter. (Or do the same for a person whom you find unattractive.) Be prepared to discuss it in class.

3 Attend a meeting of a relatively ritualized group (for instance, a church service, award ceremony, graduation, or funeral service) and write a short report on its influence on human interaction.

4 Identify the purpose (or purposes) of the next three interpersonal interactions of which you are a part, and explain how you determined the purpose and whether the other person or persons agreed with your choice.

5 Name two things you have done to help create a healthy communication climate. Then name two things you did (usually unintentional) that disrupted a good climate.

GENERAL LEARNING OUTCOMES

1 We should learn the nature of dynamic, small-group discussion.

2 We should learn that cooperative communication is essential to the success of a democratic society.

3 We should learn the contemporary forms of discussion and know when they are applicable.

4 We should learn about the reflective thinking process and its relationship to discussion agendas.

5 We should learn to distinguish among the various types and functions of leadership.

6 We should learn to develop our powers as critics of communication in small groups.

discussion: cooperative communication

THE NATURE OF DISCUSSION

This chapter is concerned with systematic, cooperative decision making in small-group discussions. The term *discussion* is derived from the Latin *discussus,* to strike asunder, to pull apart, to separate and subordinate the elements and ideas that make up a question or topic. Discussion is not to be confused with debate. Debate is two-sided; discussion is many sided. Debate is competitive, discussion cooperative. If decision is impossible through discussion, then discussion may very well lead to debate. Debate may then lead to resolution. If it does not, the group very possibly will return to discussion. Premature or unnecessary debate has interfered in many group discussions. A discussion-debate continuum is illustrated in figure 14.1.

According to communication theory, the unique aspect of discussion is that a participant is both sender and receiver at the same time—producing truly dynamic, interpersonal communication. Feedback and perception take on even greater significance in these circumstances.

The Nature of Small Groups

Most of our social interaction is in small groups. We are however interested in groups that are more than just small, casual gatherings. There must be some connecting link, some common purpose, intent, or problem that requires some modest interaction to make a "co-acting" group. We might say the members of such a group share a kind of mutual identification. The small group is a dynamic collection as long as it has *cohesiveness*. *Cohesion* is the force that binds members of a group together. Our own sense of interpersonal responsibilities and behavior greatly affects our successful interaction. We must be sensitive to our own behavior as well as to the behavior of others. The feedback is often swift and to the point in small groups; audiences are usually slower to respond and are more formal in their patterns of response.

Figure 14.1

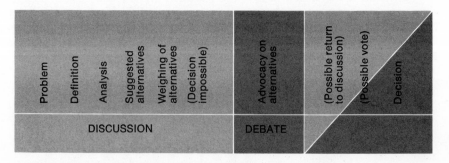

The small group differs from the larger audience in still other psychological ways. The audience is passive, the group usually active and dynamic. The group's size permits active verbal involvement and instant participation. Some members have a greater desire to take charge than others do. The interacting group often develops a spirit or cohesiveness that resembles the "collective mind" of the mob. This phenomenon, called *social facilitation*, is usually considered in positive terms, but small groups have been known to run wild, something that audiences seldom do (except in panics).

The two-part communication models in chapters 1 and 13 can be adapted here to show the complex workings of the small, co-acting group. If we consider interpersonal communication as feedback *loops*, with every pair within a larger group having its own loop, then we see quickly why three persons constitute something quite different interpersonally, than two alone (see figure 14.2). We suddenly have three times as many two-part loops to follow. The number of possible subgroups and relationships grows to seven. For example, in a group of three (A, B, and C) we can chart the following subgroups:

A–B–C	AB–C
A–B	AC–B
A–C	BC–A
B–C	

Two's company, three's a crowd!

Figure 14.2 Model for a co-acting group of three

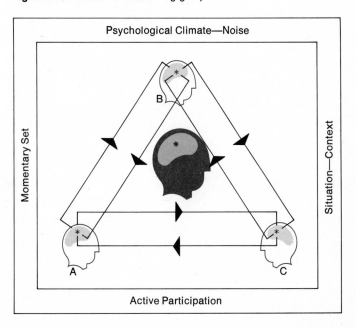

The reason most small-group experts limit their research to groups of six or seven is clear if we look at a group of eight in terms of loops and subgroup relationships. (See figure 14.3; single lines with arrows are substituted for loops in this figure.) We now find ourselves with twenty-eight two-part loops. Time is part of the equation. Perhaps over a period of days or weeks we could master that many interactions. However, the total number of relationships and subgroups is something else! Would you believe 1009![1]

[1]The formula for predicting the total number of subgroup relationships may be expressed:

$$R = \sum d\frac{n!}{d!(n-d!)+1} \text{ where } d = s\,(n-1),\,(n-2)\,(n-3)\ldots(2)$$

Figure 14.3 Model for a co-acting group of eight

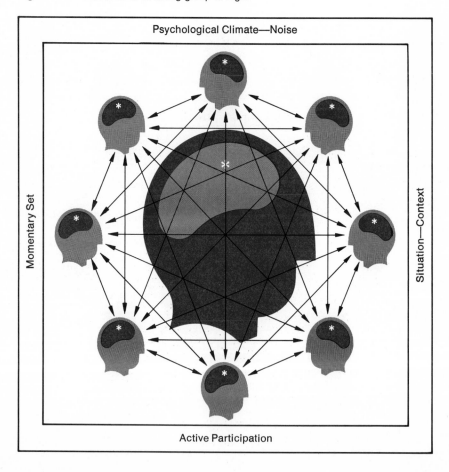

Certain *generalizations regarding the co-acting small group* are warranted from the research on such groups.[2]

1 Attitudes and behavior can be changed through group discussion.
2 On the average, small-group judgment tends to be better than individual judgment.
3 Small, agreeing groups develop more of a feeling of personal involvement and responsibility than do audiences.
4 Cooperative group communication can be improved through training.

In a broader sense, we might conclude that cooperative communication in small groups is essential to success in our society.[3]

Discussion Defined

The experts are in basic agreement about what we mean by group discussion.

Discussion is the process whereby two or more people exchange information or ideas in a face-to-face situation to achieve a goal.[4]

[Discussion groups] consist of a number of persons who perceive each other as participants in a common activity, who interact dynamically with one another, and who communicate their responses chiefly through words.[5]

Discussion occurs when a group of persons assemble in a face-to-face situation and through oral interaction exchange information or attempt to reach a decision on shared problems.[6]

. . . an orderly process of cooperative deliberation designed to exchange, evaluate, and/or integrate knowledge and opinion on a given subject or to work toward solution of a common problem.[7]

. . . a number of persons who communicate with one another over a span of time, and who are few enough so that each person

[2] See Jon Eisenson, J. Jeffrey Auer, and John V. Irwin, *The Psychology of Communication* (New York: Appleton-Century-Crofts, 1963), pp. 253–70; B. M. Bass, *Leadership, Psychology and Organizational Behavior* (New York: Harper & Row, Publishers, Inc., 1973); A. P. Hare, *Handbook of Small Group Research* (New York: Free Press, 1976); J. W. Thibaut and H. H. Kelley, *The Social Psychology of Groups* (New York: John Wiley & Sons, Inc., 1959); and Joseph E. McGrath and Irwin Altman, *Small Group Research* (New York: Holt, Rinehart & Winston, 1966).

[3] See Gerald M. Phillips and Eugene C. Erickson, *Interpersonal Dynamics in the Small Group* (New York: Random House, Inc., 1970).

[4] R. Victor Harnack, Thorrel B. Fest, and Barbara Schindler Jones, *Group Discussion Theory and Technique,* 2nd. ed. (Englewood Cliffs, N. J.: Prentice-Hall, Inc., 1977), p. 12.

[5] Dean C. Barnlund and Franklyn S. Haiman, *The Dynamics of Discussion* (Boston: Houghton Mifflin Company, 1960), p. 20.

[6] Halbert Gulley, *Discussion, Conference, and Group Process,* 2nd. ed. (New York: Holt, Rinehart & Winston, 1968), p. 5; H. Gulley and D. Leathers, *Communication and Group Process,* 3rd ed., 1977.

[7] Horace Rahskopf, *Basic Speech Improvement* (New York: Harper & Row, Publishers, Inc., 1965), p. 348.

is able to communicate with all others, not at secondhand, through other people, but face-to-face.[8]

. . . a set of activities usually executed by a small group and directed toward determining appropriate answers to controversial questions of fact, conjecture, value, or policy.[9]

Two other writers summed it up well when they said, "Discussion, then, is a means of thinking together through purposeful conversation."[10]

Assuming, then, that we have a real, interacting, face-to-face group—persons with some common goal, not just a loose collection of individuals—we might combine the above descriptions by saying that at its best *group discussion is a systematic and cooperative form of reflective thinking and communication.*

Contemporary Forms of Discussion

In this context, the word *form* refers to the type or format of discussion. In its most general sense, group discussion is a cooperative thinking effort, usually among twenty persons or less. The basic forms of group discussion are *dialogue, panel,* and *symposium.* Three techniques that may be used with any of these forms are the *buzz group, role playing,* and *brainstorming.* A *forum* is simply that part of a discussion in which the audience may speak. It can be and often is included in any of the discussion forms.[11]

A *dialogue* is a two-person interaction that may be simple conversation, an interview, or counseling. If a dialogue is held before an audience and the audience is invited to participate, the interaction becomes a dialogue forum. See figure 14.4.

The *panel* discussion is most often composed of three to seven persons pursuing a common goal in an informal climate that aids spontaneous interaction. An audience may or may not be present. A panel discussion generally calls for a procedural leader, one who plans, starts, and ends the meeting, and some *agenda* (to be discussed in the following section).

A *symposium* is a small group (three to five) that has special knowledge of different aspects of a broad topic. Each individual makes uninterrupted speeches before an audience. A procedural leader controls the order of speakers and the time limits. A forum usually follows, except when an audience is not physically present (as with radio or TV broadcasts). Fre-

---

[8] G. C. Homans, *The Human Group* (New York: Harcourt, Brace & World, 1950), p. 1.

[9] Dennis S. Gouran, *Discussion: The Process of Group Decision-Making* (New York: Harper & Row, Publishers, Inc., 1974), p. 5.

[10] Wilhelmina G. Hedde and William N. Brigance, *American Speech* (Philadelphia: J. B. Lippincott Company, 1942), p. 40.

[11] See especially Kenneth G. Hance, ed., *Michigan Speech Association Curriculum Guide 3, Discussion and Argumentation-Debate in the Secondary School* (Skokie, Ill.: National Textbook Corporation, 1968).

quently, the symposium speakers then relate to one another more informally in a panel discussion.

These forms of discussion may be used for information sharing, problem solving, or decision making, as well as for instructional purposes.

Examples of information-sharing groups are *staff meetings, study groups,* and *workshops.* The overlap among these groups is evident and probably unavoidable. A workshop, for example, may be thought of as a study group that has concentrated its work into a couple of days, or even a few hours.

Problem-solving groups include *committees, conferences,* and *governing boards* or *councils.* These discussion groups have the power of decision or at least the power to recommend action based on their collective problem solving. Their group discussions are usually closed to nonmembers.

Instructional formats of discussion include case conferences, role playing, and to some extent all the forms and techniques of discussion. A *case conference* is a discussion of a real or hypothetical incident that is meant to have a learning outcome for the participants. It may or may not be conducted with an audience present. It can be evaluated according to participant interaction, leadership, agenda setting, and the solution.

Large groups in which wider forum participation is desired may be divided into subgroups of four to six persons for more intimate, informal discussion. This technique is known as *buzz,* "Phillips 66," or "Discussion 66." The numbers refer to subgroups of six, which discuss a carefully worded question.[12] The results of the individual buzz sessions are reported to the larger group by a spokesperson. The number of people in the subgroups seems to be important: a person is more apt to speak up in a group of 6 than of 600.

The extemporaneous acting out of assigned roles or dramatic parts in a group—often a case conference—is known as *role playing,* or what Hirschfeld has described as *extemporaction.*[13] As a technique, role playing is often a good preliminary to the other forms of discussion.

Brainstorming is a technique that some speech communication instructors use to show the effect of eliminating premature and discussion-inhibiting comments of an absolute or critical nature. This technique operates in an arbitrary psychological climate complete with penalties, the purpose of which is to prohibit immediate criticism of ideas. Brainstorming permits more creative ideas to come to light in a short period of time than the more traditional climate does.[14] This technique also can be combined with other forms and used for purposes other than instruction. It can be particularly useful when a great many ideas are wanted from a group in a short period of time. It is a good technique for screening attitudes and

---

[12] Donald Phillips, "Report on Discussion," *Adult Education Journal,* 7 (October 1948), 181–82.

[13] From material supplied by Adeline Hirschfeld, director of P.A.C.E. project, "Creative and Sociodramatic Supplementary Educational and Cultural Enrichment Service," Title III, E.S.E.A., Oakland University, Rochester, Michigan, 1967.

[14] Alex F. Osborn, *Applied Imagination: Principles and Procedures of Creative Thinking* (New York: Charles Scribner's Sons, 1963).

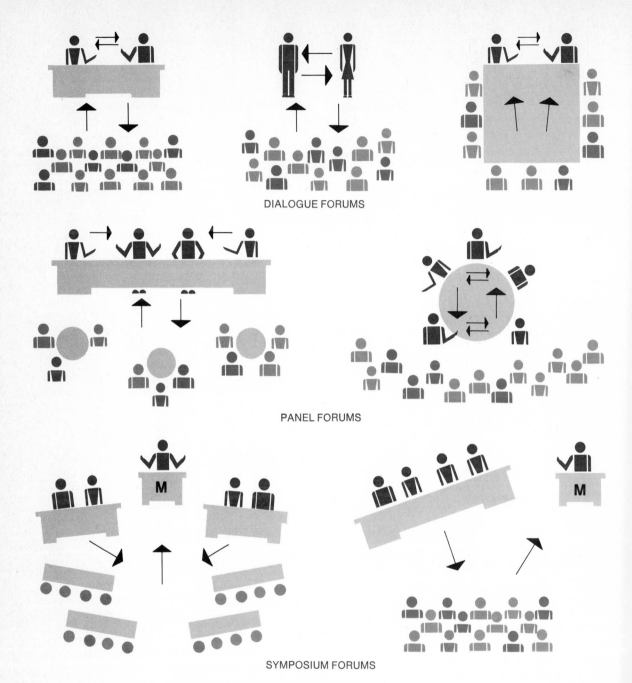

DIALOGUE FORUMS

PANEL FORUMS

SYMPOSIUM FORUMS

Figure 14.4 Participant configurations[15]

[15] For an interesting discussion of physical arrangements, see Paul Bergevin, Dwight Morris, and Robert M. Smith, *Adult Education Procedures* (Greenwich, Conn.: Seabury Press, 1963); see also Robert Sommer, *Personal Space* (Englewood Cliffs, N.J.: Prentice-Hall, Inc., 1969), pp. 58–73.

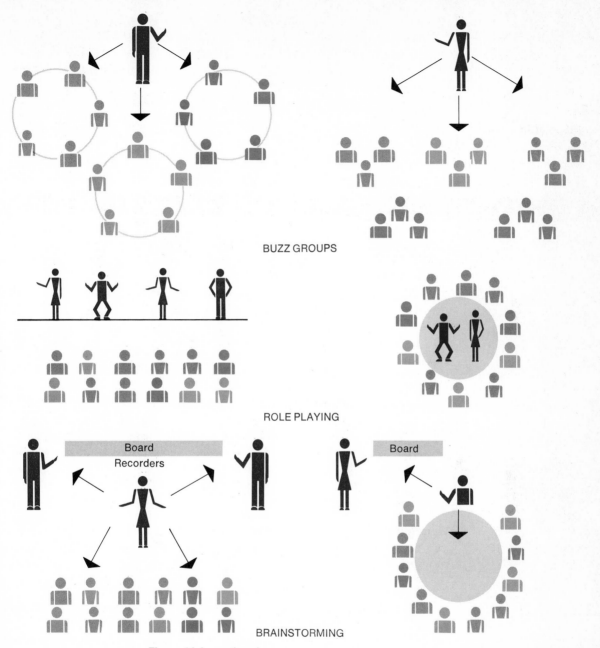

BUZZ GROUPS

ROLE PLAYING

Board
Recorders

Board

BRAINSTORMING

Figure 14.4 continued

opinions. Take the question, "What should this class use as a topic for a project discussion?" Under brainstorming rules, this question regularly produces sixty or seventy topics in ten minutes. No evaluative discussion of the topics is allowed until later. Using buzz groups to screen the list more systematically is a good follow-up.

AGENDAS

If group discussion is a *systematic and cooperative form of reflective thinking and communication,* then we had better explore reflective thinking in detail to see what kind of system or scheme it suggests for orderly *agendas*—that is, discussion outlines. That orderliness pays off in agreement is shown in a study of seventy-two conferences by Collins and Guetzkow. They report: "Those meetings in which discussion is orderly in its treatment of topics, and without backward references to previously discussed issues, tended to end in more consensus. . . . When participants discussed but one issue at a time, instead of simultaneously dabbling in two or three, it was more possible for the group to reach consensus."[16]

The Reflective Thinking Process

Reflective thinking was defined by John Dewey as "active, persistent and careful consideration of any belief or supposed form of knowledge in the light of the grounds that support it, and further conclusions to which it tends,"[17] as opposed to nondeliberate, everyday thinking. Dewey thought of reflective thinking as a scientific habit, one that consisted of acquiring the attitude of *suspended judgment* and mastering the various methods of searching for materials. Maintaining an intelligent state of doubt and practicing systematic inquiry are the essentials of reflective thinking.

Dewey's view of general education is also pertinent to group discussion, both as agendas and the way you conduct yourself. He thought of the aim of education as the establishment of a kind of *self-discipline* in students. This self-discipline consisted of *systematic observation, thorough examining,* and, most important to us, agendas, or the *methodical arrangement of thought.* The *Dewey system of reflective thinking* contains five steps:[18]

1 The occurrence or awareness of a *felt difficulty:* you know something is wrong, unexpected, or unidentified.
2 The *definition* of the felt difficulty to see what kind of problem you have and how serious it is: look carefully, don't misdefine; suspend your judgment regarding solutions.

---

[16] Barry E. Collins and Harold Guetzkow, *A Social Psychology of Group Processes for Decision-Making* (New York: John Wiley & Sons, Inc., 1964), p. 111.
[17] John Dewey, *How We Think* (Boston: D. C. Heath, 1910), p. 68.
[18] *Ibid.,* pp. 68–78.

3 The formulation of alternative suggestions, explanations, and hypotheses as *possible solutions:* inference and analysis take place here. (Review chapters 1 and 12.)
4 The rational working out of the possible solutions by gathering facts, evidence, and inferences: further analysis of the consequences of alternative solutions.
5 Further testing, rejecting, or confirming of the solution chosen in step 4—by observation, measurement, hypothetical case or model building, or actual experiment if applicable: you now have a reasoned solution in your thoughts.

AGENDA SYSTEMS

Although it is addressed to the individual, the reflective thinking system would make just as much sense to a group of individuals solving a problem or making a decision. More recent research tends to confirm the five stages of Dewey's system. Bales and Strodtbeck divided problem-solving discussions into three phases on the basis of number of interactions. They found that in the first phase, the communications pertained to *orientation, information, repetition,* and *confirmation;* in the second phase, the interactions were *analysis, evaluation,* and *communications* seeking or giving *opinions* and *feelings;* phase three consisted chiefly of acts of *control,* communications about possible directions and ways of action.[19] Bales and Strodtbeck also indicate that as a group approaches the third phase, it experiences increasing strain on the members' solidarity and social-emotional relationships. Both positive and negative reactions tend to increase. The reduction of tension is apparent as differences are resolved and agreement is reached.

The danger of oversimplifying so complicated a process is made clear by the research of Scheidel and Crowell, who suggest that the reflective thinking process as an agenda system is not a simple linear progression after all, but rather is a circular or spiraling course.[20] It's a little like a "Slinky" toy. The spirals of steel may be more compressed at the end of the spring in the

[19]Robert F. Bales and Fred L. Strodtbeck, "Phases in Group Problem-Solving," in *Group Dynamics: Research and Theory,* eds. Darwin Cartwright and Alvin Zander (New York: Harper & Row, Publishers, Inc., 1960), pp. 624–38.
[20]Thomas M. Scheidel and Laura Crowell, "Idea Development in Small Discussion Groups," *Quarterly Journal of Speech,* 50 (1964), 140–45.

Figure 14.5

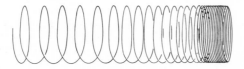

same way as ideas are compressed when a group finally nears agreement. After studying idea development in ten discussions, they concluded that members devoted one-fourth of their comments to confirming statements and another fourth to clarifying and substantiating them. The latter function is represented by the outward movement of this spiral model. The progress toward decision is represented as the onward movement.

The best agenda systems found in the literature are derived from research findings coupled with creative insight. Some excellent examples follow.

A visual aid depicting the agenda may prove helpful to participants.[21]

TWO PHASE AGENDA

I. The Analysis Phase
    A. Definitions: What does the question mean?
    B. Limitations, if any: What part of the problem do we intend to concentrate on if we cannot discuss the whole problem now?
    C. What are the important facts about this problem?
        1. What is its history?
        2. What are its causes?
        3. What has happened or is happening?
        4. What has happened elsewhere that illuminates the problem under discussion?

II. The Solution Phase
    A. What are the advantages and disadvantages of each alternative course of action?
    B. By what or whose standards must any decision be evaluated?
    C. What decision should we reach?[22]

SIX-STEP AGENDA

  I. Ventilation (general establishment of rapport)
 II. Clarification (phrasing the question)
III. Fact Finding
 IV. Discovery (finding hypotheses or solutions)
  V. Evaluation (of proposed solution)
 VI. Decision Making (putting the conclusion into words)[23]

FOUR-STEP AGENDA

  I. Are we all agreed on the nature of the problem?
 II. What would be the ideal solution from the point of view of all parties involved in the problem?
III. What conditions within the problem could be changed so that the ideal solution might be achieved?
 IV. Of the solutions available to us, which one best approximates the ideal solution?[24]

---

[21] John K. Brilhart, "An Experimental Comparison of Three Techniques for Communicating a Problem-Solving Pattern to Members of a Discussion Group," *Speech Monographs,* 33, no. 2 (June 1966), 176.

[22] Gulley, *Discussion, Conference, and Group Process,* pp. 215–16.

[23] Barnlund and Haiman, *The Dynamics of Discussion,* pp. 86–97 (material in parentheses added).

[24] R. L. Applbaum, E. M. Bodaken, K. K. Sereno, and K. W. E. Anatol, *The Process of Group Communication,* 2nd ed., (Chicago: Science Research Associates, Inc., 1979), p. 236.

```
SIX-STEP AGENDA

    Problem            1.  Problem Formulation
    Description        2.  Problem Analysis
    Phase              3.  Problem Reformation (if necessary)

    Problem            4.  Solution Proposal
    Solution           5.  Solution Testing
    Phase              6.  Action Testing[25]
```

```
ROSS FOUR-STEP AGENDA

  I.  Definition and limitation:  a concise but qualified statement of the felt
      difficulty, problem, or goal
 II.  Analysis:  the determination of the nature of the problem and its causes
        a.  Questions of fact
        b.  Questions of policy
        c.  Questions of value
III.  Establishing Criteria:  a group consensus on the standards to be used in
      judging solutions
        a.  Minimum and/or maximum limits
        b.  Rating the criteria in importance
 IV.  Solutions
        a.  Evaluation in terms of the criteria
        b.  Decision and suggested implementation or action
```

Elaborating the Agenda Systems

Using the *Ross four-step system* (E) as a point of reference, but with the understanding that what is said here will apply for the most part to all the agenda systems shown in figure 14.6, let's look at some of the finer points of an agenda.

1. THE DEFINITION STEP In most problem-solving discussions, a suggestion to take stock of the felt difficulty, to ventilate it fully, is pertinent. It helps remove emotional heat, if any, from the topic; it allows a quick audit of feelings (for example, there may be more than one felt difficulty in the group). It helps the group formulate the problem and determine goals.

The definition step consists of the *definition* and, if pertinent, the *limitation* of the problem. For example, a group may talk about unemployment and limit the problem to unemployment in Chicago. If a group defines a problem in several different ways and worse, is not aware of the differences, confusion and irritation are sure to follow. Discussion time is well spent on the definition step. Agree on the problem and/or goal *before* you proceed.

In some cases (for example, medical diagnosis), a thorough discussion of the problem and a knowledge of previous identical situations may make the solution obvious. Most often, however, a group is now ready to *analyze* its accepted problem. Agenda suggestions range from fact finding and problem restatement to a systematic determination of the *nature* of the problem.

[25] Harnack, Fest, and Jones, *Group Discussion Theory and Technique*, 2nd. ed., pp. 146–47.

	A	B	C		D	E
ANALYSIS	Definition	Ventilation	Definition and Analysis	**DESCRIPTION**	Problem Formulation	Definition and Limitation Felt difficulty Problem Goal
	Limitation	Clarification	*Ideal Solution* Analysis		Problem Analysis	
						Analysis—Nature of Problem
	Important Facts	Fact Finding			Problem Reformation	Puzzle Probability Value
SOLUTION	Alternate Courses of Action	Discovery	Problem Conditions Analysis	**SOLUTION**	Solution Proposal	Establish Criteria Limits Order of importance
					Solution Testing	
	Standards	Evaluation				
			Most ideal solution available		Action Testing	Solutions Evaluation against criteria Decision
	Decision					
		Decision				

Figure 14.6 Possible agenda systems

The nature of a problem is usually determined by *fact, policy, and value,* or, in the Ross system, by *puzzle, probability, and value.* The meaning of *fact* appears obvious to most of us. However, one cantankerous professor claims he has never heard a good definition of a fact. For the most part, facts are actions, events, or conditions that have been properly observed, described, classified, and reported. Can the phenomenon under discussion be verified by facts, to the satisfaction of group members? *Policy* is concerned with the possibility or desirability of a future course of action. Of course, facts probably also will be a part of this kind of deliberation. *Value* is concerned chiefly with judgments about attitudes, beliefs, and feelings—very often the things most difficult to measure. More will be said about value shortly.

2. THE ANALYSIS STEP

PUZZLES   In my division of the nature of a problem, the *puzzle* dimension refers to questions of *fact.* This dimension is easier to apply than the fact dimension, though it may be less comprehensive. As an illustration, consider a common jigsaw puzzle. No one would deny that a jigsaw puzzle can be difficult or frustrating (or capable of solution by group effort). Yet there is definitely a solution—and only one solution. Better yet, the solution is recognizable when you achieve it. It *is* the canals of Venice! Early detection of and agreement on a problem, as with a puzzle, can save much time and aggravation. If we were to view the jigsaw puzzle as a question of value—perhaps as a threat to our intelligence—then the problem would become more difficult and the solution (putting the pieces together) would probably be delayed.

Some puzzles are complicated. We use computers to solve engineering problems and adding machines and cash registers in supermarkets. But such problems are still puzzles, and we are well advised not to involve our emotions, morals, or value system too quickly.

PROBABILITY The *probability* dimension of the nature of a problem refers to common sense reduced to calculation. The suggestion here is that certain problems can be solved according to probability theory or to the laws of chance. Although the word *probability* itself indicates that such problems may never be solved with certainty, the mathematical chance of a solution being correct may often be treated as an operational fact. Gamblers can predict their odds with relative certainty. They know that they have a 50 percent chance of getting a head in flipping a coin. Even in simple games, however, determining probabilities can quickly become complicated. If your winning number is 5 in a dice game with two dice, you have only four possible combinations: 1–4, 4–1, 3–2, and 2–3. Since theoretical probabilities are multiplied—two six-sided dice give 36 (6 × 6) possible combinations—the odds of your winning are 4/36 or 1/9.

Figure 14.7

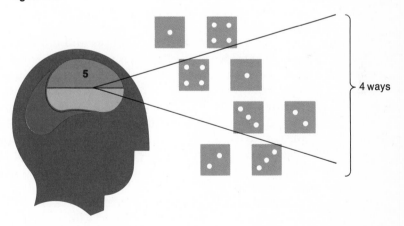

The six combinations yielding the number 7 have a probability of 6/36 or 1/6. The number of rolls is, of course, a significant variable. The larger the number of rolls, in general, the greater the likelihood that the theoretical probability becomes an established fact.

Not all probability and prediction problems have odds that are as theoretically absolute as those in a coin flip or a dice game. An insurance company never knows exactly how many accidents, deaths, and fires will occur among its policy holders, but it can make quite accurate predictions on the basis of past experiences. This science of probability prediction is called *statistics*. From statistics we learn not only to ask "What caused the difference?" but also how to test whether the difference is merely a random variation or indicates some known or unknown factor at work. *Significance tests* make it possible to express and interpret the differences mathematically. This number may be considered an indicator of the "level of confidence" we may justifiably have in the data, or it may reflect our chances of being wrong. Discussants need not be statisticians, but they should be aware of probability problems and of how theory can influence decisions about problems of large masses of data.

VALUES   The *value* dimension of the nature of a problem concerns desirability rather than probability or certainty. Value systems held by group members are commonly considered as deriving from their past experiences. It is in this light that questions of value must, partly, be evaluated.

Your general value system is determined by your past experiences; your understanding and acceptance of the concept of law as natural, universal, and/or pragmatic; and your interpretation of various concepts such as good and bad, pleasure and pain, noble and ignoble, and loyal and disloyal; as well as by a multitude of minor preferences that often defy any search for an underlying principle (preferences for certain foods, colors, architecture, and so on). By knowing the experiences, interpretations, and preferences that make up a person's general value system, it is often possible to make fairly reliable nonnumerical predictions and analyses of questions of value.

To the extent that preferences and attitudes (a form of preference) may be considered as values, it is possible to measure attitudes toward many things, from the size of next year's cars to the latest fashions. Differences in attitudes toward a given subject can, in fact, be measured fairly accurately through the use of the standard statistical techniques.

Although the *value* dimension of analysis is the part most resistant to numerical measurement, this does not mean we should not try to measure, objectify, and analyze problems. It does mean that we must know our own intelligently derived values and how they may be applied to the group's analysis of a specific problem. It also means that we must make every effort to determine the differences in preferences and values among the people in our group and among the people who may be affected by this group's decision. This kind of analysis should lead to better and more prudent group decisions regarding questions of value.

In agenda system C (figure 14.6) analysis also includes calm analysis of what an ideal solution would or should look like. It can help you find criteria that your perhaps less than ideal solution should at least try to meet.

3. THE CRITERIA STEP   Whether one thinks of this step as really a continuation of analysis or as the beginning of the solution phase is of no

great importance. It is, however, an important enough agenda item to warrant your close attention. A *criterion* is a standard or yardstick by which we may measure or evaluate something.

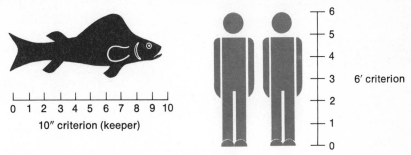

0 1 2 3 4 5 6 7 8 9 10
10″ criterion (keeper)

6′ criterion

Figure 14.8

In the case of group discussion, it refers to an *agreed-upon standard*. If a group has reasonably clear and agreed-upon criteria in mind, the evaluation or testing of suggested solutions is a lot easier, or at least more systematic. If a group were discussing the problem of a clubhouse for their organization, they would want to clearly establish the criteria of *cost, size, location, new or old,* and so on. The concept of *limits* can help a group at this point. If we are talking about cost in terms of $100,000, what do we really mean? Is that the top limit or the bottom? If the group really meant $75,000 to $110,000, it should state this, at least to itself. The same could be said for size and location. Criteria can also be negative. The group could, for example, name locations that it would not consider under any conditions.

The concept of *weighting* your criteria in terms of importance should also be considered. If size is the single most important criterion, then the group should agree on that point. Say, for example, that the old clubhouse is crowded; unless the next place is X amount larger, however beautiful a bargain, it won't solve the problem. If location is next most important (say the facilities must be close to where the members live), and then cost, parking, architecture, and so on, you have the beginnings of a subagenda for evaluating solutions. Your list of criteria should then appear in some kind of rank in terms of importance. *Weighting* may be used profitably by a group if some of the criteria are close together in importance. Assuming a 100-point weighting scale and the determination that both size and location are very important, the group might assign to size 90 points, to location 80 points, to cost 50 points, to architecture 20 points, and so on, along with specific upper and lower limits for each criterion (see figure 14.9). Such a scale gives the group considerably more insight into the distances among its ranked criteria. Further, it gives the group a more logical, systematic approach to the solution step.

4. THE SOLUTION STEP To continue the illustration of the clubhouse under the criteria step, the group may now consider solutions that individ-

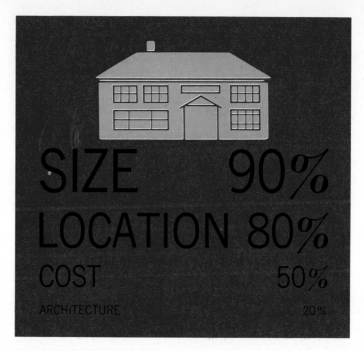

Figure 14.9 Weighting criteria

uals may offer. If Steve A. offers pictures and real estate data on a building he's found, but the building fails the criterion of size because it doesn't meet the lower limit (and no plan for enlargement is provided by the contributor), then the group is quickly and systematically ready to go on to the next possible solution. It is possible that a group may come up with several solutions that meet the major criteria; the discussion may then focus on the less heavily weighted criteria. This is progress and the group is aware of it. Without stated criteria to follow, the group might engage in lengthy argument over minor aspects of a problem while virtually ignoring the major aspects.

You may wish to discuss and evaluate your alternate solutions further, according to the puzzle-probability-value analysis suggested earlier. Or you may wish some additional firsthand observation or action testing. But in any case the group is ready for *decision*.

Remember that discussion may sometimes be called upon to solve inappropriate questions. We do not need a group to solve most questions of fact or even some questions of probability. The library, the computer, the map—these solve some problems without group discussion. Nor does discussion solve the unsolvable. Some questions of value belong here. Once past the educational value, we sometimes may be well advised to adjourn. We should, of course, always look for viable solutions of the moment if not for all time.

Figure 14.10

LEADERSHIP AND PARTICIPATION

In general, *leadership* should be thought of as any significant action by any discussant that influences group achievement.[26] A group may have an assigned leader, whose duties may range from a modest regulation of participation to near domination and control. It is possible to be in a leaderless group (that is, with no appointed leader) and still have considerable leadership, should this leadership emerge in some way from the group. By the same token, one could be in a group with a poor assigned leader; if no good leader(s) emerged, this group would really have no leadership. The distinction, therefore, between leader and leadership and leaderless and leadershipless is a critical one. All group members have a stake and often a part in leadership. Thus, what follows applies to all group discussants, whether they happen to be assigned group leader, chairperson, moderator, or whatever.

Sources of Leadership

Leadership may fall upon a person in a group because she was appointed the moderator. It may be given to a person only on certain issues because she happens to be the best informed on those issues. It may befall a person by reason of her position or status in the group (for example, she happens to be the boss, or a full professor). Particularly in leaderless groups, leadership may fall to a person who happens to perform vital group functions and procedures exceptionally well—one who knows about agendas, reflective thinking, democratic leadership, the communication process, and interpersonal relations.

[26] See especially Barnlund and Haiman, *The Dynamics of Discussion,* chap. 13; and Gulley, *Discussion, Conference, and Group Process,* chap. 10; also, see Dennis S. Gouran, "Perspectives on the Study of Leadership: Its Present and Its Future," *Quarterly Journal of Speech,* 60, no. 3 (1974), 376–81.

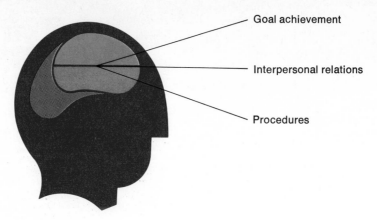

Figure 14.11

Functions of Leadership

Leadership, whatever its source (and all group members have responsibility for the source), should in general help a group move toward its goal or help it find its goal. Leadership should also promote a healthy, democratic communication climate within the group. The *major functions of leadership*, then, are *goal achievement* (content), *effective interpersonal relations* (communication climate), and *procedural functions*.

GOAL ACHIEVEMENT   Elements of leadership related primarily to content include such things as contributing and evaluating ideas, locating issues and consensus, synthesizing and cross-relating the ideas of others, and generally seeking specific contributions toward a goal.

INTERPERSONAL RELATIONS   Qualities of leadership in this area include such things as controlling emotions, setting communication and psychological climates, resolving conflict, regulating the too-talkative and the silent, and generally promoting those actions concerned with particularly social and human problems.

PROCEDURAL FUNCTIONS   Leaders, particularly when assigned or designated, must also attend to the more *practical* functions such as starting the meeting, drafting and/or following the agenda, clarifying statements, summarizing, and ending the meeting. Procedural functions may also include advanced planning and physical arrangements. As a procedural leader, you must review the purposes of the meeting. You should consider the members individually and decide the degree of formality necessary and the specific way you wish to open the discussion. You should consider group goals according to the time available.

As a procedural leader, you are also responsible for participation—that is, for preserving order, seeing that only one person speaks at a time, and fairly distributing the right to speak. You may find it necessary on occasion to clarify what has been said as well as to remind the group of the agreed-upon agenda. The agenda should be agreed on by the members unless it has already been designated.

Styles of Leadership

Style refers in part to method and in part to philosophy. Styles of leadership are variously described as laissez-faire, nondirective, permissive, democratic, supervisory, authoritarian, and autocratic. These styles are ordered on a control continuum in figure 14.12.[27] As with most spectrums of alternatives, virtue lies near the middle. Everything said so far about discussion advises that a *democratic* style is superior to an absolute or non-responsible style. However, in some groups in which *goal achievement* becomes unusually pressing, leadership should go up the scale if such an action can help. On the other hand, to achieve sincerely healthy *interpersonal relations,* particularly when emotions are strained or personalities are in conflict, it may be advisable to go down the scale. In the middle we have union-management discussions, most of which are cooperative negotiations.

An interesting study by Simons indicates that the more participation-oriented patterns or styles of deliberation, even with relatively large groups (fifteen to twenty persons), were more productive in problem-solving discussion than the more formal patterns.[28]

[27] See also Gulley, *Discussion, Conference, and Group Process,* p. 179.
[28] Herbert W. Simons, "Representative versus Participative Patterns of Deliberation in Large Groups," *Quarterly Journal of Speech,* 52, no. 2 (April 1966), 164–71.

Figure 14.12

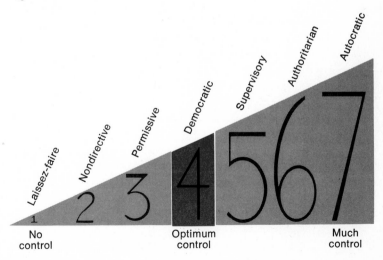

Participant Responsibilities

In addition to the general climate-setting responsibilities of all participants, more specific participant responsibilities may be described. The following participant roles tend to help *advance* the group and its goals:[29]

Encourager   +   Standard Setter
Harmonizer   Group Observer
Compromiser   Elaborator
Gate Keeper   Initiator
  (opens channels of communication)

[29] Kenneth D. Benne and Paul Sheats, "Functional Roles of Group Members," *Journal of Social Issues,* 4, no. 2 (1948), 41–49.

Figure 14.13

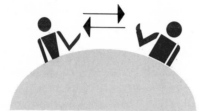

One or two members dominate.

Some members wil not talk.

Some apparently lack interest.

Discussion drifts to irrelevant matters.

Conflict occurs between members.

Discussion "techniques" backfire.

These roles tend to have a negative effect:

Aggressor (deflates status of others)	Playboy
Blocker — (opposes beyond reason)	Dominator
Recognition Seeker	Help Seeker
Self-Confessor	Special-Interest Pleader

Participants as well as leaders have an interpersonal responsibility whenever these situations arise:

A *good participant* should, in general:

1 Use tact.
2 Be enthusiastic.
3 Exhibit a sense of humor.
4 Be cooperative.
5 Minimize differences.
6 Be friendly.
7 Identify with group's goals.
8 Interact.
9 Consider rewards of membership.
10 Work to help group.

OBSERVING AND EVALUATING DISCUSSION

One of the most popular observational schemes for small-group research was developed by Bales. This system, which is called "*interaction process analysis*," is a classification of communicative acts; *act* is defined as verbal and nonverbal behavior. An observer is responsible for three areas of observation: positive social-emotional acts, "task" acts, and negative social-emotional acts. A modified outline of the system is presented in figure 14.14.

Observers' tabulations of acts in various research studies (usually of college students) indicate an average group profile of 25 percent positive reactions (category A in figure 14.14), 56 percent attempted answers (B), 7 percent questions (C), and 12 percent negative reactions (D). A self-explanatory general-discussion *rating form* for observing participants is shown in figure 14.15.

Observing and evaluating discussion can also be done by diagraming the participation. The resulting charts are called *sociograms* and may provide graphic insights into group behavior. Methods of diagraming include simply tabulating the number and length of contributions, or classifying the contributions according to categories or types, as Bales does. One can also draw circles representing the discussants, and then with lines and arrows diagram the flow and amount of interpersonal communication. One can often find graphic evidence to show to the overtalkative. (See figure 14.16, page 374)

ILLUSTRATIVE STATEMENTS OR BEHAVIOR

MAJOR CATEGORIES	SUBCATEGORIES	ILLUSTRATIVE STATEMENTS OR BEHAVIOR	Reciprocal or Opposite Pairs
Social-Emotional Area { A. Positive (and Mixed) Reactions	1. Seems friendly	Jokes, gives help, rewards others, is friendly	a
	2. Dramatizes	Laughs, shows satisfaction, is relieved	b
	3. Agrees	Passively accepts, understands, concurs, complies	c
B. Attempted Answers	4. Gives suggestion	Directs, suggests, implies autonomy for others	d
	5. Gives opinion	Evaluates, analyzes, expresses feeling or wish	e
	6. Gives information	Orients, repeats, clarifies, confirms	f
C. Questions	7. Asks for information	Requests orientation, repetition, confirmation	f
	8. Asks for opinion	Requests evaluation, analysis, expression of feeling	e
	9. Asks for suggestion	Requests direction, possible ways of action	d
Social Emotional Area { D. Negative (and Mixed) Reactions	10. Disagrees	Passively rejects, resorts to formality, withholds help	c
	11. Shows tension	Asks for help, withdraws, daydreams	b
	12. Seems unfriendly	Deflates other's status, defends or asserts self, acts hostile	a

Task Area

a. Problems of Communication
b. Problems of Evaluation
c. Problems of Control
d. Problems of Decision
e. Problems of Tension Reduction
f. Problems of Reintegration

Figure 14.14 Categories for interaction process analysis. Based on Robert F. Bales, *Interaction Process Analysis* (Cambridge, Mass.: Addison-Wesley 1950). p. 9. A. Paul Hare, *Handbook of Small Group Research* (New York: Free Press of Glenco, 1962. p. 66, and Robert F. Bales, *Personality and Interpersonal Behavior* (New York: Holt, Rinehart & Winston, 1970). pp. 91–97.

DISCUSSION EVALUATION FORM, WAYNE STATE UNIVERSITY.

1-2-3	4-5-6	7-8-9
Weak	Average	Strong

Criteria for evaluating discussion participation include the following:

A. Information about the problem (breadth, accuracy, and use of information).
B. Analysis of the problem (sensing problem's importance; finding the issues; avoiding irrelevant matters).
C. Ability to think cooperatively (open-mindedness; alertness; willingness to abandon weak arguments; ability to synthesize the contributions of others).
D. Skill in speaking (adapting voice, action, and language to the occasion; ability to state ideas clearly and briefly).
E. Good manners (listening attentively; quoting others accurately; giving others a chance to speak; general courtesy).
F. Overall effectiveness.

	1	2	3	4	5	6	7	8	9	10	11
Project											
Class Hour											
Date											
A. Information											
B. Analysis											
C. Cooperative Thinking											
D. Speaking Skill											
E. Good Manners											
F. Overall Effect											
Total Scores											
Rank Order of Participants											

General comments on the group as a whole (use back of sheet as needed):

Figure 14.15

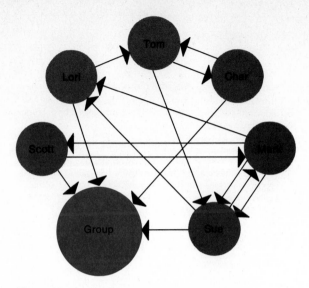

Figure 14.16   A sociogram describing participation

14 SUMMING UP

The unique aspect of discussion is that a participant is both a sender and a receiver at the same time. It is dynamic, interactive, and interpersonal. If decision is impossible through discussion, discussion may very well lead to debate. Debate is competitive and two-sided, discussion cooperative and many-sided. A discussion-debate continuum is shown in figure 14.1.

A small group is dynamic, whereas an audience is most often passive. If we consider small-group discussion in terms of subgroups and feedback loops, we quickly see why "two's company, three's a crowd." Generalizations about co-acting small groups include these:

1 Groups can change attitudes and behavior.
2 A group's consensus judgment tends to be better than individual judgment.
3 Small, agreeing groups may develop a strong feeling of personal involvement.
4 Cooperative group communication can be taught.

Assuming a real group—persons with a common goal, not just a loose collection of individuals—we can define group discussion as *a systematic and cooperative form of reflective thinking and communication.*

Group discussion uses a cooperative thinking approach among twenty persons or less. The basic forms of group discussion are *dialogue, panel,* and *symposium.* Three techniques that may be used with any of these forms are the *buzz group, role playing,* and *brainstorming.* A *forum* is simply that part of a discussion in which the audience may speak.

These forms of discussion may be used for information sharing, problem solving, and instruction. Information-sharing groups include staff meetings, study groups, and workshops. Problem-solving groups include committees, conferences, and boards or councils. Instructional formats include case conferences, role playing, and to some extent all the forms and techniques of discussion.

Systematic inquiry and an intelligent state of doubt are the essentials of reflective thinking. There are five steps in the Dewey system of reflective thinking: (1) felt difficulty, (2) definition, (3) possible solutions, (4) rational elaboration, and (5) further testing or confirming. My four-step adaptation includes (1) *definition,* (2) *analysis* using puzzle, probability, and value, (3) establishing *criteria,* and (4) *solution.* Discussion is a dynamic phenomenon that may progress in a more circular than linear course. Modern research suggests that there are three phases to problem-solving discussions. Phase 1 employs orientation, information, repetition, and confirmation. Phase 2 uses analysis, evaluation, and the seeking or giving of opinions and feelings. Phase 3 controls possible directions and ways of action. Five agenda systems that creatively reflect and synthesize the literature are shown in figure 14.6.

Leadership should be considered as any significant action by any discussant that has significant influence on group achievement. It is possible to have no appointed leader and still have leadership; it is also possible to have an appointed leader and no leadership. The distinction between *leader* and *leadership,* and *leaderless* and *leadershipless,* is a critical one. All group members have a stake and often a role in leadership.

Leadership may fall upon a person through designation, or as a result of that person's superior information, status, or special ability to perform vital group functions. The major functions of leadership are *goal achievement* and *effective interpersonal relations.* Leadership, particularly when designated, also has *procedural* functions. These functions may be planning, physical arrangements, purposes, degree of formality, goal setting, and the agenda. The procedural leader is also responsible for general control of participation and for preserving order.

Styles of leadership may be described as autocratic, authoritarian, supervisory, democratic, permissive, nondirective, and laissez-faire. The democratic style is recommended.

Interaction process analysis is an observational system that classifies communicative acts (verbal and nonverbal behavior). An observer is responsible for three major areas of observation: positive social-emotional acts, task acts, and negative social-emotional acts. These three areas and twelve subcategories of analysis are shown in figure 14.14.

A successful group discussion is the product of an interacting reflective group of individuals that is characterized by goals, systematic leadership, high cohesion, high productivity, and cooperative interpersonal communication.

1 Small-group discussion is essential to the success of a democratic society.

2 We discuss and interact for social and emotional reasons as well as to divide up the logical work of society.

3 Some people find it more difficult to interact in small groups than in larger ones.

4 Discussion is systematic, cooperative thinking, and communication.

5 A co-acting group has some common purpose and some interaction between members.

6 Our own sense of interpersonal responsibilities and behavior in a small group greatly affects our interaction.

7 Successful interaction depends on the style and amount of communication directed toward another person or persons when their reactions are taken into account.

8 Three-to-seven-member groups are different interactionally from dyads.

9 Co-acting small groups have considerable impact upon individual behavior and attitudes.

10 Once their members achieve consensus, small groups develop a feeling of personal involvement and responsibility for the solution.

11 Group conclusions and attitudes tend to be held more persistently than similar conclusions arrived at individually.

12 Orderly discussion tends more toward consensus than discussion that is not guided by any agenda system.

13 A healthy state of doubt, a belief in systematic inquiry, and an attitude of suspended judgment are essential to cooperative communication (as well as to scientific habit).

14 Leadership is any significant action by any discussant that influences group achievement.

15 The major functions of leadership are goal achievement, effective interpersonal relations, and procedural matters.

16 For most small-group discussions, a democratic style of leadership is superior to an absolute or nonresponsible style.

17 A healthy group climate is a cohesive one in which discussants, through interaction, achieve a mental state of relative psychological safety and freedom.

Specific Learning Outcomes

1 We should learn the discussion-debate continuum.

2 We should learn the classic definitions and the contemporary forms of discussion.

3 We should learn about the reflective thinking process and be able to relate it to problem-solving agendas.

4 We should learn the essential differences between "goal," "interpersonal," and "procedural" leadership.

5 We should learn the continuum of leadership control and the styles of leadership represented on it.

6 We should learn the influence of communication climate on fostering cohesion and useful interaction.

7 We should learn participant responsibilities and be able to recognize those that promote group goals and those that do not.

8 We should learn the criteria to apply as an observer and critic of discussion.

1 We should be able to participate knowledgeably and responsibly in the major contemporary forms of group discussion.

2 We should be able to recognize the difference between a co-acting small group and a simple collection of people.

3 We should have and be able to apply a knowledge of procedural leadership in group discussion exercises.

4 We should develop a sensitivity and an ability to function as an interpersonal leader.

5 We should be able to develop systematic agendas for the goals or tasks of a given discussion group.

6 We should learn to "play the scale" of leadership styles and still remain an essentially democratic leader during short discussion projects.

7 We should learn to evaluate group participation through the IPA and WSU systems shown on pages 372–73.

8 We should be able to arrange participants in various ways to accommodate the major contemporary forms of discussion.

Study Projects and Tasks

1 After being assigned to a group of three to six, pick one of the following problems and prepare for a ten-to-fifteen-minute panel discussion in which you spend the first two to three minutes setting an agenda and the remaining time following it toward a solution. (See the suggestions of veteran teachers after problem f.)

a You are a freshman in a medical school in which the lowest third of the class will be cut after final examinations. Before the exams you accidentally overhear a good friend of yours, who is inferior to you academically and whom you suspect has cheated before, making plans to cheat on the finals. Your standing might be endangered, and there isn't a formal honor system at the school. You also realize that it would be difficult to prove any accusations after the exams. You should:

(1) Ignore it.

(2) Talk to your friend about your feelings.

(3) Report your friend formally to the proper authorities.

(4) Ask other students their opinions on the matter, using fictitious names.

(5) Write an anonymous letter to your friend or to the proper authorities.

b While shopping in a grocery store, a customer noticed one of the cashiers taking money from the cash register. Startled by the incident, the customer rushed to the manager and reported what he had seen. The manager could not decide how to approach the situation at that particular moment. Finally, he decided that the best approach would be to:

(1) Go to the cashier and tell her she is fired.

(2) Investigate the matter to be certain the customer had reported accurately.

(3) Report the incident to the union.

(4) Have someone watch the girl in order to guard against a repetition.

(5) Assure the customer and forget it.

c One of your instructors, who has tenure, appears to be an alcoholic. He keeps coming to class somewhat drunk, and because of his drinking he misses 25 percent of the class meetings. Most of the students like him, and he is a qualified instructor. The material is taught if the students want it, but they end up learning most of it from the text book. The instructor doesn't push his students and gives just one test during the semester.

Your success in future courses in this field depends on how well you grasp the material and basics in this course. Your course of action should be to:

(1) Go straight to the dean and ask that disciplinary action be taken against the professor.

(2) Drink with your professor in order to get a good grade in his class.

(3) Boycott his class and try to get the other students to do the same. This way you would draw attention to the situation.

(4) Talk to the professor, explain your feelings, and ask for an explanation.

(5) Inform the department chairman of your suspicions, after checking with other students.

d George Anderson is a student in Ms. Smith's tenth-grade classroom. It seems George is fairly intelligent but doesn't care about school and spends his time getting into trouble. Ms. Smith has investigated his home situation and found two alcoholic, uncaring parents. She wants to establish George's trust and hopes he will do better.

Today when she was leaving school, George backed her against the wall with a switchblade. There is a school regulation that prohibits the carrying of a switchblade in the school at any time. Ms. Smith feels that George is testing her to see what she will do. What should Ms. Smith do?

(1) Tell George that if he puts the knife away and doesn't bring it back to school she will not report him.

(2) Report George for breaking the school regulation.

(3) Ignore the situation, hoping that her evident lack of interest will persuade him to get rid of the knife.

(4) Threaten to report him if he brings the knife back to school.

(5) Call the police.

e Mrs. Jones is not a busybody, but she's in a pinch and doesn't want to be labeled "neighborhood busybody." One day as she was shopping, she came across Johnny Barker, age sixteen, trying to sell pot to a group of his peers. She has known the Barkers for about five years and has great respect for them. She can't decide whether she should take any action. She should:

(1) Forget having seen Johnny.

(2) Go to the Barker residence and tell Mrs. Barker what she saw.

(3) Persuade a neighbor to tell Mrs. Barker.

(4) Mail Mrs. Parker an anonymous note informing her of Johnny's activities.

(5) Tell Johnny she knows about it and attempt to persuade him to quit doing it.

f Your daughter Mildred, a sixteen-year-old, announces that she has been asked to go the the high-school junior prom at the country club, with breakfast to follow at 6:00 A.M. at a classmate's house. Assuming that Mildred asks your permission to go in a pleasant manner, what should be your response as a parent?

(1) Yes, but with a warning.

(2) A flat no.

(3) No, and describe the undesirable experiences in which she might become entangled.

(4) Let Mildred make her own decision.

(5) Get more information before helping Mildred decide.

After observing several hundred similar short panel discussions, veteran teachers advanced the following conclusions. These may alert you to potential problems or faults in your own sessions.

    a Vocal subgroups often developed.
    b Seating was often awkward and disordered.
    c Leaders were seldom appointed or voted upon.
    d Time was not always well budgeted.
    e Systematic discussion was infrequent.
    f Some group members were allowed to dominate the discussions.
    g Some members should have been drawn into the discussion more frequently.
    h Initial agreement was not often challenged.
    i Language was often too absolute and unqualified for the question at hand.
    j With a few exceptions, the group thinking was relatively flexible.
    k The participants seemed to enjoy their work.
    l The expert answer was generally accepted as intelligent after discussion by the entire class.
    m The groups were interested mostly in answers—not in the problems.
    n For some, the panel discussion appeared to be a new experience in flexible thinking.

2 Select a class discussion project on an important social issue suitable for two or three days of research. Describe the issue as a question, prepare a one-hour agenda, select a procedural leader, do your research, and prepare for class discussion(s). You may use combinations of the various forms of discussion. You might choose from these topics of general interest:

Abortion	Fraternities and sororities	Gambling
Narcotics	Changing morals	Population
Welfare	Lotteries	Euthanasia
Sex education	Censorship	Prostitution
Medicare	Crime	Quarter system
Birth control	Capital punishment	Communal living
Gun laws	Busing	Space travel
Pollution	Transportation	Nudism
Advertising	Prisons	Ecumenism
Pornography	Amnesty	Big cities
Sexism	Homesexuality	UFOs
Witchcraft	Gerontology	Inflation

3 Observe a discussion group and chart the flow of communication among the participants. Use arrows to indicate direction, and use one arrow for each substantial comment (a comment other than a simple exclamation or yes or no answer). A model is shown on page 374. Discuss what the model indicates about the various participants.
4 In your next informal, out-of-class group interaction, observe the participants very carefully, and note those actions and communications typical of a person exercising interpersonal-relations leadership (those actions and communications that help hold a group together, apart from the procedures and the topic [task] itself).
5 Consider the similarities and differences between preparing for discussion and preparing for a more formal speech. What is the same? What is different? Which is easier? Be prepared to discuss the issue in class.
6 Observe a radio or television discussion and attempt to classify the various leadership functions that emerge (goal achievement, interpersonal relations, or

procedural). Be alert for changes in function by the participants. Assess their effectiveness.

7 Prepare a two-to-three-minute speech on a class-selected topic, and be ready to deliver it in a symposium format. Also be prepared for a panel discussion with the symposium members and for a possible open forum with the audience.

8 Write a two-to-three-page report of an out-of-class "contemporary form of discussion" you have observed or in which you were involved, and evaluate it according to Bales's system (see figure 14.14).

9 After you have completed this chapter, write a three-page personal, introspective report about the attitudes and behaviors you exhibit in interpersonal communication. What have you learned about yourself as a participant in cooperative communication?

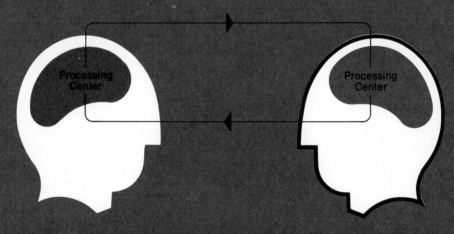

Processing
Center

Processing
Center

appendix a

COMMUNICATION
MODELS

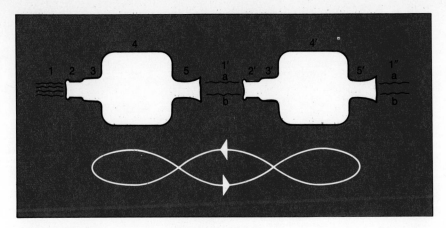

Figure A.1 **Johnson Model.** From Wendell Johnson, "The
Fateful Process of Mr. A Talking to Mr. B."
Harvard Business Review, 31
(January–February 1953), 50.

Key: Stage 1. Event, or source of stimulation, external to the sensory end organs of the
speaker.
Stage 2. Sensory stimulation.
Stage 3. Pre-verbal neurophysiological state.
Stage 4. Transformation of pre-verbal into symbolic forms.
Stage 5. Verbal formulations in "final draft" for overt expression.
Stage 1'. Transformation of verbal formulations into (a) air waves (b) and light
waves, which serve as sources of stimulation for the listener.
Stage 2'. etc.
Stage 2'. Through 1" (see diagram) correspond in the listener to stages 2 through 1'.
The arrowed loops represent the functional interrelationships of the stages in the process
as a whole.

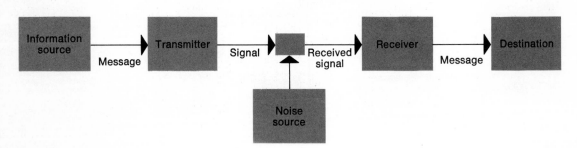

Figure A.2 **Shannon-Weaver Model.** From C. E. Shannon
and W. Weaver, *The Mathematical Theory of
Communication* (Urbana, Ill.: University of
Illinois Press, 1949), p. 98.

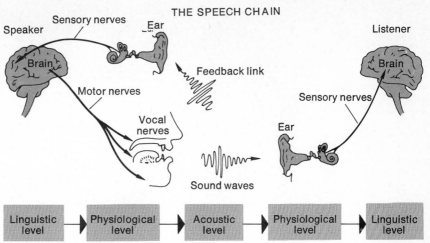

THE SPEECH CHAIN

Figure A.3 Denes-Pinson Model. From *The Speech Chain* by Peter B. Denes and Elliot N. Pinson, © 1963 Bell Telephone Laboratories, Inc. Reprinted by permission of Doubleday & Company, Inc.

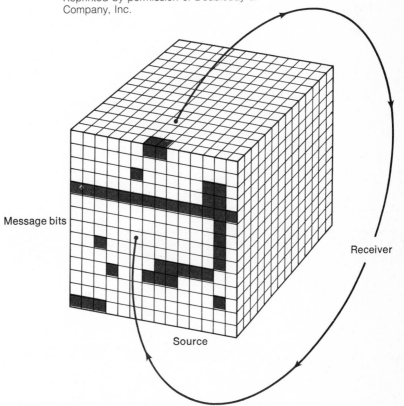

Figure A.4 Becker Model. Presented by S. L. Becker at the Wayne State University special graduate seminar, "Potpourri '70: Communication Relations," July 20, 1970.

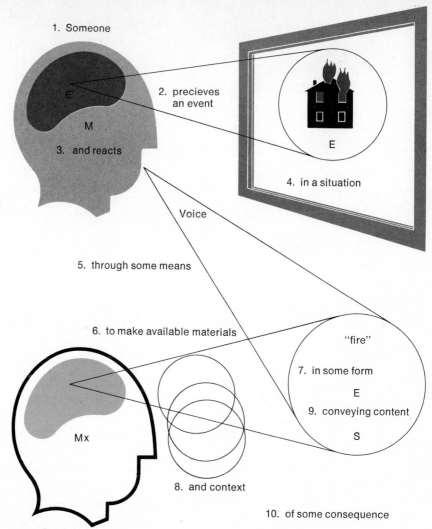

Figure A.5 Gerbner Model. From George Gerbner,
"Toward a General Model of Communication,"
Audio-Visual Communication Review, 34
(Summer 1956), pp. 172–73.

Key: E = event, S = signal, M = man. The events of someone seeing a fire and sounding an alarm are shown by the numbers:
Someone (1) is the communicating agent.
Perceives an event (2) indicates that a possibility of decoding and encoding exists, regardless of which of the senses did the perceiving.
And reacts (3) indicates that the message was received, decoded, and was being analyzed.
In a situation (4) indicates that a comparison was made to a frame of reference, stored in the communicating agent's experience and memory.
Through some means (5) indicates that appropriate action is being taken, via some channel, commensurate with the seriousness of the situation, as defined by the agent's frame of reference.
To make available materials (6) indicates that some form of communication, voice, pressure, or some other form of signal is being employed.
In some form (7) indicates that a pattern, discernible to others, was used to convey the material in (6).

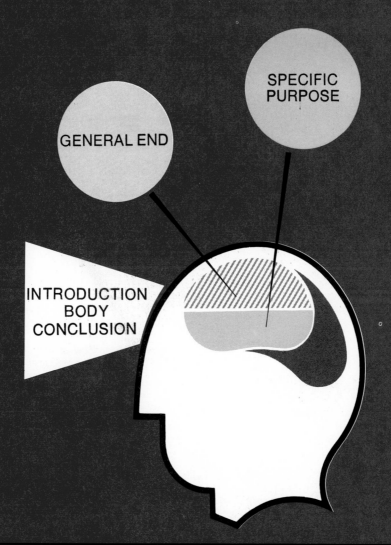

GENERAL END

SPECIFIC PURPOSE

INTRODUCTION
BODY
CONCLUSION

appendix b

OUTLINES

THE ROLE OF THE MANAGER

General End: To inform.
Specific Purpose: To explain five basic functions of managing.

Attention

I   In a well-run organization, confusion exists 25 percent of the time.
   A Visual aid with data and another with list of functions.
   B Studies show that communication breakdowns occur.
II Management is getting work done through others.
   A That makes communication the heart of all management functions.
   B That takes a knowledge of the other basic functions.

Overview

I   The planning function.
II   The organizing function.
III The directing function.
IV   The coordinating function.
IV   The controlling function.

Human relations and
communication area

Information

I   The planning function.
   A Determine objective.
   B Consider tools available.
      1 Time.
      2 Space.
      3 Personnel.
      4 Material available.
   C Consider possible lines of action.
   D Select the best line of action.
   E Determine the actual process.
      1 Who?
      2 When?
      3 What?
      4 Where?
      5 How?
II The organizing function.
   A Line of authority.
   B Span of control.
      1 Number of personnel.
         a Nature of job.
         b Ratios (1:20, 3:7)
      2 Distance.
      3 Time.

C Homogeneous assignment.
   1 Like functions grouped together.
   2 Avoid several unrelated responsibilities.
D Delegation of authority.
   1 Cannot delegate responsibility.
   2 Clearly define limits of delegated authority.
III The directing function.
   A Communication.
   B Understanding people.
IV The coordinating function.
   A Relating to lateral organizations.
   B Relating to parent organization.
V The controlling function.
   A Reporting.
   B Inspecting and evaluating.

Review

I I have tried to clarify the five basic management functions.
   A Planning.
   B Organizing.
   C Directing.
   D Coordinating.
   E Controlling.
II Communication is the heart of all management functions! It has to be: management is getting work done through people—and that takes communication.

THE DIETARY LAWS OF THE JEWISH PEOPLE

General End: To inform.
Specific Purpose: To inform the class about the ancient Jewish dietary laws that are practiced even to this day.

Introduction

I Jewish culture is interesting to study not only because of its religious aspect, but also because the laws promulgated by Moses in ancient times are still practiced by observing Jews.
II The dietary laws I will discuss are the following:
   A Consumption of meat.
   B Consumption of fish.
   C Consumption of dairy foods.
   D Consumption of a living animal.
   E Consumption of blood.
   F Ritualistic slaughter.

Body

I The Bible prohibits the consumption of meat that comes from animals that do not possess cloven (split) hoofs and that do not chew their cud.

A Animals that belong to the category that possesses both characteristics are permissible as food.
  1 Cows.
  2 Goats.
  3 Lambs.
B Animals that chew their cud but do not have cloven hoofs are prohibited as food.
  1 Rabbits.
  2 Camels.
C Animals with cloven hoofs that do not chew their cud, especially hogs, are prohibited as food.
D Animals that possess neither characteristic are prohibited as food.
  1 Dogs.
  2 Cats.
  3 Horses.
II The Jewish people are prohibited from consuming fish that do not have both scales and fins.
A Those with both characteristics are permitted.
  1 Pike.
  2 Bass.
  3 Carp.
B Those with only one characteristic are prohibited.
  1 Catfish.
  2 Bullheads.
C Those with neither characteristic are prohibited.
  1 Crabs.
  2 Lobsters.
  3 Clams.
III Another law prohibits the cooking or eating of meats and dairy foods together.
A This law is based on Exodus 23:19: "Thou shalt not seethe a kid in the milk of its mother."
B Rabbinic legislation provided that two separate sets of dishes be maintained.
IV The Bible prohibits the eating of any part of a living animal.
A This is one of the seven laws of Noah derived by the Talmud from scriptural references.
B This prohibition precludes cruelty to animals.
V The Bible prohibits the eating of blood.
A The biblical reason given for this law is that because blood is the symbol of life it must be respected.
B From this law stems the practice of koshering meats.
  1 The rabbis prescribed that before the meat could be cooked it had to be soaked in water for one-half hour.
  2 After the meat is soaked, it must be heavily salted in coarse salt for one hour and rinsed with water.
  3 Meat that is broiled need not be salted.
  4 These practices draw off the blood.
VI Only meat from an animal that has been ritually slaughtered may be consumed.
A Ritual slaughter is the severing of the jugular vein in one stroke.
B The animal is killed instantly and painlessly and the blood removed.

Conclusion

I There were probably also pragmatic reasons for the laws.
A Preserving foods was difficult for the nomadic Jews.
B Fish without both fins and scales are typically inedible.
C Many of the rules prevented cruelty to animals.
D These laws helped prevent disease.

II In review, I have discussed the dietary laws of the Jewish people. An observing Jew may *not:*

    A Consume meat that comes from animals that do not possess cloven hoofs and that do not chew their cud.

    B Consume fish that do not have both scales and fins.

    C Consume or cook meat and dairy foods together.

    D Eat any part of a living animal.

    E Consume blood (hence, koshering).

    F Consume meat from an animal that has not been ritually slaughtered.

III These laws are not merely obsolete observances, but have real meaning to observing Jews to this day.

    A The dietary laws in the total system of commandments represent submission to a divine discipline.

    B The acceptance of this discipline has served as a significant instrument of group survival for the Jewish people.

FINDING A JOB

General End: To inform.

Specific Purpose: To inform and explain briefly to the class the proper way to find and apply for a job.

Introduction

(Attention)

    I At some point soon most of us here will be seeking employment. You won't do well if you don't know how!

    II I would like to briefly explain the proper way to find a job.

        A Prepare a list of prospective employers.

        B Prepare data for an application.

(Overview)

        C Send a letter to prospective employers.

        D Plan a sales talk for an interview.

        E Take special care of personal grooming for an interview.

Body

    I Make a complete list of prospective employers.

        A List the jobs that are close to where you live.

        B List the jobs that are related to your knowledge and experience.

            1 Sources are available in telephone directories.

            2 Sources are available at your local Chamber of Commerce.

(Information)

    II Prepare data for an employment application.

        A An application gives an employer information about your past.

            1 An application states where you previously worked.

            2 An application states how your health has been in the past.

        B An application gives an employer information about your present.

            1 An application states where you live.

            2 An application states what your present job is if there is one.

    III Send a letter to prospective employers.

        A Write some personal information.

From a student speech by Mary Ann Renczak, Wayne State University.

              1 State your age.

              2 State how much schooling you have had.

(Information)   B Write some information on your experience.

              1 List the names of past employers.

              2 List the dates of past employment.

              3 List the type of work you handled.

     C Write down some references.

  IV Plan what you will say for an interview.

     A Introduce yourself to the employer.

              1 Give your age and education.

              2 State what you know about the firm.

              3 State why you are there.

     B Mention your past training.

              1 State your experience.

              2 State your qualifications.

     C Offer to furnish references.

  V Take special care of your personal grooming for an interview.

     A Dress appropriately for the job.

              1 A person applying for a job as a gas station attendant would not need to wear a dress suit to an interview.

              2 A secretary should wear a skirt or a nice pant outfit.

     B Make sure you are clean.

              1 Bad breath is an offensive odor.

              2 Stale perspiration is embarrassing to deal with.

Conclusion

  I I have explained briefly a few steps in finding a job.

     A Prepare a list of prospective employers.

     B Prepare data for an application.

(Review)   C Send a letter to prospective employers.

     D Plan a sales talk for an interview.

     E Take special care of personal grooming for an interview.

  II Seeking employment is something that most of us have experienced or will experience in the future.

Bibliography

Brown, Newell, *After College What?* New York: M. W. Lads Publishing, 1969.

Lasher, W. K., *How You Can Get a Better Job.* Chicago: American Technical Society, 1972.

ROCK MUSIC

General End: To persuade.

Specific Purpose: To persuade the audience that rock music has significant social impact.

Introduction

  I Rock music blares out on our radios and TVs.

A Radio tape demonstration.
B TV tape (audio) demonstration.
II Thousands pay to see and hear rock stars.
  A Festivals have been big.
  B Club bookings are big.
  C Records are popular.

Body

I The history and evolution of rock.
  A Originally the music was improvised from the blues.
    1 Chuck Berry.
    2 Little Richard.
  B Big stars won rock fans.

(Interest)
    1 Elvis Presley.
    2 The Beatles.
  C New electronics, advanced rock.
    1 The San Francisco sound.
    2 Electric instruments.
    3 Super amplification (short demonstration).
II Performers had impact by being daring, wild, and weird.
  A Elvis Presley's gyrations were banned from TV.
  B Jim Morrison arrested for his act.
  C Jimi Hendrix set rock afire.

(Interest)
  D The Who opened a new dimension of violence.
  E Iggy Stooge used fear to become popular.
  F Alice Cooper makes use of sadism.
  G David Bowie captured the unreal.
III Rock performers have changed our fashion codes.
  A The Beatles caused the long-hair thing.
  B Rock caused more casual dress (pictures).
  C Rock heroes caused wilder clothes (pictures).
IV Rock has had an impact on our moral standards.
  A The hippie movement is related.

(Vital Factors)
  B Drug use is related (demonstration of "drug music").
  C Rock songs aid gay liberationists (demonstration).
  D Some performers openly instigate bisexuality.

Conclusion

I Rock music has gained the attention of millions.
  A Radio, TV.

(Reinforcement)
  B Festivals.
  C New electronics.
II Rock music has had a significant social impact.
  A Brings social problems to light.
  B Affects individuals and group social behavior.

From a student speech by Robert Walker, Wayne State University.

A WAR ON WORDS

General End: To persuade.
Specific Purpose: To persuade the audience to reject the terms "man," "woman," "masculinity," "femininity," "husband," "wife," "father," "mother," etc. in their traditional form; and to effect a change in the usage and accepted meaning of such terms.

Introduction

(Attention)
I   What if this week Dr. Ross asked us to define who we are, or what our roles are? In doing so I wonder how many of us would use such terms as "man," "woman," "female," "male," "husband," "wife," "mother," "father," "masculine," "feminine"? And if so, I wonder how many of us would be stereotyping ourselves?

(Psychological Needs)
II   For far too long cliches—such as: "Little boys are made of snakes and snails and puppy dog's tails; and little girls are made of sugar and spice and everything nice"—have represented the image of the male and female in society. Traditionally, males have been depicted as heroic, active, and aggressive; while females pale in the shadow of masculinity.

Body

(Overview of Problem)
I   The problem with such stereotypes is that they pervade our culture, and threaten our psychological stability.

   A   From textbooks to television stereotypic definitions of these terms have been—and too often still are—reinforced.

(Achievement, Competence, Esteem, Self-Actualization Needs)
     1   Male and female stereotypes in student textbooks emphasize the boys as "doers" and the girls as observers.[1]

     2   Females are depicted as "sub-mankind" in basal readers.[2]

     3   In television advertising, females are primarily associated with personal hygiene products, while men are associated with cars, trucks, gas, oil, etc.[3]

(Safety Needs)
   B   The acceptance and use of such terms threatens our psychological stability by placing unreasonable pressure on us to conform to such tags.

     1   Men must be "big," "gruff," and "aggressive."

       a   Some men physically "fail" to measure up to the "big" description.

       b   Some men psychologically aren't—and don't want to be—"gruff" and "aggressive."

     2   Women must be "petite," "sweet," and "meek."

       a   Again, some women physiologically are not "petite."

       b   Not all women are—or wish to be—psychologically "sweet," and "meek."

(Objection)
   C   But, some would argue—and have argued—What's in a word?

     1   S. I. Hayakawa asserts that "words influence and to an enormous extent control future events."

     2   Benjamin Lee Worf concludes that language shapes perception.

     3   Barbara Herrnstein Smith, pinpoints the specific semantic problem.

(Both-sides Persuasion)
       a   The original adjectives are "handy" and "informative"; not "viscious" at all.

       b   But these adjectives acquire a sexual impact.

         (1)   Women are expected to be passive, so passiveness becomes a feminine trait; thus, an aggressive woman is masculine.

         (2)   Men are expected to be aggressive, so aggressiveness becomes a masculine trait; thus, a passive man is feminine.[4]

From a student speech by Marcy L. Krugel, Wayne State University.

(Solution)	II In order to solve these problems a change in the usage and accepted meaning of these words must be initiated.
	A We must sweep these stereotypic definitions from our culture.
	1 Textbooks must stop codifying roles in relation to gender.
	2 Basal readers must concentrate on equality.
	3 Television must depict men and women in diverse areas and aspects of life.
	B Further, society must objectively redefine its terms so that they no longer pose as prescriptive formulas of behavior.
(Visualization)	1 The terms "husband" and "wife" should merely denote a legal relationship.
	2 The terms "father" and "mother" should denote a legal status.

Conclusion

(Reinforcement)	I So, what is a "man"? What is a "woman"? They are both human beings who should be free of the sex-typed labels of "masculinity" and "femininity."
(Action Step) (Self-actuali- zation)	II Consequently, we must reject the traditional meaning of these terms: to liberate us *all* from a sex-typed fate; to allow our own very individual "me's" to be.

Footnotes

[1] David Sadker, Myra Sadker, and Sidney Simon, "Clarifying Sexist Values," *Social Education,* 37 (December 1973), 759.

[2] Sadker, Sadker, and Simon relate the following negative dialogue that appeared in a basal reader: "We are willing to share our great thoughts with mankind. However, you happen to be a girl." *Venture, Book 4,* (Glenview, Ill.: Scott Foresman & Company, 1965); Sadker, Sadker, Simon, "Sexist Values," 757.

[3] Joseph R. Domineck and Gail E. Rauch, "The Image of Women in Network TV Commercials," *Journal of Broadcasting,* 16 (Summer 1972), 259–65.

[4] Barbara Herrnstein Smith, "Women Artists: Some Muted Notes," *Journal of Communication,* 24 (Spring 1974), 146–47.

A RAMPANT KILLER

General End: To persuade.
Specific Purpose: To persuade the audience that they should have their chests X-rayed.

Attention

(Possible Procedures) Startling Statement Illustration Rhetorical Question Reference to the Subject	I There is a subtle killer loose in the room.
	A It killed 40,000 people last year.
	B It likes young people.
	II No one is immune to tuberculosis.
	A You may be infected now!
	B How long has it been since you had a chest X-ray?

Problem

(Development) Statement Illustration Ramification Pointing	I Despite wonder drugs, TB is our number six killer disease in America.
	A Last year 40,000 Americans died from it.
	B Nearly 2,000 died in Michigan alone.

II No one is immune to TB.

  A You can get it by contagion.

  B The most susceptible ages are from fifteen to thirty-five.

III It maims and handicaps as well as kills.

  A Many of those who recover cannot lead normal lives.

    1 They cannot travel in warm, damp climates.

    2 They cannot exert themselves.

      a Cannot run to class.

      b Cannot dance.

      c Cannot play athletic games.

  B TB may spread to other parts of the body.

    1 One may lose a limb.

    2 It often attacks the spine.

    3 One can lose a vital organ such as an eye or a kidney.

Solution

(Development)

⌈ Statement
  Explanation
  Demonstration
  Illustration
⌊ Objections

I A yearly X-ray checkup is the surest way to avoid a serious case of TB.

  A It can be stopped most effectively if caught in time.

    1 For the most part it is a slow-developing disease.

    2 Its growth depends on the resistance of the victim.

    3 Even if detected in its early stages, a cure would take at least six months.

  B An X-ray checkup is the most positive means for detecting the disease.

    1 A patch test merely indicates the presence of TB germs, but the disease may not actually be present.

    2 A lesion is the positive sign when it shows on the X-ray.

II We can benefit from an X-ray easily and quickly.

  A It is free.

    1 The money from the sale of Christmas Seals pays for the X-rays and other tests you get.

    2 The state is particularly interested in preserving the health of its young, college-age people.

  B It is convenient to get.

    1 The mobile unit comes to the campus during the first week of the semester.

      a It is open weekdays from 8 A.M. to 4 P.M.

      b It parks near the Health Center.

    2 There is also a permanent clinic in town.

      a It is open five days a week for adults from 8:30 A.M. to 4:30 P.M.

      b A special appointment may be arranged after 4:30 P.M.

      c It is located on the corner of Cass Street and Putnam Avenue.

      d The phone number there is 831–0100.

  C It is painless and quick.

    1 If you've ever had an X-ray, you know it doesn't hurt.

    2 You need only remove your outer garments, such as coats and jackets.

    3 You can be in and out in five minutes.

  D The results are mailed to you immediately.

Visualization

(Project the
Future)
(Methods)
  Summary
  Challenge
  Inducement
  Specificity

I A few minutes now can beat this killer.

  A Avoid pain and suffering.

  B Avoid years in a tuberculosis sanitarium.

  C Avoid physical handicaps.

II Enjoy a normal life physically and psychologically.

   I Get a chest X-ray this week.

  II It is simple and convenient.

     A The mobile unit is on campus at the library.

     B It will take just five minutes of your time.

     C It is absolutely free.

 III The X-ray examination program is an effective way to fight this disease.

INDEX